CONTEMPORARY STUDIES IN SCRIPTURE

An exciting new series from Greg Kofford Books featuring authors whose works engage in rigorous textual analyses of the Bible and other LDS scripture. Written by Latter-day Saints for a Latter-day Saint audience, these books utilize the tools of historical criticism, literature, philosophy, and the sciences to celebrate the richness and complexity found in the standard works. This series will provide readers with new and fascinating ways to read, study, and re-read these sacred texts.

The Anatomy of
Book of Mormon Theology

The Anatomy of
Book of Mormon Theology

Volume Two

Joseph M. Spencer

GREG KOFFORD BOOKS
SALT LAKE CITY, 2021

Paperback ISBN: 978-1-58958-783-0
Hardcover ISBN: 978-1-58958-784-7
Also available in ebook.

Greg Kofford Books
P.O. Box 1362
Draper, UT 84020
www.gregkofford.com
facebook.com/gkbooks
twitter.com/gkbooks

———————————————————

Library of Congress Control Number: 2021948608

Contents

Theological Invitations

An Epilogue of Sorts

Introduction

    This book is one of two volumes of a larger work bearing the title *The Anatomy of Book of Mormon Theology*. Taken together, the two volumes constitute a kind of archive, an attempt to account for a decade of (my own) work in a field that has only really begun to take shape since the beginning of the twenty-first century. Although people have been reading the Book of Mormon since it came off the press in 1830, and although many have done their reading with scholarly interests or intentions, the fact is that we are only right now in the midst of watching an identifiable field of Book of Mormon studies emerge. When I began writing on the Book of Mormon in earnest in about 2008, it was in no way obvious that there was such a field. A decade later, by 2018, there was little doubt that a discipline had come begun to make its way into existence. Over the course of just a few years, something hitherto unrecognizable found its way into the world. I was lucky enough to be there as this happened.

    As if it were not enough to witness the emergence of a new discipline over the last decade or two, I have also looked on as an unprecedented approach to the Book of Mormon has arisen alongside that new discipline. Major parts of the newly recognizable field have clear precedents. The proliferating creation of new editions of the Book of Mormon looks back to similar efforts at the end of the nineteenth century. The assembling of reference materials, digital and analog, mirrors work done especially in the first half of the twentieth century. Historical work, undertaken with an eye to defending the antiquity of the Book of Mormon, finds strong precedent in the second half of the twentieth century. Even literary work, which has emerged with real force and has certainly felt like a novel thing, follows up on initiatives taken in the late twentieth century (especially in the late 1970s and early 1980s). What is new in the twenty-first century, it seems, is a strong and imaginative style of *theological* interpretation of the Book of Mormon. Naturally, there have been theological investigations of the Book of Mormon before. And some of what has appeared in the past few decades looks like work done by previous generations. But there is much in recent theological work that appears to be wholly unprecedented, formally and materially.

The first—or really, the *other*—volume of *The Anatomy of Book of Mormon Theology* gathers essays that could be said to follow twentieth-century precedents, at least to a certain extent. It principally contains essays that deal with relatively traditional theological questions and concerns. That volume traces my sometimes hesitating steps as I worked my way over the course of a decade into an emerging field of Book of Mormon studies and sorted out the Book of Mormon's theological commitments. It has turned out, however, that those same sometimes-hesitating steps have been on a path toward the creation of new styles of theological interpretation. It is a path I have traveled with good friends and smart interlocutors. And so this second—or really, this *further*—volume gathers essays that directly exemplify what is new in Book of Mormon theology. Where the essays in the other volume aim just to broach the subject of doing theology with the Book of Mormon, the essays in this volume ask about what new worlds might be discovered in doing theological work on the Book of Mormon.

This volume opens with a transitional essay, meant to serve as a kind of threshold between the other volume of *The Anatomy of Book of Mormon Theology* and this one. Presented as a prologue of sorts, it directly raises questions of method, asking what interpretive options are available to the would-be Book of Mormon theologian. It puts into its rightful place the relatively traditional style of theological interpretation represented in the other volume of *The Anatomy of Book of Mormon Theology*. It then goes on, though, to introduce two more experimental kinds of theological interpretation, those represented more fully in this volume than in its companion. The essay introduces the first of these more experimental styles of theological interpretation only briefly, a style I have here labeled "microscopic" theology. This is a style of theological interpretation I have helped to develop in conversation with other theologians, and especially with all the many scholars who have been involved with the Latter-day Saint Theology Seminar (once called the Mormon Theology Seminar) over the years. The essay then introduces at greater length the second more experimental style of doing theology with the Book of Mormon, which I here call "macroscopic" theology. This is a style of theological interpretation I have developed in many ways on my own, although I have done so thanks to and in conversation with the adjacent sub-disciplines of intertextuality and reception history.

After the introductory prologue of sorts, then, this volume presents two sets of essays in succession, a first set dedicated to microscopic theology and a second set dedicated to macroscopic theology. Essays in the first set examine no more than a verse of the Book of Mormon—more often just a single phrase or two—to see what theological implications lie within the details of the text. This is what microscopic theology of the sort sponsored by the Latter-day Saint Theology Seminar looks like, and most of the essays in that section of the book were direct products of my ongoing involvement in the Seminar. Essays in the second set ask questions about the shape and intentions of the whole of the Book of Mormon, as this can be discerned through the ways it deploys biblical texts—and especially the writings of Isaiah. This is what macroscopic theology looks like, explained in detail in the prologue essay. (It is best not to go into a detailed explanation of how either microscopic or macroscopic theology works in this introduction. I leave to the prologue essay and the two sets of essays following it to explain and then to exemplify these.)

A third set of essays follows the two on microscopic and macroscopic styles of theology. To this final set I have given the title "Theological Invitations." It collects essays of two related sorts. Some are essays I wrote about some of the most interesting readers of the Book of Mormon who nonetheless work outside the boundaries of theology, usually by deploying some kind of literary style of interpretation. For me, these essays are invitations to blur the boundaries that separate different styles of Book of Mormon scholarship, so that, for example, it becomes difficult to know where literary reading ends and theological reading begins. The other essays in the same section are ones I wrote about the person I regard as the most interesting Latter-day Saint theologian who nonetheless works (or tends to work) outside the boundaries of Book of Mormon studies. I refer, here, to Adam Miller. The several essays on Miller's writings are therefore invitations to bring all Latter-day Saint theology back in the end—explicitly and overtly—to the Book of Mormon. Together, then, the third section of this volume calls on Book of Mormon scholars to move closer to theology and calls on theologians to move closer to the Book of Mormon.

Finally, the volume closes with what I have called an epilogue of sorts. It is an essay—included in some ways just for the fun of it—on the uses of the Book of Mormon in a few films from early in the twenty-first century, and on what such uses suggest about the theological stakes and status of the Book of Mormon. Including that essay allows the whole project of *The Anatomy of Book of Mormon Theology* to conclude with a discussion of

Napoleon Dynamite, a film that is experimental in all the ways I hope my own efforts in theology are experimental.

I note in the other volume of *The Anatomy of Book of Mormon Theology* that I have decided against revising or even touching up the essays in this collection. The point of gathering them together is, as I have said, to create a kind of archive, and it seems fitting to leave the timestamp of each essay's original form in place. This decision means that I need to make a caveat here, as I do in the other volume. Because everything here was originally written before President Russell M. Nelson clarified the importance of using the proper name of The Church of Jesus Christ of Latter-day Saints—and therefore of avoiding the slangy use of "Mormon" as an adjective or "Mormon(s)" as an identifying noun—these essays occasionally use terms I would avoid today. I hope that readers who are particularly sensitive to this issue will be understanding.

I should also note again here that, although I have not altered the essays in these two volumes, I have added occasional footnotes that might prove useful in orienting readers. Added footnotes (as opposed to original ones) are marked by being surrounded by square brackets. Further, each essay opens with an added introduction that explains the original occasion of its creation between 2008 and 2018, the decade I aim to archive with this collection. Full bibliographical information for previous published essays can be found in those brief introductions to each essay.

I offer a few words of thanks and a dedicatory word in the introduction to the other volume of *The Anatomy of Book of Mormon Theology*. Here I just wish to note once more the remarkable friendship I share with Chris Thomas, to whom these two volumes of essays are dedicated.

A Prologue of Sorts

Chapter One

Toward a Methodology for the Theological Interpretation of the Book of Mormon

During the second half of the twentieth century, theology was something Latter-day Saints often said they did not do. And in important ways, that was true—especially for intellectually inclined Latter-day Saints. The latter tended to give themselves either to the study of Latter-day Saint history, to the intellectual defense of the Church's faith claims, or to the systematic investigation of doctrine. Historians often and explicitly claimed that history takes—and ought to take—the place in our tradition that theology holds in other Christian traditions. Defenders of the faith took their cues from critics of the Church, who tended to build their own cases around historical issues rather than theological ones. As for those interested in doctrine, they often contrasted what they studied, which they understood as principles revealed through prophets, with theology, which they understood as a merely human endeavor, the uninspired results of abstruse reasoning.

Today, there is more space for theology. And theology is no longer being construed as a faithless appeal to reason that would usurp the place of revelation. That is, it is becoming clearer that, rightly pursued, theology is reflection on revelation. It is a way of receiving the revealed in faith, consecrating the mind by asking earnestly about the realest implications of what God has revealed in the course of the Restoration—and through scripture in particular. What might we say about the shape of the life of Latter-day Saint faith? What does it mean, really, to repent and give ourselves to the God who reveals himself in the Restoration? These are the kinds of questions driving Latter-day Saint theologians right now. But another question has to be answered before—or at least while—we answer such questions: What is the best way to go about doing theology? I wrote this essay after about a decade of reflection on that question. It was an attempt to think through that decade of reflection, drawing some consequences from what I had found. It seeks to systematize all the kinds of things pursued in the two volumes of *The Anatomy of Book of Mormon Theology*. It also serves here to introduce the essays that make up this volume.

I first presented this previously unpublished essay at "Book of Mormon Studies: Toward a Conversation," a conference held at Utah State University in October 2017.

There are, perhaps, two obvious ways to go about producing a theological interpretation of the Book of Mormon. It might be useful to present these as extremes. One approach, largely on the model of the old history-of-religions program, seeks modestly but rigorously to identify the basic theological ideas on offer within the Book of Mormon. This first approach would lay the heaviest emphasis on questions of history and context, demanding that analysis of the Book of Mormon's theological commitments be worked out with intense care for the immediate setting of each relevant pericope. The purpose of such work would be to show, within the Book of Mormon, a kind of "history of ideas" (whether or not any particular contributor to the field regards the "history" in question as real). This first approach we might call *tracing theologies within* the Book of Mormon.[1]

The second obvious approach to theological interpretation of the Book of Mormon seeks to mobilize the text of the book for the purposes of setting it in conversation with the extratextual theological concerns of the present. This approach would seek to do its hermeneutic work as responsibly as possible, but it would lay its heaviest emphasis on the theological task to which contemporary Mormonism assigns it, with care first and foremost for the discernible needs of those who confess faith in the book's truth. The purpose of such work would be to allow the authority granted to the Book of Mormon by the confessing community to play a role in shaping contemporary Mormonism, wherever texts from the Book of Mormon might address most profitably the needs of the body of Christ. This second approach we might call *producing theologies through* the Book of Mormon.[2]

---

1. If a name must be assigned to this first approach, it might be best to use that of Grant Hardy. In a talk delivered at the annual meetings of the Society for Mormon Philosophy and Theology in 2012 (but, to my knowledge, as yet unpublished), Hardy outlined what he called "the promise of Book of Mormon theology," defending an approach along exactly these lines.

2. If a name must be assigned to this second approach, it might be best to use that of Adam Miller. In an essay titled "A Manifesto for Mormon Theology," published in 2012, Miller has argued for a Mormon scriptural theology, speculative in nature, that roots itself in charity. See Adam Miller, *Rube Goldberg Machines: Essays in Mormon Theology* (Salt Lake City: Greg Kofford Books, 2012), 59–62.

In the course of this paper, I wish to argue for a third, perhaps less obvious approach to the theological interpretation of the Book of Mormon. I have no argument to make *against* these first two approaches. I hope to see them continue, and I hope to borrow heavily from their insights in doing my own work. Indeed, I hope in many ways myself to contribute directly to work done in both veins.[3] Nonetheless, I wish to outline a rather different theological project here, as well as to argue for its necessity and for why it should be privileged above other theological approaches to the Book of Mormon. Although the nature of the project will have to become clear over the course of the following discussion, perhaps we can give it a name from the outset. Rather than *tracing theologies within* the Book of Mormon or *producing theologies through* the Book of Mormon, I wish to promote the task of *constructing a theology of* the Book of Mormon.[4] The choice of preposition— "of," rather than "within" or "through"—is important to me here, but so are the presence, the singularity, and the indefiniteness of the qualifying article. I wish to promote the construction of *a* theology of the Book of Mormon, not so many *theologies*. All this, naturally, I will have to clarify.

I might productively begin by identifying a key presupposition for the argument I will present. I recognize that some might contest this presupposition, but I believe it is solid and so will not argue for it here. I take it, instead, as a given. The presupposition is this: Scriptural theology in its most robust sense must ultimately work toward the *unity* of scripture. What does this mean? For biblical theology, narrower by definition than Mormon scriptural theology, addressing this question would require producing some account of the relationship (or lack thereof) between the two biblical testaments. It would also require an assessment of the idea that there is (or is not) either a center or an organizing scheme at work in the Christian Bible as a whole.[5] For a Mormon scriptural theology, addressing the question of scripture's unity would require in addition some account of the relationship between uniquely Restoration scripture and the Christian

---

[My own experiments in this sort of theological reading are those categorized in this volume as "microscopic" theology.]

3. [Essays I have intended to contribute to this first sort of theological project can be found in the other volume of *The Anatomy of Book of Mormon Theology*.]

4. [My own experiments in this sort of theological reading are those categorized in this volume as "macroscopic" theology.]

5. For some helpful discussion of the range of contemporary approaches to these questions, see James K. Mead, *Biblical Theology: Issues, Methods, and Themes* (Louisville: Westminster John Knox, 2007), 62–68, 74–80.

Bible, as well as of any relationships among uniquely Restoration volumes of scripture. One would, moreover, have to include some assessment of whether or how uniquely Mormon scripture complicates or replaces the Bible's supposed theological center or organizing scheme. All this, it seems to me, deserves the sustained attention of any would-be Mormon scriptural theologian. Put succinctly, scriptural theology in general (like Mormon scriptural theology in particular) requires some kind of investment in—or some kind of sustainable argument against—the idea that scripture works together to communicate God's word to the world.[6] This I take for granted.

Now, if this presupposition is a good one, then the first and most fundamental question every effort at interpreting the Book of Mormon theologically must ask would be this: How might the Book of Mormon's interaction with the Bible clarify the theological center or organizing scheme at work within the larger canon of Mormon scripture—if, in fact, any such center or scheme can be discovered? Note how this question draws together into a single configuration the two major facets of what it would mean to pursue a Mormon scriptural theology, as I have just described these. The question assumes that some account of the relationship between uniquely Restoration scripture and the Bible has been worked out (this is the first facet), but then it asks how this account might itself be put to work in assessing how Restoration scripture reconfigures the Bible's theological center or organizing scheme (this is the second facet). The point here is to see how the two major tasks of a Mormon scriptural theology—or at least of a Mormon scriptural theology aimed ultimately at the unity of scripture—work together. How does the relationship *between* the Book of Mormon and the Bible help to determine the *overall* theological shape of the Mormon scriptural canon?

I need to clarify an important point before providing anything like an answer to the question I have now posed. In the preceding discussion, I have played fast and loose with the relationship between the Book of Mormon and the remainder of Restoration scripture. That is, I have spoken at times just of the relationship between the Book of Mormon and

---

6. Mormons might want to introduce into such a formulation a caveat recognizing the openness of the Mormon scriptural canon, Mormonism's commitment to continuing revelation. See, for instance, the crucial arguments in James E. Faulconer, *Faith, Philosophy, Scripture* (Provo, UT: Neal A. Maxwell Institute Press, 2010), 87–136. I fully concede the importance of this concern, but I do not believe that it requires anything more than that every fully articulated Mormon scriptural theology recognize its own provisionality.

the Bible, but I have spoken at other times of the relationship between all uniquely Restoration scripture and the Bible. Which is it? Unfortunately, the answer must be both. I hope I have outlined the most general project of a Mormon scriptural theology, one that would take into account *all* of uniquely Restoration scripture, along with the Bible. But I also mean here to narrow my focus to what might be called a "canon within the canon."[7] The Doctrine and Covenants and the Pearl of Great Price, key volumes in the specifically Latter-day Saint canon, are a good deal more canonically unstable than is the Book of Mormon or the Bible.[8] Further, these other volumes of Mormon scripture are not embraced universally across the various branches of the larger Restoration movement. Some recognize different versions of these volumes, while some do not at all recognize one or both of them. Some branches embrace still other volumes of scripture.[9] For all these reasons, it seems to me that the first step in establishing a Mormon scriptural theology—whether limited to the Latter-day Saint tradition from which I hail or not—is to consider first and as exhaustively as possible a scriptural theology that takes in the relationship just between the Book of Mormon and the Bible.[10] On such a foundation, each branch

---

7. For some discussion of the use of such a formulation within New Testament theology, see Michael J. Kruger, *Canon Revisited: Establishing the Origins and Authority of the New Testament Books* (Wheaton, IL: Crossway, 2012), 68–73.

8. When Latter-day Saints speak of the canon as open, it is usually with reference to these two volumes of scripture.

9. It might be added that the Book of Mormon itself is not equivalent in all branches of the Restoration movement. Slight differences in the actual text, as well as rather major differences in apparatus and paratext, distinguish the several major traditions' experience with the book. Helpfully, Royal Skousen's work on a critical text of the Book of Mormon allows for the possibility of a Book of Mormon theology that might be amenable to all (or at least most) of the various branches of the Restoration movement. See, naturally, Royal Skousen, ed., *The Book of Mormon: The Earliest Text* (New Haven: Yale University Press, 2009); as well as Royal Skousen, *Analysis of Textual Variants of the Book of Mormon*, 6 pts. (Provo, UT: FARMS, 2004–2009).

10. In yet a further complication, the Bible is not necessarily standard across all branches of the Restoration movement. Because of Joseph Smith's work between 1830 and 1833 on the "New Translation" of the Bible (commonly known as the "Joseph Smith Translation" in the Latter-day Saint tradition and as the "Inspired Version" in other Restoration traditions), some branches of Mormonism use a Bible fundamentally different from the standard Christian Bible. Here I focus solely on the Bible available to Joseph Smith in 1829, during the period of the

within the Restoration movement might pursue a further elaboration of its particular form of scriptural theology.[11]

The question, therefore, that I will answer here is how the Book of Mormon's interaction with the Christian Bible might serve to clarify the theological center or organizing scheme at work within the minimal canon of Restoration scripture constituted by the Christian Bible and the Book of Mormon. How might such a question be answered?

The first step, rather obviously, lies in determining the nature of the *interaction* between the Book of Mormon and the Bible. This matter might be approached in various ways, just as the relationship between the two testaments of the Christian Bible has been variously conceived in biblical theology, as well as in biblical studies more generally. From among the methodological models on offer in the latter field, one seems to me the most promising by far for constructing a theology of the Book of Mormon. I have in mind here the study of intertextuality. From the moment the volume first appeared, the Book of Mormon's close relationship to the Bible has invited the accusation of plagiarism. Mark Twain in fact famously described it in precisely such terms, although he added the word "tedious" to the word "plagiarism."[12] Despite the cheap appeal of such accusations, however, the category of plagiarism does not fit in the case of the Book of Mormon. Its use of biblical passages and turns of phrase, as well as Elizabethan language and an unmistakably King James

---

Book of Mormon's production: the King James Version. It is this upon which the Book of Mormon relies, and any assessment of the relationship between the Book of Mormon and the Bible (or Bibles) resulting from Joseph Smith's editorial work must ultimately depend first on an investigation of the relationship between the Book of Mormon and the King James Bible.

11. I recognize the still-further difficulty of disentangling the Book of Mormon fully from at least the earliest of the revelations Joseph Smith received—those received before, during, and shortly after the production of the Book of Mormon. It seems to me nonetheless that one must consider the complications these early revelations introduce only once the actual text of the Book of Mormon has been investigated in relation to the Bible.

12. Mark Twain, *The Innocents Abroad / Roughing It* (New York: Library of American, 1984), 617. For a much more recent and pretentiously systematic argument that the Book of Mormon is a work of plagiarism, see Jerald Tanner and Sandra Tanner, *Joseph Smith's Plagiarism of the Bible in the Book of Mormon*, rev. ed. (Salt Lake City: Utah Lighthouse Ministry, 2010).

style of speech, hardly hides itself from its readers.[13] The Book of Mormon deploys instead what Nicholas Frederick has recently called a "rhetoric of allusivity," a range of interactions that deliberately trade on the familiarity of biblical language and expressions for the volume's readers.[14] Rather than unreflective or deceptive thievery, the Book of Mormon exhibits an interest in artful recontextualization of biblical narratives, themes, and expressions. The study of this artful work of redeploying texts already regarded as authoritative is the study of intertextuality.

The word "intertextuality" itself can mean several things. In Roland Barthes and Julia Kristeva it has reference to the impossibility of isolating any particular discourse from the larger web of discourses within which it occurs. The very condition for the possibility of communication lies in the way that any particular attempt at communicating with others deploys figures that reproduce the recognizable contours of the total (inconsistent) network of language and talk.[15] To some extent, this more strictly literary notion of intertextuality is relevant to the Book of Mormon, since there are obvious ways in which its consistent use of King James diction and phrasing—especially when drawing from the New Testament—suggests principally a struggle to communicate meaningfully with a nineteenth-century audience whose basic form of discourse is thoroughly infused with the Authorized Version of the Bible. I wish nonetheless to restrict the definition of intertextuality here to something narrower, as does Richard Hays in his seminal work on Saint Paul's uses of scripture. That is, here I mean to focus just on the Book of Mormon's "actual citations of and allusions to specific texts."[16] It seems to me necessary to distinguish between deliberate marshaling of specifiable biblical passages and more obviously

---

13. As Grant Hardy (not entirely felicitously) puts this point, "the Book of Mormon *wants* to be seen as a companion to the Bible." Grant Hardy, *Understanding the Book of Mormon: A Reader's Guide* (New York: Oxford University Press, 2010), 5; emphasis added.

14. See, naturally, Nicholas J. Frederick, *The Bible, Mormon Scripture, and the Rhetoric of Allusivity* (Madison: Fairleigh Dickinson University Press, 2016).

15. This notion of intertextuality is discussed throughout Barthes's work, although it is in Kristeva's *Word, Dialogue, and Novel* that the word made its first appearance. See Toril Moi, ed., *The Kristeva Reader* (New York: Columbia University Press, 1986), 39. For a good collection of Barthes's writings, see Susan Sontag, ed., *A Barthes Reader* (New York: Barnes & Noble, 2009).

16. Richard B. Hays, *Echoes of Scripture in the Letters of Paul* (New Haven: Yale University Press, 1989), 15.

formulaic uses of biblical language. Important work has already been done on establishing a solid methodology for drawing such distinctions.[17]

Now, by what criterion might it be decided that intertextuality offers the ideal model for understanding the interaction between the Book of Mormon and Bible? What secures its value, in my view, is simply the fact that it uniquely allows for a fully *immanent* investigation of the relations between the two volumes of scripture. Intertextual study distinctively avoids idealizing theological approaches that would insist on taking the Book of Mormon and the Bible to be self-contained distinct wholes that then have to be put into relation to one another—perhaps through the abstract work of comparing the supposedly discernible thematic commitments of each volume. Further, such an approach refuses to regard either of the two volumes as inherently superior to, and therefore determinative of the status of, the other—whether the Bible as the more obviously sophisticated of the two, or whether the Book of Mormon as the more immediately trustworthy of the two. In short, an intertextual approach to the interaction between the Book of Mormon and the Bible recognizes their inseparability. The Book of Mormon cannot be understood independently of a close investigation of the uses to which it puts biblical texts of various sorts. And the Bible cannot be understood within the Mormon canon independently of the ways that it offers its texts and themes and language to the Book of Mormon for complex redeployment and recontextualization.[18]

This immanence of the Bible to the Book of Mormon and of the Book of Mormon to the Bible is, from my perspective, the key contribution of intertextual study to the task of theological interpretation. But what does such textual immanence mean for theological interpretation of the Book of Mormon? This question is, actually, a more specific version of the question

---

17. See, in addition to Frederick's *The Bible, Mormon Scripture, and the Rhetoric of Allusivity*, his crucial recent article: Nicholas J. Frederick, "Evaluating the Interaction between the New Testament and the Book of Mormon: A Proposed Methodology," *Journal of Book of Mormon Studies* 24 (2015): 1–30.

18. Here I largely reproduce the basic understanding of the relationship between the two testaments in intertextual study of the Christian Bible—study, as it is often put, of the "uses" of the Old Testament in the New—although I have displaced this relationship from its position between the two testament to a position between the Bible and the Book of Mormon. For what has quickly become the standard systematic work on intertextuality in the Christian Bible, see G. K. Beale and D. A. Carson, eds., *Commentary on the New Testament Use of the Old Testament* (Grand Rapids, MI: Baker Academic, 2007).

I have already asked: How does the Book of Mormon's interaction with the Bible clarify the theological center or organizing scheme at work within Restoration scripture? If it is agreed that intertextual relationships make up the hard core of the interaction between the two volumes, then it must be asked how this sort of interaction might give shape to their joint theological investigation. It should be clear to anyone reading the Book of Mormon with an eye to intertextual concerns that there can be no *one* answer to such a question. There emphatically is *not* one sort of interaction between the Book of Mormon and the Bible. The quotation of whole Isaiah chapters in literarily complex contexts and riddled with significant variants is something quite different from the use of formulaic phrases and decontextualized theologoumena drawn from the Gospels or from Paul. I think, though, that it would be a mistake to decide for that reason that nothing of substance can be said by way of a general schematization of the Book of Mormon's many intertextual ties to the Bible. It is entirely possible to establish a relatively stable typology of sorts of intertextual interaction, to discern patterns in the several sorts' usage and distribution, and to produce by such a means a general schema of the Book of Mormon's use of the Bible. And it is with a schema of this sort that serious theological work might be done.

Much work remains to be done, of course, in actually producing such a schema, but perhaps a few of its major features can already be enumerated. To be given pride of place in the schema are, certainly, the explicit uses of and discussions about the biblical books of Isaiah and Revelation. Nearly a third of the book of Isaiah appears in the Book of Mormon in one form or another, and several major voices within the book explicitly identify Isaiah as of foundational importance to the Book of Mormon project.[19] Further, the Book of Mormon explicitly associates its most grandiose vision accounts with the book of Revelation and promises a full clarification of John's apocalypse to anyone who follows the example of its prophets.[20] Far more subtle but no less essential in the schema is the role

---

19. [I have labored elsewhere on the role of Isaiah in the Book of Mormon. I have labored on the subject also in many of the essays in the section titled "Macroscopic Theology" in this volume. For work I have undertaken elsewhere, see Joseph M. Spencer, *An Other Testament: On Typology*, 2nd ed. (Provo, UT: Neal A. Maxwell Institute, 2016); and Joseph M. Spencer, *The Vision of All: Twenty-five Lectures on Isaiah in Nephi's Record* (Salt Lake City: Greg Kofford Books, 2016).]

20. [I recently published a first attempt at sketching the issues surrounding the book of Revelation in the Book of Mormon. See Joseph M. Spencer, "A Moderate

playcd in the Book of Mormon by the Gospel of John. Preliminary work has already shown John's importance to the Book of Mormon's theological commitments,[21] and there is much low-hanging fruit on this point.[22] In a kind of second tier of the schema should be included explicit references to other biblical texts (references attended by citation formulas of some sort) and unmistakable replications or manipulations of longer biblical passages,[23] as well as deliberate reproduction of biblical type-scenes.[24] In a third or final tier there would fit formulaic usage of biblical phrasing, with some privilege given to formulas that appear more often and seem to reproduce the contexts of their biblical sources.[25] Mobilizing a several-tiered schema such as this, one could begin to extract from the Book of Mormon's many intertextual interactions with the Bible a kind of "world-view-story." And with this move, one begins to move from nailing down the interaction between the Book of Mormon and the Bible to the search for the theological center or organizing schema of Mormon scripture.

Millenarianism: Apocalypticism in the Church of Jesus Christ of Latter-day Saints," *Religions* 10, no. 5 (2019): 339.]

21. See especially Krister Stendahl, "The Sermon on the Mount and Third Nephi," in *Reflections on Mormonism: Judaeo-Christian Parallels*, ed. Truman G. Madsen (Provo, UT: BYU Religious Studies Center, 1978), 139–54; and Frederick, *The Bible, Mormon Scripture, and the Rhetoric of Allusivity*.

22. Stendahl argues that the Sermon on the Mount as reproduced and lightly edited in 3 Nephi 12–14 makes of the Matthean sermon a Johannine text. Similar gestures—as yet unexplored in the literature—can be found throughout Third Nephi, among them implicit contrasts between the synoptic and fourth gospel conceptualizations of the events of the night of Jesus's arrest. The interest Third Nephi further exhibits in the idea that John the Beloved is immortal, unlike Jesus's other disciples, confirms this pattern.

23. Examples of the former would include occasional citations of Genesis 12:2 (as in 1 Nephi 15:18; 22:9; 3 Nephi 20:25, 27) or Deuteronomy 18:18–19 (as in 1 Nephi 22:20; 3 Nephi 20:23). Examples of the latter would include the development of Romans 11:11–28 (in Jacob 5) or 1 Corinthians 13 (in Moroni 7:44–48).

24. Here one might think of the unmistakable relationship the Book of Mormon posits between the escape and travels of Lehi's family and the Exodus story. [I am not sure why I did not include in this footnote before major contributions on this question. It is worth noting, though, that many have written on this subject.]

25. This third or final tier would require the most difficult work of all, to be sure. See the helpful preliminary comments in Philip L. Barlow, *Mormons and the Bible: The Place of the Latter-day Saints in American Religion* (New York: Oxford University Press, 1991), 26–32.

I borrow the term "worldview-story" from Edward Klink and Darian Lockett, who use it to explain a general methodology shared by a variety of contemporary theological readers of the Bible: Richard Hays, N. T. Wright, John Goldingay, Richard Bauckham, and Ben Witherington, among others.[26] Such interpreters "find an underlying story line running through and between the O[ld] T[estament] passages [that New Testament authors] cite."[27] Sifting the New Testament's uses of Old Testament texts, such interpreters reconstruct a story assumed by the New Testament (this regarded as a loosely coherent whole) to be at work in the Old Testament. Thus, the Old Testament finds a unity in the assumptions of the New Testament's characters (such as Jesus or Peter), authors (such as Paul or John the prophet), and editors (such as the gospel writers). If, as N. T. Wright says, "the retelling of [Israel's Old Testament] story . . . is a necessary part of the task" of the New Testament, then something much the same might be said with regard to the Book of Mormon.[28] Just as the New Testament, through its multifarious uses of Old Testament texts, leaves traces of a "worldview-story" that it assumes as a starting point for its own intervention, the Book of Mormon, through its multifarious uses of the whole Christian Bible, leaves traces of its own "worldview-story" that it assumes as a starting point for its intervention. The first task of a serious Book of Mormon theology would be, therefore, to reconstruct the relatively unified story the Book of Mormon assumes to be at work in the Christian Bible, and thereby to develop a solid account of the basic worldview the Book of Mormon presupposes.

It is here, I think, that the potential *unity* of Mormon scripture emerges. Inasmuch as the Book of Mormon presupposes a relatively coherent and consistent worldview, and inasmuch as it organizes this worldview through an articulation of the singular story it finds in (or imposes on) the Bible, the unity of Mormon scripture arises. Thus, the immanence of the Bible to the Book of Mormon and vice versa guarantees the fundamental unity of Mormon scripture, or at least of the canon within the canon with which I am here concerned. The unity of Mormon scripture, as I

---

26. See Edward W. Klink III and Darian R. Lockett, *Understanding Biblical Theology: A Comparison of Theory and Practice* (Grand Rapids, MI: Zondervan, 2012), 93–107.

27. Klink and Lockett, 99.

28. N. T. Wright, *The New Testament and the People of God* (Minneapolis: Fortress Press, 1992), 142.

understand it, is therefore *hermeneutic* in nature.[29] Within the Book of Mormon's biblical hermeneutic both a basic worldview and a set of biblical stories take shape—a worldview that presupposes a series of Christian symbols and practices, along with a set of stories about Israel's and then Christianity's global history.

Of course, as N. T. Wright emphasizes, one feels the real force of such worldview-storytelling only where its polemical intentions become clear. "Once we grasp the storied structure of worldviews in general," he explains, "we are in possession of a tool which, though not often used thus, can help us to grasp what was a stake in the [theological] debates" of particular eras in history. The theological tradition of the Abrahamic faiths has thus always been "a controversy about different tellings of the story of Israel's god, his people, and the world."[30] This is no less true with the Book of Mormon than with the Bible. Like the New Testament, the Book of Mormon *explicitly* identifies certain worldviews it aims to contest: "churches which are built up and not unto the Lord," as one passage has it (2 Ne. 28:3); people who "hiss" or "spurn" or "make game of the Jews" or "any of the remnant of the house of Israel," in another passage (3 Ne. 29:8); "the gentiles" who "mock" at things like the Book of Mormon itself, elsewhere in the text (Ether 12:25). These worldviews are, quite clearly, to be understood as built on or sustained by certain readings of the Bible and of post-biblical Christian history. Thus, there are those who "deny the revelations of God" and do so because they have "not read the scriptures" or at least do "not understand them" (Morm. 9:7–8). One voice in the Book of Mormon insists that if people in modern times "had all the scriptures," they would "know" that Israel's redemption "must surely come" (3 Ne. 28:33). And it is only because there are those who "teach with their learning and deny the Holy Ghost" that "their priests . . . contend one

---

29. As with the work of theological readers of the New Testament, there are "unintended consequences" of this approach. If "O[ld] T[estament] texts not taken up in the N[ew] T[estament] are deemphasized" in this sort of approach to the Christian Bible, it is not surprising that certain biblical texts not taken up in the Book of Mormon will be deemphasized in the approach defended here. Similarly, if "O[ld] T[estament] texts that are mentioned in the N[ew] T[estament] are usually read *only* as the N[ew] T[estament] understands them" in such approaches, it is not surprising if this theological approach will largely ignore readings of biblical texts not pursued, at least implicitly, by the Book of Mormon. Clink and Lockett, *Understanding Biblical Theology*, 101.

30. Wright, *The New Testament and the People of God*, 76.

with another" about the meaning of the Bible (2 Ne. 28:4). The Book of Mormon clearly exhibits awareness of its involvement in some kind of theological controversy.

It is necessary to underscore the fact that the controversy in which the Book of Mormon thus involves itself has less to do with particular points of traditional theology (with, say, basic Christian tenets) than with the whole reading of the Bible. Although passages within the book directly take issue with things like infant baptism or hedonistic universalism, the *primary* and certainly the *most sustained* polemic in the book concerns the general shape of the biblical story. Through its massively complex interaction with its scriptural predecessor, the Book of Mormon first and foremost presents itself as a polemic against certain non-covenantal appropriations of the Christian Bible. It outlines over and over again a history of Israel from the sixth-century before Christ to the end of time, and it repeatedly rails against gentile (European) appropriation of Christianity for its own self-serving ends—an appropriation it usually envisions as taking the shape of so-called "replacement theologies."[31] This point must be understood if the task of constructing a Book of Mormon theology is to become fully clear. Theological interpretation of the Book of Mormon cannot be reduced to investigation of *particular* doctrines of interest in the polemical context of nineteenth-century American Christianity.[32] To do so is to miss the point of the Book of Mormon's *systematic* interaction with the Bible. What is at stake, instead, is a whole worldview inextricably interwoven into a story about Israelite and Christian history.

With this last point clear, the whole task of constructing a Book of Mormon theology becomes plain. The task is to become clear about the nature of the immanence of the Book of Mormon to the Bible, to discern the ways in which that immanence articulates a coherent and singular worldview, and to set that worldview into polemical relationship with rival worldviews rooted in rival hermeneutic appropriations of the Christian

---

31. For a good overview of replacement theology, see Michael J. Vlach, *Has the Church Replaced Israel? A Theological Evaluation* (Nashville, TN: B&H Publishing, 2010).

32. In many ways, the exactly *wrong* approach to clarifying the nineteenth-century bearings of the Book of Mormon was already exemplified by Alexander Campbell's 1831 critique, and it has largely continued into the present. See Alexander Campbell, *Delusions: An Analysis of the Book of Mormon; with an Examination of Its IInternal and External Evidences, and a Refutation of Its Pretences to Divine Authority* (Boston: Benjamin H. Greene, 1832).

Bible. I believe I have made clear along the way of articulating such a project its basic motivations. All that remains to be said here by way of closure is something about why such an approach to the task of theological interpretation of the Book of Mormon should be privileged above other obvious approaches. In light of the foregoing, this point might already be obvious. Simply put, every other form of theological interpretation of the Book of Mormon text will be richer for positioning itself as a part within the whole whose construction I call for here. Themes and theologoumena, like isolated passages that might serve as spurs to philosophical and theological reflection, find their most determinate meanings only within the larger coherent whole of the Book of Mormon. To ignore this determining whole—fixed and guaranteed in many ways by the authorial and editorial control emphasized within the Book of Mormon—is to miss the most forceful theological shape of the Book of Mormon as a totality.[33]

Obviously, much more can and needs to be said about the nature of the project outlined here. And much more can and needs to be said by way of justifying it in relationship to other possible theological approaches to the Book of Mormon. I believe I have, nevertheless, outlined the key argument for a substantially fuller Book of Mormon theology than has yet been attempted. What is needed is a serious engagement with the Book of Mormon's coherence and continuity with the Bible. When this is uncovered, theological interpretation of the Book of Mormon can begin in earnest.

---

33. For a helpful, but preliminary, analysis of authorial and editorial control in the Book of Mormon, see Terryl L. Givens, *The Book of Mormon: A Very Short Introduction* (New York: Oxford University Press, 2009), 6–12. For a fuller analysis of what this kind of control looks like, see Hardy, *Understanding the Book of Mormon*.

Microscopic Theology

Chapter Two

Weeping for Zion

How much can we dig out of a few lines of scripture? We can of course reflect for hours on an insight, but this question gets at something different from that: How many insights worthy of such reflection are waiting to be discovered in even just a few words in the Book of Mormon? We tend to read the Book of Mormon at a steady pace, largely just making sure we understand the flow of the story or the basic ideas in a sermon until something arrests our attention or strikes us as meaningful. Only then do we pause. What, though, if we were to begin by pausing, paradoxical as that might sound? What if we were to determine in advance that every verse is worthy of sustained attention and careful reading? We often say that every verse is important in its own way, but what would it look like to act like that is really true?

From its origins, the Latter-day Saint Theology Seminar has worked on the premise that scripture deserves extremely slow and excruciatingly close reading. Every summer, it hosts two-week seminars on a scriptural text of no more than about twenty verses. And every summer, participants find themselves wondering by the end whether twenty verses was about two times too many to work on. Once one slows down and sees just how much there is to reflect on in these revealed words, one grows naturally impatient with the pace at which we usually read scripture. We cannot possibly take in the richness and depth of scripture when we move so fast. But what becomes visible when we slow down? This essay, I hope, is a good introduction to the kind of thing that begins to show up when we refuse to move quickly. It is the final product of my own involvement in a 2015 seminar on Jacob 7, hosted by the Latter-day Saint Theology Seminar and held at Union Theological Seminary in New York City. In it, I consider just one well-known verse late in Jacob 7.

This essay originally appeared in *Christ and Anti-Christ: Reading Jacob 7*, ed. Adam Miller and Joseph M. Spencer (Provo, UT: Neal A. Maxwell Institute, 2017), 81–110.

Readers of the Book of Mormon are familiar with the morose conclusion to the book of Jacob. Marilyn Arnold cites the passage as evidence of Jacob's "unusually tender" nature,[1] and John Tanner uses it to exhibit "the sensitivity, vulnerability and quiet eloquence" of this minor Book of Mormon prophet.[2] Hugh Nibley called Jacob's final words a "solemn dirge,"[3] Sidney Sperry wrote of the sincere nature" of the farewell,[4] and Terry Warner has said that Jacob's conclusion betrays the "emotional and spiritual tribulation" that "never ended for Jacob."[5] In a creative "street-legal version" of the Book of Mormon, Michael Hicks has more recently reworded Jacob's farewell in part as follows: "We always talked about rejoicing but were mostly overserious and glum. We had this promised land, this New Canaan, but felt sad and put down and unfulfilled all the time. I hate to end it this way. But it's true. Honest. Plain."[6] Few miss the opportunity, it seems, to highlight the almost depressive nature of Jacob's closing words.

In the following pages, however, I would like to propose a rather different reading of Jacob's farewell. He mourned, and he felt time's passage like a dream, but what might we learn if we were to read these as *normative* experiences—not as the peculiar feelings of a despairing individual, but as something Jacob as a prophet models and that we should strive to emulate?[7] Might we outline a theology of mourning that recognizes the positive and the productive in Jacob's relation to the world? In line with certain early (and other not-so-early) Christian thinkers, I want to outline here a theology of what I will call *consecrated melancholy*. Or rather,

---

1. Marilyn Arnold, "Unlocking the Sacred Text," *Journal of Book of Mormon Studies* 8, no. 1 (1999): 52.

2. John S. Tanner, "Literary Reflections on Jacob and His Descendants" in *The Book of Mormon: Jacob through Words of Mormon, To Learn with Joy,* ed. Monte S. Nyman and Charles D. Tate Jr. (Provo, UT: BYU Religious Studies Center, 1990), 267.

3. Hugh Nibley, *Teachings of the Book of Mormon: Transcripts of Lectures presented to an Honors Book of Mormon Class at Brigham Young University 1988–1990* (Provo, UT: FARMS, 1993), 1:409.

4. Sidney Sperry, *The Book of Mormon Compendium* (Salt Lake City: Bookcraft, 1968), 267.

5. C. Terry Warner, "Jacob," in *The Book of Mormon: "It Begins with a Family"* (Salt Lake City: Deseret Book, 1983), 44.

6. Michael Hicks, *The Street-Legal Version of Mormon's Book* (Provo, UT: Tame Olive Press, 2012), 105.

7. [Since I wrote this essay, a key example of a text seeking to exactly this has appeared. See Deidre Nicole Green, *Jacob: A Brief Theological Introduction* (Provo, UT: Neal A. Maxwell Institute, 2020).]

borrowing from the language of a revelation to and about Joseph Smith, I want to begin to work out the meaning of *weeping for Zion*.[8]

I will proceed as follows. In the first section, I will investigate the basic structures that underlie Jacob 7:26. My aim in doing so is to reveal some of the complexity of the passage, but also and especially to bring out the possibility that the core of Jacob's farewell exhibits a kind of progression from one psychological diagnosis of the Nephite condition to another— the first presented only in a simile but the second presented as the actual psychological state of Jacob and his people. In a second section, I will then provide a detailed philosophical assessment of the two psychological conditions mentioned by Jacob. My intention will be to clarify the basic nature of melancholy and to spell out in a preliminary way what it might mean for melancholy to be consecrated. Finally, in a third section, I will draw out what I take to be the significance of the focus of Nephite mourning, according to Jacob. The point of this last section will be to develop as fully as possible the idea of consecrated melancholy and to bring out with real force the normative features of Jacob's and his people's morose spirit.

Some questions of structure

The words Jacob uses to bid his readers farewell are deeply familiar. Unfortunately, for all its apparent familiarity, the passage's complexity passes largely unnoticed by readers. It deserves quotation in full here, since we will be looking at it in great detail:

> And it came to pass that I, Jacob, began to be old, and the record of this people being kept on the other plates of Nephi—wherefore, I conclude this record, declaring that I have written according to the best of my knowledge,

---

8. The passage is to be found in Doctrine and Covenants 21:7–8: "For thus saith the Lord God: Him [Joseph Smith] have I inspired to move the cause of Zion in mighty power for good, and his diligence I know, and his prayers I have heard. Yea, his weeping for Zion I have seen, and I will cause that he should mourn for her no longer; for his days of rejoicing are come unto the remission of his sins, and the manifestations of my blessings upon his works." For some helpful context regarding what "Zion" meant to the early Saints before the revelation concerning the actual building of a New Jerusalem, see Kerry Muhlestein, "One Continuous Flow: Revelations surrounding the 'New Translation,'" in *The Doctrine and Covenants: Revelations in Context, the 37th Annual Brigham Young University Sidney B. Sperry Symposium*, ed. Andrew H. Hedges, J. Spencer Fluhman, and Alonzo L. Gaskill (Provo UT: BYU Religious Studies Center and Deseret Book, 2008), 40–65.

by saying that the time passed away with us, and also our lives passed away, like as it were unto us a dream, we being a lonesome and a solemn people, wanderers cast out from Jerusalem, born in tribulation in a wild wilderness, and hated of our brethren—which caused wars and contentions. Wherefore, we did mourn out our days. (Jacob 7:26)[9]

At first, perhaps, the passage reads as highly disorganized, a kind of haphazard concatenation of anxieties that serially witness to Jacob's poignant feelings. Closer investigation, however, shows that it follows a careful plan and that a remarkably tight structure organizes the culminating "saying" toward which it works.

In broadest terms, a triple intention animates the passage. Three successive verbs organize this triple intention: "To conclude," "to declare," and "to say." Isolating the part of the passage in which these three verbs appear in rapid succession should help to clarify this point: "I *conclude* this record, *declaring* that I have written according to the best of my knowledge, by *saying that* . . ." Each of these moments might be considered in turn. Jacob unsurprisingly states at the outset of this fragment that the point of the farewell is to accomplish *a gesture of conclusion*: "I conclude this record." But he then immediately qualifies this move by making *a solemn declaration* regarding the relationship between his personal knowledge and the record he aims to conclude: "declaring that I have written according to the best of my knowledge." And then, apparently because he recognizes the destabilizing effect of his declaration, he finally offers *a clarifying saying* intended to justify any disparity between "the best of [his] knowledge" and a simple reality: "by saying that . . ." A gesture of conclusion, secured by solemn declaration, which then requires a clarifying saying—these are the basic elements of the plan underlying Jacob 7:26.[10]

---

9. Throughout this essay, I use as a base text—but with my own punctuation and capitalization—Royal Skousen, ed., *The Book of Mormon: The Earliest Text* (New Haven: Yale University Press, 2009).

10. Jacob shares with Moroni a sense of uncertainty when it comes to concluding his writings. Both seem to have concluded their respective contributions to the Nephite record three distinct times: Jacob at the end of Jacob 3, Jacob 6, and Jacob 7; and Moroni at the end of Mormon 9, Ether 15, and Moroni 10. It might be significant that both Jacob and Moroni write in a kind of supplementary fashion, very much in the shadow of a far more prolific and unquestionably primary author (respectively Nephi and Mormon). For an illuminating discussion of Moroni's struggles to conclude his contribution to the Book of Mormon, see Grant Hardy, *Understanding the Book of Mormon: A Reader's Guide* (New York: Oxford University Press, 2010), 248–67.

Of the three elements of this plan, the second is the simplest. This is because the first, a gesture of conclusion, arises with an odd introductory *wherefore* in the middle of what seems at first to be an interrupted thought, while the third element, the clarifying saying, has as its content the whole remainder of the verse with its own independent structure. Only the solemn declaration comes across as straightforward: the expression of an entirely understandable desire for readers to recognize Jacob's sincerity and good faith. The other two elements therefore deserve closer scrutiny. I aim here, of course, primarily to investigate the theological force of the clarifying saying (the third element), since there Jacob outlines the Nephite experience of time's passing and the psychological conditions that attend it. Nonetheless, before turning directly to the saying and its fascinating structure, I would like to say a few words about the context of the gesture of conclusion that opens the verse. At the very least, an illuminating reading of that first element of the triple plan of Jacob 7:26 should help to motivate close and charitable reading when we turn to the saying meant to clarify the solemn declaration that accomplishes the gesture of conclusion.

Jacob's gesture of conclusion seems, at best, oddly introduced. Were the opening part of the passage to be lacking the incomplete thought regarding "the record . . . kept on the other plates of Nephi," it would read far more naturally: "And it came to pass that I, Jacob, began to be old, . . . wherefore, I conclude this record." The difficulty, of course, is that Jacob inserts between his statement regarding death's approach and his gesture of conclusion a straying aside that appears never to be completed: "and the record of this people being kept on the other plates of Nephi." This clause seems to be either unrelated to the rest of the verse or inexplicable but definitively abandoned before its relevance ever manifests itself. But a closer reading, one invested in questions of structure, points to apparent motivations for Jacob's inclusion of the odd clause. A triple contrast establishes a close relationship between the statement regarding the "other places" and Jacob's gesture of conclusion. Parallel to the phrase "the other plates" in the apparently stray clause is Jacob's reference to "this record" in the gesture of conclusion. A similar parallel exists between "this people" in the apparently stray clause and the first personal "I" in the gesture of conclusion. Finally, the gerundive "being kept" of the apparently stray clause stands in parallel to the conjugated "conclude" of the gesture of conclusion. It should be noted that these parallels follow one after another in rather strict order, which suggests that they are to be read as intentional.

The record of [this people] [being kept] on [the other plates of Nephi]

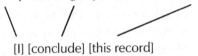

[I] [conclude] [this record]

All these parallels are contrastive in nature. Jacob seems intent on distinguishing himself, an individual prophet, from the undifferentiated mass of individuals making up "this people." His gesture of conclusion ("I conclude"), moreover, stands in contrast to the ongoing work of keeping a national chronicle ("being kept"). And this, finally, underscores the essential difference between "this record," Jacob and Nephi's small plates with their overarching theological programs,[11] and "the other plates of Nephi," the ever-proliferating annals of the Nephite people.[12] All these details make clear the close relationship between Jacob's gesture of conclusion and the only apparently stray clause that immediately precedes it. Moreover, the nature of the overarching contrast between the individual prophet who concludes his programmatic record and the nonindividualized people who keep their chronicle in an ongoing fashion marks the relevance of the still earlier reference to Jacob's approaching death. Individuals grow old and face death, but peoples do not (or do so only seldom, and under extreme circumstances).[13] The contrastive parallels between the second and third clauses of the verse rest on the foundation of the death announcement of the first clause of the verse.

Structural analysis of the opening lines of Jacob 7:26 exhibits remarkable explanatory power. What at first reads as sloppy and directionless ultimately reveals itself as complex and even sophisticated.[14] There is much

---

11. I have written extensively about the overarching theological program of Nephi and Jacob's small plates. See Joseph M. Spencer, *An Other Testament: On Typology* (Salem, OR: Salt Press, 2012), 33–104.

12. Statements regarding the differences between two Nephite records can be found in 1 Nephi 9:2–5 and 1 Nephi 19:1–5.

13. Jacob's Nephites, of course, would eventually face extinction, at a point when they had grown "ripe," as the text says (Hel. 13:14) but that time was tin the distant future for Jacob—even if he had himself prophesied of it (see Jacob 3:3).

14. It seems to me possible to explain even the odd gerundive construction of the second clause's "being kept" in light of these structural points. One most naturally takes such a construction to render the first of two clauses grammatically dependent on but explanatorily foundational for the second: "X being Y, Z must be the case." The difficulty in Jacob's farewell is, first, that the gerundive clause ("the record of this people being kept on the other plates of Nephi") reads as if it were dependent on some clause that it never states and, second, that it seems to

already in the opening lines of verse 26 that can be clarified greatly by paying close attention to structure. This is all the truer when attention turns from Jacob's gesture of conclusion to the clarifying saying that makes up the largest and most detailed part of the verse—the part of the verse to which we will give focused theological attention throughout the rest of this paper. I would like to turn to this clarifying saying now.

At the broadest level, it should be said that Jacob's clarifying saying, meant to explain the possible disparity between his account and history itself, contains three simple parts: two distinct psychologically fraught statements regarding time's passing (first, "the time passed away with us, and also our lives passed away, like as it were unto us a dream," and second, "we did mourn out our days"), and one complex description of the Nephite worldview ("a lonesome and a solemn people, wanderers cast out from Jerusalem, born in tribulation in a wild wilderness, and hated out brethren—which caused wars and contentions"). These are the basic parts of the saying. In terms of sequence, however, Jacob positions the description of the Nephite worldview between the two statements regarding time's passing, using brief rhetorical gestures to mark transitions between parts:

> [**statement**] The time passed away with us, and also our lives passed away, like as it were unto us a dream,
>> [**transition**] we being
>>> [**description**] a lonesome and a solemn people, wanderers cast out from Jerusalem, born in tribulation and in a wild wilderness, and hated of our brethren—which caused wars and contentions.
>> [**transition**] Wherefore,
> [**statement**] we did mourn out our days.

---

be in no way explanatorily foundational for the independent clause that follows it ("wherefore, I conclude this record"). The series of contrastive parallels already enumerated go some distance in alleviating these difficulties, but they do not seem to go far enough since the rhetorical construction of the verse suggests a still tighter connection. But the structural points highlighted above indicate the possibility of another interpretation. Annals and chronicles have no *one* keeper and no *identifiable* set of keepers (until the whole people have become fully extinct, anyway). Might it then be better to regard "being kept" not as a gerundive construction that marks the second clause as subordinate to the third (or to some other clause that never appears in the text) but rather as an oddly but meaningfully constructed independent clause—one that deliberately removes the grammatical subject and then eliminates the verb's indicative status by granting it instead an imperfect aspect (in the grammatical sense)?

This, then, provides the most basic structural organization of the saying. Much more, however, can and should be said about structure here.

First, it seems best to see Jacob's description of the Nephite worldview as dividing rather naturally into four parts: (1) "a lonesome and a solemn people," (2) "wanderers cast out from Jerusalem," (3) "born in tribulation in a wild wilderness," and (4) "hated of our brethren—which caused wars and contentions." A relatively clear logic organizes this fourfold sequence. Jacob follows (1) the basic character of the Nephite people of his day with (2) a word regarding their prehistory and (3) an explanation of their own beginnings, all this leading up to (4) their devastating ongoing condition: the unending conflict between Nephites and Lamanites. Jacob tells a kind of story here, that of a solemn people engaged in eternal warfare with their brothers in direct consequence of their having come into a world of conflict in exile. Jacob and his generation were born too late to see better days in Jerusalem, just as they were born too early to pass by the difficulties of travel and daily family conflict. The central description that lies at the heart of the clarifying saying of Jacob 7:26, then, provides what might be called the fourfold nature of Jacob's way of being, as well as that of his people—those of his peculiar generation.

This first further elaboration of the structure of Jacob's clarifying saying opens immediately onto a second. The transitional markers noted above clearly indicate a very specific relationship between this quadruply traumatic core of Nephite being and the Nephite experience of time's passing, described in the opening and closing statements of the saying. The "we being" that marks the transition from the first statement to the description of the Nephite worldview clearly serves to indicate that the traumas listed in the latter underlie the psychologically complex experience indicated in the former. Time passed like a dream for the Nephites precisely because they were a lonesome and a solemn people, and so on. Similarly, the "wherefore" that marks the transition from the description of the Nephite worldview to the second statement regarding time's passing indicates that the same traumas underlie the psychologically troubled experience laid out at the verse's end. The Nephites mourned out their days precisely because they were a lonesome and a solemn people, and so on. Thus, Jacob clearly wants his readers to understand that the traumas reported in the description at the saying's heart ultimately lie behind his people's psychologically fraught experience of time's passing—which is described in two parallel statements.

We might, in light of these comments, put a finer point or two on the overarching structure of Jacob's clarifying saying. The fourfold nature of Nephite trauma can be more fully articulated by lining up the several clauses of the description as sequential statements. Further, the transition markers might be presented as indicating the causal relationship between the traumatic condition of the Nephites of Jacob's generation and their psychologically complicated experience of time's passing, presented in two distinct statements. Further, the parallel presentation of those two statements might be productively marked. In all, then, the structure of Jacob 7:26, as visually represented here, brings out much more of the complexity of Jacob's saying.

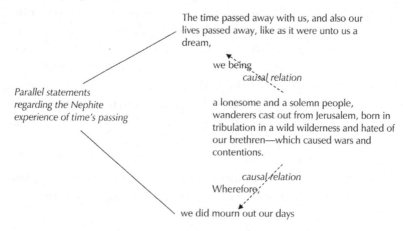

The time passed away with us, and also our lives passed away, like as it were unto us a dream,

we being

causal relation

Parallel statements regarding the Nephite experience of time's passing

a lonesome and a solemn people, wanderers cast out from Jerusalem, born in tribulation in a wild wilderness and hated of our brethren—which caused wars and contentions.

causal relation

Wherefore,

we did mourn out our days

Now, so much structural investigation demands that an answer be given to a question too seldom asked (or too noncommittally asked) when attention focuses on structure: *What light do these structural features of Jacob's clarifying saying shed on its meaning?* Because the structure outlined above exhibits at least loosely chiastic features, we must avoid the temptation to provide this question with what has become among Latter-day Saints a too-ready answer, an answer based on a rather popular understanding of chiastic structure. One too readily claims that every chiasm privileges whatever lies at its center as somehow focal, the whole point of the use of structure. But examples abound of chiasms where the point of utilizing the textual structure seems to be otherwise: in some cases to emphasize a certain mirroring or intertwining of ideas (a good example is Isaiah 5:7: "For the vineyard of the Lord of Hosts is the house of Israel, and the men of Judah his pleasant plant"); in other cases to set up boundaries within a textual unit (as in the chiastic framing of Alma 36, according to a reading I have defended elsewhere);[15] in still other cases to highlight the formal or even ritual flavor

---

15. See Spencer, *An Other Testament*, 2–7.

of what is said (for instance, in Nephi's oath to Zoram in 1 Nephi 4:32: "If he would hearken unto my words, as the Lord liveth, and as I live, even so that if he would hearken unto our words, we would spare his life"); and in yet still other cases to trace a transformation or inversion of things (as in the common scriptural formula, "the first shall be last and the last shall be first"). If there is in fact reason to stress the loosely chiastic structure of Jacob's clarifying saying—and this remains unsure—it has to be asked which of these purposes might underlie the structural features of the text.

Evidently, Jacob's way of structuring his clarifying saying has little to do with emphasizing or otherwise privileging what lies at its structural heart. The point of the saying in the first place is to help explain the existence of any possible discrepancy between actual history and what Jacob reports of history in his record. And this he accomplishes primarily in the opening and closing statements of the clarifying saying, not in the structurally central description of the Nephite worldview. The context privileges Jacob's attempts at identifying the Nephites' psychological condition, not his identification of that condition's underlying cause. For this reason, I conclude that the chief purpose for Jacob's structuring of his clarifying saying in a loosely chiastic fashion is to trace a transformation or an inversion of sorts. I take it that the point is to see how the dream simile of the saying's opening statement, after a careful rehearsal of the actual traumas underlying the Nephites' psychological condition, gives way to a more straightforward description of the Nephite experience of time's passing in terms of mourning. Jacob's saying, it seems to me, works its way from an approximate account of the symptoms to a more staid diagnosis of the actual condition of the Nephites.

A glance back at the fuller visual presentation of the structure of Jacob's saying might help to confirm this conclusion. Even as the fully articulated structure underscores the parallel nature of the opening and closing statements regarding the experience of time's passing, it marks an important lack of balance between them. The opening statement is longer and more complex. It twice attempts to state the Nephites' experience of time's passing, in subtly but significantly different ways ("the time passed away with us," and "our lives passed away"). One cannot help but wonder whether Jacob is unsatisfied with his first attempt at describing the experience but then also whether he ends up just as unsatisfied with his second attempt immediately thereafter. He goes on, of course, to compare this inadequately articulated experience to a dream state, but he inserts between the appropriate preposition ("like") and that to which he compares the experience ("a dream") two hesitating qualifications of the simile: "as it were" and "unto us." With the first of these, Jacob weakens the simile, marking its artificial character. With the second, he subjectifies the simile, limiting its force to those undergoing the experience. All this complexity stands in stark contrast to the unapologetic "we did mourn out our days" that closes the verse. And the consequent imbalance of sorts between the opening and closing statements of the clarifying saying seemingly highlights the fact that the structure marks the transformation of a hesitant and merely provisional attempt at clarification in the opening statement into a confident and conclusive diagnosis in the closing statement.

With this final point, regarding structure, it is perhaps possible at last to leave these merely preliminary considerations to one side and turn to philosophical or theological reflection on Jacob's clarifying saying. In the course of the saying, Jacob traces a shift from a comparison of the Nephite experience of time with having a dream to a straightforward equation of the Nephite experience of time with mourning. Perhaps the whole thing can be encapsulated in a formula of sorts: *From dreams to mourning, by way of an articulation of experienced trauma.* In the following sections, it is this summary formula, made visible thanks to close structural analysis, that will guide the following reflections above all.

On Matters Psychological

Interestingly, the formula of sorts with which I have concluded the above structural considerations describes not only the flow of Jacob's clarifying saying in Jacob 7:26 but also the career of the twentieth century's most influential (as well as most notorious) psychologist: Sigmund Freud. Freud's revolution in psychotherapy began in earnest when, in 1900, he announced that his discovery of the analysis of dreams provided the key to discovering the unconscious.[16] The project only came to real maturity, however, beginning in 1917, when Freud finally undertook to outline what he called his metapsychology, taking his orientation at that point in his career from the experience of mourning.[17] Moreover, what drove his work on the "talking

---

16. Freud put this point this way: "The interpretation of dreams is the *via regia* [the royal road] to the knowledge of the unconscious element in our psychic life." A. A. Brill, ed. and trans., *The Basic Writings of Sigmund Freud* (New York: Modern Library, 1995), 508.

17. The key paper marking this maturation in Freud's thought is Sigmund Freud, "Mourning and Melancholia," in *Sigmund Freud, Collected Papers,* ed. Joan Riviere (New York: Basic Books, 1959), 4:152–70.

cure" was of course, from start to finish, his careful attention to what people experiencing psychological suffering had to say about their traumatic experiences. *From dreams to mourning, by way of an articulation of experienced trauma.* Jacob's attempt at diagnosing his own and his people's condition follows, peculiarly, Freud's attempt at fixing the nature of psychoanalysis.

Of course, these parallels only go so far. Nonetheless, I would like to take them as a basic motivation for using Freud's thought to clarify at least some of the stakes of Jacob's references to dreams and mourning. I want to be clear, however, that I do not do so uncritically. There have been a few attempts to critique Freud from a specifically Mormon perspective, and I take these attempts seriously.[18] And psychologists in the English-speaking world have, of course, been less and less inclined to take Freud's work seriously in recent decades, something that cannot be ignored. Nonetheless, it seems to me that the development of scientific distaste for Freud, along with attempts at critique from a specifically Mormon perspective, often (and perhaps understandable fail to recognize the richness of Freud's thought, allowing certain definitely problematic aspects of his work to get in the way of its more fruitful aspects—aspects that I think speak in particularly poignant ways to Mormon theology.[19] Perhaps if one reads Freud as a philosopher or as a thinker rather than as a scientist in the strict sense of the word, it is possible to allow his attempts at clarifying things like trauma, dreams, and mourning to inform careful reflection. It is as a philosopher that I use his work here, aware of both the danger and the promise of his thought.

To begin to assess what Jacob says about both dreams and mourning, let me first highlight again the contrast between the respective ways he refers to them. First, he speaks of dreams, but only in a simile, which he further doubly qualifies. Jacob refers to dreams only to help his readers

---

18. Most such attempts have been indirect, actually. Representative is the collection in Aaron P. Jackson, Lane Fischer, and Doris R. Dant, eds., *Turning Freud Upside Down: Gospel Perspectives on Psychotherapy's Fundamental Problems* (Provo, UT: Brigham Young University Press, 2005).

19. Although it comes with its own problems, the larger Lacanian attempt at rehabilitating Freud's work exemplifies the ability to extract the productive from the unproductive in Freud's extant writings. Perhaps more a propos, however, is the use of Freud by someone like Paul Ricoeur, who specifically investigates his relevance to philosophical reflection. See Paul Ricoeur, *Freud and Philosophy*, trans. Denis Savage (New Haven: Yale University Press, 1977). For a good introduction to the Lacanian Project, see Bruce Fink, *A Clinical Introduction to Lacanian Psychoanalysis: Theory and Technique* (Cambridge, MA: Harvard University Press, 1977).

understand something that is *not* actually a dream, something that is only dream*like*. And his qualifications of the simile ("as it were," "unto us") seem meant to underline the fact that the simile *is* just a simile. Jacob wishes his readers to understand something of the way he and his people experienced the passing of time, but he wishes just as much that his readers recognize that his illustrative images are *only* images. All this contrasts sharply with the way Jacob subsequently talks about mourning. There he leaves off simi- les for direct description. He and his people actually *did* mourn out their days. They *really* experienced time in terms of mourning. In this descrip- tion, Jacob employs no image to help his readers grasp at what he means to convey; he assumes they can understand the brute fact he reports to them.

The contrast here works because dreaming and mourning share cer- tain features, even as they differ in important respects.[20] Their differences are, of course, much more obvious than their similarities. Dreams occur when we sleep, when our conscious awareness of the world retreats and our unconscious desires make themselves manifest. The work of mourn- ing, on the other hand, unfolds while we remain conscious—in fact, all *too* conscious, due to the depth of our loss; in mourning we are entirely aware of our desires, the intensity of which often keeps us awake at night. And this is only the first of the several obvious differences. We experience mourning in a focused way, our loss providing everything in life with a kind of focal point, deeply painful. But we experience dreams as pro- foundly disjointed and nonlinear, moving by metaphorical leaps and met- onymical bounds.[21] Where mourning seldom gives us any reprieve from the mental effort it requires, keeping us focused on what has slipped from our grasp, dreams present us with uncanny associations and comforting discontinuities—or even abruptly conclude, allowing us to wake up when they become too horrific. Other obvious differences might be named too. It certainly must be said that mourning is a difficult and painful process, even if it eventually results in healing. Dreams, however, while they might at times take the shape of nightmares, are often enough pleasurable experi- ences or at least entirely neutral, letting us forget most of them. Further,

---

20. The similarities between dreaming and mourning explicitly motivated Freud's investigation of the latter. See Freud, "Mourning and Melancholia," 152.

21. Freud used the technical terms *displacement* and *condensation* to describe the connections and disconnections that organize the experience of dreaming. Jacques Lacan has usefully shown that these two terms map nicely onto the linguistic notions of metaphor and metonymy. See Jaques Lacan, *Écrits: The First Complete Edition in English*, trans. Bruce Fink (New York: Norton, 2006), 412–41.

we might note that mourning usually comes to an end, while we go on dreaming throughout our lives.

All these differences are important, but the network they form is woven also of crucial similarities. For instance, despite the obvious disjointedness of dreams, which seems to distance them absolutely from the focused experience of mourning, it must ultimately be said that a disguised coherence underpins every dream. All of a dream's metaphoric disruptions and metonymic concatenations organize themselves into a network whose center of gravity is some kind of trauma. Whether as simple and quotidian as a passing desire for something one lacks, or whether as complex and deep as a horrified fascination with self-destruction, *some* kind of trauma serves as the principle—both causal and organizational—of every dream.[22] And it is this center of gravity in every experience of dreaming that links dreams to mourning. As dreams organize a whole network of (imagistic) associations around some kind of trauma, ostensibly in an attempt to help us cope with our frustrated or forbidden or frightening desires, the work of mourning undertakes to revise the network of our conscious associations around the experience of deep loss. Confronted with the frustration of intense desires to be with a loved one, working through the forbidden anger we feel toward the one who has abandoned us, and coming to recognize the frightening fragility of life as we know it, we mourn.[23] In essence, the work of dreaming is like the work of mourning because, in each case, we find ourselves maneuvering a landscape organized around what seems impossible to speak about—or, at least, what seems impossible to speak

---

22. It is an open question whether the initially indiscernible coherence of a dream is a feature of the dream as originally and unconsciously experienced, or whether it is instead only a feature of the dream as reconstructed afterward and in a conscious state. This is, of course, an important distinction for the psychoanalyst, but it seems to me unnecessary to give it detailed attention here.

23. Freud's succinct description of the work of mourning is perhaps worth citing: "Each single one of the memories and hopes which bound the libido to the object is brought up and hyper-cathected, and the detachment of the libido from it accomplished. . . . When the work of mourning is completed the ego becomes free and uninhibited again." Freud, "Mourning and Melancholia," 154. Another helpful description appears later in the same essay: "Reality passes its verdict—that the object no longer exists—upon each singly one of the memories and hopes through which the libido was attached to the lost object, and the ego, confronted as it were with the decision whether it will share this fate, is persuaded by the sum of its narcissistic satisfactions in being alive to sever its attachment to the non-existent object." Freud, "Mourning and Melancholia," 166.

about without somehow committing an act of sacrilege. In dreaming as in mourning, we work out our relationship to what remains inaccessible to us.

Despite important differences in outward appearance, then, dreams and mourning share much that is essential. Jacob can make sense for his readers of his people's response to their traumatic circumstances in terms either of dreams or of mourning—although, as we have seen, it is quite clear that he means to claim that his people actually mourned, while their experience was only like dreaming. That Jacob provides his readers with *both* the simile and the direct description, asking them to understand his people's experience in terms of *both* dreaming and mourning, is important because it draws attention to the shared underlying structure of the two sorts of experience. Were Jacob only to speak of mourning, readers might too easily take him to mean just that his people grumbled about their less-than-perfect circumstances. But because he couples mourning with dreams, it becomes clear that his talk of mourning indeed bears psychological significance. His and his people's time was occupied by actual mourning, by the slow process of transformation that aims at eventually stabilizing one's affairs despite deep loss. For this reason, their experience was not *actually* that of dreaming, though it was apparently very much *like* dreaming.

Implicit in the preceding few paragraphs is what seems to be the major motivation for Jacob's nonetheless drawing a contrast between dreaming and mourning in attempting to describe his generation's experience. The very first point of difference we drew above between the two sorts of experience concerns the fact that dreaming is unconscious while mourning is conscious. This distinction, presumably, plays a particularly important role in the shift from mere simile to direct description in the clarifying saying of Jacob 7:26. Dreaming is, so to speak, automatic, something that happens on its own despite our conscious intentions. We might wish for dreamless sleep, but we have no guarantee that our wish will be granted. And after being rudely awakened, we might wish to return to a pleasant dream, but we are as likely as not to move onto other dreams when we return to sleep. Mourning is a different affair entirely, however. Although we seldom have control over the events that cause or motivate our mourning, the work of mourning unfolds in anything but an automatic or unconscious way. Not only are we all too aware of our desires and our consequent pain, but we work our way toward regained normalcy only by working consciously and intentionally on seeing the world in a new way. To say that the Nephite experience during Jacob's generation was only like dreaming but was actually a matter of mourning is, it would seem, to indicate that they had to focus conscious effort on grappling with what they experienced as deep loss.

Even as we make this major point of contrast explicit, however, we should note yet another feature of Jacob's clarifying saying that brings his talk of dreams and his talk of mourning into close continuity—another feature of the saying, that is, that seems to indicate why Jacob should wish to claim that his people's mourning was *like* dreaming and therefore was *unlike* mourning to some extent. The final point of difference we drew above between the two sorts of experience concerns the fact that mourning is a work that, generally speaking, comes to a kind of resolution. Mourning comes to an end when, although we remain fully aware of our loss, we have found a way of being oriented by it or to it that allows us to go on. Something like normalcy returns. Dreams, however, as products of the incorrigibly inconsistent unconscious, do not so much end as they are interrupted, always in the middle of things. We come back from our dreams to the normal world, but we do so only by leaving the world of our dreams behind. And the world of our dreams *never* achieves normalcy. Our unconscious states never work all the way through their traumas.

This marks a further point of contrast between dreams and mourning. And yet it must be said that Jacob describes his people's mourning in the closing statement of his clarifying saying in language suggestive of dreams. When he says that he and his people "did mourn out [their] days," he clearly indicates that his people's mourning never came to an end.[24] And this is

---

24. Time's passing shows up in Jacob's talk both of dreams and of mourning, but its formulation differs. Note that in the dream simile, Jacob struggles to articulate what he has in mind. He speaks first of "the time" that passed away, but then, before he introduces the dream simile itself, he uses a different locution: "and also our lives passed away." The difference between "the time," abstract and in the singular, and "our lives," concrete and in the plural, is suggestive. Jacob seems at first unsure whether what passes should be regarded as something formal but accessible to all, or as something real but privately experienced. Whatever their differences, however, these two locutions share an important feature: objectivity. Both are sorts of things that can pass away. Jacob's formulation of time's passing in the statement that concludes his clarifying saying, however, operates in a nonobjective way. In his direct description of the experience of mourning, Jacob seems to combine the dream simile's two terms ("the time" and "our days") in a single term: "our days." This term seems to indicate something that is shared like time in general and therefore is irreducible to the privacy of a singular life, and yet that is unquestionably concrete and therefore irreducible to merely formal accessibility. Moreover, this conception of temporal experience

quite strange. Although it is certainly possible for someone never to work all
the way through the stages of mourning, and so never to achieve normalcy
again, such cases are exceptional; they are, precisely, cases that are out of the
ordinary. The sort of deep loss that leads to mourning certainly traumatizes,
but it does not usually traumatize so deeply that it cannot be overcome.
Typically speaking, one *does not* mourn out one's days. One mourns for
a time, works at reconfiguring one's world for a time, and then lives on.[25]
Jacob, however, clearly seems to say that his people *never ceased to mourn*.
They worked, quite consciously it seems, at giving a new shape to their
world, a new shape that would allow them to return to normalcy and rou-
tine. They worked, that is, at the possibility of being at last at their ease. But,
apparently, they failed. They failed ever to live on, to breathe easily, to be
consoled, to experience equilibrium. It would seem that their loss was too
deep to allow them—or at least those of Jacob's generation—ever to rest.

At this point, then, it becomes necessary to ask exactly what it was
that Jacob and his people lost. What was it that caused perpetual, unceasing mourning, preventing their coming to a point of rest or of normalcy?
Actually, Jacob states the answer to this question quite straightforwardly
in the course of his fourfold description of the traumatic experience that
underlay his and his people's dreamlike mourning. What Jacob and his
people lost was Jerusalem. In fact, he informs us that he and his people
had a particularly odd relationship to that loss, indicated by the essential
incompatibility between two things Jacob says about his people's relationship to Jerusalem. In the course of his fourfold description of Nephite
trauma, he says both that they were "born . . . in a wild wilderness" and
that they were "cast out from Jerusalem." The combination of these two
claims, of course, makes no sense. If one has been cast out of the city of
her nativity, then she must have been born there—not in "a wild wilderness." Or if she has been born elsewhere and in fact has never been to the
city in question, it makes little sense to say she has been "cast out" from
it. Yet Jacob combines these two incommensurable experiences into one
traumatic whole that underlies the Nephite psychological condition. His

---

makes time immanent to the work of mourning. People "mourn out" their days.
Despite these clear differences between the ways of talking about time in the
opening and closing statements of Jacob's clarifying saying, however, it seems
perfectly clear that the processes described in each never come to an end. Nephite
mourning is dreamlike at least in the odd fact that it does not come to an end.

25. Freud notes that occasionally the "struggle" of mourning "can be so intense
that a turning away from reality ensues." Freud, "Mourning and Melancholia," 154.

generation was at once born at a distance from Jerusalem, and yet they were always poignantly aware of their being in a kind of exile. It was thus that they "did mourn out [their] days."

I will come back to the significance of Jerusalem as the focus of Nephite loss in the final section of this paper. For the moment, it is enough just to recognize from Jacob's paradoxical description of the Nephite experience that they underwent a rather unique sort of mourning. Their mourning was not of the sort that comes to an end. Jacob and his people mourned a constitutive, irreparable loss. Helpfully, Freud has a name for this condition, or for something quite like it—a venerable name drawn, in fact, from Christian theology: *melancholia.*[26] Actually, the condition Jacob describes differs in at least one important respect from what Freud calls melancholia, since the latter emphasizes the unconscious nature of the conduction as framed by psychoanalytic practice, while Jacob, with his talk of mourning, emphasizes the conscious nature of his people's experience. Perhaps precisely for this reason, it might be useful to examine melancholia from the perspective of one of Freud's more insightful critics: Giorgio Agamben. At its real heart, Agamben explains, "Melancholy would be not so much the regressive reaction to the loss of the love object [described by Freud] as the imaginative capacity to make an unobtainable object appear as if lost." The melancholic in effect "stages a simulation where what cannot be lost because it has bever been possessed [nevertheless] *appears as* lost."[27] Put in other words, there lies at the heart of melancholic experience a paradoxical transformation of the merely inaccessible into the actually lost. And this seems to me a remarkably apt characterization of the situation Jacob describes. Although he and his people had never actually seen Jerusalem, they related to it as if it had nonetheless once been theirs; they experienced it constitutively, irreparably lost.

Not only does Agamben's slight-but-significant corrective to Freud's conception of melancholia point in the direction of Jacob 7:26, it also aims to sum up a longstanding Christian theological tradition. Agamben is explicit about the fact that the Christian tradition oddly and perhaps ironically lies behind Freud's attempt to think about melancholia. Even

26. See, again, Freud, "Mourning and Melancholia." It may be significant that Jacob speaks of mourning rather than, strictly speaking, of melancholia. Freud emphasizes the strictly *unconscious* nature of melancholic suffering, but Jacob's emphasis on mourning suggests the *conscious* nature of his and his people's experience.

27. Giorgio Agamben, *Stanzas: Word and Phantasm in Western Culture*, trans. Ronald L. Martinez (Minneapolis: University of Minnesota Press, 1993), 20; emphasis added.

more usefully, though, Agamben—unlike Freud—draws from the tradition to distinguish between two sorts of melancholy. There is on the one hand what early Christian thinkers called *tristitia mortifera*, deadly sadness, a kind of sickness unto death.[28] And there is on the other hand what early Christian thinkers called *tristitia salutifera*, saving sadness, akin in certain ways to what Latter-day Saints often call "godly sorrow."[29] Focusing on the latter of these two sorts of melancholy, Agamben speaks of an "obscure wisdom according to which hope has been given only for the hopeless"[30]— a formula very much resonant with my own recent attempt to lay out a Mormon theology of hope. Like Sarah and Abraham, confronted with the genuinely objective impossibility of a child, but precisely *therefore* free to hope for a child from the God who covenants to undermine the objective order of the world, it is "they that mourn" whom Jesus calls "blessed," because "they shall be comforted" (Matt. 5:4).[31] Agamben rightly says of melancholic or ceaseless mourning, "The greatest disgrace is never to have had it."[32] Or perhaps it would be most relevant to cite in this connection a formula Jacob first heard falling from the lips of his dying father, given in the form of a final blessing on the melancholic child: "In thy childhood thou hast suffered afflictions and much sorrow, . . . [but] thou knowest the greatness of God, and he shall consecrate thine afflictions for thy gain" (2 Ne. 2:1–2). From quite early in his life, Jacob knew of the possibility of some kind of *consecrated melancholy*.

How is one to distinguish between the two sorts of melancholy identified by the Christian tradition—between a sort of interminable mourning that results in the death of the soul and a sort of interminable mourning that somehow deserves commendation? What makes Joseph Smith's "weeping for Zion" a good thing (D&C 21:8) and what Mormon calls "the sorrowing of the damned" a clearly bad thing (Morm. 2:13)? What

---

28. I borrow this last phrase from John 11:4, but also from Søren Kierkegaard, *Fear and Trembling and The Sickness unto Death*, trans. Walter Lowrie (Princeton: Princeton University Press, 1954), 133–278.

29. The language comes, of course, from 2 Corinthians 7:10.

30. Agamben, *Stanzas, 7*.

31. I draw the story of Sarah and Abraham from Paul's discussion in Romans 4. See my discussion of Paul's analysis in Joseph M. Spencer, *For Zion: A Mormon Theology of Hope* (Salt Lake City:Greg Kofford Books, 2014), 15–23.

32. Agamben, *Stanzas, 7*. Also recommended is the treatment of melancholia in Jean-Luc Marion, *God without Being*, trans. Thomas A Carlson (Chicago: University of Chicago Press, 1991), 132–38.

differentiates the wandering "pilgrims" of Hebrews 11:13 from those condemned for having "loved to wander" in Jeremiah 14:10? Why should we not limit ourselves to speaking of the joy of the saints and the misery of the rebellious, avoiding the complexity implied by that fact that even the redeemed experience "sorrow . . . for the sins of the world" (3 Ne. 28:9)—not to mention the even starker complexity implied by Enoch's vision of "the God of heaven" who "looked upon the residue of the people, and . . . wept" (Moses 7:28)? How do we know whether our hearts are broken because we see that we cannot reach on our own what we nonetheless rightly desire, and when are our hearts broken because we see the impossibility of having what we should not but cannot help but desire?

There are, I suspect, dozens of good and productive answers to these questions. Leaving their enumeration for another occasion, however, I wish to focus in on just one possible answer—the one implied by Jacob's exclusive focus on what he and his people experienced as definitively lost: Jerusalem. It is well and good to speak of consecrated dreamlike mourning, but what lies behind that consecrated dreamlike mourning for Jacob is something quite specific. For the remainder of this theological investigation, I mean to ask what we might learn by turning our attention to what Jacob saw as forever lost.

Next Year in Zion

Everything we have said to this point makes clear that there are at least some reasons to think that Jacob's sort of melancholy, famously on display in Jacob 7:26, is redemptive rather than lamentable. It is possible and even right to speak of consecrated melancholy, a sort of saving sadness or a mourning that aligns with God's purposes. In Jacob's own words, such mourning assumes the right shape when it takes as its object or focus Jerusalem's loss, the fact that Zion has not as yet been redeemed or rebuilt. And so, it seems, to go any further in understanding what it might mean to take Jacob's mournful spirit as a guiding spirit, it will be necessary to investigate the basic meaning of his and his people's relationship to the city of Jerusalem, to the city they had never seen but nonetheless experienced as definitively lost. To do so—that is, to seek evidence concerning Jacob's and his people's understandings of Jerusalem—we can have recourse only to Jacob's words, since he is the only person from his unique generation whose words appear in the Book of Mormon. It will be necessary, then, to proceed with a survey of what Jacob has to say about the city whose inaccessibility he mourned all his life.

References to Jerusalem in the book of Jacob are few. It is perhaps telling, nonetheless, that Jacob opens his record by situating its beginnings at the time when "fifty and five years had passed away from the time that Lehi left Jerusalem" (Jacob 1:1).[33] Even before Nephi's death, but also and just as surely during the years following, it seems that the Nephites measured time itself in terms of Jerusalem's loss. That is certainly significant, but it should be noted that Jacob's formula does not, strictly speaking, refer to Jerusalem's loss. Rather, it speaks of the time that Lehi *left* Jerusalem, the family abandoning the city rather than the city exiling the family. Despite the nostalgic tone of Jacob 7:26, Jacob 1:1 suggests something of Nephite disgust for the city left behind. And what follows throughout the book of Jacob confirms this sense of antipathy for the city whose loss Jacob's final words lament so touchingly. In Jacob 4, for instance, Jacob speaks with a kind of contempt for the people of the city his family had left behind before his birth: "Behold, the Jews were a stiffnecked people, and they despised the words of plainness, and killed the prophets, and sought for things that they could not understand" (Jacob 4:14). Jacob's distaste, perhaps personal, for Jerusalem and its people is fully on display here.

Even more striking is the complex treatment of Jerusalem to be found in Jacob 2–3. There Jacob lays out less apparently personal (and therefore much more compelling) reasons for his family's having been directed to leave Jerusalem. In the course of a sermon dedicated to berating the Nephites for nascent wickedness among them—wickedness displayed most egregiously in problematic conceptions of gender relations[34]—Jacob quotes the Lord as saying the following:

> I have led this people forth out of the land of Jerusalem by the power of mine arm that I might raise up unto me a righteous branch from the fruit of the loins of Joseph. . . . I the Lord have seen the sorrow and heard the mourning of the daughters of my people in the land of Jerusalem—yea, and in all the

---

33. Note that a similar formula appears in Nephi's writings in 2 Nephi 5:28. The major difference between the two is, of course, that Jacob speaks of his father's departure, while Nephi speaks of leaving Jerusalem in the plural first person.

34. For an analysis of these and related texts, see Joseph M. Spencer and Kimberly M. Berkey, "'Great Cause to Mourn': The Complexity of Gender and Race in the Book of Mormon," in *Americanist Approaches to The Book of Mormon,* ed. Jared Hickman and Elizabeth Fenton (New York: Oxford University Press, 2019), 298–320. [Further comments of great interest on this passage appear in Green, *Jacob*.]

lands of my people—because of the wickedness and abominations of their husbands. And I will not suffer, saith the Lord of Hosts, that the cries of the fair daughters of this people, which I have led out of the land of Jerusalem, shall come up unto me. (Jacob 2:25, 31–32)

Here again the almost nostalgic feel of Jacob 7:26 is missing. Jerusalem is less something lost that should therefore be mourned than the very seat of wickedness, something that must be left behind to pursue true righteousness. In the place of Nephites mourning for a lost city, one finds in this text "the mourning of the daughters . . . of Jerusalem," the unceasing sorrow of women who have lost confidence in "their husbands." When Jacob confronts his people and their own wickedness, he sees Jerusalem primarily as the city of "David and Solomon," whose examples he does not hesitate to call "abominable" (Jacob 2:24).

In none of these texts from earlier in the book of Jacob does one find talk of the Lehites being "cast out" from Jerusalem, as in Jacob 7. Instead, in these earlier texts, the Lehites are "led out" of the abominable city—or, as in the time-measurement of the book's opening verse, they simply "left" the city as they sought their own promised land. A holistic view of the book of Jacob thus seems to complicate the deep sense of loss expressed at the book's conclusion. From the references reviewed here, it seems unlikely that what is *really* at issue in Jacob's mournful final words in Jacob 7:26 is just the fact that the Lehite peoples are no longer acquainted with Jerusalem. There is, it seems, something more complex at work in Jacob's lament concerning his people's being "wanderers cast out from Jerusalem." The key to making better sense of this situation lies, I think, in a lengthy well-known sermon delivered by Jacob but not included in his own book; it appears, rather, in 2 Nephi 6–10, gathered into the complex project of Nephi's written record.[35] To get to the heart of what interests Jacob when it comes to Jerusalem and its fate, it is necessary to turn from the book of Jacob to this sermon, even if its meaning has been channeled by Nephi's editorial interests.

The first reference to Jerusalem in the sermon of 2 Nephi 6–10 comes at the outset of a kind of commentary on a passage from Isaiah (specifically, Isaiah 49:22–23), a passage assigned to Jacob by Nephi as the text for his

---

35. I have analyzed the structure of Nephi's record, including the role played there by Jacob's sermon, in Spencer, *An Other Testament*, 34–58. I might note that I would revise many aspects of that analysis today. [I have in fact since this time published much more careful analyses of Second Nephi's structure. See discussions throughout Joseph M. Spencer, *The Vision of All: Twenty-five Lectures on Isaiah in Nephi's Record* (Salt Lake City: Greg Kofford Books, 2016).]

preaching. Describing the first of a series of events in Judah's history that Jacob understands to be relevant to the interpretation of the Isaiah text, he says: "The Lord hath shewn me that they which were at Jerusalem, from whence we came, have been slain and carried away captive" (2 Ne. 6:8). Two points seem especially salient here. First, Jacob cites as his source for this information regarding Jerusalem and its inhabitants a vision. Second, Jacob claims that the vision in question has been given him to witness Jerusalem's fall, but this destruction of the city constitutes a loss deeper than any we have mentioned to this point, resulting in an exile of world-historical significance. Observant Jews to this day mourn *this* loss and experience *this* exile, symbolized most poignantly in the glass crushed at Jewish wedding ceremonies in memory of the destruction of Solomon's temple. As the psalmist sings of Jerusalem's destruction at Babylon's hands: "If I do not remember thee, let my tongue cleave to the roof of my mouth; if I prefer not Jerusalem above my chief joy" (Ps. 137:6).

Yet Jacob's visionary witness of Jerusalem's fall only sets up his interpretation of Isaiah, and he focuses that interpretation on subsequent events in Jewish history. Significantly, the next three of Jacob's references to Jerusalem come in a lengthy quotation (of Isaiah 50:1–52:2), which he uses to provide context for the briefer Isaiah passage (Isa. 49:22–23) on which he means to comment in his sermon. The first of these Isaianic references to Jerusalem echoes Jacob's own talk of destruction and exile, even as it begins to point beyond it: "Awake! Awake!" Isaiah says to Judah, "Stand up, O Jerusalem, which hast drunk at the hand of the Lord the cup of his fury!" (2 Ne. 8:17, quoting Isa. 51:17). The other two references to Jerusalem come as a pair a few verses later in a reprise of these heartening words: "Awake! Awake! Put on thy strength, O Zion! Put on thy beautiful garments, O Jerusalem, the holy city! For henceforth there shall be no more come into thee uncircumcised and the unclean! Shake thyself from the dust! Arise, sit down, O Jerusalem! Loose thyself from the bands of thy neck, O captive daughter of Zion!" (2 Ne. 8:24–25). Beyond loss and exile, Jacob sees the promise of Jerusalem's redemption. But of course, he sees such redemption only at a distance, envisioned as occurring at a time thousands of years in the future. And so, there is much to mourn in the meanwhile.

Perhaps, then, this begins to explain Jacob's mourning. And yet there is more Jacob has to say in his sermon regarding Jerusalem. After concluding his long quotation from Isaiah and immediately before pursuing a long theological tangent regarding the nature of resurrection, Jacob refers to another event associated with Jerusalem that might give him reason to mourn. "In the body [God] shall shew himself unto they at Jerusalem, from whence we came," he explains (2 Ne. 9:5). The bad news he does not give in full until further along, however. It comes with these words: "Because of priestcrafts and iniquities, they at Jerusalem will stiffen their necks against him, that he be crucified. Wherefore, because of their iniquities, destructions, famines, pestilences, and bloodshed shall come upon them. And they which shall not be destroyed shall be scattered among all nations" (10:5–6). Unfortunately (and not without a style of language that makes twenty-first-century readers uncomfortable), Jacob sees in the crucifixion of Jesus Christ a major feature of Jerusalem's sacred history.[36] In *that* he finds reason to mourn as well. The alienation of Israel from their would-be deliverer causes him—as he explains later in his own book—a great deal of anxiety, what he even calls "overanxiety" (Jacob 4:18). It may be of real significance that such language is psychologically freighted like the language of Jacob 7:26.

Now, what is to be gathered from all these Jacobite references to Jerusalem's sad history? At the very least, it is necessary to countenance the possibility that what worried Jacob and his people was *less their own* distance from Jerusalem than the way their distance from Jerusalem symbolized the city's loss in a much larger historical sense. The exile of sorts experienced by Jacob's people was a constant reminder of the exile they had barely missed by leaving Jerusalem during Zedekiah's reign—the exile that God none-theless showed them in vision. At the very time Lehi and his family left Jerusalem for the New World, those whom they left behind subsequently left Jerusalem for lowly exile in Babylon. And of course that exile was itself a symbol of a much larger history in which Judah has been consistently home-less and traumatized, waiting for messianic redemption.[37] This the Nephite prophets of the first generation saw clearly in their visionary experiences,

---

36. Second Nephi 10:3–6 has often been labeled anti-Semitic in tone, especially because of the claim there that "the Jews" constitute "the more wicked part of the world," a claim supposedly justified because "there is none other nation on earth that would crucify their God." Perhaps one could exonerate the Book of Mormon by noting that it goes on in the same passage to provide a further point of justification by using the language of the New Testament (such that it's anti-Semitic spirit is borrowed rather than original, or by insisting that the passage explicitly limits the "wicked" to those involved in "priestcrafts and iniquities" (presumably referring just to certain opportunistic leaders). But the point stands that Jacob's language is troubling, and this should not be overlooked.

37. N. T. Wright has recently spelled out at length and quite beautifully the way the brief exile in Babylon took on a larger historical meaning. See N. T. Wright, *Pail and the Faithfulness of God* (Minneapolis: Fortress Press, 2013), 1:139–63.

and they thereby knew all too keenly that redemption for Jerusalem and the covenant people lay only in an inaccessible future, too far off to find any real joy in it.[38] The best among Jacob's people apparently mourned out their days because they were attuned to the Abrahamic in the Christian gospel, because they saw that even the Messiah's arrival could only *start* the process of redeeming Israel, as well as the process of Israel's associated redemption of the world.[39] Fulfillment would be waiting for a very long time.

There is a key theological term central to the story of Jacob's encounter with Sherem that is relevant to all this talk of the covenant and its delayed fulfillment, although the term hardly appears relevant at first sight. As the encounter with Sherem unfolds, Jacob eventually testifies that his knowledge was rooted in "the power of the Holy Ghost" (Jacob 7:12), and Sherem responds by asking for a sign executed by that same power (v. 13). Close reading of the small plates suggests that these references to "the power of the Holy Ghost" have a quite specific meaning. The phrase appears in Nephi's writings in very strategic places and with highly specific associations. Although Latter-day Saints are accustomed to conflating the power of the Holy Ghost with the witness of the Spirit of God, Nephi—and presumably therefore Jacob as well—seems to have something narrower in mind when using these words, and that something has everything to do with Jerusalem and the Abrahamic Covenant.

According to Nephi, the power of the Holy Ghost is specifically that by which one can "see and hear and know" of Israel's history. He effectively promises his readers that *everyone* can have an apocalyptic vision of the world's Abrahamic history so long as they "diligently seek" it. As he says, "the mysteries of God shall be unfolded to them by the power of the Holy Ghost"—to deny this, according to Nephi, is to deny the Lord's "one eternal round" (1 Ne. 10:19), to deny that he is "the same yesterday today and forever" (v. 18), working at one and the same massive historical project. The power of the Holy Ghost is thus not only the power by which Nephi himself witnesses in vision the whole of Israel's future; it is also a power relevant to the era in which the Book of Mormon would eventually circulate—that is, of course, our own era. In a vision of the "last days," Nephi says that "they which shall seek to bring forth [the Lord's] Zion at that day . . . shall have the gift and the power of the Holy Ghost" (13:37).

---

38. On this point, see Spencer, *For Zion*, 71–78.

39. Third Nephi 15:1–9 serves a kind of commentary on the mismatch between the Messiah's arrival and the longer history of Israel's redemption. It is, in many ways, the interpretive key to the remainder of the Book of Mormon.

To be contrasted with such repentant people, according to Nephi, are those Christians who symptomatically fail to recognize that their "bible" came "from the Jews, [the Lord's] ancient covenant people" (2 Ne. 29:4). In exasperation, Nephi quotes the Lord:

> And what thank they the Jews for the bible which they receive from them? Yea, what do the gentiles mean? Do they remember the travails and the labors and the pains of the Jews—and their diligence unto me—in bringing forth salvation unto the gentiles? O ye gentiles, have ye remembered the Jews, mine ancient covenant people? Nay, but ye have cursed them and have hated them and have not sought to recover them. But behold, I will return all these things upon your own heads, for I the Lord hath not forgotten my people! (vv. 4–5)

While culturally Christian Europe has hated and persecuted—*and massacred*—Jews, the power of the Holy Ghost, according to Nephi, has attempted to find its way into open hearts, seeking to restore a sense of the promises linked to a city not lost for thousands of years.

In closely related passages, Nephi excoriates the latter-day world, so deeply secular that even its Christians deny the power of the Holy Ghost. The symptom of this denial, Nephi says, is that they are "at ease in Zion," crying, "All is well!" (2 Ne. 28:24–25). Failing to weep for Zion, failing to mourn out their days, they—like us—ignore the very power by which one should be reminded of the Abrahamic underpinnings of the Christian gospel. Today, it would seem, the world is made up mostly of Sherems, skeptical of revelation or of any real power of the Holy Ghost. We satisfy ourselves that all is well in Zion—or, alternatively, that there is *much* to mourn in Zion while ignoring all things Abrahamic in favor of our own moral concerns, traditional or fashionable as the case may be. We continue to forget what God claims he cannot forget. And we thereby deny the very power that Jacob says lies behind his deepest theological and existential concerns. It would seem that it was always and only by that same power—the power of the Holy Ghost—that Jacob and his people mourned in a consecrated way.

To weep for Zion, or to mourn out our days as we think of Jerusalem's loss—*this* is what, according to Jacob and Nephi, the power of the Holy Ghost would lead us to do. If they are right, then perhaps the woes they pronounced upon the last days are the ones we should take more seriously. How many tears do we shed for the Zion envisaged in the Abrahamic covenant? Far too few. But perhaps, reading the small plates carefully, we might be led to shed a few more.

Chapter Three

Potent Messianism
Textual, Historical, and Theological Notes on 1 Nephi 1:18–20

Perhaps it is no surprise that a great deal can be wrung out of a long and complex verse like that of Jacob's mournful farewell. That passage is laden with pathos and rich in imagery. It is a text many recognize as provocative and interesting. The real test of theological interpretation comes when the theologian pauses over the kind of verse we tend to ignore, the kind of verse that seems at first glance—or even at second glance—to be straightforward, as if it wears its meaning on its sleeve. To find real depth in a passage that most assume is relatively simple ought to be to show that theological interpretation is onto something. But to do that, it turns out, it is not enough just to pick a random verse and start theologizing. Slow reading helps to bring interpretive questions to the surface, but to get at them theologically in the most robust way, it often proves necessary to do a good deal of non-theological work on the passage first. The depth of scripture is as much textual and historical as theological, and textual and historical work, done well, naturally opens onto rich theological possibilities. This is what microscopic theology looks like.

In this essay, I walk through all of these steps, laying the textual and then the historical groundwork necessary to pursue a rigorous theological reading of a verse that most seem to ignore. In fact, I give so much of this essay to sorting out the textual issues and surveying the historical issues that the theological work—when I finally come to it—perhaps receives too little attention. The theological aspects of the passage in question deserve a good deal more development than this essay ultimately gives them. It nonetheless puts fully on display the stages to be passed through on the way to doing good microscopic theology with scripture, and hence the difficulty and complexity of doing good microscopic theology with scripture. It too was the product of a project sponsored by the Latter-day Saint Theology Seminar—this one a seminar on 1 Nephi 1, held in 2014 in London.

This essay originally appeared in *A Dream, a Rock, and a Pillar of Fire: Reading 1 Nephi 1*, ed. Adam Miller (Provo, UT: Neal A. Maxwell Institute, 2017), 47–74.

According to a reading I will defend in this essay, it appears that Lehi, when he "went forth among the people and began to prophesy" (1 Ne. 1:18), addressed two distinct prophetic messages to his Jerusalem audience.[1] The first of these messages concerned things then present: Lehi is said to have testified of the "wickedness" and "abominations" of his contemporaries (v. 19). But the second message concerned things then still in the future: Lehi preached of the coming of "a messiah" as well as "the redemption of the world" (v. 19). Further, as I will suggest, these two distinct prophetic messages seem to have sparked two similarly distinct responses. When told of their wickedness, those at Jerusalem responded with mockery; when told of messianic redemption, they responded with anger. In fact, they "sought [Lehi's] life, that they might take it away" (v. 20). Direct prophetic accusation provoked only laughter and derision, but abstract and largely theological prophetic talk provoked murderous rage.

In the first section of this paper, I will defend the above reading at the exegetical level. However, if the narrative of 1 Nephi 1 *does*, in fact, distinguish between Lehi's accusatory preaching and his prophetic message, and if the same narrative presents blithe mockery and violent anger as distinct respective responses to these two sorts of prophetic preaching, then verses 18–20 are odd. One would expect that confrontation and accusation would invite anger and violence, while talk of some distant messianic redeemer would provoke little more than laughter. Today, to be sure, we mock wild-eyed figures that announce the world's end and reserve our political rage for those who oppose and accuse us. But historical study of the political climate of the late seventh and early sixth centuries before Christ helps to clarify why talk of messianic redemption—especially in Lehi's indefinite formulation: "a messiah," rather than "the Messiah"—might have been regarded with violent suspicion in the place and time of Lehi's preaching. It may be that, historically speaking, there is nothing at all surprising about what verses 18–20 claim. Such seems to me the upshot of the best historical research on preexilic Judean politics and religion. In

---

1. I draw all quotations of the Book of Mormon from Royal Skousen's *The Book of Mormon: The Earliest Text* (New Haven: Yale University Press, 2009), though, where it seems to me helpful to do so, I replace Skousen's suggested punctuation of the text with my own.

the second section of this paper, therefore, I attempt to explain the basic narrative of Lehi's preaching by looking to history.

However, if history can help to clarify the basic stakes of the narrative report of verses 18–20—clarifying for modern readers what would have seemed natural in ancient times—it must be said that this only sets the stage for genuine theological reflection. In a book intentionally directed to readers living after the rise of secularism, when messianic talk is universally regarded with skepticism, it is necessary to go at least one step beyond historical reflection. If part of what makes scripture scripture is the way it reorganizes history according to patterns that outline a life lived faithfully before God, it is necessary to consider the theological measure of Lehi's messianic preaching. What could talk of an indefinite, singular messiah—Lehi's talk of "a messiah" rather than of "the Messiah"—mean for the modern reader? In what way, if any, is this brief report on Lehi's preaching relevant? Sustained reflection on Lehi's prophetic gesture helps to produce a crucial theological reconceptualization of the messianic, laying the groundwork for a notion that I will call "potent messianism." In a third and final part of this paper, therefore, I outline a theology of potent messianism, a thinking of the singular Messiah.

Textual Matters

The basic interpretation of 1 Nephi 1:18–20, from which I take both my historical and my theological bearings, is not currently represented in secondary literature on the Book of Mormon. In fact, so far as I have been able to find, only one author has even hinted at the possibility that Nephi means to distinguish between two sequences or subjects of prophetic preaching and two respective responses to such preaching.[2] To a certain extent, this lack in the literature seems to be a consequence of the fact that close interpretive study of the Book of Mormon is largely nascent, not yet a discipline in its own right. However, other forces may also be at work. As I read and reread this passage in current and recent editions of the Book of Mormon, I suspect that this lacuna in interpretation is largely due to the modern textual apparatus through which 1 Nephi 1 is today presented. More specifically, the current chapter and verse breaks in this case divert the reader's attention from a theologically crucial implication of the text.

---

2. See Hugh Nibley, *An Approach to the Book of Mormon*, 2nd ed. (Salt Lake City: Deseret Book and FARMS, 1979), 40.

There is in fact much to learn from paying close attention to the logic of the current chapter and verse breaks in the Book of Mormon. They were introduced into the text in the 1870s by Orson Pratt, who was given the task of producing an edition of the Book of Mormon that looked more like the Bible and that could be referenced more easily.[3] Before Pratt's work on the text's apparatus, the Book of Mormon was printed in simple, unnumbered paragraphs, which appeared in chapters that were generally much longer than the chapters in more recent editions of the book.[4] Royal Skousen has shown that the original pre-Pratt chapter breaks were part of the dictated text of the Book of Mormon and were apparently intended elements of the text.[5] When Pratt set to work both imposing shorter chapter lengths on the text and inserting relatively natural verse divisions into the text, he was faced with an essentially *interpretive* task. The chapter breaks and verse divisions that appear in current and recent editions of the Book of Mormon thus tell us something about how at least one close reader—perhaps the nineteenth-century's most dedicated student of the Book of Mormon—made sense of the text. Studying them closely also reveals how verses and chapters might have been divided differently.

These considerations are doubly relevant to the interpretation of 1 Nephi 1:18–20. First, it should be noted that what is now 1 Nephi 1 was originally only a part—a relatively small part—of a longer chapter. What was in Joseph Smith's dictation "Chapter I" of "The First Book of Nephi" is now 1 Nephi 1–5, a complicated narrative that begins with Lehi's inaugural vision of a prophecy-inspiring record (the heavenly book) coming down to him from God's presence and ends with Lehi's subse-

---

3. For a short overview of Pratt's work, see David J. Whittaker, "'That Most Important of All Books': A Printing History of the Book of Mormon," *Mormon Historical Studies* 6 (Fall 2005): 116–17. [More work specifically on the subject of Pratt's work on the Book of Mormon has appeared since I originally wrote this essay. See especially Paul Gutjahr, "Orson Pratt's Enduring Influence on *The Book of Mormon*," in *Americanist Approaches to* The Book of Mormon, ed. Elizabeth Fenton and Jared Hickman (New York: Oxford University Press, 2019), 83–104.]

4. It should be noted that the Community of Christ—and before it, the Reorganized Church of Jesus Christ of Latter Day Saints—retained the original chapter breaks in their printings of the Book of Mormon, even after they too introduced versification into the volume. Recent republications of pre-Pratt editions of the Book of Mormon are also available, most accessibly in Joseph Smith Jr., *The Book of Mormon*, ed. Laurie Maffly-Kipp (New York: Penguin, 2008).

5. See Royal Skousen, *Analysis of Textual Variants of the Book of Mormon*, 6 pts. (Provo, UT: FARMS, 2004–2009), 44.

quent experience of a prophecy-inspiring book (the brass plates) coming down to him from Jerusalem. When Orson Pratt decided to break this originally integral story into five parts—each of today's first five chapters of 1 Nephi—he presumably felt he had found relatively natural breaks in its complicated narrative. One might suggest, however, that it would have been more natural to conclude 1 Nephi 1 with what is now verse 17, so the story of Lehi's preaching in verses 18–20 would have served chiefly as an introduction to the story of Lehi's departure into the wilderness.[6] Pratt's decision to place verses 18–20 in chapter 1, however, distances Lehi's preaching and Jerusalem's reaction to it from the subsequent commandment to leave the city. That decision, importantly, makes verse 20 the conclusion of what is now the opening chapter of the Book of Mormon, a fact that has rather heavily influenced interpretation of both Nephi's writings and the Book of Mormon as a whole. Nephi's reference in that concluding verse to the Lord's tender mercies assisting in the deliverance of the faithful has been taken as a kind of thesis statement both for Nephi's record and for the Book of Mormon as a whole.[7]

A second point of importance here concerns the verse divisions Pratt imposed on the text today known as verses 18–20, regardless of whether the passage should be included with chapter 1 or chapter 2. Pratt might have easily divided the passage into as many as five verses, perhaps (inserting my own verse numbers) as follows:

18. Therefore, I would that ye should know that after the Lord had shewn so many marvelous things unto my father, Lehi—yea, concerning the destruction of Jerusalem—behold, he went forth among the people and began to prophesy and to declare unto them concerning the things which he had both seen and heard.
19. And it came to pass that the Jews did mock him because of the things which he testified of them, for he truly testified of their wickedness and their abominations.
20. And he testified that the things which he saw and heard, and also the things which he read in the book, manifested plainly of the coming of a messiah, and also the redemption of the world.

---

6. In fact, a host of textual connections between 1 Nephi 1:1–3 and 1 Nephi 1:16–17 suggests that what is now 1 Nephi 1:1–17 forms a kind of coherent textual unit, something that can be taken independently of the rest of 1 Nephi 1–5.

7. For a good example, see James E. Faulconer, *The Book of Mormon Made Harder: Scripture Study Questions* (Provo, UT: Neal A. Maxwell Institute for Religious Scholarship, 2014), 13–14.

21. And when the Jews heard these things, they were angry with him   yea, even as with the prophets of old, whom they had cast out and stoned and slain—and they also sought his life, that they might take it away.

22. But behold, I, Nephi, will shew unto you that the tender mercies of the Lord is over all them whom he hath chosen, because of their faith, to make them mighty, even unto the power of deliverance.

As it is, however, Pratt divided the above material into only three verses, grouping what I have parsed as verses 19 and 20 into a single verse (current verse 19), and grouping what I have parsed as verses 21 and 22 into a single verse (current verse 20). Pratt's versification has, I think, determined how readers today understand the heavily abridged narrative set forth in the text. Where division into five verses might have signaled to readers that there were two distinct sequences of Lehi's prophetic preaching (my verses 18 and 20) and that each sequence produced a different response in Lehi's hearers (my verses 19 and 21), the division into three verses has caused readers to see in Lehi's preaching a single message that, consequently, solicited a largely undifferentiated response.[8]

It is worth asking what exactly may have led Pratt both to end chapter 1 where he did (immediately after Nephi's talk of tender mercies and deliverance) and to divide Nephi's summary narrative of Lehi's preaching as he did (into today's verses 18, 19, and 20, rather than in some other way). As regards the first of these interpretive moves, it seems that Pratt was attuned to the important difference between two distinct rhetorical modes operative from the beginning of the writings that appear under Nephi's name. Most often in 1 Nephi, the reader encounters a narrator's voice that describes events in the narrator's own past. Occasionally, though, the text replaces reported narration with a rather different style of discourse: the author addressing himself to his reader and describing his intentions with the record he is writing.[9] Over the course of what is now 1 Nephi 1, there is a kind of alternation of these two authorial voices: in verses 1–3, Nephi addresses his reader and describes his textual intentions; in verses 4–15, Nephi exchanges direct address for narrative; but then in verses 16–17, Nephi again resumes his form of direct address and again refers to his

---

8. For a good example, see Brant A. Gardner, *Second Witness: Analytical and Contextual Commentary on the Book of Mormon*, 6 vols. (Salt Lake City: Greg Kofford Books, 2007), 1:74–75.

9. The most sophisticated study of Nephi's authorial style is Grant Hardy, *Understanding the Book of Mormon: A Reader's Guide* (New York: Oxford University Press, 2010), 29–86.

record. These several sequences of 1 Nephi 1 are rather easy to classify, as is the long narrative sequence beginning in what is now 1 Nephi 2:1 and running through the end of what is now 1 Nephi 5.

Much more ambiguous is 1 Nephi 1:18–20. This sequence largely contains narrative, but it opens with Nephi directly addressing his readers ("I would that ye should know that . . .") and ends with Nephi again directly addressing his readers ("I, Nephi, will shew unto you that . . ."). Given that the narrative report provided between these two instances of direct address is startlingly brief, it might be best to see verses 18–20 as a continuation of, rather than a break from, verses 16–17 in terms of their rhetorical mode.[10] Pratt, it would seem, felt it better to couple what is now verses 18–20 with the rest of what is now 1 Nephi 1 than to make it a rhetorically awkward overture to the uninterrupted narrative sequence of what is today chapters 2–5.[11] Moreover, this had what Pratt may have seen as the added benefit of allowing Nephi's forceful claims regarding what he hopes to "show" his readers to be highlighted by their conclusive position at the end of today's chapter 1.

As regards Pratt's division of verses 18–20 into distinct verses, it might be suggested that Pratt was well accustomed to the more general rhetorical style of Nephi's writing. Pratt seems to have divided what is now verse 19 from what is now verse 18 because of the "and it came to pass" that opens the former. There is no mistaking that throughout the writings attributed to Nephi, this well-worn Book of Mormon formula marks progress in narrative sequences of the text. Halfway through what is now verse 19—where, as I suggested above, one might have expected Pratt to start another verse—Pratt seems to have seen enough continuity to resist the temptation to impose a division. Interestingly, if there is a distinction being drawn in the text between Lehi's preaching of repentance and Lehi's preaching concerning a messiah, the text does not indicate it by employing the usual "and it came to pass." Instead, halfway through verse 19 is a simple "and" ("and he testified that . . . "). Pratt seems to have taken the

---

10. The fact that Nephi uses the word *behold* in the course of his summary may be important. In the narrative report of this chapter, Nephi uses this rhetorical gesture only when directly addressing his readers. This may suggest that he means to provide in verses 18–20 not so much a narrative as a portrait of Lehi's preaching. He asks his readers to behold something, rather than to follow the "it came to pass" formulae that track the progress of a narrative.

11. Likely, Pratt also meant to group together all of Lehi's actions in Jerusalem in chapter 1 and all of Lehi's actions in the wilderness in chapter 2.

missing "and it came to pass" to indicate that all of what is today verse 19 reports on a single event, rather than on what I suggested above might or even should be regarded as distinct sequences of preaching. Pratt did divide what is now verse 20 from what is now verse 19, despite the fact that it too opens without an "and it came to pass" formula. Yet there is nothing surprising about this division, since the first part of what is now verse 20 clearly begins a new sentence that moves away from the narrative report of verse 19. Why, though, did Pratt not divide what is today verse 20 into two distinct verses? He might well have done so, beginning with the "but, behold" positioned halfway through the verse. Yet it seems that he saw the close connection between Nephi's intentions to show his readers something about deliverance (the second half of today's verse 20) and the report concerning the mortally dangerous circumstances in which Lehi found himself (the first half of today's verse 20). It would seem that Pratt wanted to highlight that connection rather than allow readers of the Book of Mormon to take the last part of verse 20 as a more general statement.

Orson Pratt would thus seem to have had his reasons, all of them justifiable and in many ways insightful, for giving the shape he did to the last part of 1 Nephi 1. The question, however, is whether the interpretive tendencies that result from Pratt's imposed apparatus are themselves ultimately justifiable. Is it indeed best to take Nephi's talk of tender mercies and deliverance as a rather general thesis statement, meant to guide the reader's interpretation of Nephi's writings as a whole—or even of the Book of Mormon as a whole? And is it indeed best to infer from the text that Lehi's preaching was relatively monolithic and that little needs to be said about why two different reactions to his preaching are reported? Whether Pratt foresaw that his work on the text's apparatus would shape interpretation along these lines, it seems to have done so, and it is necessary to ask whether such interpretations constitute the best reading of the text.

Although I think good theological work can be done beginning from the idea that verse 20 lays out a kind of thesis statement for the whole of Nephi's writings—a good example of which can be found in Miranda Wilcox's contribution to this volume[12]—I think that Nephi's words are

---

12. [See Miranda Wilcox, "*Tender Mercies* in English Scriptural Idiom and in Nephi's Record," in *A Dream, a Rock, and a Pillar of Fire: Reading 1 Nephi 1,* ed. Adam S. Miller (Provo, UT: Neal A. Maxwell Institute, 2017), 75–110.] For another example, see James E. Faulconer, "Sealings and Mercies: Moroni's Final Exhortations in Moroni 10," *Journal of the Book of Mormon and Other Restoration Scripture* 22, no. 1 (2013): 8–9.

probably best read as introducing only, or at least principally, the long narrative sequence that now makes up 1 Nephi 2–5. Not only does the narrative immediately go on to report the deliverance of Lehi from his would-be murderers in Jerusalem, it goes on at much greater length to report the complex deliverance of Nephi—and his brothers—from Laban. When, in what is today 1 Nephi 5, Nephi and his brothers return to camp after their dangerous encounters with Laban, Nephi provides a brief account of how their return proved to his mother ("now I know of a surety") that the Lord gave her sons "power whereby they could accomplish the thing which the Lord hath commanded them" (v. 8). These words echo not only Nephi's famous announcement of his intentions to be faithful in 1 Nephi 3:7 but also the apparent thesis statement of 1 Nephi 1:20, which speaks of God's tender mercies "mak[ing] them mighty even unto the power of deliverance." Moreover, that such tender mercies are granted only to those "chosen because of their faith" is echoed in the last words of what is today 1 Nephi 5: "thus far I and my father had kept the commandments wherewith the Lord had commanded us" (v. 20). It would seem that the immediate focus of Nephi's claim about tender mercies and deliverance is the story of the retrieval of the brass plates. To see that focus may, moreover, be interpretively important, since Nephi does not claim that God simply delivers in mercy but rather that God's tender mercies make the faithful mighty unto the power of deliverance. Nephi's brief words about divine mercy, if carefully read, are more suggestive of Nephi's ethically troubling slaying of Laban than of transcendent gifts of divine deliverance. Nephi received power to deliver his family, and this was itself a gift of mercy, it seems.

Much more important in the context of this essay, however, is the second question I asked earlier. Is it indeed best to infer from the text that Lehi's preaching was relatively monolithic and that little needs to be said about why two different reactions to his preaching are reported? At least a couple of points might be mentioned. Whatever reasons Pratt may have used to decide on his division of the passage into verses, the text does in fact mean to distinguish between two sorts of preaching on Lehi's part, as well as between two sorts of responses to these two sorts of preaching. For instance, verse 18 describes Lehi as initially making known only "the things which he had both seen and heard," while the second half of verse 19 describes him testifying concerning "the things which he saw and heard, and also the things which he read in the book." This repetition of "saw and heard," augmented ("and *also*") with a reference to the heavenly book read in the course of Lehi's visions, suggests at the very least an eventual addition to or a raising of the stakes of Lehi's initial form or style of preaching, if not a full exchange of one message for another. Further, the first part of verse 19 describes Lehi's hearers as responding just to "the things which he testified of them," while the last part of verse 19 and the first part of verse 20 describe the same people as responding to Lehi's testifying that his visions "manifested plainly" the messianic redemption of the world. However subtle, there is a distinction between testifying *of* and testifying *that*, between a message about the state of a certain people and a message about an event still to take place in the future. Most indicative of all, however, is the simple fact that, even if verse 19 seems to lump Lehi's apparently distinct messages together, verses 19 and 20 rather clearly indicate two drastically distinct responses on the part of the people.[13] Verse 19 discusses only mockery, but verse 20 mentions anger and murderous intentions. If something in the text should motivate this distinction between responses, reported successively, the most obvious solution is that there is indeed a distinction between the two messages that the text seems to tie to the respective responses.

In the end, then, I think there is ample reason to believe that the portrait of Lehi's preaching in verses 18–20 is meant to distinguish between two sorts of prophetic message, as well as to associate with each of those messages a distinct sort of typical response. It is necessary, in other words, to work against the grain of our contemporary textual apparatus in order to see what is at work in the text. At any rate, it is this typology of sorts—the preaching of repentance provokes only mockery, while messianic preaching provokes anger and violence—that calls for explanation.

---

13. The sketchiness of the details Nephi provides may be important here. He does report Lehi's apparently distinct sequences of preaching in the course of what is today a single verse, but it should be noted how much Nephi clearly skips over in this report. There is no information, for instance, about how long Lehi preached in Jerusalem. Between the commencement of the first year of Zedekiah's reign, mentioned in 1 Nephi 1:4, and the actual destruction of Jerusalem by Babylon, ten full years passed. Is the reader to think that Lehi preached on only a couple of occasions before he was commanded to flee Jerusalem? Or is one to believe that Lehi preached for months or even years before leaving the city? If his preaching is supposed to have gone on for some time, it would hardly be surprising to learn that his message shifted over the course of his ministry or that attitudes toward him changed as he fulfilled his prophetic tasks.

What is messianism, if announcing one's commitment to it inspires murderous rage?

Historical matters

In Lehi's particular case, as I have already indicated, there may be historical resources for answering this ostensibly theological question. And, after all, the text of 1 Nephi 1 explicitly ties the events it recounts to a determinate geographical setting and historical period. As stated at the outset of the record, Lehi's earliest prophetic experiences were spurred by events that took place "in the commencement of the first year of the reign of Zedekiah, king of Judah" (v. 4). Although not much is known about many parts of the ancient history of Israel, a good deal is known about the time of Zedekiah—and therefore about the time of Lehi.[14] At least a preliminary answer can be given, in light of available historical sources, to the question of why Lehi's hearers would have been so outraged by his talk of a coming messiah.

Lehi lived in troubled times. Zedekiah was made king not by his own people but by a foreign power—Babylon, the very empire that would lay waste to Jerusalem a decade later. Jehoiakim, the longest-reigning of Zedekiah's several immediate predecessors, had also been a puppet king, installed, however, by Egypt rather than by Babylon. For more than a decade, in fact, the small nation of Judah had been caught in the middle of a massive showdown between two massive empires, each vying for control of the entire ancient Near East. Since the complete collapse of the Assyrian Empire over the slow course of the preceding century, the major political-historical question had been whether it would be Babylon or Egypt that would take its place as the dominant world power. Judah found itself in the worst possible geographical position during this gigantomachy: right between the advancing fronts of the two empires. Eight years before Zedekiah was placed on the throne, the balance of power shifted heavily in favor of Babylon, and Jerusalem's kings were forced to declare allegiance to the Babylonian Empire, even as they harbored hopes that Egypt would regain power. Their political alliances with Egypt even-

---

14. Several helpful summaries of research on the political and religious history surrounding Zedekiah's reign have been made available in Latter-day Saint publications. See especially the several essays gathered in John W. Welch, David Rolph Seely, and Jo Ann H. Seely, eds., *Glimpses of Lehi's Jerusalem* (Provo, UT: FARMS, 2004).

tually cost them dearly when, ten years into Zedekiah's reign, Babylon punished them by eradicating their holy city.

Perhaps what was most devastating about all these circumstances was the fact that, only a few years before the trouble began in earnest, Judah had experienced a remarkable period of political independence. After Assyria had entirely destroyed Judah's northern neighbor, the nation of Israel, and devastated much of Judah itself—the worst destruction taking place in the last decades of the eighth century BC, one hundred years before Lehi's time—the collapse of the Assyrian Empire freed Judah from foreign oppression, ushering in a brief era of remarkable prosperity. That period of prosperity, moreover, coincided with the reign of a most re-markable Judean king—the much-discussed King Josiah, "the last of the significant kings of Judah."[15] In addition to his famous religious reform, about which Julie Smith has many illuminating things to say elsewhere in this volume, Josiah achieved remarkable success through military means in expanding Judah's borders.[16] His contemporaries clearly took him to be the greatest of Judah's kings since David, the king who, according to their tradition, first secured the nation's borders and gave the covenant people rest from their political enemies. It is most likely that Josiah under-stood himself to be—and that his people understood him to be—a kind of "second David," a restorer of the glory of the Davidic dynasty.[17] When Josiah's military might is considered alongside his piety and zeal for the religion of his ancestors, it is no wonder that his people saw in him the fulfillment of hopes that had lain dormant for many years. The historians of his day explicitly described him as a fulfiller of prophecy.[18] Indeed, one prophetic word that may well have been regarded during the height of

---

15. Volkmar Fritz, *A Continental Commentary: 1 & 2 Kings*, trans. Anselm Hagedorn (Minneapolis: Fortress Press, 2003), 395.

16. Biblical references to Josiah's efforts at expansion can be found in 2 Kings 23:15–18 and 2 Chronicles 34:6–7. See the helpful summary of Josiah's successes, combined with an analysis of their relevance for the daily life of originally Northern Kingdom families like Lehi's, in Jeffrey R. Chadwick, "Lehi's House at Jerusalem and the Land of His Inheritance," in *Glimpses of Lehi's Jerusalem*, 107–10. [See more especially, however, the paper referred to: Julie M. Smith, "Huldah's Long Shadow," in *A Dream, a Rock, and a Pillar of Fire*, ed. Adam S. Miller (Provo, UT: Neal A. Maxwell Institute, 2017), 1–16.]

17. See Jacob M. Myers, *II Chronicles: Introduction, Translation, and Notes* (New Haven: Yale University Press, 1965), 205–6.

18. See especially 2 Kings 23:15–18, meant to fulfill the prophecy recounted in 1 Kings 13.

Josiah's power as predicting his rise is Deuteronomy 18:15, attributed to Moses and often commented on in the Book of Mormon: "The Lord thy God will raise up unto thee a Prophet from the midst of thee, of thy brethren, like unto me." Much in the biblical accounts of Moses's ministry and Josiah's reign is written in a way to suggest a connection between the two.

Unfortunately for Judah, Josiah's reign of glory did not last. As tension between Babylon and Egypt mounted, confidence in the possibility of continued political independence and consequent religious freedom naturally began to dwindle. A dozen years before Zedekiah would be placed on the throne in Judah, two events happened that clearly dashed the overblown hopes of Josiah's people. First, Babylon had its first major military victory on the geographical line that led through Judah to Egypt.[19] Second, Egypt brought its military forces against Judah at Megiddo, and Josiah was killed in the course of the battle, apparently by the Pharaoh himself.[20] In the course of a single year, all the political enthusiasm associated with Josiah (heightened by the religious enthusiasm associated with the king's efforts at reform) proved to have been misguided in important ways, and Judah was forced to exchange hopefulness for a kind of hardheaded pragmatism, punctuated at dangerous moments over the ensuing decades by bouts of rash desperation.

Now, it might seem that nothing of what has just been recounted has anything to do with messianism. But in order to see just how relevant all this history is to the question of Lehi's messianism—and the violent response it apparently provoked in Jerusalem at the time of Zedekiah—it is necessary to defamiliarize messianism somewhat. Latter-day Saints tend to associate messianism only with belief in the redeeming role played in the plan of salvation by Jesus of Nazareth. To see what is at stake historically in verses 18–20, however, it is necessary to see the text through a rather different lens.

Of course, it must be said that the Book of Mormon is a deeply Christian book. Centuries before Christianity begins its historical rise in the Old World, the Nephites are granted an unmistakably Christian dispensation, thanks to startlingly specific prophecies of the coming Christ. The Nephites thus know long in advance the location of Jesus's birth and baptism; they have at least a rough sense for his ministry and his impact

19. See Mordechai Cogan and Hayim Tadmor, *II Kings: A New Translation with Introduction and Commentary* (New Haven: Yale University Press, 2008), 300–301.

20. See Fritz, *Continental Commentary*, 410–11.

long before he appears; they know of and clearly anticipate the Messiah's death and resurrection; and they are even prophetically aware of the basic contours of Christian history through the Middle Ages and into the modern world. The result of all this foreknowledge is the development in the Book of Mormon of a New World, pre-Christian Christianity: a people "look[ing] forward unto the Messiah and believ[ing] in him to come as though he already was" (Jarom 1:11). Importantly, prophetic clarity regarding the nature of the Christian dispensation comes already in some of the prophecies of Lehi. It is not difficult to see how familiarity with the Book of Mormon leads one to believe that pre-Christian messianic hopes should always have the kind of specific prophetic foreknowledge put on display throughout Nephite history. And several Nephite prophets—Lehi included—explicitly state that their Old-World predecessors "knew of Christ" and "had a hope of his glory many hundred years before his coming" (Jacob 4:4; see also 1 Ne. 10:5; Mosiah 13:33).

In the end, however, I think it is a mistake to read the implications of the Book of Mormon always in this traditional way. While it is true that passages in the Book of Mormon occasionally project its prophets' way of understanding the Messiah onto their Old World prophetic predecessors, it is equally true that other passages complicate these projections. Nephi, for instance, explicitly distinguishes between his own people's "plainness" in prophecy from the style of Old World prophecy (see 2 Ne. 25:1–8). Presumably, it is also significant that the few decades of Nephite history portrayed in Nephi's writings are portrayed as an era of increasing specific foreknowledge of Christ's coming and ministry. This includes preliminary hints in the dreams and visions of Lehi (see 1 Ne. 1:19; 10:4–11), detailed outlines in the apocalyptic experiences of Nephi (see 1 Ne. 11:13–36), helpful additions eventually discovered in scattered brass plates texts (see 1 Ne. 19:7–14), and occasional supplements in the angelic communications of Jacob (see 2 Ne. 10:3–5). In one rather telling sequence, Lehi admits that his theological convictions are woven together with some of his own speculative interpretations: "I, Lehi, according to the things which I have read, must needs suppose . . ." (2 Ne. 2:17). Nephite Christology does not appear from the beginning of the Book of Mormon as a full-blown phenomenon more or less borrowed from the clear writings of the Old World prophets. Rather, it is presented as slowly developed from a number of distinct sources and clearly distinguished from what can be found in the writings available in today's Hebrew Bible.

   In 1 Nephi 1:19, the indefinite article preceding the word *messiah* might provide a crucial—but subtle—hint that Lehi's early messianic preaching in Jerusalem should be understood as different from subsequent Nephite Christological preaching. Lehi, the text says, "testified that the things which he saw and heard, and also the things which he read in the book, manifested plainly of the coming of *a*"—note, not *the*—"messiah" (v. 19).[21] Had Lehi's hearers in Jerusalem been universally aware of a strong prophetic tradition focused on the then still-future coming of Jesus Christ, or even if all of Nephi's anticipated readers were to be aware of a similar tradition, then it would have made sense for the narrative to report on Lehi's prophecies regarding "*the* Messiah." As it is, the narrative reports his prophecies regarding "*a* messiah," some coming messianic figure who would pursue a program of redemption. The report of Lehi's preaching thus sounds much more like what secular historians today have to say about messianic belief in the seventh and sixth centuries before Christ than what Latter-day Saints tend to say about messianic belief before the beginning of the Christian era. Consequently, in order to produce a decidedly historical account of verses 18–20, I think it is best to trust secular historians of the ancient world about what messianic belief in Lehi's day would have looked like, rather than to interpret the text solely according to our own received expectations.

   What, then, did Jewish messianism look like in the years leading up to the reign of Zedekiah? The point is not just to shift from a strictly Christian to a strictly Jewish register—that is, to bracket the Christian insistence that the Messiah came in the person of Jesus of Nazareth in order to leave open the question of when, where, and in whom the Messiah might appear. Rather, the point is to recognize that this kind of messianism, familiar from both the Christian and the Jewish traditions, would have been foreign to the inhabitants of Jerusalem in the time of Josiah. Before the Jewish exile in Babylon and its aftermath back in Palestine, messianism had relatively few of the features that came to be associated with it later. The sort of messianism that would have been known to the inhabitants of Lehi's Jerusalem would have been focused much more intensely on the promises associated with the then-still-existent Davidic dynasty than on anything else. Only after that dynasty had been entirely removed from power (which occurred when Zedekiah's reign came to its

---

   21. The significance of this indefinite article (*a* rather than *the*) is all the clearer in light of the definite article attached to the other things manifested plainly in Lehi's visions: "and also *the* redemption of the world."

cnd) could messianic hopes take on the familiar shape they seem to have developed in the centuries following the return from exile.

It is not entirely clear when the theology attached to the Davidic monarchy came into existence (some scholars suggest that it already existed by David's time),[22] but it is clear that it was fully operative in some form by at least the end of the eighth century BC, during the prophetic activity of Isaiah of Jerusalem—in whose writings Nephi demonstrates such consistent interest.[23] Certainly by the time of Josiah, this theology had come into a kind of maturity, since it underpinned the massive history of Israel produced in that period: the books of Samuel and of Kings.[24] Nathan's oracle to David in 2 Samuel 7, in which an everlasting dynasty is promised to David, unmistakably "occupies an important position in the larger Deuteronomistic corpus"; that is, it explains the hopes associated with the Davidic dynasty within the larger historical narrative constructed in Josiah's days.[25] Because so few of David's successors lived up to the glorious precedent he had set for them, the history of the Davidic dynasty was at once a history of hopes for better times and a history of disappointments due to foreign control. It was because Josiah threw off the last remnants of the Assyrian yoke in the mid-sixth century BC that he was regarded as a kind of David reborn, a return to the golden age under Judah's first covenant-bound king.

All the hopes associated with the Davidic monarchy were messianic. The Hebrew word *mashiach* or "anointed one," from which the English word *messiah* derives, was applied from the earliest period of the Israelite monarchy to the kings. David was consistently careful to avoid raising his hand against the Lord's anointed, Saul the king (see 1 Samuel 24:6, 10; 26:9, 11, 23; 2 Samuel 1:14, 16). David was later himself called the Lord's anointed (see 2 Samuel 19:21; 22:51; 23:1), as were his successors (see throughout the Psalms, but also Lamentations 4:20; Habakkuk 3:13).

---

22. See, for instance, Gerhard von Rad, *Old Testament Theology*, 2 vols., trans. D. M. G. Stalker (New York: Harper & Row, 1962), 1:39–56.

23. See the general but helpful discussion in Christopher R. Seitz, *Isaiah 1–39* (Louisville: John Knox Press, 1993), 60–75.

24. Marvin Sweeney suggests that the theological shape of the earliest Isaianic writings was determined in large part by the religious and political interests of Josiah's regime. See Marvin A. Sweeney, *Isaiah 1–39 with an Introduction to Prophetic Literature* (Grand Rapids, MI: Eerdmans, 1996), 57–59.

25. P. Kyle McCarter Jr., *II Samuel: A New Translation with Introduction, Notes and Commentary* (New Haven: Yale University Press, 2008), 217.

Messianism before the Babylonian exile was largely a matter of trusting that one of David's royal successors would eventually measure up to his father's stature, giving Israel rest from its enemies anew. The clearest—and most likely the earliest—expression of this hope is to be found in Isaiah 9:6–7, the famous announcement of a new child being born—that is, of a new king ascending the throne and being adopted by the Lord as he fulfills the hopes of the Davidic dynasty. Summarily put, "the oracle apparently concerned the joyous announcement of the birth of a new Davidic king who would have the authority, resolve, and capacity to reverse the fortunes of Judah."[26] Long before messianism became a matter of eschatological hope—of being oriented to the arrival of a figure who would mark the end of history in some way—it was a basic trust that God would honor his covenant with David and see to Judah's deliverance from political enemies.

Because Josiah was the first Judean king since David to restore political independence and because he reconquered for Judah what had been obliterated of Northern Israel during the Assyrian conquest—all this while embodying a religious piety and ritual zeal that exceeded even that of his important predecessor, Hezekiah—it is not difficult to see that the hopes invested in his reign were essentially messianic. Indeed, Josiah's repetition and radicalization of the Hezekian reform of a few decades earlier was likely crucial to the messianic lens through which he was seen: Isaiah's messianic prophecy cited above was almost certainly originally focused on the rise of Hezekiah to the Davidic throne.[27] While it seems likely that pre-exilic Jewish messianism was largely a limited phenomenon in the eighth century BC, common only in the king's more intimate circles of society,[28] it seems to have become much more widely popular in Josiah's time, at the very least because of the public spectacle associated with Josiah's reform. Lehi likely reached adulthood during an era of intense messianic enthusiasm, focused heavily on the potency of the Josian monarchy.

Unfortunately, as already suggested, if Josiah was originally seen as a kind of messianic figure, he would eventually have come to be seen as a failed messiah. The unstoppable advance of Babylon's armies, combined with the surprising death of Josiah and crushed hopes for Judean independence at Megiddo, likely spoiled messianism for most of Judah—and

26. Walter Brueggemann, *Isaiah 1–39* (Louisville: Westminster John Knox Press, 1998), 82.

27. Brueggemann, 82.

28. See von Rad, *Old Testament Theology*, 2:169.

perhaps especially for the social and political elite. Only a dozen years after Josiah's tragic death, after a succession of weak puppet kings and serious problems for Judah every time one of its kings attempted to take sides, any messianic talk—any confidence in the Davidic dynasty in any form—would have sounded downright dangerous. The historically aware and socially savvy among Zedekiah's subjects would likely have responded to any messianic anticipations with a stern warning that such nonsense had been tried and had resulted only in devastating failure. Not only had the supposed messiah of a few years earlier led to oppressive subjection rather than continued independence, but now foreign rule was complete, and the political situation was dangerously volatile. Should Babylon learn that certain Judean factions hoped for messianic deliverance, armies would soon be camped outside Jerusalem, ready to replace oppressive subjection with complete obliteration.

It would thus have been one thing for someone like Lehi to claim that the Lord's covenant people had strayed in some way from the Lord. Accusations of wickedness could be laughed off—regarded as little more than the ravings of a religious factionalist. It would have been another thing entirely for someone like Lehi to claim he had plain evidence of some sort that a messianic redeemer would appear. The long-term consequences of a messianic movement in Judah would likely be irreversible, especially if it presented its teachings in a soberingly clear fashion, as Lehi's talk of "plain manifestation" would suggest he meant to do. Perhaps, then, a historical review like the one I have just provided would be enough to make the report of verses 18–20 less surprising. For Lehi to have spoken of a messiah would have been terribly dangerous in the political climate of Zedekiah's reign. That Lehi understood his announcement to have world-historical implications—after all, he announced "the redemption of the world"—would have made his message all the more potent and frightening to his contemporaries. His hearers would most likely have heard in his preaching a hope that Zedekiah would be replaced by a miraculous Judean king who would lead the Jews in a successful revolt that would mark the beginning of political independence—or even of political ascendancy. To many, it would likely have seemed better that one such wild-eyed prophet should perish than that the whole Judean nation should dwindle and perish in a sustained Babylonian siege.

Of course, given the subsequent developments of Lehi's messianic thought—his startlingly plain statement later that his anticipated Messiah would not appear for six centuries, for instance (see 1 Ne. 10:4)—it must be said that he did not at all mean to suggest what his audiences likely believed they heard in his preaching. Lehi seems to have been in the earliest stages of developing a fully Christian messianism, but his listeners likely could make little sense of his message. It took Lehi's son Nephi a fantastically detailed apocalyptic vision of the whole panorama of history even to begin to see what Lehi was after. Consequently, it would be unlikely for the average inhabitant of Zedekiah's Jerusalem to think that he or she would have had more insight into Lehi's blossoming messianism than Lehi's own son. Indeed, it is perhaps possible to suggest that Lehi's family was driven from Jerusalem toward the New World precisely because their new wine could only burst the old bottles of preexilic Jewish messianism: only in a radically new setting could a pre-Christian Christianity get off the ground. Lehi's departure from Jerusalem might well have been a theological as well as a geographical departure, in the end.

At any rate, it is along the lines I have followed here that one might begin to provide a historical explanation of 1 Nephi 1:18–20. In light of the complicated Israelite history that led up to the opening events recorded in the Book of Mormon, it is possible to make at least some preliminary sense of why Lehi's contemporaries might have been not only skeptical but also murderously angry at his messianic message. Of course, there is little reason to think that any of Lehi's hearers understood the real implications of what he preached, but given their likely misunderstanding, their reaction was not surprising.

Theological Matters

Even as the preceding historical survey helps to make some sense of verses 18–20, it does not really address the theological question I posed in connection with that passage: What is messianism, if announcing one's commitment to it inspires murderous rage? All we have glimpsed in the preceding pages is why a specific sort of messianic talk—or, rather, all messianic talk interpreted in a specific way—would have caused rage for one particular audience at a particular period of time and in a particular place. But are contemporary readers of 1 Nephi 1 supposed to recognize just the historical details reviewed above and nothing more? That is to say, is the point of verses 18–20 primarily historical in the end? Are its purposes exhausted once the passage's apparent oddity is explained away? Is it enough to know that at least one kind of messianic talk caused a genuine scandal during at least one point in history, or is the intention of the text to say something more general about the nature of messianic talk, about the nature of messianism as such?

While there is no gainsaying the fact that history is important to the Book of Mormon, it must be emphasized strongly that the book does not ask its readers to see past its words and stories to whatever ancient history can be recovered from authentically ancient documents and other artifacts. The book's aim is not so much to inspire readers to determine how to explain away oddities by doing good research as it is to inspire readers to determine how the text's oddities might inform a life lived in devotion to God. It seems to me that, once basic textual and historical questions have been dealt with—however summarily, as above—the real task of reading scripture can begin: namely, to ask what the text has to say about the life of faith. Here, then, the crucial question is this: *What is at stake in the messianic such that it is so deeply potent?* Perhaps this might be put even more directly: *Why might committed Latter-day Saints need, or at least hope, to be as much an affront to their contemporaries as Lehi apparently was to his, and what has such scandal to do with messianism?*

Of course, to make a transition from history to theology is not at all to abandon things historical. Indeed, several points from the history recounted above are of particular importance for theological reflection in this case. A first point, for instance, might be that one would do well to learn from the complex political determinations of messianism that have become clear in the preceding discussion. To speak of the messianic, it seems, is to speak of something with deeply political stakes, something whose original bearings are unmistakably political. A second and related historical point of importance qualifies this first one, however. One gathers from the historical details that messianism comes to be viewed as dangerous only after some particular messianism—the hope for a specific messiah—has been widely espoused but then proven to be a failure. In other words, the wrong or problematic rejection of true messianism seems to be connected in some way with the right or unquestionable rejection of a particular messianism. This second point might be clarified by a third one. There seems to be something crucial about the historical importance of the indefinite article in Lehi's preaching—his announcement of the coming of *a* messiah, rather than of *the* Messiah. There is, it seems, something particularly threatening in the refusal to identify the coming messiah, something dangerous about the indefinite messiah. Neither particular nor universal, the singular messiah bears a force that inspires anger and violence. Finally, this third point can be developed in light of a fourth point. What the Book of Mormon presents as right or true messianism is one that develops unforeseeably beyond its immediate setting through a series of visionary experiences that alert the prophet to problems essentially foreign to the original setting in which the messianic question is first posed. The indeterminate and conceptually indefinite messiah is one concerning which further revelation should—in fact, must—be received. Those who react violently to messianic talk therefore prove to be blind to the possibility of developing messianic thought in novel directions.

For this last part of this essay, then, I will take my theological bearings from history, beginning specifically from these four points. If one were to outline the idea of "potent messianism" (the sort of messianism that leads Lehi into his dangerous circumstances) and were to do so by drawing on the historical insights just summarized, it is possible to begin from four theological theses:

1. Potent messianism is essentially political.
2. Potent messianism is founded on the ruin of particular messianisms.
3. Potent messianism is indefinite or singular.
4. Potent messianism is revisable or, we might say, reenvisionable.

In the space that remains, I would like to begin to articulate the theological importance of these several theses.

To begin, what does it mean to say that potent messianism, as the first thesis above states, is essentially *political*? Clearly, the messianic idea has its roots in a political situation. To be a messiah is to be an anointed one—that is, to be invested with authority by the established institutional apparatus and according to the established protocol (the anointing ritual that invested kings in the specifically Israelite tradition). In the Davidic context, moreover, to be a messiah is also to be a successor or an heir—the product, therefore, of a function that assigns one a dynastic place within a genealogical history. Further, when messianism comes eventually (at the latest, by the eighth century before Christ) to be woven with expectation, being a messiah becomes a matter of repetition and restoration, of making certain forms of being-with or being-together possible anew—a certain peace and political independence. In short, to the extent that messianism has reference to messiahs, it cannot fully break with the strictly political determinations that governed the investiture of kings in the ancient Near East. To speak of a messiah at all is always to speak of a certain confidence or of certain hopes associated with either political stability or political change.

The first thesis concerning potent messianism is thus relatively straightforward. Part of what makes messianism potent is its irremediable connection to political institutions, as well as to political transformation. Weaving the religious and the political—those two taboo topics never to be broached in polite company—messianism of *whatever* sort is always already effectively potent. It is impossible to divorce messianism in any absolute sense from questions of what it means to live together. Whatever one's view of the ideal social order, there is a messiah—already established or still to come—who represents and secures its goodness. The messianic institution of ancient Israel was, arguably, originally conservative in nature, an apparatus meant to ensure the long-term preservation of a certain social order. The messianic anticipations of ancient Israel that developed over the course of the monarchy's history were, however, clearly liberal in nature, an orientation aimed at welcoming the harbinger of a social order more than just the status quo. Whether conservative or liberal (using such terms extremely broadly, obviously), one's commitments tie into some sort of messianism, it would seem. Again, then, to the extent that messianism has reference to messiahs, it cannot fully break with the strictly political determinations that governed the investiture of kings in the ancient Near East.

Messianism cannot fully break with political determinations, but it must in its most potent form be said to operate only and always at the borders of such political determinations. This, it seems, is the basic implication of the second thesis above. The determinations laid out in the preceding two paragraphs are the trappings only of certain particular messianisms that were associated first with the original Davidic monarchy and eventually with the possibility of restoring Davidic political independence and peace through the arrival of a better king. According to the second thesis, however, the most potent messianism is founded only on the ruins of such particular messianisms. The conservative messianism of the Israelite monarchy eventually gave way to the liberal messianism of Isaianic and post-Isaianic hopes. But that liberal messianism in turn eventually collapsed after investing all its hopes in the specific reigns, successively, of Hezekiah and especially of Josiah. By the time Lehi could preach a radically potent messianism, all particular messianisms had fallen apart. It was entirely clear that the monarchy as an established institution would never deliver Judah anew from its political enemies. And, after Josiah's death and the installation of a series of puppet kings, it became equally clear that there was no reason to hope for an enlightened messianic hero who would liberate Judah after turning the nation back onto the right track.

To speak in a general vein, potent messianism dawns specifically when it is no longer possible to orient one's messianism by tying the anointed one to an identifiable inherited institution or by locating the anointed one in an identifiably needed restoration. Messianism's potency reaches extreme intensity only when what is in view is no longer the stabilization or the redemption of a particular nation with its peculiar institutions. Genuinely potent messianism dawns only when what is in view is more global—"the redemption of the world," as Lehi puts it. Potent messianism, in other words, is what is glimpsed in a visionary experience that outstrips the determinations of a particular messianism that has already proven itself a failure—twice over, in fact. It is in this sense that potent messianism, while nonetheless political, cannot be reduced to any particular politics. It is what works in the interstices between actual, observable political institutions and possible, imaginable political institutions. Potent messianism is what calls for thought when both the knowably actual and the knowably possible prove themselves to be fully inadequate. Only at that point is it possible to embrace the most potent messianism, the sort of messianism that always and inherently scandalizes.

It is, of course, difficult to know what all this implies. It would seem that the potently messianic does not weigh in on political debates but rather cuts their Gordian knots. But what can that mean? It would seem that the potently messianic does not take sides but cuts diagonally across every opposition, or perhaps zigzags between opposed poles. But, again, what can that mean? It would seem that the potently messianic neither slavishly obeys nor slavishly rebels against political institutions, opting rather to subject all such apparatuses to a kind of free play. But, yet again, what can that mean? At the very least, it seems to mean something like the following. Potent messianism is so profoundly scandalous because it fails—in fact, refuses—to carve up the world according to the categories determined by everyday political discourse. Its political nature lies only in the way it produces entirely new configurations of political discourse. It is easy to mock someone who has assumed an opposing political position. But it is far more difficult to know how to deal with someone who refuses to recognize as valid either of basically opposed political positions. And the anxiety that accompanies every encounter with such a person can very quickly inspire anger and violence.

How can such a reconfiguration of political discourse be accomplished? Here, it is necessary to turn to the third thesis above, that potent messianism is indefinite or singular. Potent messianism places its hopes neither in the particular nor in the universal—neither in some specifiable individual (this or that uniquely nameable person) nor in whoever happens to fit a definite conceptual description (someone who accomplishes a specifiable set of aims). The potent messiah is neither a self-identical person nor a well-formed category. And yet—this is the difficult theological point here—the potent messiah is nonetheless an unmistakable figure of fulfillment. Every messianism dreams of fulfillment, but potent messianism dreams differently. Every specific messianism dreams of seeing the peculiar desires of a determinate political apparatus fulfilled. Potent messianism, it would seem, asks after the meaning of fulfillment without commitment to any determinate political apparatus. Fulfillment of hopes, but without particular hopes that require fulfillment—that, it seems, is the orientation of potent messianism. It dreams of fulfillment as such, fulfillment per se, fulfillment without qualification, fulfillment without end, fulfillment of life.

Crucial to understanding this point is the ability to distinguish between two philosophical concepts, often equated: that of the particular and that of the singular. Where the particular can be identified because of the weave of predicates that assigns it a place in the world—one could say that the particular is identified by the parts it plays in larger categories that allow for identification—the singular is effectively indiscernible because it suspends predication in its indefiniteness: "a messiah," still "coming," whose arrival marks "the redemption," it turns out, of the whole "world." It is thus that the word *potent* in *potent messianism* gains its true resonance. The potent messiah is the potential messiah, the messiah still-to-come, the messiah who, because not yet actual, gathers into a single figure all predicates in latent form, holding them together in a kind of infinite contradiction. With such a messiah on the horizon, anything could happen, and that is what makes potent messianism so threatening. But what is crucial is that with the full arrival of the messiah, no one thing will have happened. Instead, everything will be redeemed, the infinite contradiction being sustained indefinitely. It is only with the coming of a messiah that it is possible to speak of world redemption. The web of actual objects and actual relations making up the realm of experience, even if this realm is considered diachronically—that is, over the course of history—is nonetheless only a relatively small part of the much larger web of potential objects and potential relations. For the world to be redeemed, everything actual has to be traced back in some way to its potentialities, to what might have been.

It seems to me that it is precisely for this reason that potent messianism must be visionary, and even revisionary or reenvisionary—as the fourth thesis above states. To recognize potency or potentiality is to develop a certain ability to see, to envision, to reenvision. To see what might have been, and especially to see why that matters, requires a visionary capacity that can only be called prophetic. Those who fail to understand the message of potent messianism reject it so violently at least in part because they fail to discern radically different configurations of the real latent possibilities operative in every situation. To reject potent messianism is to fail to see—or to refuse to see—the fullness of the present. It is thus to give up on fulfillment as such, apparently because the fulfillment of this or that particular messianic hope has proven so disastrous. The fullness of the world is to be found in its potentialities, its as-yet-undetermined or indefinite possibilities, rather than in the right sorts of actualities. For this reason, it is easy to come to hate potent messianism because it is difficult to see how the failure of every actual messiah to be messianic is in fact productive, indicative that the actual cannot contain the fullness that arrives with the potent messiah. In proverbial terms, the light can shine in the darkness, but the darkness cannot comprehend it.

I am led, as I think more carefully about this fourth thesis, to believe that what is at stake in visionary experience is not at all some kind of straightforward witnessing of actual historical events that take place elsewhere or at a time different from one's own. I find myself believing that what is at stake here is rather a prophetic ability to see the potentialities of a concrete situation, to see what the apparent face of a situation masks. It is for that reason that prophecies and knowledge and languages inevitably fail, while faith, hope, and love remain. To be a prophet, it seems, is to know as well as one's contemporaries that every messianic anticipation has been and should have been dashed. But it is also to know that the despairing have nevertheless been too quick to give up on the messianic. The prophet sees something potent organizing and structuring the terrifying situation of the present, something others are far too quick to dismiss. There are, in the end, two miserably wrong responses to the repeated collapse of every hope. It is wrong, of course, to go on believing that next time will be different. But it is also wrong to believe that, because the next time will not be different, the current situation is one of pure chaos without structure, without possibilities or potentialities. It is wrong to fantasize, starry-eyed, that something is coming in order, effortlessly, to solve all problems; but it is also wrong to pretend, hollow-eyed, that it only remains to give oneself to pragmatic efforts at ensuring endurable survival.

What fires descend onto what rocks before us today, in whose dancing flames we might, with enough care and enough study, begin to recognize the latent potency of our own situation? What book descends from heaven today that, once we have been bidden to read it, fills us with prophetic insight enough to see the fullness rather than the emptiness of the world? What preaching ought we today to pursue—if, that is, we still have the courage to hope to scandalize our own contemporaries by insisting that the messianic remains relevant? And then, what wilderness should we be prepared to flee to?

Chapter Four

Seams, Cracks, and Fragments
Notes on the Human Condition

Readers of the Book of Mormon are eager to explain away every oddity. This is entirely understandable. The Book of Mormon has been under attack from the moment it went on sale in Grandin's bookshop in Palmyra, New York, in 1830. The history of the Church is in many ways the history of Latter-day Saints defending the book against its critics. Long habit makes us quick to assume a defensive posture, makes us quick to worry that any puzzle or peculiarity in the text had better have an explanation—and had better have one soon!—if the Book of Mormon is to continue in its role as the ambassador of our faith. This defensive posture, however, can make our relationship to the Book of Mormon a frail one. We too easily become doubtful readers, looking at the book through the eyes of its detractors and therefore feeling too often worried that the whole thing might be a sham. The relief Latter-day Saints express after having some oddity explained to them is a symptom of this unfortunate—but again, understandable—approach to the book.

The kind of sensibility necessary for microscopic theological reading is wholly at odds with this usual way of coming at the Book of Mormon. A theological reader has to have a penchant for the peculiar. Awkward phrasing, non-standard grammar, interrupted thoughts, ambiguous claims, impossible punctuation—these are the kinds of things that spur a theological reader. Rather than so many minor scandals, things to be explained away or covered up, the oddities of the Book of Mormon text are occasions for reflection. Might God be hidden and waiting for us behind a textual hiccup? This essay—yet another product of the Latter-day Saint Theology Seminar—illustrates the theologian's interest in the stranger moments in the text, the moments we tend to wish to ignore. What if we invest all the significance we can in a brief moment of apparent and awkward restatement within the text? That was the question I asked in the course of reading parts of Alma 12–13 with my fellow seminarians in a 2016 seminar held at the Pacific School of Religions in Berkeley, California.

This essay was originally published in *A Preparatory Redemption: Reading Alma 12–13*, ed. Matthew Bowman and Rosemary Demos (Provo, UT: Neal A. Maxwell Institute, 2018), 64–81.

According to the Book of Mormon, seams and cracks and fragments serve as geological witnesses to the plan of redemption. Nephi captures this idea early in the book in a kind of theological formula. "The rocks of the earth must rend," he says, when "the god of nature suffers" (1 Ne. 19:12). Apparently for this reason, what before the death of Christ was "one solid mass" of stone has since been—and is apparently "ever after" to be—"found in seams and in cracks and in broken fragments upon the face of the whole earth" (Hel. 14:21–22). Of this Samuel prophesies a few years before the birth of Christ, and then Mormon reports some chapters later that, although "the earth did" eventually "cleave together again" after Christ's death (3 Ne. 10:10), "the rocks" were nonetheless irreversibly rent, such that "they were found in broken fragments and in seams and in cracks upon all the face of the land" (8:18). Highlighting the fact that these geological phenomena bear witness of the plan of redemption, Mormon urges his readers to "search" the scriptures to "see and behold" if "all these things are not unto the fulfilling of the prophecies of many of the holy prophets (10:14).

This material geotheology in the Book of Mormon runs parallel to a formal cosmotheology spelled out in the volume—or so I have come to think as I have worked on Alma 12–13 in conversation with my fellow seminarians. Just as Christ's actual death rends the one solid mass of rock, making it a matter of seams and cracks and fragments, Christ's virtual death, his being "slain from the foundation of the world" (Rev. 13:8), rends *eternity* and gives rise to *time*, which is characterized by its own seams and cracks and fragments. In both cases, both the geological and the cosmological, Christ's death and the possibility of redemption break up the continuous and leave us with the discrete. But further, because Alma outlines his understanding of the relationship between time and eternity most fully in the course of responding to a question about the human condition (see Alma 12:20–21), a certain anthropotheology (a theological account of human nature) mirrors his cosmotheology (his theological account of time and eternity). Alma arguably understands human beings, those most time-bound of all creatures, as finding *themselves* only in seams and cracks and fragments. The cherubim who guard the way to the tree of life (see v. 21) serve as scriptural ciphers for the fracture of eternity, but also for the split that divides human beings against themselves.

In this paper, I wish primarily to develop just the last of these three theologies: Alma's anthropotheology. The body of the paper is therefore given to this task. Beyond that, however, I wish to develop at least in outline Alma's cosmotheology as well. Because of the technical nature of that task, and because I wish to do it more briefly, I have relegated this second task to an appendix, following the main argument of the paper. (As for the Book of Mormon's geotheology, because it does not derive from Alma 12–13, I leave its elaboration for another occasion, drawing from it only a guiding image for this paper: that of seams and cracks and fragments.) Although I displace my elaboration of Alma's cosmotheology into an appendix, I would like to note that I take it to be intertwined with—or at least in a mirroring relationship to—his anthropotheology. A fuller elaboration of the connection, however, awaits another opportunity.

Twice in the course of Alma 12–13 Alma focuses directly on the question of human nature. The first, which appears in Alma 12:24, briefly presents the human condition as "a probationary state," "a time to prepare." According to this passage, the human condition is bounded at its horizon by "the temporal death," but it is also oriented beyond that horizon to an "endless state" that comes "after the resurrection of the dead." Elsewhere in this volume, Adam Miller provides a beautiful analysis of this and related texts within Alma's discourse.[1] I am quite happy to leave verse 24's theological exposition to him while focusing my attention more or less solely on the second of Alma's two discussions of human nature. That second discussion appears in Alma 12:31, a brief aside within a larger passage focused on God's having given commandments to human beings after their exile from Eden. The verse opens with a reference to this giving of commandments, but then it diverts itself by attempting to describe the basic motivations for God's giving of commandments. That motivation is, summarily put, the human condition itself. "Men," Alma says, "transgressed the first commandments" given to them: their instructions not to eat from the tree of knowledge. And the consequence was that they became human; they became the sort of creature we still are today. It was for this reason that "God gave unto them commandments" (v. 32).

---

1. [See Adam S. Miller, "A Preparatory Redemption," in *A Preparatory Redemption: Reading Alma 12–13*, ed. Matthew Bowman and Rosemary Demos (Provo, UT: Neal A. Maxwell Institute, 2018), 82–92.]

What does the human condition, as Alma describes it, look like? Unfortunately, there is no simple answer to that question, at the very least because there are several quite distinct ways Alma 12:31 can be read. And crucially, none of the several possible readings should be preferred over the others solely on syntactical grounds. To decide among possible interpretations of Alma's description of the human condition is to make a *theological* decision, a decision for one reading over another because one wishes to pursue the theological implications of that reading. It seems to me best to lay out three possible interpretations of the text before pursuing the one that seems to me the most theologically promising.

Here is the description of the human condition from Alma 12:31, presented without punctuation (it should be remembered that Joseph Smith did not dictate punctuation along with the words of the Book of Mormon):

> becoming as Gods knowing good from evil placing themselves in a state to act or being placed in a state to act according to their wills and pleasures whether to do evil or to do good

Interpretation of these words, it seems to me, turns on the scope and function of the *or* that appears more or less at the center of the text. Both the scope and function of this *or* deserve some description and development.

By scope, I refer to how many phrases the *or* in Alma connects. Does the *or* simply connect "placing themselves in a state to act" with "being placed in a state to act"? If so, the later phrase, "according to their wills and pleasures," would qualify both instances of the verb "to act." This first possibility might be represented by the following approach to punctuating the text:

> Becoming as Gods, knowing good from evil, placing themselves in a state to act (or being placed in a state to act) according to their wills and pleasures—whether to do evil or to do good

A second option would be to assume that the *or* connects all the phrases following in verse 31, from "being placed in a state to act" onward—with the implication that everything following the *or* is presented as an alternative to everything that precedes the *or*. This might be represented by a rather different approach to punctuating the text (even inserting some bracketed numbers to signal the alternatives presented):

> [1] becoming as Gods, knowing good from evil, placing themselves in a state to act *or* [2] being placed in a state to act according to their wills and pleasures, whether to do evil or to do good

These two approaches cover the range of options as regards the scope of the *or* in Alma 12:31.

Before turning to the question of the function of the *or*, I might note that the first of the above two approaches to the scope of the *or* is by far the more familiar—and perhaps in some sense the more natural—of the two. The fact that "in a state to act" appears immediately following both "placing themselves" and "or being placed" certainly makes the reader feel as if, once she has come to the end of the repetition of "in a state to act," she has caught back up to the point where the *or* interrupts the flow of the text. She therefore naturally assumes that the interruption has run its course by that point and that the scope of the *or* extends only to being placed in a state to act." But, however familiar this approach to the text might be, and however natural it might in some sense feel, it must be emphasized that nothing in the syntax of the passage requires that it be read this way. It is entirely possible, syntactically speaking, that the reader is presented with alternative descriptions of some "state to act," one description before and the other description after the *or*. Any decision in favor of either interpretation of the scope of the *or* must be decided on theological grounds.

Next, by function, I refer to the question of whether the *or* is inclusive or exclusive—that is, whether it presents alternatives that might both be true, or whether it presents alternatives, only one of which may be true. The inclusive use of the word *or* is exemplified in a sentence like "Karen or Kim will suggest a good place to eat." This sentence would not turn out to be false if both Karen and Kim make suggestions about where to eat, but neither would it turn out to be false if only one of the two makes a suggestion. It is in this sense that this sentence's *or* is inclusive; the truth of one alternative does not preclude the truth of the other alternative presented. By contrast, the exclusive use of the word *or* is exemplified in a sentence like the following: "Either Jenny or Sharon will get the last available seat at the restaurant." Here the truth of the sentence depends on only one of the two alternative situations proving to be the case; if both Jenny and Sharon were to get the last seat, the sentence would turn out to be false (just as it would if neither got the last seat). This sentence's *or* is exclusive. The question of the function of the *or* in Alma 12:31 thus means to ask whether the alternatives marked by the *or* (whatever the scope of the *or* may be) should be understood as presenting rival or consonant possibilities. Does the *or* mean to present the same idea in two distinct ways, or does the *or* mean to present ultimately inconsistent ideas?

This question of function might seem abstract at first. But its significance becomes much clearer when it is brought to bear on the text of Alma 12:31. I will, over the next several pages, outline three distinct interpretations of this verse in light of the scope and the function of the *or*. These will clarify greatly the stakes of inclusive and exclusive interpretations of the term.

A first interpretation of Alma 12:31 would understand the scope of the *or* to be limited to "being placed in a state to act," and it would understand the function of the *or* to be exclusive. This might be called the "corrective" interpretation, because it takes the interjection of the *or* (along with what it covers) as intended to correct a mistake. On this interpretation, Alma (or the narrator, or the editor, or perhaps even the translator) spoke (or wrote) too quickly at first, infelicitously attributing to Eve and Adam the Godlike ability to *place themselves in a state to act.* From this perspective, it would be true enough that Adam and Eve became "as Gods" and came to know "good from evil," but it would be wrong to think that they could "plac[e] themselves in a state to act." Who could believe that the first human beings had any such power of self-determination? Luckily, Alma (or the narrator, editor, or translator) immediately recognized the error and corrected it by saying (or writing): "or, *being placed* in a state to act." The clear trace of the error, however, remains present in the final form of the text.

This corrective interpretation clearly limits the scope of the *or* since it understands only the words "being placed in a state to act" (not the remainder of the verse) to be required to correct the inadvertent error; the original thought about being "in a state to act" resumes immediately after the corrective clause, beginning with the words "according to." Further, this interpretation clearly regards the function of the *or* to be exclusive, because it sees talk of Eve and Adam's "being placed in a state to act" as true to the exclusion of any talk of them "placing themselves in a state to act." Ultimately, on this first interpretation, the appearance of the *or* in the verse is largely unfortunate and accidental—or perhaps instructive. Some who espouse the corrective approach would certainly think that it would have been preferable if the mistake had never been made—that is, if the verse had read simply as follows: "becoming as Gods, knowing good from evil, . . . being placed in a state to act according to their wills and pleasures, whether to do evil or to do good." Others espousing this interpretation, however, might regard the retention of the error in the text as deliberate or at least useful; it potentially makes clear to readers the theological error of thinking that the first human beings had any power of self-determination.

Either way, adherents of this first interpretation would certainly wish to say that only one of the two alternatives—specifically that following the *or*—is true.

A second interpretation of Alma 12:31 would similarly understand the scope of the *or* to be limited to "being placed in a state to act," but it would understand the function of the *or* to be inclusive rather than exclusive. This interpretation might be called the "synthetic" interpretation, because it advocates the idea that it is impossible to assign with accuracy either activity or passivity to Adam and Eve at the moment they entered the human condition. This approach, which is represented in some of the other papers in this collection, sees a paradox at work in the beginnings of human agency.[2] It would seem ultimately inappropriate to say that Eve and Adam actively placed themselves in a state to act, since then they would have to have acted before they were in a state to do so. At the same time, it would seem just as inappropriate to say that they were passively placed in a state to act, since they could only come into such a state by deliberately eating from the tree of knowledge. Agency would thus appear to have its beginnings in a necessarily paradoxical leap. The world as we know it—divided into "things to act" and "things to be acted upon" (2 Ne. 2:14)—arose out of an event that, because the fundamental division between activity and passivity was its result, cannot itself be properly described in either active or passive terms. But we have no other choice in using language than to use active or passive terms. Hence, according to this second interpretation, Alma describes the origins of human agency by describing it twice—once in active language ("placing themselves in a state to act") and once in passive language ("being placed in a state to act").

This, then, is the synthetic approach, which sees Alma synthesizing the active and the passive in order to highlight the inappropriateness of either kind of language for describing the origins of agency. It, like the corrective interpretation, limits the scope of the *or* in Alma 12:31, since it assumes that the active and passive alternatives concern just the arrival of Adam and Eve in "a state to act"; the *or* in no way concerns the remainder of the verse. But this interpretation differs from the first because it understands the function of the *or* to be inclusive. That is, the synthetic approach understands "placing themselves in a state to act" and "being placed in a state to act" as alternative expressions of one and the same (inexpressible) idea. The two might be true together (however paradoxical that seems from our

---

2. [See papers throughout Bowman and Demos, *A Preparatory Redemption*.]

present perspective), or, better, the two are ultimately false or at least misleading together. For this reason, this second interpretation differs from the first in another way. Where the corrective interpretation regards the presence of the *or* as largely unfortunate and accidental (or perhaps, by way of its mistake, as instructive), the synthetic interpretation regards the use of the *or* as essential to communicating the truth of the matter. The *or* allows for a formulation of the paradoxical origins of agency, one that does not misconstrue—or at least comes close to not misconstruing—the nature of such origins.

Now, despite the important differences just discussed, these first two interpretations of the *or* clause in Alma 12:31 have much in common. Obviously, as I have already emphasized, they share an interpretation of the scope of the *or*, despite their distinct approaches to its function. But this point of similarity has larger interpretive consequences. In the end, it must be said that there is no real difference in these first two approaches' understandings of the human condition. This is because what distinguishes these first two approaches from each other is not their respective views of human nature but rather their respective views of how human beings *come into* human nature. They differ only on the relationship between the two phrases "placing themselves" and "being placed." For both, the *or* in Alma 12:31 only briefly interrupts an otherwise seamless presentation of human nature—whether to correct a misconstrual of God's role in producing human nature (the corrective interpretation) or to underscore the paradoxical leap involved in the emergence of human nature (the synthetic interpretation). Consequently, for both of these first two approaches to the text, human nature is simply that "state to act" where human beings are "as Gods, knowing good from evil" and fully able "to act according to their wills and pleasures, whether to do evil or to do good." That is, for every interpretation that limits the scope of the *or*, the human condition is a Godlike (but nonetheless nondivine) condition of *knowing* and *doing*—of knowing good and evil, and of being able to act by doing good or evil.

Because the corrective and the synthetic interpretations of Alma 12:31 share a basic understanding of human nature, one that assumes a certain continuity between knowledge and ability to act, it seems relatively clear what it would mean to construct a theological anthropology beginning from either of these two approaches to the text: one would have to proceed to investigate as probingly as possible the apparent continuity between knowing and doing, when it comes to good and evil. But, for reasons Sheila Taylor spells out elsewhere,[3] I must confess that claims of supposed continuity between knowing and doing make me theologically suspicious. These first two interpretations seem to me too Pelagian, too convinced that human agency is sufficient to itself—as if *knowing* did not in fact more or less constantly get in the way of *doing*. My experience has consistently left me to find myself only in the seams and cracks and fragments of any supposed continuity between knowing and doing. Human nature, before or apart from or resistant to its redemption in the Messiah's grace, seems to me always to be *divided between knowing and doing*, rather than *situated at the point of their coincidence*.

Something like what I have just described certainly seems to characterize the experience of the Apostle Paul. In one of Paul's most famous texts, one finds a poignant expression of radical discontinuity between knowing and doing. Knowing the good, and even wanting it, is not enough to make it possible to do it. As in Alma's words, Paul's text focuses on the moment when God "gave commandments unto men" (Alma 12:31). And Paul directly connects the commandments to knowledge of good and evil: "If it had not been for the law, I would not have known sin" (Rom. 7:7 NRSV). But as soon as the commandments assist Paul in knowing good and evil—as soon as he can "agree that the law is good" (v. 16)—he finds that he cannot bring his actions into conformity with what he knows to be good. "I do not do what I want, but I do the very thing I hate," he says (v. 15); "I can will what is right, but I cannot do it. For I do not do the good I want, but the evil I do not want is what I do" (vv. 18–19). The frustration Paul experiences in connection with this ongoing state of affairs leads him to near despair: "Wretched man that I am!" he exclaims (v. 24).

Paul is hardly alone, as any reader of the Book of Mormon knows. Nephi expresses the same self-critical exclamation: "Notwithstanding the great goodness of the Lord in showing me his great and marvelous works—my heart exclaimeth: O wretched man that I am!" (2 Ne. 4:1). He goes on: "When I desire to rejoice, my heart groaneth because of my sins" (v. 19); and he finds he has to ask himself "why" he should "weep" and "linger in the valley of sorrow" and "waste away" and "slacken" and become "angry because of [his] enemy" (vv. 26–27). Nephi, like Paul, suggests that knowledge of the good, far from simply enabling one then to set about doing good, more often than not reveals just how disinclined one naturally is to doing good. And this is something Nephi might well

---

3. [See Sheila Taylor, "Obtaining Divine Mercy," in *A Preparatory Redemption*, 54–63.]

have learned from his father, Lehi, who claims that "men are instructed sufficiently that they know good from evil" in that "the law is given" to them, but by this knowledge-granting law "no flesh is justified" and "men are cut off" (2:5). In the end, numerous scriptural voices give us reason to think that there is a fundamental *disjunction* between knowing good and evil and having the ability to do good or evil.

Perhaps Alma feels the same way. If he does, or if the passages just discussed give us motivation enough to explore the possibility that he does, then we might venture to interpret the *or* of Alma 12:31 in a way quite distinct from that of the corrective and synthetic approaches. This third approach would understand the scope of the *or* of our text to extend to the conclusion of the verse, rather than just to the end of the clause "being placed in a state to act." And it would understand the function of the *or* to be exclusive, rather than inclusive, as if the verse means to outline alternative possibilities that cannot both be true (or, in this case, false) at the same time. This third approach might rightly be termed the "parallax" interpretation. According to it, the text disjoins or—at least in the last instance—renders discontinuous *knowing* good and evil and the ability to *do* good or evil. That is, the *or* here presents us with a forced alternative. This forced alternative needs some articulation. And here I might simply describe my own representative experience—fundamentally similar to what I see Paul, Nephi, and Lehi describing. In setting such a description forth, however, I will limit myself to the language and ideas of Alma 12:31.

In my fallen or my lost situation, I invariably find myself alternating between two mutually exclusive "states." On the one hand or at certain moments, I find myself in the state of possessing Godlike knowledge and being able to determine my intentions. That is, at times I find that we human beings "have become as Gods, knowing good from evil, placing ourselves in a state to act." A kind of euphoria or even delirium attaches itself to this state. The clarity with which I can see the world reaches to the heavens, and I can deliberate decisively about what I ought to do with myself. Yet, to the extent that I find myself in this first state, I find also that I am entirely unable to do the good or the evil that I see with such clarity and in terms of which I wish desperately to determine myself. I know exactly what I ought or what I wish to do, but I find that I cannot actually do it. Although I place myself in a state to act, my actions end up unaligned with my will and disconnected from any pleasure I might take in deliberately doing good or evil. I know the good, and I wish to do it, but I find myself being selfish and vindictive. I fall devastatingly short of what I can outline in my mind perfectly well. In short, precisely to the extent that I see human beings as knowing good and evil, I find that we *cannot* "act according to [our] wills and pleasures, whether to do evil or to do good."

This first state is nicely illustrated by the situation in which Eve and Adam found themselves immediately after eating the fruit of the tree of knowledge. At that moment, they saw for the first time their nakedness, and they knew shame. Each felt responsible before the other for the first time, but what each felt responsible for was something over which she or he had no real or at least no ultimate control: her or his body. They had been granted Godlike knowledge, but the result was that—although they could see everything with perfect clarity—suddenly, they could not do much of anything, except perhaps awkwardly (certainly never with any real grace). And in fact, there is no better way to end up entirely unable to act than to be fully self-conscious, fully aware of being in a situation where it is necessary to act while awaiting the judgment of others. The fact is that the more fully knowledgeable we are about things, and therefore the more deeply aware we are of the indefinite complexity of things, the more we find ourselves immobilized, unable to do anything at all.

But then, on the other hand or at certain other moments, I find myself in a rather different state: a state where I am fully capable of getting things done, taking real pleasure in what I do and experiencing no hindrance to my will. That is, at times I find that we human beings can in fact "act according to our wills and pleasures, whether to do evil or to do good." A rather different sort of euphoria or delirium descends on me when I find myself in this state. My ability to act appears boundless, and real pleasure attends my action. Yet, to the extent that I find myself in this second state, I find also that I am entirely ignorant of what in my actions really serves the good and what ultimately serves the purposes of evil—and I experience a kind of all-too-human feeling of impotence. I do exactly as I wish, and deep feelings come over me unbidden, but I have no idea how to decide whether what I am doing is what I ought to be doing. Although I exercise my will and experience pleasure, I suffer desire passively, as a foreign imposition, and I feel that I could not be more unlike a heavenly being. I do good and evil, but I find that I fail to understand what I am doing. In short, precisely to the extent that I see human beings as good or evil, I find that we *have not* "[become] as Gods, knowing good from evil."

This second state is nicely illustrated by what Jesus Christ describes as happening at the end of time, when the final judgement arrives. Whether we find ourselves at his left hand or at his right, he says, we will be told that we did good or evil *without* knowing it. "When saw we thee an hungered . . . ? or thirsty . . . ? When saw we thee a stranger . . . ? or naked . . . ? Or when saw we thee sick, or in prison . . . ?" (Matt. 25:37–39). From Jesus's parable, it would seem that the righteous and the wicked alike have little understanding of what they do. From the cross, in fact, Jesus pleads for our collective forgiveness because we "know not what [we] do" (Luke 23:34). At the final judgement, when everything can be seen for what it really is, we will apparently learn that we have been rather poor at guessing at our real motivations. If we try to make honest sense of even half of what we do, we must confess that we often make mere conjectures about our reasons for doing things, and we are wrong about much or most of it. And, of course, it is unquestionably true that every time we wish to think carefully about our actions, we must *stop* acting in order to do so. Inevitably, we act in ignorance, letting thought and reflection fall to the wayside while we attempt to get things done.

Here, then, is the human condition according to the parallax interpretation of Alma 12:31. The *or* at the heart of the verse divides knowing from doing, and doing from knowing. It fractures human being at its very core, in parallel to the fracturing of eternity that produces the time in which human being unfolds. Trapped in time, we discover that the more we know, the more impotent we are, and the more that we can do, the less we can make sense of what we do. At any given moment, we sustain some kind of relation to good and evil, and we are in some sort of "state to act." But the question at any given moment is whether our relation to good and evil is principally a matter of knowledge (in which case we are guaranteed infinite frustration at our inability to do what we know we ought, despite placing ourselves in a state to act) or whether our relation to good and evil is principally a matter of action (in which case we are guaranteed infinite frustration at our inability to understand what we do, since we have been alienatingly placed in a state to act).

Knowingly impotent or ignorantly active—we alternate between these two inconsistent "states." *That* is the human condition.

I cannot help but wonder whether this strict divide between knowing and doing, glimpsed in the third possible interpretation of Alma 12:31 (the parallax interpretation), helps to make sense of Alma's description of the human condition as "preparatory." I said before that I am happy to leave the interpretation of Alma's other brief discussion of the human condition, found in Alma 12:24, to Adam Miller. But perhaps I might add just one comment to Miller's rich analysis.[4] Why do we, as fallen human beings, spend our time preparing? Might it not be a way of compensating for the dilemma I have attempted to articulate above? In preparing, we pretend that the divide between knowing and doing is simply a *temporal* divide, a divide between before and after. We work on knowing *now*, pretending that we will thus be ready to do something *later*. And thus, in our preparations, we pretend that we are the ones who divide knowing from doing, as if we *intentionally* separate knowing from doing so as to make the former's exhaustive execution the gateway to successful accomplishment of the latter. But this is, of course, sheer fantasy, pretending that the void that traumatically divides us from ourselves is really just a feature of our own brilliant strategizing about how to do things in the best way possible. Ultimately, this fantasy just masks our procrastination. Generally speaking, we prepare so that we do not have to be redeemed. Or better, we prepare so that we can ignore the fact that we have always already been redeemed, according to the redemption that was prepared from the foundation of the world.

Until we give up and allow God, at last, to redeem us, we are condemned to endless preparation. In the human—the *unredeemed*—condition, we are fragmented and cracked, just like eternity in the Book of Mormon's cosmotheology and the rocks in the Book of Mormon's geotheology. But then there is the possibility of redemption. And in redemption, the *or* of Alma 12:31 might assume a fourth meaning: one where its scope is as broad as in the third or parallax approach, but one also where its function is inclusive rather than exclusive. In redemption, it might at last be true *both* that we know *and* that we act. The fragments that result from the crack at the heart of human nature might be sewn together in a seam. In redemption, we might concede Alma's radical disjunction, the fracture between knowing and doing. But we might at the same time receive both our impotent knowing and our ignorant doing as things that work together for good. We remain cracked, and our parts remain in fragments, but a seam stitches us together in a way that good becomes possible.

God has been preparing us for just such a possibility since the foundation of the world. And we are likely to bear the scars of our passage through the human condition not only for time but for all eternity.

---

4. [See, again, Miller, "A Preparatory Redemption."]

Appendix: Alma's Cosmotheology

The time of the world, according to Alma, begins with a seminal event or series of events, to which he returns again and again in his discourse in Alma 12–13. He illuminatingly assigns this event or series of events to an inaugural temporal moment, which he consistently calls "the foundation of the world." At no point does Alma pause to describe this event or series of events in systematic fashion or sustained detail. Instead, he refers to it only occasionally, providing mere glimpses of its basic nature. It seems, though, according to his account, to have been primarily a matter of *preparation*, since Alma refers to several things that were "prepared from the foundation of the world." These include "the plan of redemption" (Alma 12:30), "priests" who are both "called" and prepared (13:2–3), and a certain "holy calling" (v. 5). Hence, whatever else might have taken place at the foundation of the world, Alma clearly believes that a good deal of *preparatory* work was accomplished then.

As if to underscore the importance of preparation in each of these passages, the several prepared things Alma mentions *look forward* in one way or another—and each looks forward always, significantly, toward redemption. The plan of redemption, the first thing Alma mentions as having been prepared from the foundation of the world, is in and of itself clearly provisionary, looking forward to what Christ would accomplish. As for the second thing Alma attaches to the foundation of the world—priests called and prepared at that time—he says they are ordained typologically, such that "the people might know in what manner to look forward . . . for redemption" (Alma 13:2). And finally, the holy calling Alma also says was prepared from the foundation of the world was, he claims, prepared "with and according to a preparatory redemption" for those who receive it (v. 3). Hence, all things prepared from the foundation of the world can be said, from Alma's perspective, to have been laid out "according to the foreknowledge of God" (v. 3).

It seems safe to say that, if Alma indeed believes that time interrupts eternity, it is the event or the series of events taking place at the foundation of the world that "initially" accomplishes this interruption. And thus the world and its time, separated out from eternity, find their foundation in *preparation*. Timeless eternity fractures and fragments from the moment that something is *prepared*. One might in fact say that preparation necessarily fractures and then fragments eternity because the preparatory looks forward from one time to another, provisionally. To put the point formulaically, time supplants eternity through preparation—even though what is prepared for, in all of Alma's talk about the foundation of the world, is redemption. One might say that redemption dawns as a possibility only where eternity gives way to time, that is, where life becomes first and foremost a "preparatory state" (Alma 12:26) rather than a kind of continuous existence.

Now, these are suggestive ways of reading Alma's text, but one might well wonder whether they are really justified. What justifies this interpretation in my mind is a further passage, Alma 13:7, where Alma once more refers—*but in a fundamentally distinct way*—to the foundation of the world. In this further passage, he refers to something he consistently regards as eternal, rather than to something he regards as having had its preparatory beginnings only at the foundation of the world. That is, where in previous passages Alma speaks of things that were apparently ordained only in the course of the event or series of events that took place at the foundation of the world, in this further passage he speaks of something that apparently already *was* when that event or series of events "initially" interrupted eternity. The plan of redemption, priests themselves, and the holy calling: these all had their beginnings at the foundation of the world. But *the holy order,* or "the order of (God's) Son," Alma explicitly describes as "being without beginning of days or end of years" (13:7). The holy order is eternal, not prepared from the foundation of the world. And yet Alma *does*, as he goes on, nonetheless connect the holy order to *both* preparation and the foundation of the world. But he makes these connections in an odd way, thus distinguishing the holy order from the callings and priests and plan that were all "prepared from the foundation of the world."

In effect, when speaking of the holy order, Alma separates "preparation" from "the foundation of the world." The holy order is, like all the other things Alma talks about, something *prepared*, but it was not prepared *from the foundation of the world*. While the holy order is in some way oriented to *the foundation of the world*, that orientation is in no way one of *having been prepared at that time*. What Alma says is simply that the holy order "was from the foundation of the world," and that it is "prepared *from eternity to all eternity*" (Alma 13:7). Each of the two parts of Alma's usual formula ("being prepared," "from the foundation of the world") is in Alma 13:7 separated from the other and attached to something else (the one to "from eternity to all eternity," the other simply to "was").

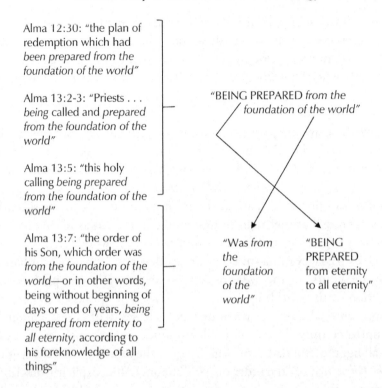

Alma 12:30: "the plan of redemption which had *been prepared from the foundation of the world*"

Alma 13:2-3: "Priests . . . *being* called and *prepared from the foundation of the world*"

Alma 13:5: "this holy calling *being prepared from the foundation of the world*"

Alma 13:7: "the order of his Son, which order *was from the foundation of the world*—or in other words, being without beginning of days or end of years, *being prepared from eternity to all eternity,* according to his foreknowledge of all things"

"BEING PREPARED *from the foundation of the world*"

"Was *from* the foundation of the world"

"BEING PREPARED from eternity to all eternity"

Clearly, Alma wishes his hearers and, eventually, his readers to understand that the holy order is in some fundamental way distinct from the other things he discusses. It is eternal, and so its relationship both to preparation and to the foundation of the world is unique.

What is most theologically intriguing in Alma 13:7 is Alma's odd claim that the holy order is "prepared from eternity to all eternity." At one level, the formula just seems paradoxical, as if it made sense to speak of something *being prepared eternally.* At another level, however, the formula might be interpreted as itself pointing to the fracturing and fragmentation of eternity. In the formula, perhaps, one might discern *eternity dividing itself,* dividing itself into "eternity" and "all eternity"—the former open and oriented (the order is prepared *from* eternity) and the latter complete and at rest (the order is prepared *to* all eternity). Perhaps provisional plans and typological ordinations and preparatory redemptions take initial shape inasmuch as God's eternal order, without beginning of days or end of years, finds its place in time somewhere between "eternity" and "all eternity." Thus, at the foundation of the world, when many other preparatory things had their beginnings, the eternal order opened a seam or produced a crack in eternity and therefore assumed a kind of preparatory shape. The holy order, eternal rather than provisionary, nonetheless gives itself over to "being prepared" as eternity divides itself into eternity *before* (not yet finished, not yet "all") and eternity *after* (apparently total, "all eternity").

If this interpretation is not too far off the track, then it might be said that Alma 13:7 understands time to follow a kind of movement toward wholeness, toward "all eternity" and "according to (God's] foreknowledge of all things." Perhaps time is a kind of detotalization of eternity that then organizes a movement—through so much preparation toward re-totalization or renewed wholeness. Incidentally, the Apostle Paul seems to say something quite similar. Paul sees time as a melee, over the course of which "all enemies" must be put down—"the last" of which is "death" (1 Cor. 15:25–26). And he says that this whole process comes to an end, time finally giving way to eternity anew, when God is at last "all in all" (v. 28). It may well be that Alma shares this Pauline conviction, anticipating in eternity the becoming whole of what for the moment is only partial. "When that which is perfect is come, then that which is in part shall be done away" (13:10).

Chapter Five

As Though, As Though Not
Time, Being, and Negation

Latter-day Saint theologians who do microscopic theology on the Book of Mormon have their counterparts outside the Latter-day Saint tradition. Although the vast majority of scholars working in the field of biblical theology use methods quite distinct from the work being done by, say, the Latter-day Saint Theology Seminar, there are readers of the Bible who do work that is strikingly similar. The best such work, though, has been undertaken not by trained theologians so much as by philosophers. (It is probably important to emphasize that the Latter-day Saint thinkers who have devised the microscopic style of theological interpretation also tend to have their academic training in the field of philosophy, rather than directly in the fields of theology or biblical studies.) Philosophical readers of biblical texts often pause over the potential significance of minor phrases, hoping to draw from them massively important philosophical implications.

A particularly interesting philosophical reader of the writings of the Apostle Paul is the Italian thinker Giorgio Agamben. Agamben has written about Paul in a number of contexts, but his most sustained treatment is a lecture series published as *The Time That Remains: A Commentary on the Letter to the Romans*. The book's subtitle is somewhat deceptive. Agamben offers a commentary on just the first verse of Romans, although he ranges across Paul's writings as he explores the meaning of just that one verse. The book is filled with subtle readings of this or that phrase, this or that formula, this or that peculiar moment in Paul's letters. Among the most poignant investigations, however, is Agamben's study of Paul's use of the phrase "as though not." Reading that treatment was enough to spur in me an interest in seeing whether uses of "as though" and "as though not" in the Book of Mormon might prove as philosophically rich as Paul's. This essay is the result, the only example of microscopic theology in this volume that did not originate in a project hosted by the Latter-day Saint Theology Seminar.

I originally presented this piece at the 2015 meetings of the Society for Mormon Philosophy and Theology (held at Brigham Young University). It then appeared in a volume produced by the Book of Mormon Academy, an institution housed in the Department of Ancient Scripture at Brigham Young University. It was thus first published in *Abinadi: He Came Among Them in Disguise*, ed. Shon D. Hopkin (Salt Lake City and Provo, UT: Deseret Book and BYU Religious Studies Center, 2019), 263–86.

Abinadi's story and prophecies can be approached from a variety of perspectives.[1] In this essay, I provide a philosophical and theological approach to Abinadi. This analysis is motivated in large part by philosophical work that pays careful attention to a phrase—if not, in fact, a theological formula—that appears in the writings of the Apostle Paul. What draws my attention here is the fact that this phrase or theological formula appears not only in Paul's writings but also in Abinadi's defense before Noah's priests. I wish to ask what light Abinadi's use of the formula might shed on the philosophical implications of his defense. Thus, in an important way, this paper asks whether the Book of Mormon might be as rich a philosophical resource as the Bible has long been recognized to be. And, it will be seen, I believe that the answer to this question must be positive.

At any rate, recent philosophical work on the writings of Saint Paul—quite in line with recent exegetical and theological interpretation of Paul's letters—has focused on 1 Corinthians 7:29–32.[2] The point in such work, undertaken in parallel across several disciplines, has been to privilege what seems in Paul's thought to serve as a kind of theological or philosophical operator, the phrase "as though not." In my own work—most extensively in my book, *For Zion*, but also in an as-yet-unpublished paper presented to the Society for Mormon Philosophy and Theology—I have given attention to how Paul's "as though not" might speak to and within Mormonism. In *For Zion*, I argue that the underlying structure of the law of consecration as laid out in Doctrine and Covenants section 42 closely resembles the form of thought expressed in 1 Corinthians 7.[3] Further, in

---

1. [See essays throughout Shon Hopkin, ed., *Abinadi: He Came among Them in Disguise* (Salt Lake City and Provo, UT: Deseret Book and BYU Religious Studies Center, 2019)—in which this essay originally appeared.]

2. This alignment between exegesis and philosophy is perhaps clearest when N. T. Wright, a New Testament scholar, speaks with startling approval of Giorgio Agamben's work on Paul. See N. T. Wright, *Paul and the Faithfulness of God* (Minneapolis: Fortress Press, 2013), 556, 559, 835. For a more systematic assessment, see N. T. Wright, *Paul and His Recent Interpreters* (Minneapolis: Fortress Press, 2015), 315–23.

3. See, generally, Joseph M. Spencer, *For Zion: A Mormon Theology of Hope* (Salt Lake City: Greg Kofford Books, 2014).

the unpublished paper just mentioned, I argue that Joseph Smith's revisionary attention to 1 Corinthians 7 in his work on the New Translation (often called the Joseph Smith Translation) outlines a remarkable development of Pauline thought.[4]

Here I mean to continue in the same vein I have pursued before, but here I turn my attention from the Doctrine and Covenants and the New Translation to the Book of Mormon. As already noted, I want to look closely at a passage from Abinadi's preaching to see how it might cause us to think still more closely about the Pauline formula. But where in my earlier studies of the formula in the context of the Restoration I have focused much attention on Paul's own contribution, here I mean to leave Paul largely (or really, almost entirely) out of the conversation just to focus on the use of the formula in Abinadi's preaching. Whether or how Abinadi's "as though not" formulas might connect up with Paul's lies just beyond the scope of the present study, and there seems to be little reason to think that Abinadi's uses are meant to serve as direct intertextual references to Paul's formula.[5]

The passage that we will consider here can be found in Mosiah 16:5–6, and it concerns the nature of redemption. Coming to the conclusion of his long polemical encounter with Noah's priests, Abinadi outlines in Mosiah 16 a few thoughts regarding resurrection and redemption. And in verses 5 and 6 in succession, he uses both the strictly Pauline formula found in 1 Corinthians 7, "as though not," and also a slight (less-Pauline) variation of it, simply "as though." Here I wish to look at these two formulas in their Abinadite context, asking what might be learned, theologically, from their use in the most emphatically Mormon volume of Mormon scripture.

Although textual analysis and philosophical argument will have to clarify the stakes of my conclusions, it might be useful to state them here at the

---

4. See Joseph M. Spencer, "Are There Predicates in Zion?," presented at the annual conference of the Society for Mormon Philosophy and Theology, "The Atonement," held at Utah Valley University, October 31–November 2, 2013. [It should be noted that this essay, although delivered to the same society as the first version of the present paper, is not an earlier version of the same one. This is a different and as-yet unpublished paper.]

5. There is too little about the contexts of Paul's and Abinadi's uses of the formula to assume that they are meant to be deliberately related. For some analysis of the critera for recognizable allusions to New Testament texts in the Book of Momron, see Nicholas J. Frederick, "Evaluating the Interaction between the New Testament and the Book of Mormon: A Proposed Methodology," *Journal of Book of Mormon Studies* 24 (2015): 1–30.

outset. In general terms, I find philosophical significance in the fact that the negative formula, "as though not," appears in the part of the Abinadite passage that focuses on questions of being, while the positive formula, "as though," appears immediately thereafter where the text instead focuses on questions of time.[6] In light of this, I argue that the presence of negation in the first use of an "as though" formula marks the deficiency of the world inhabited by those who rebel against God, while the absence of negation in the second "as though" formula marks the deficiency of the world the faithful place in brackets. Developing the implications of this interpretation, I conclude that the use of the two formulas in Abinadi's words helps to draw a distinction between time and being in the operation of the Atonement—at least as Abinadi might be said to conceive it.

I

We will, in the course of this paper, eventually provide an interpretation of both verses 5 and 6 of Mosiah 16. For the first two sections of the paper, however, we will address just verse 5, developing the implications of the first use of the Pauline formula there.

Verses 1b–5 of Mosiah 16 form a clear textual unit.[7] A narrative transition (found in verse 1a) divides it from the material preceding it in Mosiah 15, just as a rhetorical transition at the beginning of verse 6 ("and now") divides it from the material that follows in Mosiah 16. Further marking out the boundaries of this textual unit is a kind of repetition: a repetition of material from verses 2–3a in verse 5. These structural points need not receive detailed attention,[8] but the fact that the passage to which

---

6. I assume no particular philosophical conception of the notions of—or relationship between—being and time here. Despite what the subtitle of this paper might suggest, I do not aim to provide a Heideggerian reading of Abinadi's words, though it *is* worth noting that Heidegger too was interested in Paul's "as though not" formula. His discussion might well be consulted, but they do not directly affect my interpretation here. See Martin Heidegger, *The Phenomenology of Religious Life*, trans. Matthias Fritsch and Jennifer Anna Gosetti-Ferencei (Bloomington and Indianapolis: Indiana University Press, 2004), 83–89.

7. Throughout this paper, I quote from Royal Skousen, ed., *The Book of Mormon: The Earliest Text* (New Haven: Yale University Press, 2009)—though I use my own punctuation where it seems useful to do so.

8. Unfortunately, I am unaware of any published attempts at fixing the basic textual structures of Mosiah 16. It seems to me, however, that the resumption of verses 2–3 in verse 5 may be one feature of a larger structure organizing the whole

we hope to give our attention here resumes or reprises material from a few verses earlier proves to be of some interpretive importance. Verses 2–3a speak of "the wicked," explaining that "the Lord redeemeth them not, for they are carnal and devilish, and the devil hath all power over them." Verse 5 unmistakably harks back to this when it announces that "he that persists in his own carnal nature and goes on in the ways of sin and rebellion against God, he remaineth in his fallen state and the devil hath all power over him—therefore he is as though there was no redemption made." Parallels between the two passages are obvious; both talk of carnality, of the devil having power, and especially of some persons who fail to receive redemption. But differences between the two texts deserve notice as well. The most relevant of these differences, it seems, is this: verse 2 straightforwardly negates redemption ("the Lord redeemeth them not"), while the later part uses the odd Pauline formula ("*as though* there was no redemption made").

Why should straightforward negation of redemption in verse 2 be replaced within just a few verses by the more complex gesture of what might be called "quasi-negation"—the "as though . . . no" formulation of verse 5? Perhaps something of an answer might be found in verses 3b–4. Verses 2–3a, as we have already noted, address the subject of "the wicked," but then verses 3b–4 turn their attention from "the wicked" to "all mankind." At first it seems as if there is little to distinguish the two groups. According to verse 3a, the wicked "are carnal and devilish, and the devil hath power over them." Similarly, according to verse 3b, the devil's work in Eden "was the cause of all mankind's becoming carnal, sensual, and devilish—knowing evil from good, subjecting themselves to the devil." All mankind, like the wicked who form a particular subset of them, are "devilish," and all end up at least temporarily in subjection to the devil. What seems to distinguish these two groups, then, is less the form of each's relationship to the devil than the permanence or the temporariness of each's subjection. Verse 4 is key: "Thus all mankind were lost, and, behold, they would have been endlessly lost were it not that God redeemed his people from their lost and fallen state." What distinguishes at least some human beings from others is the fact they are "redeemed" and so eventually escape subjection to the devil—while others ("the wicked") remain in subjection.

---

of verses 1b–5—perhaps in a chiastic fashion. I will have to leave to others the task of discerning such structure. For my purposes, it is enough just to recognize the reprise of verses 2–3 in verse 5.

Abinadi gives a title of sorts to the redeemed in verse 4. They are "his people"; that is, God's people. How should this title be understood? One might naturally interpret it in the broadest possible terms, as a simple description of the redeemed; because God redeems them or buys them back, they are God's people.[9] Certainly, drawing on other features of Abinadi's sermon, this is how *Alma* interprets Abinadi's talk of God's people when he establishes the first Nephite church a few chapters later (see Mosiah 18:8–10).[10] Nevertheless, we might interpret Abinadi's reference to God's people in a rather different way: as a reference, quite specifically, to the house of Israel or to the children of Abraham. In certain contexts, the meaning of such a title could *only* point in the direction of Israel and its historical covenant, and it may be that Abinadi means to make such a reference as well.[11] The meaning of Mosiah 16:4 depends on which of these two options is to be preferred. If we decide in favor of the broader or less specific interpretation, then it seems that Abinadi simply finds in Christ's redemptive work a certain reversal for "all mankind," even if only those who eventually constitute God's "people" receive the full benefits of redemption. But if we decide in favor of the narrower or more specific interpretation, then it seems that Abinadi believes that the specific redemption of historical Israel somehow plays a role in reclaiming "all mankind" from their "lost" condition.

This specificity matters for the interpretation of verse 5, because only the latter of these two interpretations of verse 4 helps to motivate the shift from verse 2's straightforward negation ("the Lord redeemeth them not") to verse 5's murkier form of negation ("he is as though there was no redemption made"). If we interpret verse 4 as claiming just that God's

---

9. Jennifer Lane has consistently written on the theme of redemption in Latter-day Saint scripture. For a good overview of the idea in the Book of Mormon, see Jennifer C. Lane, "Choosing Redemption," in *Living the Book of Mormon: Abiding by Its Precepts*, ed. Gaye Strathearn and Charles Swift (Salt Lake City and Provo, UT: Deseret Book and BYU Religious Studies Center, 2007), 163–75.

10. Alma's conception of what constitutes God's people draws heavily on Abinadi's interpretation of Isaiah 52:7–10 and Isaiah 53:8–10. Whether Abinadi meant to link his interpretation of these Isaiah passages to his passing reference to God's people remains unclear, however.

11. In the Book of Mormon, one should point especially to Nephi. I have elsewhere argued that Abinadi is far less interested than Nephi in Israel's historical covenants, but I do not think that their distinct theological perspectives directly imply that Abinadi's reference to God's people could not here have reference to historical Israel. See Joseph M. Spencer, *An Other Testament*, 2nd ed. (Provo, UT: Neal A. Maxwell Institute Press, 2016).

"people" are the redeemed—those among "all mankind" who escape the destiny of "the wicked"—then it seems that the text assumes some kind of (inexplicable) equivalence between the two formulas. The wicked both *are* not redeemed and are *as though* not redeemed. But if we instead interpret verse 4 as claiming that Israel's redemption opens up possibilities of redemption for "all mankind," then verse 5's formula would apply to something other than the simply-and-straightforwardly wicked. When in verse 5 Abinadi speaks of him who "persists in his own carnal nature and goes on in the ways of sin and rebellion against God," it would seem that he has reference not to the wicked in general, but specifically to the wicked among Israel—to the wicked among God's redeemed people. The wicked generally simply *are* unredeemed (v. 2), but the wicked among God's redeemed people are *as though* unredeemed (v. 5). When it comes to "every nation, kindred, tongue, and people" (v. 1), it seems it is possible to employ a simple division between those who are and those who are not redeemed. But when it comes instead to God's people, no such simple operation of division works. Instead, it is necessary to utilize a logic of exception; the whole of God's people is redeemed, but there are nonetheless certain exceptional individuals among them who exist as though that full redemption were not, in fact, accomplished.[12] In other words, the wicked among Israel experience the world in terms of non-actual possibilities, hypothetical situations, or counterfactual states of affairs.

Now, it may ultimately be that this more complex interpretation of verses 4–5 is erroneous. Nonetheless, there are reasons to think it the better of the two interpretations, at the very least because it helps to motivate the distinction between the formulas of verses 2 and 5—a distinction that otherwise would be without obvious explanation. But this more complex interpretation also serves well because of the way it points to the larger theology of Paul's first letter to the Corinthians. It points not only to 1 Corinthians

---

12. Various formalizations of such a logic of exception might be cited for the purposes of fuller elaboration, although any strictly formal presentation of such a logic would likely avoid using the language of Paul's "as though (not)." For this reason, it is perhaps best to cite the extended discussion of exception, which draws on formal work, found in Giorgio Agamben, *The Coming Community*, trans. Michael Hardt (Minneapolis: University of Minnesota Press, 1993). The extremely lengthy discussion among logicians and mathematicians about the concept of the exception has been gathered in its essentials in Jean van Heijenoort, ed., *From Frege to Gödel: A Source Book in Mathematical Logic, 1879–1931* (Cambridge: Harvard University Press, 1967).

7:29–32, with its use of the "as though not" formula, but to the whole of the letter, which serves as an extended reflection on the notions of totality and exception, especially as these apply to covenant Israel.[13] These were, of course, themes that Paul developed even more fully in Romans 9–11.[14] For present purposes, however, we will leave fuller investigation of the theme of covenant—and of Paul's commentary on it—for another time.[15] For now, perhaps it is enough just to allow these connections to motivate further the interpretation offered here of Mosiah 16:4–5.

To summarize things so far, then, we might say that what, for Abinadi, distinguishes covenantal and non-covenantal relationships to redemption is the distinct role played by negation in each. On the one hand, negation simply divides non-covenantal peoples in two, into the redeemed and the unredeemed. On the other hand, negation more complexly organizes the experience of exceptionality among the covenant people, attaching itself to an "as though" that brings with it the hypothetical or the counterfactual. We might make this same point by drawing on another facet of the text. Gentiles are either redeemed or not redeemed, such that negation negates always and only the individual's redemption; either "the Lord redeemeth them" or "the Lord redeemeth them not." But Israel as a whole apparently just *is* redeemed, and therefore what exceptional individuals among God's people face is not their own individual non-redemption, but rather, it seems, the (non-actual) possibility of the non-redemption of the whole of God's people. Abinadi's wording is quite suggestive here. He does not claim that the unrepentant among God's people are as though they were not redeemed; he says, rather, that these are "as though there was no redemption made." The "as though not" applies not to the individual's own particular redemption, but to what that individual experiences with regard to the whole people's redemption.

---

13. This is a point made especially by Jacob Taubes, who calls 1 Corinthians "one great fugue around this single word *pan* ['all']." Jacob Taubes, *The Political Theology of Paul*, trans. Dana Hollander (Stanford: Stanford University Press, 2004), 1.

14. See Giorgio Agamben, *The Time that Remains: A Commentary on the Letter to the Romans*, trans. Patricia Dailey (Stanford: Stanford University Press, 2005), 53–57.

15. For my own discussion of Romans 9–11, see Spencer, *For Zion*, 57–68.

II

At this point, in order to clarify what is at stake here, it seems best to take a step back from the text to ask about what happens, rather generally, when something like an "as though not" appears in language. What do we mean by "as," by "as though," and by "as though not"? And how might clarity on these points help to shed some light on Abinadi's use of the formula?

There are, of course, numerous ways one might make sense of the word "as." Among the many possibilities, we will focus here on what might be learned from the field of philosophical hermeneutics. According to the hermeneutic tradition (launched by Friedrich Schleiermacher, brought to a first maturation with Wilhelm Dilthey, given an ontological bent thanks to Martin Heidegger, and coming into its own with the conversation spurred by Hans-Georg Gadamer),[16] every "as" concerns an implicit understanding, a certain assumed bearing among things—a *world* in the Heideggerian or even the Wittgensteinian sense.[17] That is to say, the word "as" always already marks an individual's involvement in a set of relationships and meanings, a totality of significations that serves as the basic context for sense. If I say that my friend works "as a teacher," then I indicate that she does her work in the world of education, a world that is roughly determinate or determinable if not necessarily explicit for her or for me. Similarly, if I say that I regard the Book of Mormon "as scripture," then I suggest that my reading of it ideally exhibits an implicit trust in its canonical or authoritative status both for me and for the larger religious community of which I form a part (a certain religious world), whether or not I or others in that community consciously think about what it means for the Book of Mormon to serve

---

16. The story of the hermeneutic tradition here summarized is told by Gadamer himself. See Hans-Georg Gadamer, *Truth and Method*, 2nd rev. ed., trans. Joel Weinsheimer and Donald G. Marshall (New York: Continuum, 2004), 172–382. For the basic texts, see the excellent collection: Kurt Mueller-Vollmer, ed., *The Hermeneutics Reader* (New York: Continuum, 1994).

17. See the discussions in Martin Heidegger, *Being and Time*, trans. John Macquarrie and Edward Robinson (New York: Harper & Row, 1962); and Ludwig Wittgenstein, *Tractatus Logico-Philosophicus*, trans. D. F. Pears and B. F. McGuinness (New York: Routledge, 2001). For a full formalization of this notion of worlds, see Alain Badiou, *Logics of Worlds: Being and Event II*, trans. Alberto Toscano (New York: Continuum, 2009).

in this way.[18] And so it goes with every "as," each serving as the indicator of some roughly determinate or determinable world.

What, then, occurs when one adds "though" to "as"? First, of course, it should be noted that there is a crucial element of negativity present in the word "though," such that to say "as though" is always already to recognize that the world indicated by *this* "as" is non-actual or at least in some sense foreign to the context into which it is introduced. When we use the phrase "as though," then, we recognize that the actual world we inhabit in some way precludes or excludes the world we gesture toward with the word "as." At the same time, our use of "as though" clearly means to indicate some kind of relevance to the actual world of the nonactual world we introduce by the words "as though."[19] When I say that my friend acts "as though she were a student," I clearly imply that my friend is not a student in the actual world even as I simultaneously note the relevance to the actual world (thanks to my friend's behaviors) of some non-actual world in which she is a student. Similarly, when I say that I regard the Bhagavad Gita "as though it were scripture," I indicate at once that the Gita is not authoritative or binding in the actual religious world I inhabit and that my devoted reading of it is suggestive of a non-actual world in which I would participate in a community of devoted readers of the Gita's account of Krishna's grace. So it goes with every "as though," each serving to indicate a point of connection between the actual world and some non-actual world.

This description of the "as though" might be put in other, more philosophically fruitful terms. In every "as though," one finds a layering of worlds: a layering of a *possible* world on top of the *actual* world. Further, in every "as though," one discerns an intention to reveal something about the actual world: an intention to mark a suggestive feature of structure,

---

18. This example suggests that a more careful regard for the various sorts of things Latter-day Saints read the Book of Mormon *as* might prove useful. It is one thing to read the Book of Mormon as scripture and another to read it as history; it is one thing to read it as literature and another to read it as a theological resource; it is one thing to read it as comparative text and another to read it as material artifact. Each of these approaches to the text brings with it a larger world or context that determines the possibilities of interpretation.

19. It is worth noting that there has been a systematic attempt—not as yet widely recognized for its importance—at a "philosophy of as if." I do not here pursue a close reading of this approach, but it deserves at least mention. See especially Hans Vaihinger, *The Philosophy of "As If": A System of the Theoretical, Practical, and Religious Fictions of Mankind*, 2nd ed., trans. C. K. Ogden (New York: Barnes and Noble, 1968).

to highlight some potential incongruity, or to underscore a focal point of passion or desire.[20] In short, the "as though" performs an intellectual (because linguistic) operation by which two orders of things, one actual and one possible, are brought into relation in a revealing way. Perhaps we could say that the two orders enter into a differential network, like x and y axes that, in the slopes and curves and singularities one can trace in their plotted interaction, reveal much about each other.[21] Or perhaps we could say that the two orders come into a comparative framework through which much becomes visible about each that would remain invisible if it were considered on its own.[22] At any rate and whatever metaphor one uses, in every "as though," someone draws the possible toward the actual in order to reveal both the contingencies and the necessities of the latter.[23]

What, next, does the "not" of "as though not" add to the already philosophically rich gesture of the "as though"? What do we mean when we say "as though not"? Here, it seems clear, we are still involved in layering possible and actual worlds, just as in the slightly simpler formula of the "as though." What distinguishes the "as though not" from the "as though," then, is just that the differential point of contact between the

---

20. See Jacques Derrida, *Writing and Difference*, trans. Alan Bass (Chicago: University of Chicago Press, 1978), 279: "As always, coherence in contradiction expresses the force of a desire."

21. I take this example from calculus, not without some violence, with an eye to the remarkable exposition provided in Gilles Deleuze, *Difference and Repetition*, trans. Paul Patton (New York: Columbia University Press, 1994). For a helpful commentary, see Manuel DeLanda, *Intensive Science and Virtual Philosophy* (New York: Bloomsbury, 2013).

22. Here one might in fact point to the concrete work of comparative philosophy of religion. For a rich experiment in this discipline that is focused specifically on Mormonism, see Jad Hatem, *Postponing Heaven: The Three Nephites, the Bodhisattva, and the Mahdi*, trans. Jonathon Penny (Provo, UT: Neal A. Maxwell Institute Press, 2015); for a shorter example somewhat more explicit about methodological questions (and interested in the same examples of scripture used here), see Joseph M. Spencer, "Christ and Krishna: The Visions of Arjuna and the Brother of Jared," *Journal of Book of Mormon Studies* 23 (2014): 56–80. [This last-mentioned essay appears in the other volume of *The Anatomy of Book of Mormon Theology*.]

23. Drawing on the resources of model theory (and comparative study of two philosophers: Alfred Tarski and Alain Badiou), I have elsewhere provided a formal analysis of this procedure. See Joseph M. Spencer, "Formalism and the Notion of Truth" (PhD dissertation, University of New Mexico, 2015).

actual world and the relevant possible world concerns something lacking rather than present in the possible world. Where the "as though" identifies something (curiously or symptomatically) lacking in the actual world by imagining a possible world in which it is present, the "as though not" identifies something (curiously or symptomatically) present in the actual world by imagining a possible world in which it is lacking. When I say that my friend behaves "as though she were not a teacher," I make clear that she *is* a teacher in the actual world, although her behavior suggests the relevance of a non-actual or possible world in which she is *not* a teacher. Similarly, when I say, as a theologian, that historians regard the Book of Mormon "as though it were not scripture," I indicate my firm belief that the Book of Mormon fundamentally *is* scripture, even if historians sometimes inhabit a (for me) non-actual world in which the book is *not* primarily scripture. And so it goes with every "as though not," each serving—like the "as though"—to indicate a point of connection between the actual and the possible, but by reversing the relationship of presence and lack that obtains in the "as though."[24]

What might we say by way of summary regarding the philosophical force of both the "as though" and the "as though not" formulas? We have seen that the word "as" already invokes the philosophical notion of a world, serving as a kind of linguistic indicator of some roughly determinate or determinable world. When "as" is coupled with the word "though," however, what is at issue is a layering of worlds, one actual and one possible, and the point of contact between these serves to reveal something about the nature of the actual world. Where "as though" appears without a subsequent negation (without a "not"), the point of contact between the actual and the possible concerns something lacking in the actual but present in the possible. Reciprocally, where "as though" appears with a subsequent negation ("as though not"), the point of contact between the actual and the possible concerns something lacking in the possible but present in the actual. The "as though" formula, we might say, thinks the actual through a possible world that is *in excess of* the actual, while the "as though not" formula thinks the actual through a possible world that is *deficient by comparison to* the actual.

---

24. My discussion here differs in important ways from that of Giorgio Agamben, but it should be noted that his comments focus quite specifically on the use of "as though not" when the layered worlds are, curiously, identical (as in 1 Corinthians 7). See Agamben, *The Time that Remains*, 23–25; and also my own commentary in Spencer, *For Zion*, 150–53.

This might be illustrated quite concretely by coming back to Mosiah 16:5, where "he that persists in his own carnal nature and goes on in the ways of sin and rebellion . . . is as though there was no redemption [of God's people] made." Here in Abinadi's words there is no need to go looking for the actual world at issue, since it is *the* actual world—the world we all inhabit—but one should note well that Abinadi sees as a key feature of the actual world we all inhabit a certain event, for him still future, namely "God himself . . . com[ing] down among the children of men and . . . redeem[ing] his people" (15:1).[25] If this is the actual world in question, what is the possible world with which Abinadi's "as though" brings it into contact? Quite straightforwardly, it is the possible world in which "there was no redemption made."[26] So far as Abinadi is concerned, this possible world approximates the actual world at every point, except that it *lacks* one thing: God's redemption of his people. The "not" of Abinadi's "as though not" draws the reader's attention to the chief (if not sole) point of tension between the two worlds he layers by using the "as though" formula. He inhabits a world in which God does in fact redeem his people, but he regards as relevant to the experience of certain individuals within the world the possible (but non-actual) world in which God does *not* redeem his people.

Of course, more needs to be said here because we have, to this point, ignored a crucial feature of the text in Mosiah. So far, we have spoken as if we always and only use "as though" language when attempting, in a kind of abstract way, to *think* about things—as if it were only or at least chiefly an *intellectual* matter. But, without discarding anything worked out about the use of the formula, we must now take careful note of a curious fact: Abinadi does not, in Mosiah 16:5, undertake anything like a thought experiment (like that to be found later, for instance, in Alma 42:11–13). The possible world he mentions, taken in its deficiency (lacking a redemption event), is not something someone *thinks about*; rather, it is something someone *lives through*. That is, Abinadi does not *speak* as though there was no redemption made; rather, the rebellious person to whom he refers

---

25. The importance of this claim to Abinadi should not be missed. It clearly forms the central feature of his sermonizing before Noah's priests, and Noah subsequently cites this particular teaching as his chief offense, the reason for his state-sponsored murder (see Mosiah 17:7–8). Importantly, a generation later, Noah's son Limhi explicitly recalls that the basic motivation for Abinadi's murder was his insistence that God would come in the flesh to redeem his people (see Mosiah 7:26–28).

26. This is, incidentally, a possible world on which Book of Mormon prophets seem to reflect often. See, for instance, Alma 11:41; 12:18; 42:11–13; Moroni 7:38.

just *is* as though there was no redemption made. Here, then, what usually passes as a kind of intellectual exercise becomes an *existential* matter. And Abinadi in fact makes this a question of being: "he *is* as though there was no redemption made."[27]

The existential stakes of Abinadi's "as though not" require us to revise, however minimally, some of what we have said about the entanglement of the actual and the possible in the operation of the "as though (not)" formula. In the intellectual use of "as though (not)," one aims—quite intentionally—to reveal something about the actual through an explicit thinking of the possible. But here in Abinadi's preaching, we find a reference to someone effectively unaware of the difference between the actual and the possible. Abinadi's point, it seems, is to insist that those among the covenant people who continue in rebellion despite their redemption live out their lives in what is really only a possible world, never in the actual world (where redemption has irreversibly occurred). The rebellious thus do not bring up the possible in an attempt to get clearer about the actual; rather, they live in the possible in a way that renders them constitutively blind to the actual.[28] And the "not" that Abinadi couples with his "as though" makes clear that the merely possible world inhabited by the rebellious among the covenant people is a deficient world, a world essentially lacking.

These points should be brought to bear on our conclusions from the first section of this paper. At issue in Mosiah 16:5 is what certain people actually experience, what Abinadi does not hesitate to present as their way

---

27. Obviously, such language would seem to gesture toward Heidegger—and toward existential phenomenology more generally. As will become clear in the course of this paper, however, the sort of being presupposed in Mosiah 16:5 is far more static than dynamic, and thus far more reminiscent of classical conceptions of being than of any conception set forth by Heidegger. The title of this paper does *not* mean to align Abinadi with Heidegger's thought.

28. In effect, Abinadi might be said to accuse the rebellious of living ideologically, while those attuned to the actuality of redemption occupy what philosophers would call a more strictly "scientific" position. See, for instance, the careful delineation of science and ideology in Louis Althusser, *For Marx*, trans. Ben Brewster (New York: Verso, 2005); and Louis Althusser, *"Philosophy and the Spontaneous Philosophy of the Scientists" and Other Essays*, ed. Gregory Elliott, trans. Ben Brewster et al. (New York: Verso, 1990). For an extremely useful commentary on the larger conversation within which this point of view takes shape in French philosophy, one in which "the lived" (as viewed in phenomenological circles) is definitively associated with the ideological, see Knox Peden, *Spinoza Contra Phenomenology: French Rationalism from Cavallès to Deleuze* (Stanford: Stanford University Press, 2014).

of being ("he is as though"). But we saw earlier that this sort of experience, this sort of way of being, is something Abinadi regards as exceptional. Hence, the rebellious among the covenant people are, quite unawares, condemned to the *exceptional* experience of a world that is not—that is, of a merely possible world. As we put it before, an odd logic of exception replaces the simple logic of division that holds outside the bounds of the covenant. Consequently, what operates outside the covenant as simple negation—some are redeemed, some not—we now recognize as operating inside the covenant in a rather different fashion. Within the covenant and as part of an "as though" formula, negation marks the deficiency of the merely possible world unconsciously inhabited by the rebellious, oblivious as they are to the actual world in which redemption has irremediably taken place.

All this might be adumbrated in two points. First, the Abinadite "as though not" is a matter of the lived, presented in terms of being (being, then, in its existential form: being-in-the-world). Second, the Abinadite "as though not" removes negation from its role as divisor (outside the covenant) and assigns it instead to the role of marker of worldly deficiency—that is, as what marks the world-in-which-the-rebellious-are as in some way lacking.

III

We might now turn our attention to Mosiah 16:6, the very next verse in Abinadi's defense before Noah's priests.

If, as we noted above, verses 1b–5 of Mosiah 16 form a determinate textual unit, then it should not surprise that with verse 6 Abinadi begins a transition in his sermon toward a new theme (signaled in part by the words "and now" at the outset of the verse). The transition is effected over the course of verses 6–7 through a bit of literary artistry.[29] The point, rather

---

29. There is, of course, some question of whether the literary artistry in question should be understood as the sermonic work of Abinadi or the literary endeavors of Alma (who apparently produced the first transcription of Abinadi's words; see Mosiah 17:4) or some subsequent editor (Mormon, for instance). Commentators have generally argued that Abinadi's preaching as contained in the Book of Mosiah reflects Mormon's editorial hand. See Joseph Fielding McConkie and Robert L. Millet, *Doctrinal Commentary on the Book of Mormon*, 4 vols. (Salt Lake City: Bookcraft, 1987–1992), 2:249; Brant A. Gardner, *Second Witness: Analytical and Contextual Commentary on the Book of Mormon*, 6 vols. (Salt Lake City: Greg Kofford Books, 2007), 3:316.

clearly, is to replace talk of "redemption," accomplished by Christ's having "come into the world" (v. 6) with talk of "resurrection," accomplished by Christ's having subsequently "risen from the dead" (v. 7). This shift from redemption to resurrection allows Abinadi to bring out his final theme in addressing Noah's priests: the event of final judgment that accompanies resurrection (the topic of the remainder of Mosiah 16). The bit of literary artistry that makes the transition work so effectively lies in the fact that the two verses share an identical structure, but with the place occupied by "redemption" in verse 6 occupied in verse 7 by "resurrection." Each verse presents a straightforward hypothetical statement (an "if-then" statement) that is interrupted at its heart by a point of clarification. The antecedent of each hypothetical statement opens identically, with "if Christ had not . . . ," and the consequent in each case opens identically, with "there could have been no . . . ." What replaces the ellipses in each verse differs just in that verse 6 focuses on redemption and verse 7 on resurrection. As the reader moves from verse 6 to verse 7, the clear repetition of structure highlights this thematic shift, from what Christ accomplishes by coming into the world to what Christ accomplishes by leaving it again to return to heaven.

What concerns *us* is what one finds in the interruption of the hypothetical statement in verse 6, immediately before Abinadi accomplishes, in verse 7, his full transition away from the central themes of verses 1b–5. Between "if Christ had not come into the world" and "there could have been no redemption," we get the following clarifying aside: "speaking of things to come as though they had already come."[30] The parallel interruption in verse 7—namely, "that the grave should have no victory and that death should have no sting"—is of no importance to our philosophical interpretation here. What is essential is just that in verse 6, in Abinadi's final word regarding redemption before he turns his attention quite fully to resurrection, he (or a scribe or an editor) lets the reader know that the prophet is "speaking of things to come as though they had already come." Crucially, here—only a breath after Abinadi has given us a theologically robust "as though not" formula, and while he remains for at least a moment longer on the topic of redemption—he (or a scribe or an editor) gives us

---

30. I have provided a preliminary theological interpretation of this and similar phrases in the Book of Mormon in a piece investigating the thought of Adam Miller. See Joseph M. Spencer, "Notes on Novelty," *SquareTwo* 6, no. 1 (Spring 2013), http://squaretwo.org/Sq2ArticleMillerSymposiumSpencer.html. [This essay appears later in this same volume.]

also an "as though" formula.[31] The striking proximity between the two "as though" formulas, one with and one without a negation, is already quite suggestive. That the proximity of the two formulas comes coupled with a set of differences between their respective uses is only *more* suggestive.

Now, we might note that the framing hypothetical statement of verse 6 might itself seem to be related to all we have already had to say about verse 5, quite apart from the clarifying aside that interrupts it with an "as though" formula. Because the hypothetical statement refers to a "world" into which the Messiah "had not come" and for which there had consequently "been no redemption," it seems already straightforwardly to be focused on possible worlds and counterfactual situations, much in the way any "as though" statement is.[32] And certainly verse 6's use of the words "no redemption" directly echoes verse 5's use of the same two words! Nevertheless, we need to distinguish strictly verse 6's "if not, then" from verse 5's "as though not." The hypothetical statement in verse 6, like the formula in verse 5, certainly concerns itself with a merely possible world—and in fact with the *same* possible world explored in verse 5—but it does so in a strictly intellectual fashion (again, as in Alma 42:11–13), rather than in an existential fashion. In verse 6's "if then, not" statement, no one *experiences* the actual world as anything other than what it is, and in verse 5's "as though not" statement, no imaginary *consequences* of the counterfactual are drawn.[33] The point of the hypothetical statement in verse 6 is in fact just to draw on the resources of a non-actual or a possible world to establish a relationship of necessary conditionality that holds across *all* worlds, possible or actual (Christ's coming into the world is a necessary condition for the redemption of his people). The fact that the framing hypothetical statement concerns God's success or failure in redeeming his people will prove relevant to the interruptive aside at the heart of verse 6—at the very least because of the way it determines the *thematic* and *temporal* significance of the aside—but its hypothetical con-

---

31. The possibility that an editor, rather than Abinadi, provides the second formula should not be overlooked.

32. In essence, the "if" of the hypothetical statement operates in a manner quite similar—if not identical—to that in which the "though" of every "as though" formula operates. Obviously, the "no" or the "not" operates in each case in a similar—if not identical—fashion as well.

33. In other words, what distinguishes the hypothetical "if then, not" from the existential "as though not" is both (1) the absence in every "as though not" formula of a "then" and (2) the absence in every hypothetical statement of an "as."

struction must be viewed as distinct in crucial ways from the construction of an "as though" formula.

It is, then, in the clarifying aside of verse 6 that the spirit, if not also the letter, of verse 5 makes itself felt—perhaps simply because we are there again confronted with an "as though" formula. And in interpreting verse 6, we can move more quickly than we did with verse 5, since we have already done the philosophical work necessary to make sense of the "as though" formula in general. Here again, then, we face a layering of worlds, one possible and one actual. This time, however, the "as though" formula lacks a negation, a "not," which, as our philosophical work above clearly shows, means that here the *actual* world, rather than the possible world, is what is found lacking.[34] In verse 6's "as though" statement, the possible world exceeds the actual world (rather than vice versa, as is the case in verse 5), since the actual world lacks a key feature of the possible world.

Now, at this juncture, we might well assume that the difference between actual and possible worlds in verse 6's aside *cannot* be the same as the difference between actual and possible worlds in verse 5. In verse 5, the difference between actual and possible concerns the actuality of redemption; the actual world is the world in which God redeems his people, while the merely possible world (certainly *non*actual) is the world in which God fails to redeem his people. Since Abinadi has made perfectly clear which world is the real world (the world of redemption), we would naturally assume that the "as though" formula of verse 6 focuses us on the revealing relationship between the actual world invoked in verse 5 and some possible world other than that invoked in verse 5. The point, we cannot help but think, must here be to see how some *other* possible world might be brought to bear on the actual world in yet *another* revealing way. And yet the hypothetical statement that frames the interruptive aside of verse 6 makes perfectly clear that the subject matter throughout the verse is, quite precisely, the world without redemption, the world into which "Christ had not come." The "as though" formula of verse 6, quite against the grain of verse 5, understands the actual world to be the world (at least

---

34. Giorgio Agamben finds in the simple gesture of the "as though" the basic nature of the parabolic, an already-messianic function because of the way Jesus uses parables in the Gospels. He ties this notion, moreover, to Franz Kafka's interest in parables. See Agamben, *The Time that Remains*, 24, 41–43. In some sense, to be sure, Mosiah 16:6's use of the "as though" formula is parabolic, opening up the actual world toward the possible in a messianic embrace of the coming Kingdom of God. The way this is so should become clear as this paper proceeds.

as yet) without redemption. The "things to come," about which Abinadi "speak[s] as though they had already come," are just Christ's "com[ing] into the world" and there being a "redemption." But the fact that these are only spoken of *as though* realized makes perfectly clear that they remain, from the temporal perspective of Abinadi's (pre-Christian) era, questions of *possibility* rather than *actuality*. In verse 6, redemption for God's people has irreversibly occurred only in the merely possible world, nonactual because still future for Abinadi.

This perfect reversal in verse 6 of verse 5—signaled by the exchange of the "as though not" formula for the "as though" formula and confirmed by close interpretation—necessarily surprises. Just a verse earlier, Abinadi presents the world eternally without redemption for God's people as a kind of fantasy world experienced only by the rebellious. But now he (or a scribe or an editor) presents the world without redemption for God's people as the real world of the present, such that only in "speaking" can one allow the future possibility of a world of redemption to occupy one's attention.[35] Putting it this way, however, already helps to highlight a crucial element, introduced only in verse 6 but playing a vital role in effecting the reversal of the possible and the actual: *time*. In verse 5, Abinadi effectively brackets time in his presentation of the *being* of the rebellious among the covenant people. In verse 6, however, he (or a scribe or an editor) complicates matters by bringing time into consideration, along with a recognition that Christ comes into the world at a determinate moment in history and that, until that actually happens, redemption must in some sense be regarded as a possibility (rather than an actuality).[36] And it is clearly *this* that effects the surprising inversion of the actual and the possible. The implication might at first seem to be that Abinadi, at least when

35. I will return to the question of speaking, but it is worth providing at least one point of contact here with Agamben's thought. See his discussion of speaking in Paul's thought in *The Time That Remains*, 126–37.

36. Here it becomes particularly clear why it should be important whether Abinadi himself is the author of the aside in verse 6, or whether it is the work of a subsequent scribe or editor. Does Abinadi himself recognize the reversal of verse 5's basic conception of things in verse 6? Does he see himself as enmeshed in time at all, or does his way of "speaking" in fact suggest that his prophetic anticipations provide him with a nonlinear experience of the temporal? For a brilliant exposition of the difficulties of prophetic time in the Book of Mormon, see Jacob Rennaker, "Divine Dream Time: The Hope and Hazard of Revelation," in *Christ and Anti-Christ: Reading Jacob 7*, ed. Adam S. Miller and Joseph M. Spencer (Provo, UT: Neal A. Maxwell Institute Press, 2017), 43–54.

"speaking of things to come as though they had already come," *himself* inhabits a fantasy world (a merely possible future world) and is therefore willfully blind in some way to the real world. But, of course, this way of putting things is misleading, since it ignores the way in which time operates in verse 6, as well as the way time operates in faith.

At issue in Mosiah 15:5–6, then, is a brilliant contrast between being and time, or between being and becoming.[37] The reversal of the possible and the actual, rooted in opposed uses of the "as though (not)" formula, concerns principally the radically distinct experiences of, on the one hand, those trapped in static being as if the to-come did not unsettle being at every moment and, on the other hand, those enmeshed in dynamic becoming such that the crystallization of being is postponed (if not entirely eradicated). The too-stable experience of the rebellious is one of desperate fantasy, while the self-transformative experience of the faithful is one of hope and faith. For Abinadi, it seems, being and time are strangers to one another, and this clearly has something to do with the actual and the possible in redemption.[38]

These points need clarification, but we might fruitfully pause here to draw a few points of summary before turning to the twin tasks of clarification and conclusion. We have seen that verses 5 and 6 of Mosiah 16 both use "as though" formulas, and that each use concerns a layering of worlds—a layering of some possible world on the actual world. In both cases, what distinguishes the two worlds involved in the layering is the presence or absence in them of God's redemption of his people; one world has as an essential feature the realization of that event, while the other lacks this. Strikingly, however, each verse layers these two worlds in a different—in fact, inverse—manner. In verse 5, the *actual* world features redemption, while the relevant possible world lacks redemption; but in verse 6, the *possible* world features redemption, while the actual world

---

37. It may be most appropriate to speak of becoming rather than of time, in light of the actual wording of the two verses. Verse 5 speaks of the person who "*is* as though . . . ," while verse 6 speaks of things "*to come* as though . . . ." This suggests *becoming* much more directly than it does *time* as such.

38. Nothing in Abinadi's words directly contests the viability of philosophies— like Heidegger's, for instance, but like those of many others as well—that find the dynamic instability of time at the heart of what is. "Being" and "time" operate as stipulative technical terms in this theological or philosophical reading of Abinadi, rather than as generalizable terms that can be put, acontextually, into conversation with philosophers using similar language.

lacks redemption. What underlies this inversion as one verse gives way to the other is, apparently, the fact that the one uses the language of being and entirely ignores time or becoming, while the other uses the language of time or becoming and entirely ignores being. Where time is bracketed and being is foregrounded, the actual world features redemption, though one might exceptionally be "as though there was no redemption made" (living in a kind of fantasy world). But where the reverse is the case, the actual world as yet lacks redemption, though one might exceptionally "speak of things to come as though they had already come." In a few concluding paragraphs, these final points deserve some exposition and development.

IV

What conclusions might we draw from this discussion, and how might we utilize them to clarify all we have said? For my part, I am deeply struck that the complex arrangement of Mosiah 16:5–6 allows "as though" formulas to be used to frame *both* rebellion against the Redeemer *and* faithful anticipation of the Messiah. Both the rebellious and the faithful live "as though" something, and that "something" has to do in each case with whether or not God accomplishes the redemption of his people. Consequently, both the rebellious and the faithful live their lives through and in the element of the possible, which overlays the actual. Now, at the end of this philosophical textual analysis, and thanks to the set of clear similarities between the two sorts of experience outlined in the text, it is possible to attempt to distinguish at the theological level between faithful submission to God and faithless rebellion against God.[39] As we have already intimated, what is at issue is some kind of distinction between being and time—between the static nature of what is and the dynamic nature of what comes—as well as between being and speaking. But these points now deserve at least brief exposition.

We might begin with faith. Abinadi (or a scribe or an editor) gives us to understand that faith is a phenomenon at once temporal and verbal. The faithful *speak*, we learn from the text, and they speak in a manner that assumes something about the structure of *time*. That is, the faithful are those "speaking of things to come as though they had already come." The

---

39. This notion that difference becomes clear only thanks to a larger network of discernible similarities is one I have discussed elsewhere. See, again, Spencer, "Christ and Krishna." [This essay, once more, appears in the other volume of *The Anatomy of Book of Mormon Theology.*]

faithful live out their faith by bringing the distant future directly into the present through their speech—that is, by assuming in their speech that what remains to come has in some sense always already come. Their speech, so to speak, *actualizes the possible*, or perhaps *potentializes actuality* through consistent attunement to the future as present. The faithful dwell in the possible, tapping into the potency of the potential, but they do so in a way that never loses sight of the present or actual world. Instead, we might say, it seems they work at depicting the halo of the possible that encircles the head of the actual. Peculiarly attuned to the possibilities with which the present is pregnant—*especially* to the possibility of redemption—they open the actual directly onto its future, to what remains to come.

Now, how does this contrast with rebellion, with sin? For Abinadi, sin seems not to be just a kind of languishing in the actual. Rather, it constitutes a certain flight into the merely possible, but one that fails to see how the possible is ultimately entangled with the actual. In essence, the rebellious *replace the actual with the merely possible*. Like the faithful, they are attuned to the possible, but unlike the faithful, they in no way open the actual onto the possible; instead, they close off the actual entirely by insisting that what is really only merely possible exhausts the actual. Sin thus effectively gives up on time (with its forced disenclosure of the present and the actual) thanks to a preference for a kind of stable state: mere timeless, fantastical being.[40] The sinful neither actualize the possible nor potentialize actuality, refusing to weave the actual and the potential in a more complex arrangement. Rather, they simply equate the actual and the possible in such a way that the latter entirely supplants (or closes) the former.

What we have in all this is, I think, two radically distinct ways of overlaying the possible and the actual. Sin and faith, that is, are two different ways of layering worlds. Faith amounts to a layering of the possible and the actual in such a way that the two interpenetrate, the future possible interrupting the present actual and all actuality opening directly onto its fundamental possibilities. Sin, however, amounts to a layering of the possible and the actual in such a way that one entirely obscures—if not eradicates—the other, the merely possible posing as and in the place of the actual. Faith denies only the radical independence of the actual and the

---

40. I borrow the language of "disenclosure" from Jean-Luc Nancy. See Jean-Luc Nancy, *Dis-Enclosure: The Deconstruction of Christianity*, trans. Bettina Bergo and Gabriel Malenfant (New York: Fordham University Press, 2008).

possible, but sin pretends that there is only the actual, which happens for the sinful to be what is really only the possible.[41]

We might make all of this more concrete by returning one last time to Abinadi and what he has to say. What is actual and possible in Abinadi's words is divine redemption. Hence we might say that faith denies only the radical independence of the world as it currently stands (without redemption) from the world as it is promised to become (the scene of divine redemption). These two cannot be extricated because they are bound by time, and the faithful weave them into a still more remarkable arrangement where the present disarray of God's people itself bears the halo of gathering and redemption, as though the Messiah had always already come in advance to set all things right. Sin, on the other hand, affirms the static continuation of the world as it currently appears, without redemption. It insists that there is only the world where God's people—if such there be—are in disarray and will remain so. But of course, as the honest can see, static continuation of the way things appear right now is only one among so many possibilities. And the sinful must therefore be said to take the merely possible as the actual, failing to see the potency of the present.

Faith and sin, to *speak as though the redemption were eternally sure* or to *be as though there were no redemption*. These are, it seems, the only options Abinadi means to examine. How will we sort out the entanglement of the actual and the possible? Are we content with the despair of being, or are we willing to turn to the hope of time? But these questions are ones we have to answer with our lives, and not through our philosophical discourse.

---

41. These categories of the actual and the possible might productively be triangulated with the third category of the "impotential," as articulated by Giorgio Agamben (throughout his works). This I leave for another occasion.

Chapter Six

Law, Grace, and Sovereignty in 2 Nephi 2

If any chapter in the Book of Mormon deserves close and careful theological reading, it is 2 Nephi 2, Lehi's famous sermon to his son Jacob just prior to his death. The chapter includes reflections on humankind's fall from paradise, the nature of law, the shape of human agency, the ontological necessity of opposition, the world's need for redemption, the purposes of the creation, and so much more. Generally speaking, although Latter-day Saints have read this chapter as a theologically rich and philosophically fraught one, we have avoided the task of reading it slowly and carefully. We tend to see it as deep, but we take the meaning of any particular passage within it to be relatively straightforward and stable. We have not yet begun, on the whole, to give it anything like the theological attention it really deserves, despite our recognition of its richness.

In 2013, the Latter-day Saint Seminar decided to sponsor two simultaneous and interrelated seminar projects—one on 2 Nephi 2 and one on Genesis 2–3. The idea was to spur parallel reflections on the Christian notion of the Fall, one set of reflections oriented by a text unique to the Restoration, and another oriented by a text the Restoration shares with the rest of Christianity. Participants discussed the texts online, gathering in person only for a final symposium. I was a part of the seminar on 2 Nephi 2. The seminars proceeded all the way to the joint symposium, but circumstances prevented the various papers written for the seminar on 2 Nephi 2 from appearing in print (although the seminar on Genesis 2–3 did produce a published volume: *Fleeing the Garden: Reading Genesis 2–3*). It is just as well. Despite our best efforts, I think the participants in the seminar only really just began to grapple with this richest of Book of Mormon texts. This paper, previously unpublished, is what I presented at the final symposium before the project was effectively abandoned.

I originally presented this paper in June of 2013 at "Mormon Conceptions of the Fall," a symposium held at Utah Valley University.

Preliminaries

When Nephi's brothers refused to help him build the ship that would carry their family to the New World, Nephi apparently made the mistake of showing his disappointment. "When they saw [it]," Nephi writes, "they were glad in their hearts, insomuch that they did rejoice" (1 Ne. 17:19).[1] Among his brothers' gloatings, Nephi records their defense of those in Jerusalem whom their father had prophetically condemned: "We know that the people which were in the land of Jerusalem were a righteous people, for they keep the statutes and the judgments of the Lord, and all his commandments according to the law of Moses—wherefore we know that they are a righteous people" (v. 22). Nephi's lengthy response to this particular point of defense is fascinating—and terribly understudied.[2] Nephi, curiously, never refutes his brothers' claim that the people of Jerusalem were keepers of the *law*. Instead, he suggests—through a retelling of Israelite history—that the problem lay in their relationship to the *covenant*. In short, Nephi seems to have been willing to concede the Jerusalemites' lawfulness but not their dedication to the covenant that underpinned true lawfulness.

The relationship in the Book of Mormon between the Mosaic law and the Abrahamic covenant is complex. The Nephites were from the start a people who understood the law messianically, as something given precisely in order to be rendered inoperative. Beginning from Nephi himself, they wrestled with the implications of living a law with an expiration date, and different Nephite prophets provided different interpretations of that problem.[3] Despite the commitment of the prophets to providing solutions to it, the problem remained until Christ himself made a visit to the New World and clarified what it meant to say "that old things had passed away, and that all things had become new" (3 Ne. 15:4). The inseparability of

---

1. Throughout this paper, I use the critical text of the Book of Mormon produced by Royal Skousen, though I insert my own (rather than borrow Skousen's) punctuation. See Royal Skousen, ed., *The Book of Mormon: The Earliest Text* (New Haven: Yale University Press, 2009).

2. The most interesting study of Nephi's sermon in 1 Nephi 17 is unquestionably Noel B. Reynolds, "Nephite Kingship Reconsidered," in *Mormons, Scripture, and the Ancient World: Studies in Honor of John L. Sorenson*, ed. Davis Bitton (Provo, UT: FARMS, 1998), 151–89. Reynolds, however, says little about what concerns me in this paper.

3. I review the two major varieties of Nephite response to this problem in Joseph M. Spencer, *An Other Testament: On Typology* (Salem, OR: Salt Press, 2012).

the law from the covenant, of Moses from Abraham, had to be reemphasized and clarified again and again in Nephite history.

Nephi's own writings are best read as a systematic exposition of the Abrahamic covenant, almost to the detriment of attention that might have been paid to the Mosaic law. The law, he was happy to announce, was "dead" for him (2 Ne. 25:25), since his attention was focused on the covenant and on the Messiah who would prepare the way for the fulfillment of the covenant. Paying attention first and foremost to Nephi's own direct contributions to his small plates record, one could get the sense that the law was for him little more than a test of obedience. After all, he procured a copy of the law through his own most trying test of obedience (see 1 Ne. 4:10–18)! Thus, one could come from a reading of Nephi's writings asking why God bothered with the law of Moses at all, except perhaps, as subsequent Nephite prophets would indicate, as a kind of punishment for stiffneckedness (see Mosiah 13:29–32).

One *might* come from a reading of Nephi's writings with such a question, but only by skipping over 2 Nephi 2, where Nephi records his father's great sermon on *the necessity of law*, perhaps even on the necessity of the *Mosaic* law. There is reason to suspect that Nephi's interest in Lehi's sermon—his willingness to include it in its entirety in his record, and his decision to couple it with Lehi's words to his rebellious brothers—was rooted ultimately in the sermon's brilliant defense of law.[4] It was the kind of theologizing Nephi seems to have been unable to do himself, but from which he was more than content to learn.[5] I suspect that we as readers of Nephi have as much as Nephi had to learn from it.

In what follows, then, I will read 2 Nephi 2 as a theological exposition of law's necessity. What Lehi has to say is difficult, and theological work on this text is demanding. Nonetheless, I think real sense can be made of

---

4. 2 Nephi 2 was originally coupled with 2 Nephi 1 as a single chapter. It was only with Orson Pratt's work on the text late in the nineteenth century that Lehi's sermon to Jacob was separated from his instruction for Laman and Lemuel.

5. Nephi seems to have included the teachings of others in his writings at times because they provided answers to questions he was not himself inclined to ask. This seems to explain his interest in Jacob's sermon on atonement (2 Ne. 9), from which he seems to have borrowed his own understanding of the resurrection. (The direct dependence of 2 Nephi 25:23 on 2 Nephi 10:24 is suggestive of Nephi's theological dependence on Jacob on questions of soteriology.) It is not unlikely that Nephi's interest in Lehi's words to Jacob was rooted in a similar relation of dependence.

the text. My basic thesis—likely unintelligible at this point—is that Lehi, in order to defend the necessity of law, distinguishes between the *force* and the *enforceability* of the law. I will suggest, moreover, that if this distinction is drawn as Lehi draws it, it becomes possible to reconceptualize, and in a startlingly modern way, the sovereignty of God.

The Ends of the Law

Lehi opens his sermon in 2 Nephi 2 with a problem, largely implicit. Verses 5–6 read as follows:

> The law is given unto men, and by the law no flesh is justified, or by the law men are cut off—yea, by the temporal law they were cut off, and also by the spiritual law they perish from that which is good and become miserable forever. Wherefore, redemption cometh in and through the Holy Messiah, for he is full of grace and truth.

Straightforwardly interpreted, these words identify the source of redemption. The law ultimately serves only to cut human beings off from God, so redemption comes not through the law, but through the Messiah. Happy as that last news might be—God be praised that grace is extended through the Messiah!—the first bit of news presents a theological puzzle that needs solving. If the law serves only to cut human beings off from God, necessitating the intervention of a messiah, why should it have been given in the first place? Is law not characterized by a certain superfluity?

Of course, Latter-day Saints have ready answers to that question. Jumping rather too quickly to verses 11–13, we eagerly respond that opposition is necessary to God's eternal purposes, that without law there can be no sin and therefore no righteousness and happiness, punishment and misery, and so on. Although Lehi does eventually make those sorts of moves, and although we are quite right to be excited about them, there is something wrongheaded about skipping over verses 7–10. Indeed, as I hope to show, there is an important sense in which we cannot understand Lehi's theological claims in verses 11–13 until we have made better sense of verses 7–10—and *that* we are reluctant to do. Our reluctance is not without some justification. Verses 7–10 are very difficult.

If verses 5–6 leave us wondering about the purpose of law, we should pay close attention to verse 7, which takes as its explicit theme "the ends of the law"; in fact, their complex fulfillment: "Behold, he [the Messiah] offereth himself a sacrifice for sin, to answer the ends of the law unto all those which have a broken heart and a contrite spirit—and unto none else can the ends of the law be answered." As it turns out, even a basic exegesis of this verse requires a fair bit of work, let alone a theologically satisfactory one. This is in part because of an all-too-natural interpretation that almost forces itself on Latter-day Saint readers, an interpretation that—I hope to show—ultimately fails to make sense of the text.

The first problem of interpretation concerns the use of the word "sacrifice." A survey of the text of the Book of Mormon reveals that the word is used in connection with the Messiah's death only in this passage in 2 Nephi 2 (where it appears once) and in Amulek's sermon among the Zoramites in Alma 34 (where it appears eight times).[6] It should give us pause that the language of sacrifice appears so infrequently in the Book of Mormon, with its many sermons on atonement—only once in Lehi's discourse, and a handful of times in Amulek's discourse. *Generally* speaking, it should be said that the Nephite prophets were uninterested in a theology that takes sacrifice as the lens through which to view the atonement. Amulek's discourse is a kind of anomaly or outlier, and Lehi's passing reference to sacrifice is—as will become clear—very difficult to interpret.

Further, there is reason to avoid taking Amulek's words in Alma 34 as a kind of interpretive key for unlocking the meaning of Lehi's words in 2 Nephi 2. Certainly the differences between their approaches to the question of sacrifice are important. Readers of the Book of Mormon too quickly take Amulek's theology to provide a straightforward translation of Lehi's brief formulation: when Lehi says "offereth himself a sacrifice for sin," we hear Amulek's "sacrifice his own blood" to "atone for the sins of another" (Alma 34:11); and when Lehi says "to answer the ends of the law," we hear Amulek's "satisfy the demands of justice" (Alma 34:16). But it is far from clear that Lehi's unqualified "sacrifice" is the equivalent of Amulek's fleshed-out "sacrifice" of "blood," that Lehi's singular "sin" is the equivalent of Amulek's plural "sins," that Lehi's abstract reference to "sin" is the equivalent of Amulek's concrete reference to "the sins of another," that Lehi's ambiguous "answer" is the equivalent of Amulek's theologically determinate "satisfy," that Lehi's unimaginative "ends" is the equivalent of Amulek's evocative "demands," or that Lehi's juridical "law" is the equivalent of Amulek's cosmic "justice."[7]

---

6. All other references in the Book of Mormon to sacrifice are references to religious rituals, Mosaic or otherwise.

7. Some readers of Alma 34 have argued that Amulek explicitly rejects the notion of sacrifice. I think this is a provocative, but ultimately a forced, reading. See R. Dennis Potter, "Did Christ Pay for Our Sins?" *Dialogue: A Journal of Mormon*

For my purposes here, I am happy to bracket Amulek's theological interests in order to pursue other interpretive possibilities with Lehi's words. Key to thinking carefully about what Lehi might mean by his reference to sacrifice, it seems to me, is a clear understanding of his reference to "the ends of the law" being "answered." As even a brief glimpse at the theological literature available at the time and place of the Book of Mormon's translation makes clear, talk of answering the ends of the law was not uncommon. Occasional debates concerned exactly how the ends of the law were (or were not) answered by Christ's atonement, as well as how the ends of the law might be compromised by certain styles of preaching. I am no historian of theology and so am entirely unprepared to recount the debates concerning the ends of the law in any detail—although I suspect that a full account of those debates would be helpful to see how the Book of Mormon would have been seen as intervening in them. Instead, with a nod to recent work by Christopher Jones,[8] I want to focus on one particularly interesting intervention in those debates—that of John Wesley, the founder of the Christian movement to which Joseph Smith often said he felt the strongest affinities (Methodism).

Wesley's statement about the ends of the law appears in a polemic directed at those who, by failing to focus on the law in their preaching, "make void the law through faith" (Romans 3:31). Beginning from "the deepest ignorance of the nature, properties, and use of the law," Wesley states, such preachers believe that "speaking of nothing but the sufferings and merits of Christ" somehow "answers all the ends of the law." According to Wesley, however, this approach to preaching "does not answer the very first end of the law, namely, The convincing men of sin, the awakening those who are still asleep on the brink of hell."[9] It is anything but sure whether Lehi would have agreed with Wesley that the *first* end of the law was "to convict sinners by [it],"[10] but I think there is merit in suggesting that 2 Nephi 2:7 be read along those lines. The ends of the law

---

Thought 32, no. 4 (Winter 1999): 73–86; and Jacob Morgan, "The Divine-Infusion Theory: Rethinking the Atonement," *Dialogue: A Journal of Mormon Thought* 39, no. 1 (Spring 2006): 57–81. Cf. Mark Thomas, "Revival Language in the Book of Mormon," *Sunstone Magazine* 8.3 (May–June 1983): 22–23.

8. See Christopher C. Jones, "Mormonism in the Methodist Marketplace: James Covel and the Historical Background of Doctrine and Covenants 39–40," *BYU Studies* 51, no. 1 (2012): 67–98.

9. John Wesley, *Works*, 10 vols. (New York: J. & J. Harper, 1826), 5:375–76.

10. Wesley, 5:376.

are, according to Lehi, answered *only* for those with "a broken heart and a contrite spirit"—only, that is, for those who experience a certain convictedness; all *others*, Lehi later makes clear, have to look forward to "the punishment of the law at the great and last day" (2 Ne. 2:26).

What does 2 Nephi 2:7 say if we thus assume, in a Wesleyan vein and not without a certain confirmation in the spirit of Lehi's teachings, that the first and chief end of the law was to bear a certain *affective* or *convicting* force? Somewhat paradoxically, it would say that Christ offered himself as a sacrifice precisely in order to ensure that the law would not lose its convicting force for those who, because their hearts are broken and their spirits contrite, will never actually be punished by the law. This way of putting things might lead one to suspect that among Lehi's theological worries in delivering his sermon to his son Jacob was whether the grace associated with the atonement does not somehow compromise or conflict with the ends of the divinely given law. How is law to retain any real force if the punishments associated with its transgression are simply unexecuted? On the other hand, how is the atonement to have any effect if all punishments associated with the law's transgression are meted out? In a word, how is it possible to ensure that law retains its *force* for those who repent, even as it is not *enforced* for them?[11] Lehi's answer to these questions, on the reading I am developing here, is sacrifice. In the Messiah's self-sacrifice, the law's force is uncoupled from its enforcement, in a way that the former has its full and necessary sway for those who, through the atonement, escape punishment.

2 Nephi 2:7 thus seems to provide a basic outline of an answer to the puzzle posed by 2 Nephi 2:5. Why should God have given a law in the first place, if the law serves only to cut human beings off from God? At the very least because one of the ends of the law—perhaps the primary end of the law—is to give human beings to feel a certain convictedness. And apparently, so that that can happen without the law *simply* and *irreparably* cutting human beings off from God, some kind of self-sacrifice on the part of the Messiah was necessary. Why sacrifice should accomplish any such thing remains, however, a question.

---

11. A not-dissimilar uncoupling of force and enforcement in law is presented in Jacques Derrida, "Force of Law: The 'Mystical Foundations of Authority,'" in *Acts of Religion*, ed. Gil Anidjar (New York: Routledge, 2002), 230–98. That Derrida has more recently begun to connect such an uncoupling with the figure of the sovereign is reminiscent of further directions I pursue in this paper. See Jacques Derrida, *The Beast and the Sovereign*, 2 vols., trans. Geoffrey Bennington (Chicago: University of Chicago Press, 2010–2011).

The Inflicting of the Punishment

Verse 7 of 2 Nephi 2, on the interpretation I am setting forth, answers the question implicitly asked in verse 5. What text, if any, might serve to answer the lingering question implicitly asked by verse 7—namely, concerning the possibility that sacrifice can answer the ends of the law by ensuring that law retains its convicting force even if the transgressors go unpunished? The answer, I think, is to be found in verse 10, what might be called Lehi's unfinished thought.

After abandoning the theme of the ends of law briefly, Lehi returns to it in verse 10. In a sentence that never ends, Lehi says the following: "Wherefore, the ends of the law which the Holy One hath given unto the inflicting of the punishment which is affixed—which punishment that is affixed is in opposition to that of the happiness which is affixed to answer the ends of the atonement . . . ." This thought is incomplete, interrupted by the remarkable thoughts contained in verses 11–13, but even in its incompletion, it can be said to communicate two things, both of them qualifications or clarifications of the ends of the law.[12] In the first part of the thought, we are told something about one way the ends of the law are accomplished: through "the inflicting of the punishment which is affixed." In the second part of the thought, talk of the ends of the law is doubled with talk of "the ends of the atonement," although Lehi fails to clarify satisfactorily what the relationship between these two sorts of ends ultimately is. Somewhere between these two qualifications or clarifications, I believe one can find an answer to the question concerning sacrifice left lingering in verse 7.

At a first and largely unreflective glance, the first part of Lehi's unfinished thought in 2 Nephi 2:10 might be taken to suggest that "the inflicting of the punishment which is affixed" is among the ends of the law, in addition to or alongside whatever else might be the law's ends. This would be a problem for the interpretation of 2 Nephi 2:7 worked out above, since

---

12. Two emendations to 2 Nephi 2:10 have been suggested, both meant to give the verse a kind of closure. The first would insert the verb "are" between "given" and "unto": "the ends of the law which the Holy One hath given *are* unto the inflicting of the punishment which is affixed." The second would entirely delete (as an instance of dittography) "which punishment that is affixed": "the ends of the law which the Holy One hath given unto the inflicting of the punishment which is affixed . . . is in opposition to that of the happiness which is affixed to answer the ends of the atonement." Royal Skousen has presented both of these possibilities and, on good grounds, rejected them. See Royal Skousen, *Analysis of Textual Variants of the Book of Mormon*, 6 vols. (Provo: FARMS, 2004–2009), 1:493–94, 6:3985–86.

it would be difficult to hold together as two conjoined ends of the law (1) to ensure that the punishment associated with transgression of the law *is* indeed inflicted and (2) to ensure that, while the punishment associated with transgression of the law is *not* inflicted, it has a convicting force. Here, though, it is important to read quite carefully. Lehi's unfinished thought states not that punishment's execution is among the ends of the law, but that the ends of the law are accomplished by the execution of the punishment. The inflicting of the affixed punishment, it seems, is a means, rather than an end—auxiliary rather than equivalent to the ends of the law.

With this more careful reading in mind, we might here surmise that Lehi intends to refer to one and the same event with his reference to the Messiah's self-offering in sacrifice (in verse 7) and his reference to "the inflicting of the punishment which is affixed" (in verse 10). The punishment associated with transgression of the law was inflicted precisely in the sacrifice of the Messiah. By offering himself *in the place of others*—that is, sacrificially—the Messiah allows the punishment of the law to be executed, *but not on those in whose place he positions himself.* There is little by way of surprise here. The idea of vicarious atonement is abundantly familiar to Latter-day Saints, even to those unacquainted with academic theology. Indeed, the idea of vicarious atonement is familiar enough to have become the target of criticism by certain Mormon theologians, those who are (rightly) troubled by the idea that some abstract cosmic justice, because it *has* to be satisfied through some balancing of the books, requires that *someone* suffer.[13] In light of such criticisms and the worries that motivate them, it is important to move most carefully at this point in interpretation. It seems clear, from Lehi's talk of sacrifice, that he conceived of the Messiah as suffering vicariously. What is *not* clear, however, is that that vicarious suffering was meant on Lehi's conception to satisfy the demands of abstract cosmic justice.[14]

---

13. See here especially Potter, "Did Christ Pay for Our Sins?"

14. Terryl Givens has suggested that the Book of Mormon works out a notion of justice that breaks with every conception of it as an abstract cosmic force that demands satisfaction. See Terryl L. Givens, *By the Hand of Mormon: The American Scripture that Launched a New World Religion* (New York: Oxford University Press, 2002), 205–7. Because the notion of justice developed by Givens appears in the teachings of Alma delivered to his sons shortly after Amulek's discourse was given, it is possible that it was meant in part by way of clarification or even critique of Amulek's conception of justice. Obviously, a full argument for such a conclusion cannot be included here. [I explore this theme further in "Amulek and Alma: Atonement," included in the other volume of *The Anatomy of Book of Mormon Theology*.]

What, though, could "the inflicting of the punishment which is affixed" accomplish if it does not serve to balance the books of justice?[15] Because we are concerned here with the punishment of an innocent (but willing) substitute, we cannot say that punishment is meant to accomplish the reform or rehabilitation of the one punished—which is what punishment has, on a certain line of argumentation, come in the modern era to be.[16] We *might*, however, say that punishment is meant to accomplish the reform or rehabilitation of the *un*punished, of those for whom the substitute substitutes himself. We might, in other words, play with the possibility that the Messiah offers himself a sacrifice for sin not to ensure that some cosmic debt is taken care of, but to produce a certain affect for, a certain conviction in, those escaping punishment.

In that the punishment is indeed executed, the weightiness of the law can be felt by those who witness its execution—even if that execution produces punishment for someone other than those who have transgressed the law. In a vicarious sacrifice that allows the affixed punishment to be inflicted on the innocent substitute, the Messiah frees the infinite demand bound up with the law from its direct association with readily identifiable duties and responsibilities. Law's force, uncoupled from concrete enforcement (through a substitutionary atonement performed by an infinite being), is freed to be felt *fully*—or at least in tension with "the happiness which is affixed to answer the ends of the atonement." Where the ends of the law are answered, the second half of Lehi's unfinished thought suggests, the ends of the atonement are answered as well. Happiness, it seems, cannot be disentangled from the experience of the force of law. Or, as 2 Nephi 2:25 has it, "Adam fell that men might be, and men are that they might have joy."

What I have produced here through this reading of Lehi's words is, I think, best described as a penal substitution theory of atonement— "substitution" because of the sacrificial role played by the Messiah, and "penal" because the sacrifice in question is understood to be tied to the in-

---

15. I leave out here the answer provided to this question by Saint Anselm of Canterbury, to which—for all their interest in Anselmian satisfaction more abstractly—Latter-day Saints have not subscribed, and for important theological reasons (discussed further along in this essay). Anselm's answer was that it was God's honor that demanded reparation. See Saint Anselm, *Basic Writings*, ed. and trans. Thomas Williams (Indianapolis: Hackett, 2007), 266–67 (*Cur Deus Homo*, I.16).

16. See Michel Foucault, *Discipline and Punish: The Birth of the Prison*, trans. Alan Sheridan (New York: Vintage, 1991).

flicting of a punishment affixed to the law. Now, those words alone ("penal substitution theory of atonement") are enough to worry many theologians, but it is crucial to recognize that Lehi, as I am reading him, has provided us with a penal substitution theory *subtracted from any theory of satisfaction*. Nothing somehow lying beyond or outside the Messiah requires satisfaction for Lehi. There is no abstract cosmic justice that has to be settled through a suffering-based balancing of the books. Instead, Lehi's theological gesture is to see in the Messiah's *self*-offering ("he offereth himself") a complexly double move. *The law acquires real force when the lawgiver both (1) suspends the law* (in terms of the execution on the deserving of its affixed punishment) *and (2) enforces the law* (in terms of the execution of its affixed punishment). Only in such a gesture does the law become *pure* law, the law that consummates itself in the lawgiving Messiah.[17]

On the interpretation I have offered, 2 Nephi 2:10 provides the clues necessary to develop an answer to the question left lingering at the end of 2 Nephi 2:7, just as 2 Nephi 2:7 provides the clues necessary to develop an answer to the question left lingering at the end of 2 Nephi 2:5. Does 2 Nephi 2:10 leave any questions lingering at its end? It seems to me that it does, though this may not be obvious. It leaves open, I think, the question of divine sovereignty.

The Wisdom of God

The question of God's sovereignty is addressed further along in Lehi's discourse, but it seems to me necessary to motivate the question before turning directly to the relevant passages. To do that, it is necessary to say a bit more about what it means to subtract penal substitution from satisfaction. I have already noted that the idea of penal substitution is very familiar to Latter-day Saints. Just as familiar—if not in fact determinative of most Latter-day Saint interpretations of penal substitution—is the notion of satisfaction, the notion that Christ's atonement serves to pay some kind of debt incurred by human sins. What is seldom noted, however, is that Latter-day Saints generally understand satisfaction in a way quite different from other Christians. This difference must be clarified if the question of divine sovereignty is to be fully grasped.

Most Christians trace the satisfaction theory of atonement to Saint Anselm of Canterbury, an eleventh-century theologian whose *Cur Deus*

---

17. I provided a preliminary analysis of this conception of the Law of Moses in Spencer, *An Other Testament*, 95–97.

Homo spelled out the basics of the theory. On Anselm's account, human sins require satisfaction because simple forgiveness without exaction of the affixed punishment would compromise God's honor or glory. So that God remains fully God, the slight against his honor has to be repaired through punishment. The atonement, construed as an event of penal substitution, serves to pay the necessary debt and so to protect God's honor.[18] Many have noted how heavily Anselm's theory of atonement relies on medieval (feudal) notions of honor, marking the theory's cultural distance from the spirit of the New Testament despite its general popularity among average Christians.[19] The twentieth century has rather generally seen among New Testament scholars a return of sorts to what was arguably the earliest Christian theory of atonement—that of Christ as victor over death (a conception arguably on display in 2 Nephi 9, the atonement sermon of Lehi's son Jacob).[20]

Latter-day Saints have been as generally given as non-Mormon Christians to a certain satisfaction theory of atonement (most likely under the influence of Alma 34). But due to some of Mormonism's theological commitments—in particular, to the idea that God is not absolute in the sense he is generally held to be in the Christian tradition—Latter-day Saints have largely assumed a rather non-Anselmian conception of satisfaction. For the average Latter-day Saint, it is not *God's honor* that requires satisfaction through penal substitution, but *justice as such* (what I have been calling "abstract cosmic justice" in the course of this discussion), something to which God himself is seen to defer. Imported into a traditional Mormon context, satisfaction becomes the requirement imposed on God by the unchangeable laws of nature, by the way things simply (and inertly) are. Satisfaction is usually, for the Latter-day Saint, a requirement the necessity of which God divinely recognizes and executes out of

---

18. See Saint Anselm, *Basic Writings*, 237–326.

19. An entire literature has developed in recent years defending Anselm against this common criticism. The defense is perhaps summarized most succinctly in the words of R. W. Southern: "Everything of importance in Anselm's argument can survive the removal of every trace of feudal imagery." R. W. Southern, *Saint Anselm: A Portrait in a Landscape* (New York: Cambridge University Press, 1990), 221. See, however, the helpful rebuttal in Anthony Bartlett, *Cross Purposes: The Violent Grammar of Christian Atonement* (Harrisburg, PA: Trinity Press, 2001), 76.

20. The push in this direction began with the publication of the now classic Gustaf Aulén, *Christus Victor: An Historical Study of the Three Main Types of the Idea of the Atonement*, trans. Arthur Gabriel Hebert (London: SPCK, 1931).

love for human beings—his literal offspring with the potential, through redemption, to become like him.[21]

What is significant for present purposes about the Latter-day Saint transformation of the notion of satisfaction is what it does with the idea of divine sovereignty. Anselm's worry, clearly, was that forgiveness without satisfaction would somehow compromise God's full sovereignty. The Latter-day Saint's worry, however implicit, has traditionally been that forgiveness without satisfaction would somehow compromise not God's sovereignty, but rather the laws of nature that, because they lie *beyond* his power, themselves mark a certain limit to God's sovereignty. Put another, more radical way, the Latter-day Saint's worry has traditionally been that forgiveness without satisfaction would somehow grant God *too much* sovereignty; that is, sovereignty enough that he might become afresh the God of the very tradition the Restoration called into question. Rather than serving to save God's sovereignty, the satisfaction theory of atonement as often as not serves in the Latter-day Saint's hands to save God's *non*-sovereignty.[22]

The consequence of all this, it seems to me, is that any argument undertaken, in an explicitly Mormon context, on behalf of penal substitution but without an appeal to satisfaction amounts to an attempt to restore a notion of divine sovereignty to the God of Mormonism. There is, of course, a danger in such a gesture—namely the risk of returning to the God of the tradition, a bodiless God beyond all passion and removed from his humanity (except in the short passage of the Incarnation). The risk is real but worth assuming, at the very least in order to discover what might be at work in Lehi's words in 2 Nephi 2.[23] What is the notion of sovereignty on offer in Lehi's discourse? Does the reading I have been developing here imply a certain return to notions of divine sovereignty that Mormonism has rightly rejected?

---

21. The classic articulation of this view in Mormonism (albeit with little emphasis or insistence on atonement) is, of course, John A. Widtsoe, *A Rational Theology: As Taught by The Church of Jesus Christ of Latter-day Saints* (Salt Lake City: General Priesthood Committee, 1915).

22. This formulation is, of course, too strong. It nonetheless helps to illustrate the difference between two remarkably different notions of satisfaction.

23. Lest I be misinterpreted here, I might note that I could not myself be more committed to the theological vision of Joseph Smith's Nauvoo sermons. It is a question here not of returning to pre-Restoration traditions, but of allowing the various texts of the Restoration to enter into appropriate tension with one another.

2 Nephi 2:11–13 is obviously the text that requires consideration. It is there if anywhere in the Book of Mormon that Latter-day Saints have found an indication of how the nature of things imposes certain limits on God.[24] It is there that Lehi again and again uses the phrase "it must needs be that," and it is there that Lehi is willing to predicate God's very existence on the maintenance of a certain order of things ("if these things are not, there is no God"). What, if any, are the limits Lehi imposes on God's power in these verses?

First, it should be said that one goes well beyond the text of Lehi's discourse if one begins to speak of the laws of nature—the laws of physics and chemistry, for instance—as being imposed on God. Although Lehi countenances the possibility that God's very existence is predicated on a certain order of things, he insists that without the existence of God "there could have been no creation of things, neither to act nor to be acted upon" (2 Ne. 2:13). John Widtsoe's heavily scientific theology cannot be read into Lehi, regardless of whether it can or cannot be read into the teachings of Joseph Smith.[25] On what is God's existence then predicated, according to Lehi? The most conservative interpretation, it seems to me, would be a certain set of transcendental conditions, conditions for the possibility of (human) experience.[26] It would seem that, for human beings to *be* human beings, for them to experience the world *as they do*, certain conditions must be met: minimally, the imposition of some kind of possibilizing "opposition" at the core of "all things" (v. 11).[27] A close reading of the text, however, makes clear that that minimal requirement, the imposition of a possibilizing opposition at the core of all things, is fulfilled precisely by God's giving a law. Verse 15 reveals that the opposition in question was that between "the forbidden fruit" and "the tree of life," a founding opposition established by what verse 5 already labels "the temporal law,"

---

24. See, for instance, B. H. Roberts, *The Truth, the Way, the Life: An Elementary Treatise on Theology*, ed. Stan Larson (Salt Lake City: Signature Books, 1994), 377–83.

25. See, again, Widtsoe, *A Rational Theology*.

26. I assume the language here of Kantian critical philosophy. It should be noted, however, that the idea that some kind of transcendental framework provides the basic bounds of possible experience need not remain within a specific Kantian framework. See, for instance, Alain Badiou, *Logics of Worlds: Being and Event II*, trans. Alberto Toscano (New York: Continuum, 2009), 101–2.

27. See LaMar E. Garrard, "Creation, Fall, and Atonement," in *Studies in Scripture: 1 Nephi to Alma 29*, ed. Kent P. Jackson (Salt Lake City: Deseret Book, 1987), 87–98.

to which was attached—as Lehi's son Jacob would later put it—"the first judgment" (2 Ne. 9:7).[28]

If this interpretation is not amiss, it seems best to suggest that what imposes a limit on God's sovereignty in Lehi's discourse is only what has already been reviewed: the necessity, if a certain conviction is to be felt by human beings, of introducing a law and securing its real force. But that, it seems to me, is to say that nothing really imposes a limit on God's sovereignty in Lehi's discourse. The only thing that, in Lehi's words, could "destroy the wisdom of God and his eternal purposes" (2 Nephi 2:12) would be *God's* decision not to pursue the ends of the law he himself desired to pursue. And it is hard to know how one could justify ignoring the weight of verse 24, Lehi's concluding thought regarding the aftereffects of the temporal law's transgression: "all things have been done in the wisdom of him who knoweth all things."

In light of the above, I think it advisable to restore to what seems its rightful place in Lehi's discourse a notion of God's full sovereignty. And if this is coupled with what I have, rightly or wrongly, read into Lehi's words concerning sacrifice and the ends of the law, it is possible to see Lehi as outlining a theological picture in which God's sovereignty is on display *precisely* in his uncoupling of the law's force from its enforcement. It is possible to find in Lehi's teachings, in other words, the idea that God's sovereignty is somehow *constituted* by the paradoxical gesture by which he purifies the law. In that the pure force of the law is separated out from the law regarded solely as a set of practices, divine sovereignty—the absolute authority of *the* Lawgiver—comes fully into its own or is realized in its most radical sense. Sovereignty in its strictest sense is realized in a certain suspension of the law that transforms the law into a deeply felt force, a certain sort of anxiety.[29] As a revelation from the Doctrine and Covenants has it, it is only when niggling commandments meant collectively to manage all human affairs are replaced by a generalized injunction to "bring to pass much righteousness" that one comes finally to be "*anxiously* engaged

---

28. The link between verse 11 and verse 15 is essential to the interpretation of Lehi's discussion of "opposition." Textual parallels between them make clear that the singular "opposition" that Lehi says must be in "all things" is that introduced through the prohibition placed on the forbidden fruit in Eden. Thus the link between the two verses makes clear that it is law that creates opposition in the first place.

29. This idea can be traced to Carl Schmitt, but is most productively presented in the analyses of Giorgio Agamben, *Homo Sacer: Sovereign Power and Bare Life*, trans. Daniel Heller-Roazen (Stanford: Stanford University Press, 1998).

in a good cause" (D&C 58:26–27; emphasis added). And it is apparently *that* sort of anxiety that constitutes human agency.

This model of divine sovereignty—one in which God's authority is a function first and foremost of his ability to *deoperationalize* the law *without destroying* it—is strikingly modern. The classical Christian model of divine sovereignty is one in which God's authority is a function first and foremost of his ability to operationalize whatever he desires. Sovereignty has been linked with a certain notion of power *without remainder*, with a certain idea that authority cannot be disentangled from perfect immunity. The sovereign God of the tradition has too often been a God who could hold together *both* the force of law and its enforcement.[30] Lehi gives us reason, I think, to wonder about the possibility that the sovereign God is a God whose sovereignty is constituted by his willingness to be *paradoxically* sovereign, by his willingness to be *so* sovereign that the law undoes itself in a certain way. Lehi spurs me, at the very least, to play with the possibility that God's sovereignty is so absolute that the very law cannot hold together in his presence. It, like us, falls to pieces as it comes before God's glory.

Self-sacrifice may be the *ultimate* gesture of sovereignty. It is neither surrender nor self-deliverance. Rather, it is in Christ's case undertaken in full recognition of what gives law to be law: namely, its force. Self-sacrifice presents the broken-hearted and the spiritually contrite with law in its purest form: grace.

The Merits and Mercy and Grace

What motivation, apart from the pure joy of doing speculative theology, could drive a Latter-day Saint to reassert divine sovereignty? Why try to save sovereignty? The answer, for me, is simple: *for the sake of grace*.

The most radical notion of grace to issue from the Protestant Reformation was that of John Calvin, and Calvin saw the ultimate inseparability of sovereignty and grace. Whatever must be said, in the end, about Calvin's talk of predestination, it has to be said that he saw that sovereignty and grace are paired. Calvin's worrisome idea that a certain arbitrariness attached to God's election—whether to heaven or to hell—is best interpreted as a remarkable insistence on the fact that divine sovereignty could not be compromised (by, for instance, some determining force that decided for God what the eternal fate of this or that human be-

---

30. This is true, oddly, despite the apostle Paul's vigorous insistence in Romans 7 that these cannot be held together.

ing should be) without grace being compromised as well. To that extent, I think, he was right. If Lehi has anything to say about the matter, it would seem that Calvin went theologically awry not in that he coupled grace and sovereignty, but only in that he misunderstood the nature of sovereignty. In Lehitic terms, at least as I have developed them here, the problem with Calvin's theology is that his God simply is *not sovereign enough*. The problem with Calvin's theology, in other words, is that his God simply is *not graceful enough*.

That, of course, remains to be shown. And I do not have the space here to show it even to my own satisfaction. For the moment and unsatisfactorily, then, I will allow Lehi's words from 2 Nephi 2:8 to suffice: "there is no flesh that can dwell in the presence of God save it be through the merits and mercy and grace of the Holy Messiah, which layeth down his life according to the flesh and taketh it again by the power of the Spirit, that he may bring to pass the resurrection of the dead." Somewhere in those words, I think, arose the dawn of a Nephite theology of grace, the most radical theology of grace of which I am aware, worked out in myriad ways over the millennium of Nephite theological reflection that followed.[31]

I believe we would do well to spend some time in the traces of that millennium of reflection that have been left to us.

---

31. I have tried to spell out in an as-yet-unpublished paper a preliminary analysis of the Nephite theology of grace. See Joseph M. Spencer, "Resurrection and Grace: Toward a Nephite Theology of Atonement." [This paper appears in the other volume of *The Anatomy of Book of Mormon Theology*.]

Macroscopic Theology

Chapter Seven

Mormon Conversion, Christian Conversion

Comparing Conversion Narratives in the Book of Mormon and the New Testament

Among the more puzzling aspects of the Book of Mormon is the infusion throughout it of New Testament language. Readers have long wondered at the similarities between Moroni 7 and 1 Corinthians 13, for instance. The truth is, though, that New Testament language appears all over the Book of Mormon, making it a definite and unmistakably significant dimension of the book's presentation in English. There are good scholars working on how to make sense of this issue (see especially the work of my colleague Nicholas J. Frederick). Far beyond just the bare question of how to understand why there are echoes of and allusions to the New Testament all through the Book of Mormon, though, there is the question of what the entanglement of the Book of Mormon with another text might signify at the theological level. Does the Book of Mormon in some sense borrow or even just reproduce the Bible's theological commitments? Or do differences both small and large between otherwise similar elements of the two books suggest that the Book of Mormon carves out its own theological path?

For my part, I think there are good reasons to think that places where the Book of Mormon draws near to the New Testament are sites for theological exploration. Looking at the question from a position of faith, I find myself convicted that, as God gave the English text of the Book of Mormon to Joseph Smith, he deliberately wove New Testament language into it for a specific purpose. I think, in short, that he wove into the English text of the Book of Mormon allusions and echoes that bring the Book of Mormon near enough to the familiar New Testament to make us see the significance of the real differences between them. When the two are so similar that we simply have to ask why they are not ultimately identical, there is reason to start asking theological questions about the non-identity of the two texts. This essay, previously unpublished, is one in which I explore in a theological way one of the more apparent connections between the Book of Mormon and the New Testament: the obvious similarity between the stories of Paul's and Alma's conversions. It introduces here a first take on macroscopic theology.

I presented this paper at the Pacific Northwest regional meetings of the American Academy of Religion, held at the University of Calgary in May of 2014.

In speaking to you of conversion today, I'll have reference to what William James called conversion "by self-surrender."[1] Because such conversion comes unbidden—at least at the level of consciousness—it represents a kind of paradigm case: conversion against one's will and due to a call from beyond. The archetypal such conversion story in the Christian tradition is, of course, that of Saint Paul, recounted in the Acts of the Apostles. A startlingly similar archetypal conversion story is to be read in Mormonism's founding scripture, the Book of Mormon presented to the world by Joseph Smith in 1830. The story of a certain Alma who was converted from his idolatrous way to an ancient American Christian church serves as a point of reference for Mormon thinking about conversion as much as Saint Paul's story does for Christian reflection. In the few minutes I have here today, I want to outline a comparative study of these two narratives. My thesis, summarily put, is that the Book of Mormon text reworks the New Testament text in a series of identifiable ways that highlight the basic differences between the respective experiences of conversion in these two religious traditions. At the heart of those differences, as will be seen, lies a shift in perspective from the *political* to the *familial*.

I should note from the beginning that I'm hardly the first to notice striking similarities between the narratives recounting Paul's and Alma's respective conversion experiences. Believers as much as skeptics have long noted the parallels—the former to suggest that the Book of Mormon bears crucial authority-granting similarity to the Christian Bible, the latter to suggest that Joseph Smith's scripture is principally an exercise in plagiarism.[2] Whatever conclusions might be drawn, the parallels are clear: both

---

1. See William James, *The Varieties of Religious Experience* (New York: Mentor, 1958), 169.

2. See classic examples of each approach in Bruce R. McConkie, *Doctrinal New Testament Commentary*, 3 vols. (Salt Lake City: Deseret Book, 1972), 2:89; and Fawn M. Brodie, *No Man Knows My History: The Life of Joseph Smith, the Mormon Prophet*, 2nd ed. (New York: Vintage, 1995), 62–63.

Paul and Alma go about attempting to destroy the church; both are traveling on a country road when they're confronted by a divine call; both are left physically depleted by their experience with the divine; both are subsequently taken helpless to a servant of God, who provides healing; both give themselves for the remainder of their lives to preaching the gospel of Christ; and both recount their conversion experiences to others at subsequent points in the narrative. My point of departure, however, is this: Such broad *similarities* serve best to highlight crucial but subtle *differences* between narratives, differences that prove to be theologically significant.

The principal—and at first glance the only apparent—difference between the two narratives I'll consider lies in the fact that Paul's conversion begins with a confrontation by the risen Christ *himself*, while Alma's begins with a confrontation by a merely *angelic* messenger. That difference is surprising, but its real significance only emerges when a set of subtler distinctions receives close attention. Paul's and Alma's first-person retellings of their conversion experiences especially help to highlight these subtler distinctions. Each retells his story in the first person twice. Both of Paul's retellings take place in markedly public, politically charged settings—first immediately after his arrest and addressed to the crowds who had attempted to kill him for his (supposed) failure to maintain ethnic boundaries between Jews and Gentiles, and second before Agrippa and Bernice, arrayed in all the pomp of state. Both of Alma's retellings, by contrast, take place in the quiet privacy of a family ceremonial of some kind—first to his oldest son, Helaman, who was on the occasion receiving the charge of the church and its sacred records, and second to Helaman's brother Shiblon, a dutiful officer in the church who would many years later be given the charge of the church for a few uneventful years. Thus, where Paul's focus in recounting his conversion is on sharpening the blurry boundary line between the revolutionary nature of the Christian message and political revolution pure and simple, Alma's focus is uniquely on ensuring that his sons understand the full theological import of his private experience—apparently in particular because they are being called to serve in ecclesiastically significant positions.

The settings and purposes of these first-person retellings of the conversion experience retroactively reveal the sharply distinct narrative framing of each figure's conversion experience as recounted originally in the third person. The New Testament narrative frames the wickedness from which Paul turns in terms of the apparently law-based killing of Stephen and the petition for letters to imprison Christian Jews in foreign territory. Paul's conversion thus takes place in a politically charged setting. At issue are complex questions of ethnic conflict—conflict between Jews and Gentiles—and the legal status of the new Christian sect, the political fragility of which was manifest from the beginning by the fact that its celebrated Messiah was executed by the Roman state in a manner that indicated his political radicalism: crucifixion. Although there are important political questions at issue in the chapters surrounding the story of Alma's conversion, they are deliberately subordinated to more domestic concerns in the conversion story itself. Hence the rebellion against the church in which Alma participates begins when "many of the rising generation" make clear their lack of belief in "the traditions of their fathers" (Mosiah 26:1). Just as Alma would later recount his conversion story directly to his sons, his conversion experience has its origins in his own relationship to his father. At issue in Alma's conversion is the ostensibly private question of familial harmony and generational succession.

The clearest indication of the strictly familial character of Alma's conversion story in the Book of Mormon is marked by another string of striking—but at first subtle—differences between the two narratives. After his confrontation with the risen Christ, Paul is blindly led to Damascus, where he is, so far as the narrative reports events, left on his own. No accompanying figure is said to be with him when "he was three days without sight, and neither did eat nor drink" (Acts 9:9). Apparently in control of his wits but intentionally fasting as he prays for deliverance, Paul is alone until the Lord speaks to a certain Ananias—presumably one of the original targets of Paul's machinations—about seeking Paul out to heal him. It's Ananias who at this point has a vision ("to him said the Lord in a vision, Ananias"—Acts 9:10), and he then finds and heals Paul. The parallel events in Alma's conversion experience are distinct in crucial ways. It isn't blindness but muteness and physical immobility that afflicts Alma ("he could not open his mouth" and "he could not move his hands"), with the result that he is "carried helpless" rather than led in blindness to his destination (Mosiah 26:19). Rather than being led to a foreign city and there left alone to fend for himself, Alma is "carried" and "laid before his father," the high priest over the church (v. 19). Alma *is* afflicted for three days, like Paul, but he's in something like a coma, with the result that it isn't he but his father and "the priests" who "assemble themselves together" and "fast" and "pray" over Alma's condition (v. 22). Anything but alone, then, Alma is in his suffering surrounded by "a multitude" intentionally "gathered together that they might witness what the Lord had done" (v. 21). And it isn't Alma's would-be healer who has a vision in the course of these events but Alma himself, as he reports to his sons later: "methought I saw . . . God sitting upon his throne, surrounded with numberless concourses of angels, in the attitude of singing and praising their God; yea, and my soul did long to be there" (v. 21).

The domestic setting of Alma's recuperation is drastically highlighted by this string of crucial differences—lending emphasis to and in turn emphasized by Alma's triple mention of being "born of God" in the speech he delivers upon being healed (see Mosiah 26:24–25, 28). His conversion less marks a kind of radical alienation from community that's then overcome when two political enemies are made brothers through the healing power of Christ than it marks a kind of radical alienation from family that's then overcome when father and son come to share a vision of what Christ's church is supposed to accomplish. Indeed, Alma later reports to his sons that the days he spent in a kind of comatose state came to their end only when he finally focused his attention on what he had learned from his father. It was, that is, only when he "remembered also to have heard [his] father prophesy unto the people concerning the coming of one Jesus Christ" that he found the way to forgiveness and was granted a vision of God enthroned—a vision he connects with his "father Lehi," the first prophet of the Book of Mormon and Alma's distant direct ancestor (Alma 36:17, 22). Where Paul's conversion takes place at the borders between nations and world religious traditions, Alma's conversion takes place at the borders between generations and visions of what an ecclesiastical tradition means.

So much for the sharp contrast between the political and the familial in these two conversion narratives. How might this contrast help in turn to clarify what I've already identified as the starkest difference between Paul's and Alma's respective conversion stories—namely, the fact that Paul is confronted by the risen Christ while Alma is confronted only by an angel? Of course, it makes perfect sense that Paul's conversion is rooted in an encounter with the Messiah—that is, with the figure who had actually accomplished the event that, Paul would argue throughout his correspondence, problematizes the ethnic boundary between the Jews and the Gentiles. What's peculiar, really, is just that the Book of Mormon portrays its parallel conversion account by having a mediating angel rather than Jesus Christ himself interrupt Alma's persecution of the believers. What sense is to be made of that detail in Alma's conversion story, and how might the familial framing of Alma's experience help to clarify things? And how, in turn, might a clarification of the role played by the angel help to clarify the focus on the family at issue here?

The key to these questions, it seems to me, is the largely overlooked angelology of the Book of Mormon. Students of Mormonism tend in their discussions of Mormon angelology to focus of Joseph Smith's mature teachings—developed most clearly only some ten years after the Book of Mormon's publication—according to which angels are material resurrected persons from biblical times who serve as messengers from a divine council held in heaven. The Book of Mormon, however, has a robust angelology of its own—the important first seeds of which are planted in two sermons by the very Alma whose conversion I'm considering here.[3] The clearest articulation of this angelology, however, comes late in the Book of Mormon, in a sermon by the book's author and compiler. In an excerpt worth quoting at some length, Mormon discusses the role of angels:

> And the office of their ministry is to call men unto repentance, and to fulfill and to do the work of the covenants of the Father, which he hath made unto the children of men, . . . by declaring the word of Christ unto the chosen vessels of the Lord, that they may bear testimony of him. And by so doing, the Lord God prepareth the way that the residue of men may have faith in Christ . . . ; and after this manner bringeth to pass the Father the covenants which he hath made unto the children of men. (Moro. 7:31–32)

This passage, it's to be noted, opens and closes with references to "the covenants of the Father." The Book of Mormon couldn't be clearer about which covenants are meant by this phrase, since the book declares at the outset that its chief purpose is to restore to biblical Christianity an emphasis on the Israelite or Abrahamic covenant of the Old Testament, which, the Book of Mormon has the resurrected Christ himself announce, "is not all fulfilled" (3 Ne. 15:8). Malachi's prophecy of "fathers" and "children" being reconciled "before the coming of the great and dreadful day of the Lord"—a prophecy that the same resurrected Christ quotes verbatim in the Book of Mormon (see 3 Ne. 25:5–6)—is the eschatological horizon the Book of Mormon projects. And angels, it announces, are those who ensure that that generational reconciliation takes place by showing themselves to "chosen vessels of the Lord," "call[ing them] unto repentance," and sending them "to fulfill and to do the work of the covenants of the Lord."

It's thus perhaps *entirely* appropriate that it's an angel rather than Christ himself who confronts Alma and thereby launches his conversion experi-

---

3. See Alma 12:28–30 and especially Alma 32:22–23. See also Joseph M. Spencer, "Faith, Hope, and Charity: Alma and Joseph Smith," in *An Experiment on the Word: Reading Alma 32*, ed. Adam S. Miller (Salem, OR: Salt Press, 2011), 57–69. [This essay appears in the other volume of *The Anatomy of Book of Mormon Theology*.]

ence. The Book of Mormon has as its focus when it comes to questions of conversion: not the necessity of negotiating ethnic boundaries overcome by complex fidelity to a messianic event of world-historical proportions, but the necessity of negotiating generational boundaries overcome by the resettlement of Christian worship on the deeply familial ground of the Hebrew Bible's covenants—covenants explicitly said in the Book of Mormon to find their fulfillment not in the messianic triumph over death, but rather in the angelic work of reconciling children to parents on questions of religion. Where the New Testament begins from the question of determining the implications of messianic fulfillment for determining the political or ethnic boundaries of religion, the Book of Mormon might be said to begin from the question of determining the implications of angelic ministration for reconciling successive generations as they split over the inheritance of messianic religion. Each religion, beginning from its founding text, consequently has a unique conception of conversion.

A curious confirmation of this interpretation might be found directly in the early experiences Joseph Smith, Mormonism's founding prophet, claimed to have had in connection with the religion's beginnings. Two distinct revelatory encounters with divine beings might be said to have marked Mormonism's genesis. The first of these, a visit of Jesus Christ, took place in 1820, when Smith was fourteen years old. The second took place three years later, when Smith's visitor was not the risen Lord but the angel Moroni, guardian of the record the young man would be inspired to translate. First, like Paul, an encounter with Christ himself; second, like Alma, an encounter only with an angel. Both encounters Smith portrayed as divine responses to his personal feelings of spiritual waywardness. Regarding the first vision, Smith wrote that he had "become convicted of my sins" and "felt to mourn for my own sins and for the sins of the world" and so retired to the woods to pray. The Lord's first words to him in response to his prayer, he reported, were "Joseph my son thy sins are forgiven thee."[4] Concerning the second vision Smith reported, in what would become the canonical account, that the bedside prayer that resulted in a manifestation began when he sought "forgiveness of all my sins and follies," because he "often felt condemned for my weakness and imperfections" (JS–H 1:29).

Significantly, the first of these visions—Smith's being encountered, Paul-like, by the risen Christ—seems to have resulted in a mediocre con-

---

4. Scott H. Faulring, *An American Prophet's Record: The Diaries and Journals of Joseph Smith* (Salt Lake City: Signature Books, 1989), 5.

version. Smith himself spoke of the years following his first vision as years in which he remained largely as he had been. Moreover, his report when he arrived home from the experience seems only to have exacerbated what was already a real conflict within his family over which branch of Protestant Christianity was the true one: "As I leaned up to the fireplace, mother inquired what the matter was. I replied, 'Never mind, all is well—I am well enough off.' I then said to my mother, 'I have learned for myself that Presbyterianism is not true'" (JS–H 1:20). In fact, Smith's deeper convictions and the full reconciliation of his religiously divided family came only when he had his Alma-like experience with an angelic messenger a few years later—with an angel, it might be noted, whose message included a full quotation of the same passages from Malachi made so much of in the Book of Mormon. From the visit of the angel to his violent death two decades later, Smith's family was united by his prophetic responsibilities, and Smith was deeply committed to the vision of Christianity he had developed. The tension between Paul's and Alma's apparently identical conversion stories was thus repeated in the earliest history of Mormonism—in Joseph Smith's own encounters with the divine.

What I've outlined here suggests the following: Mormon conversion is diachronic in nature, while Christian conversion is synchronic in nature—the one a matter of generational succession and the other a matter of community affiliation. These conclusions, however, speak only to what's to be read in the founding scriptural texts of these two traditions. Taking Mormonism as a moment in the historical unfolding of Christianity, it wouldn't be difficult to see how a shift from the synchronic to the diachronic, from questions of community affiliation to generational succession, was rather generally taking place in the Christianity of the young American republic. And, ironically, the largest branch of Mormonism so quickly took on a kind of ethnic identity in the nineteenth century, as well as gave itself to such a profound missionizing spirit, that it exchanged the diachronic for the synchronic shortly after its founding, replacing questions of reconciling children and parents with questions of bringing diverse peoples into a single religious way of life. And yet, with the rise of widespread secularism in the West, there is perhaps a way in which Christianity is being forced again to ask synchronic rather than diachronic questions. And Utah-based Mormonism at least is arguably passing, currently, through a kind of self-transformation largely in response to diachronic questions, rather than synchronic questions, that young Mormons are posing.

These, however, are questions for another occasion. What I've laid out in much more detail here, hopefully, helps to clarify the starting points for two drastically distinct conceptions of conversion—set forth in narratives that can only strike readers as startlingly similar. Within the category of conversion "by self-surrender," of conversion in response to a call from beyond, it's possible to speak of two fundamentally distinct experiences: one synchronic in orientation, and one diachronic in orientation. Mormonism perhaps, due to its scriptural resources, provides a unique source for pursuing a hermeneutic investigation of the latter.

Chapter Eight

The Book of Mormon as Biblical Interpretation
An Approach to LDS Biblical Studies

There is much grist for the theological mill in the nearness between the Book of Mormon's English text and the King James New Testament. There is arguably much more grist for the theological mill in the far more apparent—because often simply stated—interest the Book of Mormon has in the biblical book of Isaiah. All told, the Book of Mormon quotes nearly twenty chapters from Isaiah, not to mention dozens of minor allusions and borrowings and other forms of dependency. It is in Isaiah that the Book of Mormon finds its closest point of contact with the Bible. And because the Book of Mormon is so overt about its uses of Isaiah, those interactions are particularly useful occasions for reflecting on how the Book of Mormon positions itself theologically with respect to the larger Judeo-Christian tradition.

It seems to me a terribly unfortunate thing that basically everything written about Isaiah in the Book of Mormon over many, many decades entirely ignored the theological implications of the whole affair. For about a century now, the chief intellectual concern regarding Isaiah in the Book of Mormon has been simply about whether its inclusion does not spell out historical problems for believers. For nearly as long, the chief devotional concern has been simply about how to make any sense at all of Isaiah's increasingly foreign prophecies. For years, however, I have made it my most central project to investigate the theological significance of the many roles Isaiah plays in the Book of Mormon. All the remainder of the papers here exemplifying macroscopic theology attend in one way or another to Isaiah's place in the Book of Mormon, and to what that might mean for the overarching theological picture the Book of Mormon presents. This essay amounts to a programmatic statement of how a study of Isaiah in the Book of Mormon might illustrate a good way forward for Latter-day Saint students of the Bible in general.

I presented a version of this paper at the 2015 annual meetings of the Society for Biblical Literature, held that year in Atlanta, Georgia. The final version of the essay then appeared in *Studies in the Bible and Antiquity* 8 (2016): 130–56.

Recent years have witnessed a growing recognition in the academy that the Book of Mormon deserves closer attention than it has received. Not surprisingly, adherents to the various Mormon faiths have long read the book with some care. But larger numbers of believing and nonbelieving academics have come to recognize that, despite its often didactic style and relative literary artlessness, the Book of Mormon exhibits remarkable sophistication.[1] This is perhaps nowhere truer than in those passages where the volume interacts—whether explicitly or implicitly—with biblical texts (always in or in relation to the King James rendering).[2] Close reading of the Book of Mormon makes clear that Mormonism's founding text models a profoundly inventive biblical hermeneutic that deserves a place in the burgeoning field of reception history. How does Mormon scripture understand and react to particular biblical texts, and what might be learned about the potential meanings of those biblical texts in light of such interactions?[3]

In this paper, I want to argue that one form—one particularly promising form—that Latter-day Saint biblical studies might take is to bring the implicit and explicit engagements with biblical texts present in the Book of Mormon into conversation with other work being undertaken in reception

---

1. The sophistication of the Book of Mormon (along with its didactic style and relative artlessness) has been argued for most forcefully in Grant Hardy, *Understanding the Book of Mormon: A Reader's Guide* (New York: Oxford University Press, 2010). A growing interest in the sophistication of the Book of Mormon is signaled with plans for a forthcoming collection of essays, *The Book of Mormon: Americanist Approaches*, edited by Elizabeth Fenton and Jared Hickman, set to be published by Oxford University Press. [This volume appeared in 2019 under the title *Americanist Approaches to* The Book of Mormon.]

2. A watershed in close study of the Book of Mormon's interaction with biblical texts was Krister Stendahl, "The Sermon on the Mount and Third Nephi," in *Reflections on Mormonism: Judaeo-Christian Parallels*, ed. Truman G. Madsen (Provo, UT: Religious Studies Center, Brigham Young University, 1978), 139–54. The best work on biblical texts in the Book of Mormon has followed in Stendahl's wake.

3. A general but nonetheless helpful analysis of how biblical texts are treated in the Book of Mormon can be found in Philip L. Barlow, *Mormons and the Bible: The Place of the Latter-day Saints in American Religion* (New York: Oxford University Press, 1991), 26–32.

history.[4] Rather than argue for the usefulness of such an approach simply in the abstract, however, I wish to demonstrate this usefulness by carrying out the approach in question, at least in outline, with respect to a specific text. Among so many biblical texts that make their appearance in one way or another in the Book of Mormon, I select for this exhibition of sorts Isaiah 6:9–10.[5] A number of considerations make this a particularly illustrative example. First, the importance of Isaiah to the project of the Book of Mormon is immense, obvious to anyone familiar with the volume, and this particular Isaiah text is part of a larger pericope that plays a crucial structural role in the first portion of the Book of Mormon.[6] Second, this Isaiah passage is one of many in which interpretively significant alterations to the biblical text have been made in the Book of Mormon, and in this case those alterations seem clearly to be motivated by a long-recognized theological provocation contained in the Isaianic original: the suggestion in the biblical text that God wills to harden his people's hearts against the prophetic word, leading to their destruction and exile.[7] Third and particularly useful for a brief study

---

4. One suggestive example, not without its problems, of this approach in rather general terms might be found in Eran Shalev, *American Zion: The Old Testament as a Political Text from the Revolution to the Civil War* (New Haven: Yale University Press, 2013). For an indication of certain difficulties with Shalev's treatment of the Book of Mormon, see Benjamin E. Park, "The Book of Mormon and Early America's Political and Intellectual Tradition," *Journal of Book of Mormon Studies* 23 (2014): 167–75.

5. Treatments of this passage in the Book of Mormon are few and far between, and none have paid sufficient attention to certain difficulties in the preprinting manuscripts of the Book of Mormon. For examples, see Victor L. Ludlow, *Unlocking Isaiah in the Book of Mormon* (Salt Lake City: Deseret Book, 2003), 117; Monte S. Nyman, *I Nephi Wrote This Record: Book of Mormon Commentary* (Orem, UT: Granite, 2004), 522; and Brant A. Gardner, *Second Witness: Analytical and Contextual Commentary on the Book of Mormon*, 6 vols. (Salt Lake City: Greg Kofford Books, 2007), 1:244.

6. The most detailed scholarly treatment of Isaiah in the Book of Mormon to date is Donald W. Parry and John W. Welch, eds., *Isaiah in the Book of Mormon* (Provo, UT: FARMS, 1998). On the basic structural roles played by Isaiah's writings in the Book of Mormon, see Joseph M. Spencer, "Prolegomena to Any Future Study of Isaiah in the Book of Mormon," *Claremont Journal of Mormon Studies* 1, no. 1 (April 2011): 53–69. [This essay appears in the other volume of *The Anatomy of Book of Mormon Theology*.]

7. For what remains the most detailed treatment of variants in the Isaiah texts found in the Book of Mormon, see John A. Tvedtnes, *The Isaiah Variants in the Book of Mormon* (Provo, UT: FARMS, 1981). A substantive critical treatment

such as this, productive reception-historical work has already been done on this particular Isaiah passage, allowing for ready comparison between the Book of Mormon's handling of the passage and that of other traditions.

I will proceed as follows. In a first, rather brief section of the paper, I outline the basic theological puzzle contained in Isaiah 6:9–10, as well as common responses to the puzzle that can be traced in early Jewish and Christian translations of the passage. In four further sections, I look at how the Book of Mormon structurally privileges its quotation of Isaiah 6, provides an important variant reading of verses 9–10, offers a few words of commentary on the larger block of Isaiah text within which Isaiah 6 appears, and weaves a larger network of passages that allude to this text or develop its central themes. Along the way, I unfold an argument that the Book of Mormon's handling of Isaiah 6:9–10 carves out a space irreducible to either traditionally Jewish or maturely Christian responses (although it might be said to align in interesting ways with the use of the passage in the earliest texts of the New Testament). Finally, at the end of the paper, I outline a few conclusions regarding what it might mean to develop a discipline of Latter-day Saint biblical studies along the lines pursued here.

Puzzles

Isaiah 6:9–10, rather faithfully translated from the Masoretic Text, reads as follows in the King James Version of the Bible (with some quotation marks inserted into the text for clarity):

> And he [the Lord] said, "Go, and tell this people, 'Hear ye indeed, but understand not; and see ye indeed, but perceive not.' Make the heart of this people fat, and make their ears heavy, and shut their eyes; lest they see with their eyes, and hear with their ears, and understand with their heart, and convert, and be healed."[8]

---

can be found in David P. Wright, "Isaiah in the Book of Mormon: Or Joseph Smith in Isaiah," in *American Apocrypha: Essays on the Book of Mormon*, ed. Dan Vogel and Brent Lee Metcalfe (Salt Lake City: Signature Books, 2002), 157–234. Important shortcomings of all published analyses of the variants have been noted in John A. Tvedtnes, "Isaiah in the Bible and the Book of Mormon," FARMS Review 16, no. 2 (2004): 161–72.

8. For detailed critical commentary on these verses, see Hans Wildberger, *Isaiah 1–12: A Commentary*, trans. Thomas H. Trapp (Minneapolis: Fortress Press, 1991), 271–73. [Today I would recommend H G. M. Williamson, *A Critical*

This instruction—or rather, this theologically paradoxical command—comes to Isaiah in the course of his famous encounter with the Lord in the temple, which took place, according to the text, in the year of Uzziah's death. Seeing the Lord seated on an exalted throne and attended by worshipful seraphs, as well as being cleansed by one of the seraphs and thereby prepared to speak the divine word, Isaiah receives a startling commission. Despite a long tradition of attempts at explaining away the relatively obvious meaning of the text, the twentieth century saw the development of a consensus of interpretation that takes the passage at its word while situating its meaning within the larger context of ancient Hebrew thought. Thanks especially to Gerhard von Rad, most interpreters today understand Isaiah's commission to represent a watershed in Hebrew thinking regarding the sovereignty of God.[9] Like the God of the exodus story, Isaiah's God is even sovereign enough to harden human hearts to see to his larger purpose. But where the God of the exodus story hardens only the hearts of noncovenantal people, Isaiah's God here goes so far as to harden his own people's hearts against the prophetic message for a time in order to accomplish a "strange work" (Isa. 28:21). Only this sort of God, one willing even to "hide his face from the house of Jacob" (8:17) at times, is fully master of history. And such a paradoxical move, it turns out, is necessary because part of God's plan with his people involves reducing them to a holy remnant that is finally prepared to represent God to the world (see Isaiah 6:13 and, more generally, Isaiah 7–12).[10]

---

and Exegetical Commentary on Isaiah 1–27, vol. 2, *Commentary on Isaiah 6–12* (New York: Bloomsbury T&T Clark, 2018), 24–26, 72–83.]

9. See Gerhard von Rad, Old Testament Theology, trans. D. M. G. Stalker, 2 vols. (New York: Harper & Row, 1962), 2:153–55; as well as a helpful exposition of the basic theological problems in Brevard S. Childs, *Isaiah* (Louisville: Westminster John Knox Press, 2001), 56–57. Craig Evans, in his study of the reception of this text, has provided a good survey of modern critical scholarship on the passage. See Craig A. Evans, *To See and Not Perceive: Isaiah 6.9–10 in Early Jewish and Christian Interpretation* (Sheffield: JSOT Press, 1989), 17–52. The success of von Rad's approach can be glimpsed in the fact that it is reflected at quite opposite extremes of the ideological spectrum of commentaries. See both Joseph Blenkinsopp, *Isaiah 1–39: A New Translation with Introduction and Commentary* (New Haven: Yale University Press, 2000), 223–24; and John N. Oswalt, *The Book of Isaiah, Chapters 1–39* (Grand Rapids, MI: Eerdmans, 1986), 188–90.

10. On the remnant theme in the Hebrew Bible, and especially in Isaiah, see Gerhard F. Hasel, *The Remnant: The History and Theology of the Remnant Idea from Genesis to Isaiah* (Barrien Springs, MI: Andrews University Press, 1972).

Ancient readers were as confused by—or at least as concerned with—Isaiah 6:9–10 as are modern readers. In fact, in an important study, Craig Evans has traced in broad outlines the ancient reception of this provocative pericope. Looking at ancient Greek, Aramaic, and Syriac translations of the passages, as well as at quotations of and allusions to Isaiah 6 in early Jewish and Christian texts into the early medieval era, he marks out a few clear patterns. In ancient Jewish translations, he finds "a marked tendency to move away from the harsh, telic understanding of the Hebrew text," discerning nonetheless several distinct forms in which this tendency manifests itself.[11] Representative is the rendering in the Septuagint, where several subtle grammatical alterations of the Hebrew in the Greek text make the hardness of the people's heart into a simple historical fact—presumably the consequence of their own sins—rather than something the Lord aims to bring about.[12] Evans traces this same general approach to the text into the rabbinical tradition, where "the text is moralized and applied in a way that has little to do with the original sense."[13]

Interestingly, Evans finds this general trend among ancient Jewish interpreters to have been reversed in the singular case of nascent (and therefore still-Jewish) Christianity. This took place in a first form already with Jesus (in Mark 4), but then also with Paul (in Romans 9–11).[14] For both Jesus and Paul, the Isaiah passage was transmitted in a form closer to the Hebrew original and was apparently helpful in explaining how "rejection and ostracism" of early followers of Jesus "unwittingly furthered God's purposes in producing a new remnant of the faithful."[15] Instead of reworking Isaiah's words to soften their impact, the earliest Christians understood them as referring to God's surprising intention to establish a chosen people *within* the chosen people, a believing persecuted remnant that would be

---

11. Evans, *To See and Not Perceive*, 163.

12. See Evans, 62–63. Here is Evans's translation of the Septuagint rendering: "And he said, 'Go and say to this people: "You shall indeed hear but never understand, and you shall indeed see but never perceive." For this people's heart has grown dull, and their ears are heavy of hearing, and their eyes they have closed, lest they should perceive with their eyes, and hear with their ears, and understand with their heart and turn for me to heal them'" (p. 62).

13. Evans, 166; see also 137–45.

14. See especially Evans, 81–106.

15. Evans, 165.

involved in the eschatological fulfillment of the promise made to Israel that the Gentiles would come to worship the true God with them.[16]

Unfortunately, as Christianity developed into a religious movement increasingly estranged from and even antagonistic toward its Jewish origins, this earliest approach to Isaiah 6:9–10 was supplanted by another, according to Evans. Beginning with later New Testament writings and then more starkly in the writings of the early Christian fathers, interpreters shifted away from affirming the production of a remnant within Judaism, moving instead toward positioning Jews as radical outsiders. From that point on, the passage—along with much of the remainder of Isaiah's writings—came to serve the purposes of Christian anti-Semitism.[17] For Christians, Isaiah's commission came to mean that God mysteriously announced long in advance that he would deliberately harden the hearts of Jews against the Messiah, thereby inaugurating the wholesale replacement of one chosen people with another. This played into a fully revitalized, but deeply troubling, theology of divine sovereignty.

Such is the framework provided by the general trends Evans traces: (1) general Jewish discomfort with Isaiah 6:9–10, (2) Jesus's and Paul's reinvestment in the passage's original implicit remnant theology, and (3) subsequent Christian use of the passage in the construction of an anti-Semitic salvation history. Crucially, this schematic outline of the ancient interpretive tradition proves helpful for making sense of the Book of Mormon's handling of this same Isaianic text. But, naturally, we must first explore how the Book of Mormon handles it.

Structures

The first major portion of the Book of Mormon presents itself as the writings of Nephi, a barely preexilic Jerusalemite whose family escapes before Zedekiah's rebellion and the consequent devastation of the city. Decades after removing to the New World, where the fledgling colony tragically divides into two warring factions, Nephi produces a record of

---

16. This depends on a careful interpretation of Romans 9–11, helpfully worked out from a Jewish perspective in Mark D. Nanos, *The Mystery of Romans: The Jewish Context of Paul's Letter* (Minneapolis: Fortress Press, 1996). See also, of course, Isaiah 2:1–4, where this expectation is given one of its richest expressions.

17. This is something John Sawyer has also noted; see various discussions in John F. A. Sawyer, *The Fifth Gospel: Isaiah in the History of Christianity* (New York: Cambridge University Press, 1996).

the family's travels and travails, using the narrative to contextualize his and his father's prophetic experiences.[18] The focal point of the narrative is an apocalyptic vision obviously—and explicitly—connected to the New Testament Apocalypse of John, which Nephi places in a mutually interpretive relationship with a host of texts from the canonical book of Isaiah.[19] Nowhere else in the Book of Mormon does Isaiah become such a consistent focus as in Nephi's record. More important, nowhere else in the Book of Mormon are Isaiah's writings woven into the organizing structure of the text. And Isaiah 6:9–10 makes its chief appearance in the Book of Mormon in Nephi's record, where it plays an important structural role.

Late in his record, Nephi reproduces in one massive block the whole of Isaiah 2–14 (see 2 Ne. 12–24), albeit with a great number of variants (many quite minor, many others interpretively significant). These Isaiah chapters appear in the center of a triptych, preceded and followed by prophetic sermons by Nephi (2 Ne. 25–30) and his brother Jacob (2 Ne. 6–10) that quote from other Isaianic texts (specifically Isaiah 11, 29, and 48–52) and provide commentary. The entire triptych constitutes what Nephi describes as the core of his record, "the more sacred things" (1 Ne. 19:5). It is at the structural center of this already-central block of Isaiah text that Isaiah's temple theophany appears.[20] These first details preliminarily clarify that Isaiah 6 is of some importance to the Book of Mormon's interest in the writings of Isaiah. Not only is the story of Isaiah's commission included in the record, it receives a structurally privileged position at the heart of the most Isaianic portion of the record.

Isaiah 6 occupies its place in Nephi's "more sacred things" for what seems a relatively apparent reason. The Book of Mormon arguably interprets the long quotation of Isaiah 2–14 as telling a three-part story.[21] The

---

18. For a good introduction to Nephi as a figure in the Book of Mormon, see Hardy, *Understanding the Book of Mormon*, 29–86.

19. A helpful general analysis of this mutually interpretive relationship can be found in the "summary report" of the Mormon Theology Seminar project from 2009 on 2 Nephi 26–27. See Joseph M. Spencer and Jenny Webb, eds., *Reading Nephi Reading Isaiah: 2 Nephi 26–27*, 2nd ed. (Provo, UT: Neal A. Maxwell Institute for Religious Scholarship, 2016), 7–17.

20. Here I only summarize these structures. I have provided a full analysis of and argument for them elsewhere. See Joseph M. Spencer, *An Other Testament: On Typology* (Provo, UT: Neal A. Maxwell Institute for Religious Scholarship, 2016), 33–68.

21. The Book of Mormon as originally dictated divided the quotation of Isaiah 2–14 into three larger blocks of text: Isaiah 2–5, Isaiah 6–12, and Isaiah

first part of the story, consisting of Isaiah 2–5, draws a sharp contrast between Israel's eschatological destiny as a redeeming force in the world and its always-sinful status in the present.[22] The second part of the story, consisting in turn of Isaiah 6–12, describes God's historical interventions with Israel, in particular his use of prophets to warn the covenant people before winnowing them down to a holy remnant that, joined by a messianic deliverer, is finally prepared to receive the divine word. The third and final part of the story, consisting of Isaiah 13–14, describes the final elimination of all those (primarily Babylon) who had persecuted and tormented Israel before its ultimate redemption. In this larger three-part story, Isaiah 6 reports the beginnings of the divine response to Israel's corruption: commissioning a prophet to provide the covenant people with a call to repentance and transformation before it becomes necessary to reduce Israel to a small band of survivors. For the Book of Mormon, Isaiah 6 provides a paradigmatic story of how God begins to involve himself in covenantal history.[23] More specifically, this seems to imply that the Book of Mormon regards Isaiah 6:9–10 as containing a paradigmatic prophetic commission.

Another structural feature of Nephi's record reveals that the Book of Mormon regards Isaiah's temple theophany as paradigmatic. Accounts of divine encounters clearly parallel to Isaiah's appear in two other places in Nephi's writings: one as part of the record's opening narrative, which describes the prophetic experiences of Nephi's father in Jerusalem before the family flees the Old World (1 Ne. 1:8–15), and the other as part of the record's exhortative conclusion, where Nephi enjoins his readers to join the heavenly chorus as his father had done back in Jerusalem (2 Ne. 31).[24]

13–14. This is most easily glimpsed in the first edition of the Book of Mormon. See Joseph Smith Jr., *The Book of Mormon* (Palmyra: E. B. Grandin, 1830), 86–102. For a much fuller analysis of how Nephi develops this three-part story, see Joseph M. Spencer, *The Vision of All: Twenty-Five Lectures on Isaiah in Nephi's Record* (Salt Lake City: Greg Kofford Books, 2016), 143–249.

22. This it does twice, first by contrasting the vision of Isaiah 2:1–5 (or 2 Nephi 12:1–5) with the accusation of Isaiah 2:6–4:1 (or 2 Nephi 12:6–14:1), and then by contrasting the vision of Isaiah 4:2–6 (or 2 Nephi 14:2–6) with the accusation of Isaiah 5 (or 2 Nephi 15).

23. That Nephi's record interprets Isaiah's writings as paradigmatic—rather than solely as historical—is explicit. The technical term employed in numerous places in the Book of Mormon in connection with the interpretation of Isaiah is "likening." See, for instance, 1 Nephi 19:23–24; 22:8; 2 Nephi 6:5; 11:2, 8.

24. The key connection between 2 Nephi 31 and 1 Nephi 1 is the reference to angels and their songs of praise (see 2 Ne. 31:13; 1 Ne. 1:8).

In each of these visions, the recipient witnesses the divine, describes being overcome by the experience before being ministered to (thanks to some kind of mediating element like Isaiah's glowing coal), and finally joins the divine council to receive a prophetic commission.[25] Nephi's record thus uses Isaiah's encounter in the temple, alongside the similar encounter of Nephi's own father, as the basic outline for an experience that it then, quite audaciously, recommends that all of its readers seek to replicate. Not only does the Book of Mormon place Isaiah 6 at the turning point of the structurally privileged center of Nephi's writings, it also draws on Isaiah 6 to outline the aim of the true Christian disciple.

All these structural details, reviewed here only in passing, collectively suggest that the Book of Mormon means to privilege Isaiah 6. That chapter, and therefore Isaiah 6:9–10, is thus of real importance to the Book of Mormon. But structural privilege alone does not make clear what this uniquely Mormon volume of scripture has to say about the meaning of this theologically complex passage. Beyond granting a certain pride of place, Nephi reproduces Isaiah 6:9–10 with some variation from the biblical version. In considering the variants within the Book of Mormon's version of this key passage, readers might most clearly identify the contribution of Isaiah 6 to a larger history of interpretation.

Variants

By presenting a variant reading of Isaiah 6:9–10, rather than attempting through interpretive commentary simply to explain the passage, the Book of Mormon positions itself within a fascinating history of direct manipulation of this peculiar text.[26] But as it turns out, determining exactly how the Book of Mormon's version of Isaiah 6:9–10 varies from the biblical version requires some work. That is, several difficulties attend the transmission of the Book of Mormon's rendering of Isaiah 6:9–10, making it necessary to address a few textual-critical concerns.

---

25. For a detailed comparison of these three texts, see Spencer, *An Other Testament*, 55–56. It might be noted that the Book of Mormon expresses no particular interest in either of the closest (and therefore often-noted) biblical parallels to Isaiah's commissioning: 1 Kings 22:19–23 and Amos 9:1–6.

26. It would, of course, require a separate study to compare the Book of Mormon's largely implicit interpretation of Isaiah 6:9–10 with explicit commentaries on the passage available in early nineteenth-century America, where the Book of Mormon made its first appearance in English. I leave such a study for another occasion.

Unfortunately, the original manuscript of the Book of Mormon, produced in the course of the volume's dictation by Joseph Smith, is no longer
extant for Isaiah 6:9–10. The result is that the only preprinting manuscript
available for study is the so-called printer's manuscript, a handwritten copy
of the original manuscript produced for the use of the book's first printer.
And, as can be seen by comparing the printer's manuscript with the original
where portions of the latter have survived, the printer's manuscript is an inconsistent guide to what Smith originally dictated.[27] Making matters worse,
enough confusion exists in the printer's manuscript where Isaiah 6:9–10
appears that Smith or one of his assistants felt compelled to change the text
for the second edition of the Book of Mormon in 1837.[28] As a result, at least
three possible reconstructions of Smith's original dictation of Isaiah 6:9–10
provide at least three possible variant texts to consider. Fortunately, Royal
Skousen has done detailed textual-critical work on this passage, reconstructing what was most likely the original dictated text. Skousen's reconstruction
is convincing, and I will use it here, but it should be noted that it is not
the only possible reconstruction—and it is, moreover, emphatically a reconstruction (Skousen's reconstructed text does not appear in any extant manuscript or in any printed edition apart from Skousen's own critical edition).[29]

---

27. For a good summary introduction to the printer's manuscript, see Royal
Skousen and Robin Scott Jensen, eds., *The Joseph Smith Papers, Revelations and
Translations Volume 3: Printer's Manuscript of the Book of Mormon*, 2 vols. (Salt
Lake City: The Church Historian's Press, 2015), 1:xi–xxviii, 3–11. For extensive
discussion of the relationship between the original and printer's manuscripts, see
Royal Skousen, *Analysis of Textual Variants of the Book of Mormon*, 6 vols. (Provo,
UT: FARMS and Neal A. Maxwell Institute Press, 2004–2009).

28. For the text of the printer's manuscript, along with a photographic reproduction
of the manuscript page, see Skousen and Jensen, *Printer's Manuscript of the Book of
Mormon*, 1:162–63. This 1837 revision to Isaiah 6:9–10 as quoted in the Book of
Mormon has unfortunately been reproduced in all subsequent official editions of the
book from all branches of Mormonism. The result has been that the vast majority of
readers and even scholars have been entirely unaware of the difficulty in the printer's
manuscript. This has, moreover, compromised most scholarly discussions of the
variant in the Book of Mormon's version of Isaiah 6:9–10.

29. For Skousen's discussion and conclusions, see Skousen, *Analysis of Textual
Variants of the Book of Mormon*, 2:697–99. The earlier *Book of Mormon Critical Text*,
3 vols. (Provo, UT: FARMS, 1986), 1:217–18, largely the work of Robert F. Smith,
retains the reading of the printer's manuscript but includes in a footnote several
variant readings found in the New Testament and other ancient versions. Skousen's
critical edition (published without a critical apparatus), is Royal Skousen, ed., *The*

According to Skousen's reconstruction of the original text, then, the Book of Mormon's revision to Isaiah 6:9 is relatively minimal in terms of actual words altered, while no revisions at all appear in Isaiah 6:10.[30] The King James Version's "hear ye indeed, but understand not" becomes "hear ye indeed, but *they* understand not," while "see ye indeed, but perceive not" becomes "see ye indeed, but *they* perceive not." However minimal these revisions actually appear—the mere addition of two pronouns!— they alter the meaning of the text substantially. Two major consequences of the revisions deserve notice.

First, the inserted pronouns in both clauses alter the mood of the verbs following them, which are imperative in the original but indicative in the Book of Mormon's revised text. In the latter, Isaiah's Judean audience is not *commanded* to fail to understand or to perceive; rather, the text just reports that Isaiah's audience *in fact* fails to understand or to perceive. In the Book of Mormon version of the passage, Isaiah commands Judah to hear, but they do not understand—to see, but they do not perceive. This first consequence of the variant reading leads directly to a second. Because the inserted pronouns alter the mood of the verbs they precede, they make unclear exactly who is supposed to be talking when the mood of the text's verbs shifts from the imperative to the indicative.[31] That is, while it remains clear that the Lord instructs Isaiah to say to the people both "hear ye indeed" and "see ye indeed," it is unclear in the Book of Mormon version whether the Lord means Isaiah to say also to the people that "they understand not" and that "they perceive not"[32] or whether perhaps the Lord rather uses

---

Book of Mormon: The Earliest Text (New Haven: Yale University Press, 2009). All quotations from the Book of Mormon in this paper come from this edition.

30. Smith revised a portion of Isaiah 6:10 for the 1837 edition of the Book of Mormon, directly annotating the printer's manuscript (the active "convert" Smith changed to the passive "be converted"). This revision has been retained in subsequent official editions from all branches of Mormonism. See, again, Skousen, *Analysis of Textual Variants of the Book of Mormon*, 2:699–700.

31. In a critical analysis of the Book of Mormon rendering, Wesley Walters rightly points out—though he too quickly and facilely draws larger implications from the fact—that the revised text seems to "confuse the persons in the verb, jumping from second to third person." Wesley P. Walters, "The Use of the Old Testament in the Book of Mormon" (Master's thesis, Covenant Theological Seminary, 1981), 61–62. Wright, "Isaiah in the Book of Mormon," 230, makes the same unilluminating move.

32. The sense of this interpretation might be conveyed by using the following punctuation of the Book of Mormon text: "Go and tell this people, 'Hear ye indeed, but they understand not,' and 'See ye indeed, but they perceive not.'"

these further words to explain to Isaiah the reaction he can expect from his hearers[33] or whether Isaiah here inserts awkward anticipatory asides to his audience about how his preaching was later received[34]—or whether in fact some *other* interpretation than these should be sought.[35]

However the ambiguity just noted should be interpreted, it seems relatively clear that the Book of Mormon's version of Isaiah 6:9 works to soften the theological force of the biblical version. In this respect, the Book of Mormon might in fact be fruitfully set side by side with the Aramaic rendering of the passage in *Targum Jonathan*: "And he said, 'Go, and speak to this people that hear indeed, but do not understand, and see indeed, but do not perceive.'"[36] It should be noted that the Targum removes the imperative mood from all the verbs (rather than just from two of them, as the Book of Mormon does), making "hear indeed" and "see indeed" into descriptions as much as "do not understand" and "do not perceive." In this way it avoids the ambiguity of the Book of Mormon version, reading somewhat more smoothly. Yet, this last difference notwithstanding, the Book of Mormon and targumic renderings appear to soften the impact of the Hebrew text in similar ways, making factual descriptions out of paradoxical commands.

Interestingly, while the Book of Mormon arguably softens the theological impact of Isaiah 6:9, it in no way softens the theological impact of

---

(It should be noted that Joseph Smith did not dictate punctuation as part of the Book of Mormon.)

33. The sense of this interpretation might be conveyed with slightly different punctuation: "Go and tell this people, 'Hear ye indeed,' but they understand not, and 'See ye indeed,' but they perceive not."

34. The sense of this third interpretation might be conveyed with yet another way of punctuating the text: "Go and tell this people, 'Hear ye indeed'"—but they understand not!—"and 'See ye indeed'"—but they perceive not!

35. Brant Gardner suggests without sufficient argument that "the Book of Mormon reading solves the problem in the KJV that God has commanded his people not to understand his message by creating a command/response structure rather than seeing both clauses as part of the command." Gardner, *Second Witness*, 2:244. That the alternation between the imperative and the indicative moods amounts to a "command/response structure" requires further motivation.

36. Bruce D. Chilton, *The Isaiah Targum: Introduction, Translation, Apparatus and Notes* (Collegeville, MN: Liturgical Press, 1987), 15. For discussion, see Evans, *To See and Not Perceive*, 69–76. Note that Evans provides his own translation of the Aramaic text.

Isaiah 6:10, since it offers no variant reading of that verse at all.[37] Even if in the Book of Mormon the Lord does not tell Isaiah to command Judah neither to understand nor to perceive, he nonetheless seems to burden the prophet with the responsibility to harden his hearers against the prophetic word, "lest they see with their eyes, and hear with their ears, and understand with their heart, and convert, and be healed." Because the Book of Mormon in no way attempts to revise the equally provocative "lest" of Isaiah 6:10, it is difficult to argue that its softening of the implications of sovereignty in the Hebrew original is either complete or uniform.[38] In this way, interestingly, the Book of Mormon distinguishes itself from the Targum, where the Hebrew פֶּן ("lest") is translated by אמלד, which, while it *can* mean "lest," seems in context to have been intended to mean "unless" or "until" (it is so used elsewhere in the Isaiah Targum) and was certainly understood in this way by later rabbinical interpreters of the passage, as Evans points out.[39] The Targum revises both Isaiah 6:9 and Isaiah 6:10 in similar ways, while the Book of Mormon oddly provides a variant reading of only one of the two verses. It leaves at least half of the biblical text's theological provocation in place.

This inconsistency in the Book of Mormon rendering of Isaiah 6:9–10 proves quite surprising on further inspection. Close study of the many variant readings in the Book of Mormon's long quotations of Isaiah suggests remarkable consistency, especially where theological motivations seem to underlie the differences between the Book of Mormon and the biblical pre-

---

37. It might, of course, be suggested that either Nephi or the translator failed to reproduce certain textual variants in verse 10. In the absence of any concrete evidence for such a possibility, however, I pursue here a reading of what appears in the text of the Book of Mormon itself.

38. Commentators implicitly recognize this. It should be noted, for instance, that Latter-day Saint interpreters who address in some detail the possibility that the Book of Mormon's rendering of Isaiah 6:9 solves the theological conundrum posed by the Isaianic text as it stands in the Bible feel compelled to offer creative interpretations of Isaiah 6:10, which the Book of Mormon does not alter in a similar way. See, for instance, the discussions in Monte S. Nyman, *"Great Are the Words of Isaiah"* (Salt Lake City: Bookcraft, 1980), 50–51; and Ludlow, *Unlocking Isaiah in the Book of Mormon*, 117–19. Such interpreters can be seen as seeking ways to make Isaiah 6:10, which is not changed in the Book of Mormon, follow suit with Isaiah 6:9, which is changed in the Book of Mormon.

39. See Evans, *To See and Not Perceive*, 71.

sentations of Isaiah.[40] Thus, given the patterns of revision found in the Book of Mormon's presentation of Isaiah quite generally, something odd seems to be afoot in the fact that a revision appears in Isaiah 6:9 but not a corresponding one in Isaiah 6:10. Whatever degree of theological softening is implied by the revision in one verse thus seems clearly to be lessened by the lack of revision in the other. Although the Book of Mormon version of Isaiah 6:9–10 seems unwilling to make Isaiah's message to Judah one of commanding them neither to understand nor to perceive, it nonetheless prefers not to deny that God's will in commissioning Isaiah involves an intentional desire

---

40. A rather striking example might be cited to illustrate this point. In two passages similar in theme but separated by several chapters of text, extremely nuanced revisions are made, both apparently connected to an underlying and profoundly subtle theological conception of history. The passages in question are Isaiah 7:20 and Isaiah 10:5. In the former, the Book of Mormon removes just the word *namely* from the King James rendering of the verse, an italicized interpolation by the King James translators meant to ward off an ambiguity that might result without it. By removing the italicized word, the Book of Mormon version of the text restores the ambiguity skirted by the King James Version. The passage can thus be said either to mean that the Lord will use Assyria as a razor with which to shave Judah or to mean that the Lord will use some person or persons hired out by Assyria's king as a razor with which to shave Judah. The second of these possible interpretations introduces a three-tiered conception of divine intervention in history. Rather than directly mobilizing Assyria to punish Judah through military force, the Lord uses Assyria's already-existent military purposes (hiring mercenaries, apparently, for its campaign for dominance) to accomplish his own purposes with Judah. That this, rather than the other interpretive possibility, is meant becomes clear only when the other passage is considered. In Isaiah 10:5, a single possessive pronoun is replaced in the Book of Mormon text: "mine [the Lord's] indignation" becomes "their [Assyria's] indignation." Here again the Lord's instrumental relationship to Assyria is at issue. The revision in the Book of Mormon this time produces no ambiguity but directly implies the three-tiered conception of divine intervention. Where in the King James rendering the only anger or indignation spoken of belongs to God, in the Book of Mormon a distinction is drawn between the Lord's anger (Assyria is "the rod of mine [the Lord's] anger") and Assyria's own anger ("the staff in their hand is their indignation"). Here again, then, the implication is that the Lord's anger is expressed through the Assyrians' anger, rather than through some sort of direct manipulation of Assyria's destiny. The fact that two extremely nuanced revisions in texts several chapters apart from each other can result in a remarkably consistent— but subtle—theology of history in Book of Mormon Isaiah suggests that greater consistency should be expected from the revisions made to Isaiah 6:9–10.

that the prophet's hearers *not* "see with their eyes, and hear with their ears, and understand with their heart, and convert, and be healed."

Peculiar though this inconsistency may be, it proves to be suggestive as well, especially when one attempts to frame the Book of Mormon's approach to Isaiah 6:9–10 in terms of the earliest Jewish and Christian approaches to the passage. In a preliminary approximation, it should be said that the Book of Mormon's presentation of Isaiah's commission falls somewhere *between* two of the three major trends Evans traces in the earliest reception of the text. With the earliest Jewish interpreters, the Book of Mormon exhibits discernible concern about the idea that the Lord would send a prophet with a message directly commanding his audience not to understand or not to perceive. But with the earliest Christian interpreters, the Book of Mormon nonetheless exhibits interest in the idea that God might for a time mysteriously but intentionally harden his covenant people against a prophet's message—and against Isaiah's message in particular. (Importantly, the Book of Mormon expresses *no* interest in the later Christian approach in which Isaiah's commission perceives Judah as excluded from the covenant, excluded specifically in order to be replaced by gentile Christians as the new Israel. Rather generally, the Book of Mormon insists that Gentiles receive salvation only by assisting in the redemption of historical Israel. In this regard, it is unmistakably Pauline in its theological orientation.)[41] In attempting to make sense of a particularly difficult Isaiah passage, then, the Book of Mormon aligns itself with the perspective of earliest New Testament Christianity, even as it exhibits a certain pre-Christian Jewish interpretive sensibility.

This, however, is only a preliminary approximation. To make the stakes of the Book of Mormon's theological middle position clearer, we might look at the volume's other treatments of this particular Isaiah passage, as well as at its treatment of associated themes. It is not in this one passage alone that the Book of Mormon weighs in on the idea of Israel's hearts being hard.

Comments

As it turns out, numerous resources distributed throughout the Book of Mormon might be gathered together to produce an exhaustive study of its relationship to Isaiah 6:9–10. At least two of these must, unfortunately, be set aside for present purposes, left for another occasion when they might

---

41. See Joseph M. Spencer, *For Zion: A Mormon Theology of Hope* (Salt Lake City: Greg Kofford Books, 2014), 71–78.

be developed fully, though they ought to be mentioned here. The first is the book's extensive treatment of the Isaianic theme of the remnant, something in the Book of Mormon that has not yet received systematic study. Reconstructing the volume's remnant theology would provide a larger context for its approach to Isaiah's mysterious commission, since the latter is best interpreted as part of a larger divine plan to winnow the covenant people down to a holy remnant.[42] A second important resource I will not pursue here is the general theme, prevalent in the Book of Mormon, of the hardened heart. The litany of passages in the book that draw on this image deserves systematic exposition, and such an exposition would certainly help to clarify the book's relationship to the biblical hardening theme more generally—of which Isaiah 6:9–10 is a particularly poignant example.[43]

These two helpful (perhaps crucial) resources I must, unfortunately, set aside here so as to focus instead just on a singular passage in which Nephi provides the closest thing available in the Book of Mormon to a commentary on Isaiah's commission. This is to be found in Nephi's brief but nonetheless informative attempt to summarize, in his own prophetic voice, the general meaning of Isaiah 2–14, within which Isaiah 6:9–10 appears.[44] Nephi does not in this summary *directly* address Isaiah's theologically provocative commission, but he nonetheless provides a larger interpretive framework within which its place in the Book of Mormon can be considered.

---

42. I am aware of no serious treatment of the remnant in the Book of Mormon available in publication. In 2010, I dedicated a series of blog posts to a preliminary clarification of the topic, though they present sketches of research rather than finished studies. The first of them, introductory to the series, can nonetheless be accessed at http://feastuponthewordblog.org/2010/02/05/towards-a-thinking-of-remnant -theology-in-the-book-of-mormon/.

43. I am unaware of any scholarly treatment of this important theme in the Book of Mormon, but a largely devotional treatment—which, at the very least, gathers important references—can be found in Michael J. Fear, "Blind Eyes and Hard Hearts: Apostasy in the Book of Mormon," in *Selections from the Religious Education Student Symposium 2003*, ed. Robert C. Freeman et al. (Provo, UT: Brigham Young University Religious Studies Center, 2003), 49–58.

44. That the purpose of 2 Nephi 25:1–20 is to explain the quotation of Isaiah 2–14 is evident from the following two details: (1) in verses 1–8, Nephi concedes to his people their bafflement at Isaiah but offers to provide them a prophecy of his own to help them interpret the prophet; (2) in verses 9–20, then, Nephi outlines a summary prophecy of his own that maps onto Isaiah 2–12 (but perhaps not Isaiah 13–14) rather cleanly.

Nephi's commentary of sorts appears immediately following the full quotation of Isaiah 2–14, and it is apparently meant to provide an outline of the meaning of at least Isaiah 2–12.[45] Those particular chapters the Book of Mormon presents in two blocks of text, dividing Isaiah 2–5 from Isaiah 6–12.[46] In the course of what the text calls Nephi's "own prophecy," offered up in "plainness," he provides a key to these chapters, with a focus primarily on Isaiah 6–12 (2 Ne. 25:7). In just a few words, Nephi appears to summarize the content of Isaiah 2–5 (as he is supposed to have understood these chapters): "As one generation hath been destroyed among the Jews because of iniquity, even so have they been destroyed from generation to generation according to their iniquities" (2 Ne. 25:9). There then follows immediately what appears to be a one-sentence summary of Isaiah 6 (which serves as the opening of the longer stretch of text from Isaiah 6 through Isaiah 12): "And never hath any of [these generations] been destroyed save it were foretold them by the prophets of the Lord" (2 Ne. 25:9).[47] Obviously, such a brief summary interpretation of Isaiah 6 sheds little light on how Nephi is supposed to have understood Isaiah's prophetic commission. Yet as Nephi's summary interpretation continues and summarizes the chapters following Isaiah 6, the commentary begins to

---

45. The commentary in question appears in 2 Nephi 25:9–20. Interestingly, the commentary there offered does not obviously attempt to explain Isaiah 13–14, the final two chapters of Isaiah quoted by Nephi. Other passages in Nephi's record, however, arguably present a summary of what he is supposed to have understood those particular chapters to mean. Seemingly, he understood their prophecy of Babylon's collapse to be readily likened to the fall of what he calls "the great and abominable church," while he understood their discussion of the fall of Babylon's king to be readily likened to the final binding of Satan at the time of Israel's ultimate redemption. See 1 Nephi 14:8–17; 22:13–28; 2 Nephi 30:8–18.

46. This is according to the original chapter breaks of the Book of Mormon, no longer preserved in official editions of the book published by The Church of Jesus Christ of Latter-day Saints (though they are retained in official editions published by Community of Christ, the second-largest branch of Mormonism). Royal Skousen has made clear that the original chapter breaks are to be regarded as a structural feature of the text of the Book of Mormon. See Skousen, *Analysis of Textual Variants of the Book of Mormon*, 1:43–45.

47. I have elsewhere provided a basic analysis of the larger context in which Nephi's prophecy quoted here appears. See Joseph M. Spencer, "What Can We Do? Reflections on 2 Nephi 25:23," *Religious Educator: Perspectives on the Restored Gospel* 15/2 (2014): 33–35. [This essay appears in the other volume of *The Anatomy of Book of Mormon Theology*.]

provide a basic sense of how the Book of Mormon apparently understands the difficult passage of Isaiah 6:9–10.

First, Nephi describes the response of Jerusalem's inhabitants to his own father's prophetic interventions with the following, clearly Isaianic words: "They hardened their hearts" (2 Ne. 25:10). Similarly, a few lines afterward, when he summarizes the response of the same city's later inhabitants to Jesus Christ, Nephi says that "they will reject him because of their iniquities and the hardness of their hearts and the stiffness of their necks" (v. 12). In both of these interpretive statements, Nephi is presented as assuming that the hardening of the covenant people results from human willfulness, rather than from divine imposition. Human beings harden their hearts, do iniquity, and reject those who are divinely appointed to come to their assistance. In no way is the reader asked to believe that there is a strictly divine hardening of human hearts. In this, Nephi follows the rendering in 2 Nephi 16 of Isaiah 6:9.

And yet, as Nephi's commentary of sorts continues, it begins to use language more indicative of divine sovereignty, as in 2 Nephi 16's rendering of Isaiah 6:10. After the destruction of Jerusalem by Rome, Nephi prophesies, "The Jews shall be scattered among all nations" (2 Ne. 25:15). This event and its unfortunate aftermath the text directly (and uncomfortably, for modern readers) makes into the work of the Lord: "They have been scattered and the Lord God hath scourged them by other nations for the space of many generations" (v. 16).[48] Although the Book of Mormon does not attribute the hardening of the covenant people's hearts directly to God,

---

48. One might, from a twenty-first-century perspective, be naturally inclined to find traces of anti-Semitism in Nephi's description of these events, though there is reason to recognize why Nephi might have harbored strong feelings regarding Jerusalem's inhabitants (they tried to kill his father; see his strong comments in 2 Nephi 25:2). Much more troubling are the words of Nephi's brother Jacob (found in 2 Nephi 10:3–5), though there it should be noted that Jacob narrows the scope of those he blames for Christ's death to Jews involved in "priestcrafts"—presumably the Sadducees. Worries about Mormonism's ethical relationship to Judaism have been expressed on occasion in connection with the Book of Mormon—although I personally remain unsatisfied with the treatments that have been as yet made available on these questions. The most widely read discussion of the topic is Steven Epperson, *Mormons and Jews: Early Mormon Theologies of Israel* (Salt Lake City: Signature Press, 1992). See also the extensive bibliography in Seth Ward, "A Literature Survey of Mormon-Jewish Studies," in *Covenant and Chosenness in Judaism and Mormonism*, ed. Raphael Jospe, Truman G. Madsen, and Seth Ward (Madison: Fairleigh Dickinson University Press, 2001), 195–211.

it nonetheless claims here that the long subsequent history of their persecution has its origins, at least in part, with God. This seems perfectly consistent with the other half of Nephi's rendering of Isaiah 6:9–10.

Here there is a clear confirmation of the variant text of Isaiah 6:9–10 from the Book of Mormon. Nephi's apparent refusal, in what appears to be his own commentary on Isaiah 6–12, to attribute the hardening of Jewish hearts directly to God (in some kind of confession of God's mysterious sovereignty) echoes the slight variation in the Book of Mormon's rendering of Isaiah 6:9, where the prophet commands Judah to hear and to see, but they apparently elect of their own free will neither to understand nor to perceive what the prophet points out to them. But then Nephi's willingness immediately thereafter to attribute the long history of Jewish persecution to the divine will echoes the nonvariant text of Isaiah 6:10 as it appears in the Book of Mormon, where God expresses his intent to prevent any short-term return of Judah to its God. Destruction and diaspora are apparently supposed to intervene before real redemption takes place—as in the point of view of Jesus and Paul in the New Testament as they develop their remnant theologies. (Further, once again, the Book of Mormon expresses no interest in the post-Pauline Christian development of the idea that Jews were to be replaced by non-Jewish Christians as the true Israel.) In all this, the Book of Mormon confirms its complicated position somewhere between the earliest Jewish and the earliest Christian appropriations of Isaiah 6:9–10.

Nephi's commentary of sorts on Isaiah 6–12 thus seems clearly to underscore the consistency of the Book of Mormon's perspective on Isaiah's prophetic commission. And this is not the only corroborating evidence that can be brought to bear on the question. Elsewhere in the Book of Mormon—both within and without the boundaries of Nephi's record specifically—one can find direct and indirect textual echoes of Isaiah 6:9–10. A consideration of these intertextual echoes should help to demonstrate still more convincingly the Book of Mormon's consistency in its approach to Isaiah's commission.

Intertexts

Twice, quite late in the Book of Mormon, the careful reader notices echoes of Isaiah 6:9–10. Both of these appear at the volume's climax—that is, in connection with the eventual visit of the resurrected Christ to Israel in the New World some six centuries after Nephi's time. Both allusions to Isaiah 6:9–10 at this later point in the text are, moreover, attributed directly to Jesus

Christ: once as he speaks from the heavens before his actual physical arrival in the New World, and then once during his sermonizing after his arrival.

Unfortunately, however, several factors make these later allusions to Isaiah's commission less than helpful for making sense of the Book of Mormon's general approach to Isaiah 6:9–10. First, both of Christ's allusions to the passage are arguably formulaic—rather than substantive—in nature. That is, rather than using the language of Isaiah 6:9–10 in contexts where questions about remnant theology or Israelite history are at issue, Christ alludes to Isaiah's commission in the context of relatively private or individual instances of potential repentance. In the first of them, Christ speaks from heaven to ask the survivors of a devastating calamity whether they are prepared to repent: "Will ye not now return unto me and repent of your sins and be converted, that I may heal you?" This is followed immediately by a promise of "eternal life" to all those who "come unto" Christ, since his "arm of mercy" is extended (3 Ne. 9:13–14). A similar context prevails in Christ's second allusion, where he provides instructions to the leaders of his newly established church. The unrepentant should not be "cast . . . out" of their "places of worship," since, he explains, "Ye know not but what [such persons] will return and repent and come unto me with full purpose of heart, and I shall heal them, and ye shall be the means of bringing salvation unto them" (18:32).

That these passages allude to Isaiah 6:9–10 is relatively obvious, but that they have anything interpretively significant to offer is unclear. Neither alludes to the text for which Nephi provides a variant (the allusions allude to verse 10, not to verse 9, of Isaiah's commission). Moreover, the noncovenantal contexts of the two allusions are quite significant given the fact that the visiting Christ of the Book of Mormon dedicates much of his sermonizing in the New World to an exposition of, quite precisely, remnant theology and the themes first developed by Nephi.[49] That Christ has much to say about themes deeply relevant to Isaiah's commission elsewhere during his visit, but that he alludes to Isaiah's commission only in

---

49. See especially 3 Nephi 15–16, 20–26. Note that the first of the two allusions appears *before* these sermons on remnant theology, while the second appears *between* them. One might object that at least the first of these two allusions presents itself as an address specifically to the New World remnant of Israel, but the text never belabors this point. For the connections between Christ's sermonizing and Nephi's teachings, see Spencer, *An Other Testament*, 164–69.

these less-relevant places, suggests that these allusions have no light to shed on the interpretation of Isaiah 6:9–10 in the Book of Mormon.[50]

This irrelevance is compounded when one notes that the wording of the allusions seems in important ways to draw on New Testament versions of Isaiah 6:10, rather than directly on Isaiah 6:10 itself.[51] It would seem almost as if the point is to draw on formulaic language familiar from the New Testament rather than on Isaiah's actual words. Moreover, it is quite clear that both allusions are woven with starkly Christian theological language (with talk of "eternal life" and "coming unto Christ" with "full purpose of heart"), and this language only further distances the allusions from the original context of Isaiah 6.

Much more relevant than such distant allusions to Isaiah 6:9–10, then, is the handling in the Book of Mormon of Isaiah 29:10, a passage closely related to Isaiah's commission both in theme and theological provocation.[52] This verse from elsewhere in Isaiah is also reproduced in the Book of Mormon; significantly, it is quoted (like Isaiah 6:9–10) by Nephi relatively early in the volume. Crucially, like Isaiah 6:9–10, this passage contains interpretively significant variants in Nephi's reproduction. Passages quoted by Nephi from Isaiah 29 are more heavily revised than any other Isaiah texts that appear in the Book of Mormon, and readers are to understand that many—if not all—of the variants in Isaiah 29 in the Book of Mormon are the intentional work of Nephi himself.[53] But whether or not the variants in Isaiah 29:10 are to be understood as deliberate or received, they closely corroborate the implications of the variants in Isaiah 6:9–10 earlier in Nephi's record.

In the biblical version of Isaiah 29:10, one finds the now-familiar theme of divine hardening. Isaiah tells Judah that "the Lord hath poured

---

50. [Today I would need to qualify the sharpness of this claim. See the excellent essay, Jason R. Combs, "The Narrative Fulfillment of Isaiah 6 in 3 Nephi 11," *Journal of Book of Mormon Studies* 29 (2020): 289–98.]

51. For details, see the discussion in Skousen, *Analysis of Textual Variants of the Book of Mormon*, 2:699–700. On the difficulties surrounding New Testament language in the Book of Mormon more generally, see Nicholas J. Frederick, "Evaluating the Interaction between the New Testament and the Book of Mormon: A Proposed Methodology," *Journal of Book of Mormon Studies* 24 (2015): 1–30.

52. See Blenkinsopp, *Isaiah 1–39*, 404.

53. For a helpful analysis of the ways in which Isaiah 29 is molded to Nephi's purposes, see Heather Hardy and Grant Hardy, "How Nephi Shapes His Readers' Perceptions of Isaiah," in *Reading Nephi Reading Isaiah*, 37–62.

out upon you the spirit of deep sleep, and hath closed your eyes: the prophets and your rulers, the seers hath he covered." In the Book of Mormon, however, this passage is revised to read as follows: "For behold, the Lord hath poured out upon you the spirit of deep sleep—for behold, ye have closed your eyes, and ye have rejected the prophets and your rulers—and the seers hath he covered because of your iniquity" (2 Ne. 27:5).[54] Several revisions made to the text here emphasize that human sin begins with human beings rather than with any divine initiative. It is not God who has closed anyone's eyes; rather, human beings have elected to close their own eyes. Further, other revisions make clear that, from the Book of Mormon's perspective, the divine acts of pouring out a spirit of deep sleep on people and of covering their seers are direct responses to human iniquity.[55] Throughout the passage, the idea that God hardens his people in response to their own elective hardening replaces any suggestion that God hardens his people for his own sovereignly determined reasons.

Significantly, these revisions are once again consistent with the variants in the Book of Mormon's quotation of Isaiah 6:9–10. The revision of Isaiah 29:10 exhibits a certain aversion to the idea that God would intentionally harden his people's hearts against their will—at least before they make any show of rebelliousness on their own part. At the same time, however, the revision does not excise from the text its several references to the Lord nonetheless pouring out a spirit of deep sleep on his people or covering their seers for a time. The Book of Mormon's Isaiah understands God to have orchestrated a larger history within which Judah's conversion and healing are deliberately postponed, even as the prophet refuses to believe that God would send messengers to command the covenant people to turn aside from righteousness in order to launch such an unfortunate history.

Here once again, then, it seems best to see the Book of Mormon's treatment of Isaiah's hardening theme as drawing both on early Jewish worries about some of the implications of the prophet's strong notion of sovereignty and on still–Jewish Christian interest in a divine mystery through

---

54. There is some ambiguity about how this text should be punctuated. Is "and your rulers" to be included with "the prophets" as what has been "rejected"? Or is "and your rulers" to be regarded as the beginning of the next clause, such that rulers and seers have together been "covered"? Note that Skousen punctuates the text differently than I do.

55. It should be noted that the preceding verse in Isaiah 29 is also revised to make clear that this larger passage is addressed to "all" those who "do iniquity." See 2 Nephi 27:4, and compare Isaiah 29:9.

which a temporary prevention of some Jews' conversion would help to produce the long-promised remnant, a winnowed people ready to assume the divinely granted assignment of redeeming gentiles alongside the remainder of Israel. Similarly, yet once more, the Book of Mormon shows no commitment to the later Christian notion that Jews were somehow to be replaced by gentile Christians as the true Israel. Indeed, Nephi goes so far as to apply Isaiah 29:10 to *both* Jews *and* gentiles—to "all the nations of the Gentiles and also the Jews" (2 Ne. 27:1).[56] The consistency of the Book of Mormon's approach to this passage is striking, to say the least.

Conclusions

Over the course of this paper, I have provided the beginnings of an argument that the Book of Mormon exhibits a consistent theological perspective relative to the provocation contained in the biblical version of Isaiah 6:9–10. This theological perspective, moreover, appears consistent across a variety of contexts—not only in various passages in the Book of Mormon, but in distinct sorts of settings (direct manipulations of Isaianic texts, summary comments on the history outlined by Isaianic prophecy, and scattered references throughout the text). This consistency is suggestive, indicating a kind of program of interpretation that deserves closer and more exhaustive attention. The Book of Mormon, it seems, does not haphazardly quote from well-worn passages of Isaiah without any probing investigation of their implications. Rather, at least in certain places within the text, it organizes its presentation of themes around specific Isaiah passages that it then probes in theologically interesting and strikingly consistent ways.

Moreover, I have demonstrated that the position the Book of Mormon comes to inhabit in its treatment of at least one particular Isaianic passage (or perhaps one more general Isaianic theme) is relatively novel. It suggests a certain closeness to the use of the same Isaiah text in the New Testament while nonetheless simultaneously exhibiting a consistent point of difference in interpretation from New Testament interpreters. Interestingly, that point of difference places the Book of Mormon in rather close proximity to early Jewish interpretation, and in a suggestive way. That the Book of Mormon carves out a space that is at once irreducible to classic early Christian interpretations and irreducible to classic early Jewish interpreta-

---

56. [On the Book of Mormon's resistance to replacement theology, see Nicholas J. Frederick and Joseph M. Spencer, "Remnant of Replacement? Outlining a Possible Apostasy Narrative," *BYU Studies Quarterly* 30, no. 1 (2021): 105–27.]

tions while nonetheless drawing on both deserves further development. This pattern is indicative of the Book of Mormon's rather general conflation of Jewish and Christian perspectives—most visible, perhaps, in the volume's portrayal of a pre-Christian Jewish Christianity.

Beyond these more localized conclusions, however, I hope that this exercise has made clear the advisability of pursuing closer and more extended treatment of biblical texts in the Book of Mormon. By looking with care at the inventive use of the Bible in Mormon scripture, one might begin to develop a clearer sense for the ways in which Mormonism intervenes in the larger world of religion. How does the interpretive use of Isaianic texts in the Book of Mormon compare to other uses in the larger history of Isaiah interpretation? How does it distinguish itself in the setting of its emergence in nineteenth-century America? How does it compare to virtuosic treatments of biblical texts in other traditions more removed in time and space? Are there productive ways of placing Mormonism's often-audacious theology into a variety of religious contexts that might reveal more about the meaning of this particular biblical tradition? These are, I think, questions especially worth pursuing in a deliberately Latter-day Saint subdiscipline of biblical studies.

Chapter Nine

Isaiah 52 in the Book of Mormon
Notes on Isaiah's Reception History

Every reader of the Book of Mormon knows that quotations of Isaiah are not distributed evenly through the text. Nothing in Mormon's long history of the Nephites or in Moroni's capstone contributions at the end of the volume comes anywhere close to Nephi's obsessive examination of Isaiah's prophecies in the first part of the Book of Mormon. Closer readers note also that different Book of Mormon figures express interest in different parts of the book of Isaiah. Nephi gives his attention to early chapters from the book of Isaiah—quoting the whole of Isaiah 2–14, for instance—as much as he gives it to chapters later in that book, chapters like Isaiah 48–49. By contrast, Mormon and Moroni really only ever borrow from or allude to a very narrow range of Isaiah texts, all taken from just Isaiah 52–54. There are clear variations in styles of interpretation of Isaiah as well. All this has implications for a theological reading of the Book of Mormon that begins from the question of how the volume handles Isaiah.

A striking detail too easy to overlook, however, is the simple fact that one particular passage of Isaiah appears in some fashion or form in every major Book of Mormon engagement with Isaiah. Nephi borrows from and alludes to it. Abinadi has it quoted to him by King Noah's priests and then goes on to explain it. Jesus Christ himself quotes it and then adapts it to his audience during his climactic vision among the Nephites and the Lamanites. This passage is Isaiah 52:7–10. The consequence of this sustained interest across the Book of Mormon is that this one passage might be among the most important keys to sorting out the stakes and status of Isaiah in the Book of Mormon. And this essay represents an attempt on my part to sort out—both exegetically and theologically—just how the Book of Mormon, in its various contexts, deals as a whole with this one passage.

I originally presented a shorter and less developed version of this paper at the Pacific Northwest regional meetings of the American Academy of Religion, held at the University of Idaho in May of 2016. The complete version of the paper then appeared in *Relegere: Studies in Religion and Reception* 6, no. 2 (2016): 189–217. It was aimed at a non–Latter-day Saint readership.

Recent years have witnessed drastically increased interest in the reception history of the book of Isaiah.[1] Serious efforts are being made to provide English-language translations of Greek and Latin commentaries on Isaiah,[2] and renewed attention has been given to early Reformation-era interpretations.[3] Many have begun to analyze critically the rise of modern Isaiah scholarship,[4] and some recent commentaries draw on pre-critical approaches to the text.[5]

In this paper, I wish to look at an important but overlooked aspect of Isaiah's reception history: the use of Isaiah texts in uniquely Mormon scripture. Despite increasing recognition of Mormonism's importance to the American religious experience, little attention has as yet been given to the novel uses of Isaiah in foundational Mormon texts.[6] Much might

---

1. This began in earnest with the publication of John F. A. Sawyer, *The Fifth Gospel: Isaiah in the History of Christianity* (Cambridge: Cambridge University Press, 1996).

2. See, most recently, Jerome, *Commentary on Isaiah: Including St. Jerome's Translation of Origen's Homilies 1–9 on Isaiah*, trans. Thomas P. Scheck (New York: Newman, 2015).

3. See the rich treatment, for instance, in Brevard S. Childs *The Struggle to Understand Isaiah as Christian Scripture* (Grand Rapids: Eerdmans, 2004), 181–229.

4. For examples, see Claire Mathews McGinnis and Patricia K. Tull, "Remembering the Former Things: The History of Interpretation and Critical Scholarship," in *"As Those Who Are Taught": The Interpretation of Isaiah from the LXX to the SBL*, ed. Claire Mathews McGinnis and Patricia K. Tull (Atlanta: Society of Biblical Literature, 2006), 1–27, as well as Childs, *Isaiah as Christian Scripture*, 230–90.

5. See not only compilation like those in the *Ancient Christian Commentary on Scripture* series, edited Thomas C. Oden and published by InnerVarsity Press, but also commentaries published in the *Historical Commentary on the Old Testament* series: Willhelm A.M. Beuken, *Isaiah II*, trans. Brian Doyle, vol. 2, *Isaiah Chapters 28–39* (Leuben: Peeters, 2000); and Jan L. Koole, *Isaiah III*, trans. Antony P. Runia, vol. 3, *Isaiah Chapters 56–66* (Leuben: Peeters, 2001).

6. The only available literature on Isaiah in the Book of Mormon, for instance, is directed to a largely lay readership interested either in developing a basic understanding of Isaianic texts or in deciding the implications of Isaiah's inclusion in the Book of Mormon for the volume's claims to historicity. For the best of the literature, see Victor L. Ludlow, *Unlocking Isaiah in the Book of Mormon* (Salt Lake City: Deseret Book, 2003); Donald W. Parry and John W. Welch, eds., *Isaiah in the Book of Mormon* (Provo: Foundation for Ancient Research & Mormon Studies, 1998); John A. Tvedtnes, ed., *Isaiah Variants in the Book of Mormon* (Provo: Foundations for Ancient Research & Mormon Studies, 1981); David P. Wright, "Isaiah in the Book of Mormon: Or Joseph Smith in Isaiah," in

therefore be gained by crossing two lines of inquiry: Mormon studies and the reception history of Isaiah.[7] It may yet prove to be no coincidence that Mormonism's deep investment in Isaiah in the early nineteenth century coincides historically with the rise of modern critical study of the book of Isaiah. For this paper, however, a narrower scope is necessary. Joseph Smith, Mormonism's founder, produced several volumes of new scripture,[8] attempted a full revision of the Christian Bible,[9] preached several volumes' worth of sermons,[10] and left behind diaries, histories, letters, and numerous other texts.[11] All these sources draw extensively on the language of Isaiah. In addition, there is the literary output of Smith's followers, sources that might also be mined in reconstructing early Mormon understandings of Isaiah. Faced with so much material, how might one establish a foothold? Here I will focus just on the Book or Mormon, the earliest and most influential of published Mormon sources. Further narrowing my scope, I will look here only at how the Book of Mormon uses just one passage from Isaiah—specifically Isaiah 52:7–10—and ignore the other twenty-or-so chapters of Isaiah on which the Book of Mormon explicitly

---

American Apocryphal Essays on the Book of Mormon, ed. Dan Vogel and Brent Lee Metcalfe (Salt Lake City: Signature Books, 2002), 157–234.

7. Several studies look at early Mormonism's relationship to biblical culture in its historical context, albeit without focusing in any substantial way on the Isaianic corpus that plays such a dominant role in Mormon texts. See Philip L. Barlow, *Mormons and the Bible: The Place of the Latter-day Saints in American Religion* (New York: Oxford University Press, 1991); Paul C. Gutjahr, *An American Bible: A History of the Good Book in the United States, 1777–1880* (Stanford: Stanford University Press, 1999); and David F. Holland, *Sacred Borders: Continuing Revelation and Canonical Restraint in Early America* (New York: Oxford University Press, 2011).

8. These are the Book of Mormon, The Doctrine and Covenants, and The Pearl of Great Price, available in print in a variety of editions.

9. This was not published during Smith's lifetime, but the manuscripts of the revision have been made available in full since. See Scott H. Faulring, Kent P. Jackson, and Robert J. Matthews, eds., *Joseph Smith's New Translation of the Bible: Original Manuscripts* (Provo: Religious Studies Center, Brigham Young University, 2004).

10. That most significant of these have been collected, in a preliminary form, in Andrew F. What and Lyndon W. Cook, *The Words of Joseph Smith: The Contemporary Accounts of the Nauvoo Discourses of the Prophet Joseph* (Provo: Religious Studies Center, Brigham Young University, 1980).

11. Joseph Smith's collected papers are currently being published serially, with a projected completion date in the next few years. Twenty-three volumes are projected. See http://www.josephsmithpapers.org.

draws.[12] The volume's use of this particular text from Isaiah is, I believe, illustrative of Mormonism's earliest engagement.

My thesis is that the Book of Mormon outlines several distinct interpretations of Isaiah 52:7–10.[13] In essence, the book presents itself as (in part) the history of a debate regarding the interpretation of this passage. That it couples this history with an attempt to address nineteenth-century American Christianity directly makes it clear that the Book of Mormon should be read as contributing to Isaiah's reception history. It seems that the Book of Mormon is aimed in part at recommending that Western Christianity, struggling with secularism at the time of the book's appearance, revisit the prophecies of Isaiah.[14] And the book suggests that the meaning of Isaianic prophecy is unstable, outlining possible approaches to Isaiah and adjudicating among them—apparently in hopes of assisting in Christianity's struggle in an increasingly secular context.

---

12. The Book of Mormon directly quotes the whole of Isaiah 2–14, most of Isaiah 29, and the whole of Isaiah 48–54 (minus a few verses of Isaiah 52). Except in the case of Isaiah 29, the text explicitly identifies the book of Isaiah as its source for the quotations (although it claims to draw on an ancient manuscript kept on brass plates, and hence it often provides variant readings of the text). In addition to these lengthier quotations, passages in the Book of Mormon often draw in obvious but unacknowledged ways on the language of Isaiah. Several scholars have attempted to produce comprehensive lists of the Isaiah passages quoted or alluded to in the Book of Mormon. For the best available lists, see Royal Skousen, "Textual Variants in the Isaiah Quotations in the Book of Mormon," in Parry and Welch, *Isaiah in the Book of Mormon*, 369–71; and the citation footnotes throughout Grant Hardy, ed., *The Book of Mormon: A Reader's Edition* (Urbana: University of Illinois Press, 2003).

13. Certain of these interpretations have been helpfully reviewed in Dana M. Pike, "'How Beautiful upon the Mountains': The Imagery of Isaiah 52:7–10 and its Occurrences in the Book of Mormon," in Parry and Welch, *Isaiah in the Book of Mormon*, 249–91; and Joseph M. Spencer, *An Other Testament: On Typology*, 2nd ed. (Provo: Neal A. Maxwell Institute, Brigham Young University, 2016).

14. The Book of Mormon is explicitly aware of the secular context in which it makes its nineteenth-century appearance. Prophets especially at the volume's opening and closing focus intensely on the secular "gentiles" (read "people of European descent") who are among its intended readers. On this aspect of the book, see Grant Hardy, *Understanding the Book of Mormon: A Reader's Guide* (New York: Oxford University Press, 2010), 217–47; and Jared Hickman, "*The Book of Mormon as Amerindian Apocalypse,*" *American Literature* 86, no. 3 (2014): 429–61.

Isaiah 52:7–10 for Nephi

The Book of Mormon's narrative opens in ancient Jerusalem "in the commencement of the first year of the reign of Zedekiah, king of Judah" (1 Ne. 1:4).[15] This setting makes the book's sustained interest in Isaiah 52 perfectly sensible. Zedekiah's reign (which ended in 587 BCE) resulted in the exile of Judah in Babylon, to which exile (and its imminent end with Babylon's demise) Isaiah 52:7–10 and surrounding prophecies directly respond. Whether one approaches questions of Isaianic authorship conservatively (the whole book can be dated to the eighth century) or liberally (major portions of the Isaiah had their origin in and after the exile), more or less all interpreters agree that Isaiah 52 and the texts surrounding it focus on the period of Judah's sixth-century exile in Babylon.[16] It is immediately prior to this exile that the Book of Mormon's story begins. The first year of Zedekiah's reign marked the first major deportation of Jerusalem's inhabitants, anticipatory of the destruction of the temple and a fuller deportation a decade later; between these two events of deportation, according to the Book of Mormon, a small group of Jerusalemites left the city to journey to the New World.[17] According to the Book of

---

15. Throughout this essay, I use the critical text produced by Royal Skousen for citations from the Book of Mormon. But because Joseph Smith, in dictating the Book of Mormon to a scribe, dictated no punctuation, I provide my own punctuation of the text, at times consonant and at times not with Skousen's suggested punctuation. For references, I use the standard versification used in editions published by The Church of Jesus Christ of Latter-day Saints. For the full text, see Royal Skousen, ed., *The Book of Mormon: The Earliest Text* (New Haven: Yale University Press, 2009)

16. Mormon scholars have generally preferred conservative Isaiah scholarship for relatively obvious reasons. If much of Isaiah 40–55 originated only during or after the exile, it should not have been available in any form to the peoples of the Book of Mormon, who, according to the volume, took their leave from Jerusalem before the exile began in earnest. Thus, consensus liberal scholarship on Isaiah raises serious questions about the historicity of the Book of Mormon, which is taken to be a cornerstone of Mormon Faith. For the most recent Latter-day Saint defense of conservative Isaiah scholarship, see Kent P. Jackson, "Isaiah in the Book of Mormon," in *A Reason for Faith: Navigating LDS Doctrine and Church History*, ed. Laura Hales (Provo: Religious Studies Center, Brigham Young University, 2016), 69–78.

17. Throughout this essay, I attempt to provide enough context to make clear relevant portions of the Book of Mormon without reviewing unnecessary details. For a good overview of the book, see Terryl L. Givens, *The Book of Mormon: A Very Short Introduction* (New York: Oxford University Press, 2009), 3–59.

Mormon, these escapees were in no way unaware of the exile they were escaping. Their patriarchal leader, Lehi, is a prophet who himself anticipates the exile. His family and the remainder of the company leave Jerusalem precisely because Lehi's prophecies concerning destruction and exile create opposition among the city's elites. And after the group has arrived and settled in the New World, Lehi announces having "seen a vision, in which I know that Jerusalem is destroyed—and had we remained in Jerusalem we should also have perished" (2 Ne. 1:4). From the very beginning of the Book of Mormon, the text presents its main characters as aware of having just barely missed a definitive event in Jewish history. They, as much as their fellow Israelites who remained in the Old World, seek to make sense of Jerusalem's destruction and Judah's exile.[18] And it should be no surprise that they also turn to prophecies in the book of Isaiah to do so.

The theological perspective worked out in the book of Isaiah makes of the exile a crucial moment in the unfolding of a larger historical project undertaken by Israel's God.[19] The exile, according to Isaiah, is only "for a small moment" (Isa. 54:7), and on the other side of the exile lies restoration for a holy remnant of the covenant people.[20] This passage through exile and return—through abandonment and reconciliation—serves the divine purpose because it draws the attention of the whole world to the faithfulness and kindness of YHWH, Israel's unique God. The purpose of the exile, in short, is supposed to have been both to bring ancient Jews into closer cultural contact with non-covenantal peoples and to place them in a compromised situation. Together, these two aspects of Judah's situation would allow its redemption and restoration to have a determinate effect on non-Israelites. The book of Isaiah anticipates mass gentile

18. A second-generation prophet and Lehi's direct spiritual heir later claims that he and his people experienced their own longing for Jerusalem after its loss, as if their escape were a kind of parallel to the exile experienced by their Old-World contemporaries. "The time passed away with us-and also our lives passed away like as it were unto us a dream-we being a lonesome and solemn people, wanderers cast out from Jerusalem, born in tribulation in a wild wilderness, and hated of our brethren, which caused wars and contentions. Wherefore, we did mourn out our days" (Jacob 7:26).

19. For an astute and detailed assessment of the theological commitments of Isaiah 40–55, see John Goldingay, *The Message of Isaiah 40–55: A Literary–Theological Commentary* (New York: T & T Clark, 2005).

20. I use here and throughout this article the King James renderings of Isaianic texts, since the Book of Mormon, when it quotes from Isaiah, uses the King James rendering.

conversion, although the exact status of converted Gentiles vis-a-vis the covenant people remains ambiguous in the book.[21]

All of these themes interest the Book of Mormon at a fundamental level, but especially in the first major portion of the book (that is, especially in the First and Second Books of Nephi).[22] Those who make up the story's first generation worry about Israel's covenantal standing, and they wonder about the relationship between gentiles and the covenant people. Early in the book, Lehi prophesies of the coming of "a messiah" (1 Ne. 10:4) who, after being killed and rising from the dead, "should make himself manifest, by the Holy Ghost, unto the gentiles" (v. 11). This would occur in the course of a history involving "the dwindling of the Jews in unbelief" (v. 11), a consequent scattering for Jews while Gentiles receive "the fullness of the gospel" (v. 14).[23] In an attempt to explain these prophecies to the family, Lehi's son Nephi draws on his own (and his father's) visions, but also on a biblical resource: "I spake unto them concerning the restoration of the Jews in the latter days, and I did rehearse unto them the

---

21. For a nice exploration of some historical consequences of the ambiguity of the book of Isaiah's position on the status of converted Gentiles, see Delio DelRio, *Paul and the Synagogues: Romans and the Isaiah Targum* (Eugene: Pickwick, 2013).

22. The first major portion of the Book of Mormon is presented as the work of a series of writers over the course of four centuries, recorded on what the volume calls the "small places" of Nephi (Jacob 1:1). The tone and style of this first part of the book (stretching from the First Book of Nephi to the book of Omni) differ substantially from those of the remainder of the book, which is presented as the work of two editors, father (Mormon) and son (Moroni), who write their abridgement of Lehite history from the perspective of their own time, some ten centuries after Lehi's departure from Jerusalem, when one half of Lehi's descendants are wiped out by the other half. Importantly, for various reasons, Joseph Smith dictated the contents of the Book of Mormon out of their published order, beginning with the third-person historical accounts gathered under the names of Mormon and Moroni and only then coming to the first-person records that now open the volume. For a brief account of the events surrounding Smith's dictation and his reasons for dictating things out of final order, see Richard Lyman Bushman, *Joseph Smith, Rough Stone Rolling: A Cultural Biography of Mormonism's Founder* (New York: Alfred A. Knopf, 2005), 57–83. For a systematic argument that the first major portion of the Book of Mormon was dictated last, see Brent Lee Metcalfe, "The Priority of Mosiah: A Prelude to Book of Mormon Exegesis," in *New Approaches to the Book of Mormon: Explorations in Critical Methodology*, ed. Brent Lee Metcalfe (Salt Lake City: Signature Books, 1993), 395–444.

23. Hardy has outlined the basic nature of this history in *Understanding the Book of Mormon*, 61–62.

words of Isaiah, which spake concerning the restoration of the Jews (or of the house of Israel)" (15:19–20). It is specifically in Isaiah that Lehi's family finds scriptural resources for making sense of Israel's history and destiny. And it is there, too, that they find an outline of the complex place occupied by Gentiles in that history.

The specific texts presumably referred to in the just-quoted passage are not difficult to determine. Although the Book of Mormon quotes from and draws on various Isaianic texts, in an important scene Nephi instructs Lehi's family regarding covenantal history by quoting specifically from Isaiah 48–49 (see 1 Ne. 20–21). It is clear that the Isaianic source the Book of Mormon regards in its first major sequence as particularly relevant to understanding Israel's history begins with Isaiah 48, at the heart of the portion of Isaiah meant to address the return of Judah from Babylonian exile. In the remainder of his contribution to the Book of Mormon, Nephi goes on to quote (in bits and pieces) the whole of Isaiah 48:1–52:2, in addition to drawing on earlier portions of Isaiah.[24] To explain Jewish history, the Book of Mormon's opening voices thus turn again and again to key prophecies of Second Isaiah.[25]

---

24. These quotations are found in 1 Nephi 20–21 and 2 Nephi 7–8.

25. There is some ambiguity in the first portion of the Book of Mormon about whether Isaiah's prophecies are limited in their original historical scope just to the events of the eighth through the sixth centuries, or whether they are instead focused also on the events of specifically Jewish history from the time of the exile to the time of the eschaton. At times or on one reading, the Book of Mormon seems committed to the idea that the prophecies of Second Isaiah focus solely on the events surrounding the exile, and that one must do some work of extrapolation in order to apply them, somewhat inventively or certainly prophetically, to the whole of Jewish history. At other times or on another reading, however, the Book of Mormon seems committed to the idea that the prophecies of Second Isaiah themselves focus on the whole of Jewish history. As the book presents the data, interestingly, the latter of these two readings would seem to be associated more closely (or at least initially) with Nephi's brother Jacob, as if it were his innovation. For some discussion of this, see chapters 11 and 12 of Joseph M. Spencer, *The Vision of All: Twenty-Five Lectures on Isaiah in Nephi's record* (Salt Lake City: Greg Kofford Books, 2016). It might be noted that the longer-historical interpretation of Isaiah that is certainly operative in certain places in the Book of Mormon shares much with the intertestamental interpretation of Isaiah (and the prophets more generally) as interpreted by E. P. Sanders and N. T. Wright (what the latter calls the "continuing exile"). See especially N. T. Wright, *Paul and the Faithfulness of God* (Minneaoplis: Fortress, 2013), 114–63.

What makes the Book of Mormon's approach to these prophecies unique is that it sees them as a resource for thinking about a history somewhat broader than that of the Jews, narrowly defined (that is, as direct descendants of Judah). In the very first story told in the Book of Mormon, Lehi and Nephi discover from a genealogical record that they are *not* in fact Jews, strictly speaking, because they hail from Judah's brother Joseph, rather than from Judah himself (see 1 Ne. 5:14–16). The Book of Mormon thus tells the story of a Josephite, rather than a strictly Jewish, transplant from Jerusalem to the New World during the era of Judah's exile in Babylon. The result is that, while the Book of Mormon's first voices find in Isaiah's words a direct analysis of specifically Judahite history, they find themselves inspired to extrapolate from that history an indirect analysis of the covenant God's ways of dealing with *all* of Israel—and therefore with Joseph's descendants as well as with Judah's. Nephi and his priestly brother Jacob even give to this interpretive approach to Isaiah a name, used consistently in the text: "likening."[26] Throughout the first portion of the Book of Mormon, to liken is both to recognize the specifically Jewish determinations of the historical text of Isaiah and to see in Isaiah's prophecies resources for understanding non-Jewish-but-still-Israelite patterns of history.

This point is essential. A too-casual reader might come away from a reading of the first portion of the Book of Mormon believing that it understands Isaiah to have prophesied of Israel's whole story—from the time of exile to the end of history, focused as much on Joseph's descendants as on Judah's.[27] Such a reading, however, is inaccurate because the text explicitly recognizes the historically limited scope of Second Isaiah's prophecies (they are about exile and restoration in the sixth century, or perhaps, more expansively, about the history of Judah more generally). At the same

---

26. See, for instance, 1 Nephi 19:23–24; 22:8; 2 Nephi 6:5; 11:2, 8. Perhaps the most illuminating of these passages is 2 Nephi 6:5: "And now the words which I shall read are they which Isaiah spake concerning all the house of Israel," Jacob says to the people of Nephi. "Wherefore they may be likened unto you, for ye are the house of Israel. And there are many things which have been spoken by Isaiah which may be likened unto you because that ye are of the house of Israel."

27. Incidentally, this is how even Latter-day Saints traditionally understand the Book of Mormon's uses of Isaiah. And in parallel, Latter-day Saints generally understand the book's talk of likening to recommend a general practice of life application, rather than a specific hermeneutic approach of Isaianic prophecy. For a good example of both of these approaches, formulated in full, see Joseph Fielding McConkie and Robert L. Millet, *Doctrinal Commentary on the Book of Mormon*, vol. 1, *First and Second Nephi* (Salt Lake City: Bookcraft, 1987).

time, the Book of Mormon pursues a deliberate extrapolation from the Isaianic text to apply its basic patterns to a history of wider scope (a history the Book of Mormon's inaugural prophets claim to have witnessed in apocalyptic visionary experiences).[28] In effect, the first major sequence of the Book of Mormon finds in Isaiah a basic pattern for God's historical dealings with covenant Israel, illustrated primarily through events happening to Judah between the eighth and sixth centuries before Christ; and then it extrapolates that basic pattern or schema to apply it to the history of the Josephites, whom the book identifies with certain inhabitants of ancient America.[29] In short, Isaiah's prophecies, despite their limited historical scope, can be "likened" to the longer history of Israel, which is only known by an independent revelatory source.

For this reason, the events discussed in Isaiah 48:1–52:2 can be lined up, point by point, with the Josephite events anticipated prophetically by the Book of Mormon's first characters: (1) the exile of Jerusalem's population to Babylon Nephi likens to the departure of the Book of Mormon's Jerusalemites for the New World six centuries before Jesus; (2) Jews' suffering in Babylon he likens to the subjugation of the Book of Mormon's New-World Israelites when European Christians come to the Americas two thousand years later, devastating native populations; (3) the restoration of the Jewish remnant of Joseph, to the knowledge of its Abrahamic heritage; and, finally (4) the rise of gentile interest in the Jewish God Nephi likens to growing awareness among gentile Christians of the covenantal status of Native American peoples, which in turn is supposed to reorient modern Christianity to its Abrahamic roots (like the Persians with barely-post-exilic Jews, European Christians are to assist New-World Israelites

---

28. For the fullest of these apocalyptic visions, of central importance to making sense of everything the Book of Mormon has to say about Isaiah, see 1 Nephi 11–14.

29. For many years, Latter-day Saints assumed that the Book of Mormon recounted the ancient history of all native peoples of the American continent, but numerous circumstances have led many more recently to believe only that a relatively small proportion of indigenous Americans is related to the Book of Mormon's narrative. Relatively recently, the institutional church itself altered the editorial introduction to official editions of the book to indicate that the descendants of Lehi "are among the ancestors of the American Indians." See the useful discussion in Armand L. Mauss, "Rethinking Retrenchment: Course Corrections in the Ongoing Campaign for Respectability," *Dialogue: A Journal of Mormon Thought* 11, no. 4 (2011): 5–6.

in building up a New Jerusalem, but the latter in the New World).[30] The Book of Mormon thus works out a point-by-point quasi-allegorical reading of Second Isaiah, and this reading is explicitly acknowledged to be a quasi-allegorical reading (a "likening").

Whether understood historically in terms of sixth-century Jewish history, or whether understood quasi-allegorically in terms of New-World history, this four-part schema is sketched most economically in Isaiah 52, specifically in verses 7–10.[31] In no way coincidentally, these same four verses comprise the most frequently quoted Isaiah text in the whole of the Book of Mormon.[32] In their King James rendering, they read as follows:

> How beautiful upon the mountains are the feet of him that bringeth good tidings, that publisheth peace; that bringeth good tidings of good, that published salvation; that saith unto Zion, Thy God reigneth! Thy watchmen shall lift up the voice; with the voice together shall they sing: for they shall see eye to eye when the Lord shall bring again Zion. Break forth into joy, sing together, ye waste places of Jerusalem. The Lord hath made bare his holy arm in the eyes of all the nations; and all the ends of the earth shall see the salvation of our God.

Here the entire four-part schema appears: (1) removal into exile is implied, since good tidings have to be brought from afar, just as (2) suffering in exile is also implied, since good tidings are so appreciatively received; and then (3) the announcement is one of restoration and return, with waste places themselves finding reason to rejoice, all this (4) leading to the demonstration of God's power to deliver before all the gentile nations. In

---

30. A good summary of this schema and its use in the Book of Mormon can be found in Garold N. Davis, "Pattern and Purpose of the Isaiah Commentaries in the Book of Mormon," in *Mormons, Scripture, and the Ancient World: Studies in Honor of John L. Sorenson,* ed. Davis Bitton (Provo: Foundation for Ancient Research & Mormon Studies, 1998), 277–303.

31. Commentators often note that these four verses, taken together, provide a succinct statement of the whole of Second Isaiah's prophecy. See, for instance, the comments of Brevard S. Childs, *Isaiah: A Commentary* (Louisville: Westminster John Knox, 2001), 406. For a brief summary of the towering influence of this passage in the biblical tradition, see Joseph Blenkinsopp, *Isaiah 40–55: A New Translation with Introduction and Commentary* (New York: Doubleday, 2000), 344; see also John Goldingay and David Payne, *A Critical and Exegetical Commentary on Isaiah 40–55,* 2 vols. (New York: T & T Clark, 2006), 2:261–64.

32. Pike also notes the frequency of allusions to or borrowings from this passage elsewhere in early Mormon sources. Pike, "Imagery of Isaiah 52:7–10," 251–54.

a profound way, this passage serves as a synopsis of everything about Isaiah that interests the Book of Mormon.

And yet, curiously, even as Isaiah 52:7–10 is the most frequently quoted passage of Isaiah in the Book of Mormon more generally, it appears only in passing and rather formulaic allusions in the first part of the book, where otherwise Nephi is presented as having given such detailed interpretive attention to Isaiah.[33] The careful reader cannot help feeling that this particular passage inspired Nephi, and yet Isaiah 52:7–10 never becomes the clear or explicit focus of the Book of Mormon in any sustained way until long after Nephi's death. Thus, despite Isaiah 52:7–10 serving as a particularly beautiful encapsulation of the whole of Second Isaiah's prophetic output, and despite the first portion of the Book of Mormon serving as the volume's most sustained engagement with Second Isaiah quite generally, this particular passage never becomes a major focus there. All that gets quoted of Isaiah 52 in the first sequence of the Book of Mormon is its first two verses, and even these are quoted somewhat perfunctorily.[34]

---

33. The first of these two allusions appears in 1 Nephi 13:37, in which Nephi quotes an angelic messenger's word to him regarding those who "seek to bring for [the Lord's] Zion at that [the last] day": "Whoso shall publish peace—that shall publish tidings of great joy—how beautiful upon the mountains shall they be!" The second appears in 1 Nephi 22:10–11, where Nephi attempts an explanation of Isaiah 48–49 by tying it to Genesis 12:3 ("In thy seed shall all the kindreds of the earth be blessed," that verse is rendered in 1 Nephi 22:9): "And I would, my brethren, that ye should know that all the kindreds of the earth cannot be blessed unless he [God] shall make bare his arm in the eyes of the nations. Wherefore, the Lord God will proceed to make bare his arm in the eyes of all the nations in bringing about his covenants and his gospel unto they which are of the house of Israel." These allusions together make clear that Nephi is supposed to be read as having been perfectly familiar with Isaiah 52:7–10, but neither amounts to a particularly probing investigation of the text. The latter of the two does suggest something of an interesting interpretive gesture—at the very least by connecting the text explicitly to Genesis 12:3 and by providing some kind of explanation of exactly what is supposed to be meant by God making his arm bare. But these gestures are quite remarkably less intense, interpretively, than those Nephi makes with respect to other Isaiah passages, and than those that other Book of Mormon voices make with respect to Isaiah 52:7–10.

34. Isaiah 52:1–2 is quoted not in its own right but as a kind of conclusion to Isaiah 50–51, two chapters that are in turn quoted as a continuation and partial explanation of Isaiah 49:22–26. (All these are quoted in the course of 2 Nephi 6–8.) The use of Isaiah 52:1–2 to conclude the quotation of Isaiah 50–51 seems to be motivated—this is what makes its quotation somewhat perfunctory—by

But despite the relative lack of direct interest in Isaiah 52:7–10 in the first part of the book, one can easily make the case that more or less all attention given to Isaiah in the Book of Mormon after Nephi's death focuses *solely* on interpreting this one passage. If the volume were missing its first sequence,[35] the whole of the book could be justifiably read as an investigation just of Isaiah 52:7–10. But because the writings attributed to Nephi open the book, saturated with a variety of close and inventive readings of Isaianic texts, it is impossible to say that the whole book amounts to an investigation of Isaiah 52:7–10. Nephi's sustained interactions with Isaiah focus instead primarily on Isaiah 11, 29, and 49—never on Isaiah 52. Yet Isaiah 52:7–10 *is* there in the first major portion of the book. Although the light there shines squarely on different texts from Isaiah, Isaiah 52:7–10 seems in crucial ways to be hovering just outside the circle of light, as already noted. And the remainder of the Book of Mormon, focused intensely on Isaiah 52:7–10, asks that the reader look to the edge of the circle in connection with Nephi's writings to see what they have to say about the meaning of the passage.

Of course, as I have shown, what Nephi's writings have to say about Isaiah 52:7–10 is largely implicit. The first part of the Book of Mormon just seems to assume that the passage outlines the events of exile and restoration in the sixth century, along with the effects of these events on Gentiles, before it then assumes that the passage can also be "likened" to the parallel (and prophetically anticipated) history of the New-World Israelites (Josephites). Nephi's two passing allusions to Isaiah 52:7–10, mentioned above, make perfectly clear that he is meant to be understood as applying the passage to the subjugation of New-World Israelites by Gentiles in the early modern era, and to the subsequent possibility of a reorientation of European Christianity to its Jewish roots.[36] Significantly, this largely im-

---

the repetition of "Awake! Awake!" from Isaiah 51:9, 17 in Isaiah 52:1. It also makes the full quotation of Isaiah 50–51 end on a more clearly positive note than it would if the quotation ended with the conclusion of Isaiah 51.

35. That is, were Smith to have concluded his dictation of the text when he came to what is now the end of the book, instead of then proceeding to dictate the lengthy portion of text that serves now as the volume's opening sequence, in other words, from the First Book of Nephi through the book of Omni (see note 22 above).

36. In 1 Nephi 13:37, those publishing peace are pretty clearly to be understood as gentile Christians who, by taking the Book of Mormon to native American peoples, make the identity of Josephites known. In 1 Nephi 22:10–11, the making bare of the Lord's arm in the eyes of all nations is accomplished in that ancient

plicit interpretation of Isaiah 52:7–10 finds itself effectively at odds with several other interpretations—all of them explicit—offered over the course of the remainder of the book. These deserve separate treatment.

Isaiah 52:7–10 for Abinadi and His Opponents

The first significant treatment of Isaiah in the Book of Mormon after Nephi's death comes in a situation of overt conflict—a situation of conflict, moreover, between rival conceptions of true religion. Although this conflict is presented as occurring some four centuries after Nephi's time, the intervening history is narrated in such abbreviated form that the conflict comes more or less as the very next story in the book. And crucially, the conflict seems, on close reading, to be intentionally presented as growing out of Nephi's attempt to make sense of Isaiah.[37] Further, once the conflict is resolved, the reader naturally feels as if the whole question of Isaiah's meaning has been fully decided, since references to Isaiah almost entirely disappear from the Book of Mormon for three hundred pages of text. More than a century and a half of the book's chronology passes with just a few fleeting allusions to Isaiah.[38] Eventually, questions concerning the interpretation of Isaiah return to the foreground, significantly doing

---

Israel's covenants and ancient Christianity's gospel are both made known, in full view of gentile Christians, to native American peoples.

37. The Book of Mormon, after Nephi's record (and several minor contributors to it), presents itself as largely the work of Mormon, from whom the book takes its name. Beginning with the Book of Mosiah and running through the Book of Mormon, the narrative unfolds as a third-person story told by Mormon, who is positioned historically at the end of the story. Mormon has relatively clear agendas, nicely traced by Hardy in a recent book (*Understanding the Book of Mormon*, 87–213). Importantly, those agendas are presented as having taken their orientation in an important way from a close reading of Nephi's record (see the brief Words of Mormon that intervene, in the Book of Mormon, between Nephi's record and Mormon's record). Because Nephi's record is so unmistakably taken up with the question of interpreting Isaiah's writings, it seems significant that Mormon's history is organized around two particularly important events where the interpretation of Isaiah's writings become a central question anew. For a general interpretation of the Book of Mormon along such lines, see Spencer, *An Other Testament*.

38. In the first (1830) edition of the Book of Mormon, nothing concerning the book of Isaiah or its interpretation appears between pages 190 and 486—that is, in current chaptering, between Mosiah 17 and 3 Nephi 15. The events recounted in Mosiah 11–16, moreover, are presented as having occurred at some point

so at the climax of the book, when the resurrected Jesus Christ makes a New-World appearance.[39] But until that point, the much-earlier conflict concerning Isaiah 52:7–10, along with its apparent resolution, determines the status of Isaiah's meaning for the Book of Mormon.

As noted, the conflict arises four centuries after the days of Nephi (though only a few pages after Nephi's story). Naturally, major changes have occurred by that point. During Nephi's time, the children of Lehi divide into rival nations—the Nephites and the Lamanites (the latter named after Nephi's oldest brother)—and the intervening centuries are characterized by continual warfare. A generation before the opening of the Book of Mormon, the Lamanites gain the upper hand, sacking the Land of Nephi. Only a few Nephites escape, resettling in the Land of Zarahemla (an already inhabited territory nearby). Thereafter, a small group of zealots, hoping to reclaim lands lost to the Lamanites, establish a treaty with the Lamanite king and begin recolonizing the Land of Nephi. Under their first king, Zeniff, the colonists win several battles against their Lamanite neighbors, with the result that a false sense of security settles over the colony as the second king, Noah, comes to the throne. Adding to this false sense of security is a period of economic prosperity. Noah lives in Solomonic splendor while his debauched priests justify the regime's oppressions through ideological preaching; the text speaks not only of the priests "spend[ing] their time with harlots" (Mosiah 11:14), but also of the "lying and vain words" they use while addressing the people (v. 11).

What emerges as the story unfolds is that the priests use Isaiah 52:7–10 as a kind of scriptural touchstone for justifying Noah's regime. When a classic Hebrew prophet figure named Abinadi appears among Noah's people—predicting first that Noah's wickedness will bring the people "into bondage" (Mosiah 11:21) and then, when repentance is not forthcoming, that the people "shall be slain" and Noah's life "shall be valued even as a garment in a hot furnace" (12:2–3)—the priests find themselves confronting the prophet in a show trial.[40] To clinch their case, they propose

---

substantially earlier than 120 BCE, while the events recounted in 3 Nephi 15–26 are presented as having occurred in 34 CE.

39. Average Latter-day Saints readers of the Book of Mormon tend to downplay the Isaianic focus of the book's account of Jesus Christ's ancient visit to the New World. For a good survey of what usually interests most readers, see the summary treatment in Andrew C. Skinner, *Third Nephi: The Fifth Gospel* (Springville: CFI, 2012).

40. In an essential study, John Welch has investigated the Abinadi story carefully from the perspective of biblical legal practices. In the course of his study,

a hermeneutic contest, asking Abinadi to defend himself with a viable interpretation of Isaiah 52:7–10. They introduce the passage as "the words which are written, and which have been taught by our fathers" (Mosiah 12:20). Readers are clearly meant to assume that the passage has developed a relatively standard interpretation among the Nephite colonists (apparently already established before Zeniff's death and Noah's ascendancy), an interpretation the priests believe Abinadi would both know and espouse. The twist of the story comes when Abinadi produces an entirely novel interpretation of the Isaiah passage, shifting the gravitational center of the Book of Mormon's approach to Isaiah substantially.

The priests' interpretation is left largely implicit in the text, but it proves easy to reconstruct.[41] Loosely following Nephi's program of "likening," the Nephite colonists see in Isaiah 52:7–10 an outline of their own then-recent colonizing experience, as if their adventures in Lamanite territory have fulfilled the prophecy: Isaiah anticipated that the Lord would "bring again Zion," and the colonists have seen their own lost lands of inheritance restored to them; the "waste places" of their "Jerusalem" can "sing together" because it has been "redeemed"; undoubtedly, they feel that God has "made bare his holy arm in the eyes of all the nations"—at least of those nations that matter to them: the Lamanites—given their belief that their military victories amount to divinely granted "salvation." It seems readers of the Book of Mormon are intended to understand that the colonists under Zeniff and Noah have come to see Isaiah 52:8–10 as applicable not only to exiled Judah's return to Jerusalem, but also to the restoration of certain Nephites to the lands of their inheritance.[42] And so

---

moreover, he produces some of the best available exegesis of the Abinadi story as well. See John W. Welch, *The Legal Cases in the Book of Mormon* (Provo: Brigham Young University Press, 2008).

41. See Joseph Fielding McConkie and Robert L. Millet, *Doctrinal Commentary on the Book of Mormon*, vol. 2, *Jacob through Mosiah* (Salt Lake City: Bookcraft, 1988), 208; Hugh Nibley, *Teachings of the Book of Mormon: Transcripts of Lectures Presented to an Honors Book of Mormon Class at Brigham Young University, 1988–1990*, 4 vols. (Foundation for Ancient Research & Mormon Studies, 1993), 2:71; Pike, "Imagery of Isaiah 52:7–10," 264; Welch, *Legal Cases*, 176; Spencer, *An Other Testament*, 142–45.

42. It is interesting that the Book of Mormon leaves the colonists' interpretation of Isaiah 52:7–10 unstated, even if it is relatively obvious what it is supposed to be. At this point, the Book of Mormon invites speculation and reconstruction of the text's assumed historical background, where one might instead expect—given the volume's unquestionably didactic style—a kind of point-by-point summary of the

readers are intended also to understand that the priests, and perhaps the colonists more generally, understand the basic meaning of Isaiah 52:7, with its talk of beautiful feet and "good tidings of good," to be that prophets will not only speak of restoration and deliverance. Abinadi's dour prophetic message contradicts the spirit of this interpretation.

The uneasy proximity between this priestly interpretation in the Book of Mosiah and the implicit interpretation attributed to Nephi earlier in the Book of Mormon deserves careful notice. Both extract from Isaiah certain historical patterns that are then reapplied to events more relevant to Book of Mormon peoples. But while Nephi's interpretation reapplies Isaianic patterns to events he sees in visions, events thousands of years in the future, the priests reapply Isaianic patterns to events in their own time—events they themselves live through. This difference is surely important, but it does not make irrelevant the more general proximity between the two interpretations. Readers of the Book of Mormon who come to the story of Abinadi after dutifully imbibing the spirit of Nephi's approach to Isaiah should feel as if Noah's priests represent just a slightly corrupted version of Nephi's interpretive strategy. The priests' question regarding the meaning of Isaiah 52:7–10 seems intended to suggest that something has gone awry in Nephi's long-standing Isaianic program, revealing it as potentially dangerous. Unless subtle differences between Nephi's original approach to Isaiah and that of Noah's priests can be teased out, the weaknesses of Nephi's approach might outweigh its strengths.[43]

Strikingly, Abinadi's response to the priests' question concerning Isaiah is not to draw out the subtle differences between Nephi's and their ap-

---

colonists' point of view. Although the Book of Mormon makes the interpretation of Isaiah 52:7–10 a central question beginning with the story of Abinadi, it never strains itself in presenting the whole panoply of interpretive options; instead, it leaves to the reader to do the detective work necessary to reconstruct certain interpretations that the authorial voices in the text clearly mean to reject as viable options. This is in itself a noteworthy bit of literary artistry. As Hardy (borrowing from Mark Twain's description of Wagnerian opera) says of the Book of Mormon more generally, it is "better than it sounds." Hardy, *Understanding the Book of Mormon*, 273.

43. Perhaps the Book of Mormon wishes its readers to understand that Nephi himself was aware of this potential difficulty. After all of his careful interpretive work on Isaiah, he concludes his record in mourning "because of the unbelief, and the wickedness, and the ignorance, and the stiffneckedness of men—for they will not search knowledge, nor understand great knowledge, when it is given unto them in plainness, even as plain as word can be" (2 Ne. 32:7).

proaches to the prophet.[44] Instead, he offers a drastically distinct—and entirely non-Nephi-like—interpretation of the Isaianic text, one that develops over the course of several pages. Abinadi entirely abandons the idea of "likening" the text, assuming instead that Isaiah's prophecies are straightforward prophecies of very specific events, events quite distinct from those surrounding Judah's sixth century exile in Babylon. Furthermore, the events of which Abinadi sees Isaiah prophesying transcend the whole larger history of covenant Israel. Where Nephi and Noah's priests interpret Isaiah as speaking forcefully and directly to the historical experience of covenant peoples (Judah, the New-Word remnant, and even the Nephites of Zeniff's generation), Abinadi takes Isaiah's prophecies as describing events that, from his perspective, supersede covenantal history. In a word, Abinadi develops an emphatically Christological interpretation of Isaiah 52:7–10.[45]

Abinadi's interpretation is in no way presented as straightforward, however. In a remarkably sophisticated interpretation, Abinadi uses Isaiah 53 as a hermeneutic key for Isaiah 52:7–10, apparently motivated by two linguistic or thematic connections between Isaiah 52:7–10 and Isaiah 53:1. Both passages focus on preaching or reporting (compare Isaiah 52:7 and 53:1),[46] and both contain references to "the arm of the Lord" (compare

---

44. It seems to be significant that Noah's priests never identify Isaiah by name, though they quote four full verses from Isaiah 52. It is only Abinadi who goes on to identify the author of the passage (see Mosiah 14:1), almost as if the priests knew the words only as an authoritative saying, rather than as a specifically Isaianic word.

45. Of course, messianism—and therefore every Christology—unquestionably has its original context in Jewish thought and history. In saying that Abinadi's Christological interpretation of Isaiah focuses on events superseding covenantal and non-covenantal history, I mean just to indicate that the sort of Christianity Abinadi represents is so deeply universalist that it never raises the question of its universalism. That is, Abinadi's sort of Christianity never points out that the universal implications of Christian atonement undermine the difference between covenantal and non-covenantal peoples; it simply is universal. In Abinadi's teachings and those presented in the Book of Mormon as having been influenced by him, there simply is no talk whatsoever of Jews/Israelites or of Gentiles. Christianity is a message presented simply and solely to human beings, the children of God. It is in this sense that Abinadi clearly shifts the basic nature of Nephite interpretation of Isaiah.

46. It should be noted that Saint Paul explicitly draws a connection between these two passages in Romans 10:13–17, in connection with his theology of preaching. As it reads in the King James Version, here is the passage: "For whosoever shall call upon the name of the Lord shall be saved. How then shall they call on him

Isaiah 52:10 and 53:1). What Isaiah 53:1 has to say about preaching—that many fail to "believe" the prophet's "report"—indicates that the priests' optimistic interpretation of Isaiah 52:7 ("good tidings of good") moves far too quickly. Similarly, what Isaiah 53:1 has to say about the Lord's arm— that it remains a question "to whom" exactly it is "revealed"—in turn indicates that the colonists' interpretation of Isaiah 52:10 ("in the eyes of all the nations") assumes too much. According to Abinadi, the book of Isaiah itself directly complicates the meaning of Isaiah 52:7–10. And the fact that Isaiah 53:1 introduces what Abinadi understands—in classically Christian fashion—to be a clear prophecy of Jesus's suffering is supposed to indicate that the meaning of Isaiah 52:7–10 has more to do with Jesus and with Christian atonement than with anything else.[47]

Abinadi's use of Isaiah 53 as a hermeneutic lens for Isaiah 52:7–10 is more complicated still, however. After quoting the whole of Isaiah 53 as

---

in whom they have not believed? And how shall they believe in him of whom they have not heard? And how shall they hear without a preach? And how shall they preach, except they be sent? As it is written, How beautiful are the feet of them that preach the gospel of peace, and bring glad tidings of good things! But they have not all obeyed the gospel. For Esaias saith, Lord, who hath believed our report? So then faith cometh by hearing, and hearing by the word of God." Abinadi's (somewhat implicit) linking of these same two texts suggests some kind of intertextual connection with Romans 10, but not enough to draw out the full weight of Paul's argument, which concerns quite precisely the relationship between Jews and gentiles. On questions of the relationship between the Book of Mormon and New Testament language and ideas, see Nicholas J. Frederick, "Evaluating the Interaction between the New Testament and the Book of Mormon: A Proposed Methodology," *Journal of Book of Mormon Studies* 24 (2015): 1–30.

47. It seems significant that the Book of Mormon nowhere contests or complicates Abinadi's Christological interpretation of Isaiah 53—though it must be said that no one apart from Abinadi ever really says a word about Isaiah 53. It is not clear whether this is supposed to suggest that all prophetic voices represented in the Book of Mormon would have agreed on the Christological meaning of Isaiah 53, or whether readers are to assume that Nephi (for instance) would have had a non-Christological interpretation of Isaiah 53. This remains an open question—and a deeply interesting one, given the long history of debate concerning the meaning of the song of the suffering servant. To get a good sense of the current status of the discussion, see Bernd Janowski and Peter Stuhlmacher, eds., *The Suffering Servant: Isaiah 53 in Jewish and Christian Sources* (Grand Rapids: Eerdmans, 2004). For a careful but largely traditional approach to Isaiah 53 in the Book of Mormon, see John W. Welch, "Isaiah 53, Mosiah 14, and the Book of Mormon," in Parry and Welch, eds., *Isaiah in the Book of Mormon*, 293–312.

evidence that "all the prophets which have prophesied ever since the world began" have "said that God himself should come down among the children of men" (Mosiah 13:33–34), Abinadi presents a fascinating interpretation of the song of the suffering servant, an interpretation focused most intensely on just two aspects of the text: its talk of "generation" ("And who shall declare his generation?") and its talk of "seed" ("When thou shalt make his soul an offering for sin, he shall see his seed").[48] The former detail Abinadi appears to interpret in a patristic fashion, understanding the prophet's question about the servant's generation to express awe at the mystery of divine incarnation (see Mosiah 15:1–10).[49] The reference to seed, however, proves more essential to Abinadi's interpretation of Isaiah 52:7–10. Making up Christ's seed, according to Abinadi, is "whosoever hath heard the words of the prophets . . . and believed [before the event] that the Lord would redeem his people" (Mosiah 15:11), along with "all the holy prophets" themselves, those who prophesied of the redemptive event (v. 13).

What makes the prophets and their disciples Christ's seed is, according to Abinadi, the fact that they are to rise with him at his resurrection. Abinadi explains:

> The Son reigneth and hath power over the dead; therefore he bringeth to pass the resurrection of the dead. And there cometh a resurrection—even a first resurrection—yea, even a resurrection of those that have been and which are and which shall be, even until the resurrection of Christ (for so shall he be called). And now, the resurrection of all the prophets, and all those that have

---

48. Some Mormon interpreters have noted the similarity between the Hebrew term translated "arm" in Isaiah 53:1 and the Hebrew term translated "seed" in Isaiah 53:10, reading some significance into the possible connection. See, for instance, George Reynolds and Jane M. Sjodahl, *Commentary on the Book of Mormon,* ed. Philip C Reynolds, 7 vols. (Salt Lake City: Deseret Book, 1972), 2:155.

49. The passage in which Abinadi offers his interpretation of the servant's "generation" is among the most difficult in the Book of Mormon and one that often frustrates lay Latter-day Saint readers, because it seems to espouse a theological conception of God eventually rejected by Joseph Smith and officially rejected by the Latter-day Saint Church today. Nonetheless, it does seem that the passage can be consistently read as consonant with current Latter-day Saint theological commitments. For a standard such interpretation, see McConkie and Millet, *Jacob through Mosiah,* 225–34. For examples of the patristic interpretation, see Mark W. Elliott, ed., *Isaiah 40–66,* Ancient Christian Commentary on Scripture (Downers Grove: Inter-Varsity Press, 2007), 167–68; Robert Louis Wilken, Angela Russell Christman, and Michael J. Hollerich, eds. and trans., *Isaiah Interpreted by Early Christian and Medieval Commentators* (Grand Rapids: Eerdmans, 2007), 419, 427, 429.

believed in their words—or all those that have kept the commandments of God—these shall come forth in the first resurrection. (Mosiah 15:20–22)

Abinadi here imagines that pre-Christian prophets (whom he understands as prophesying directly of Jesus) and their believing disciples will rise together at Christ's resurrection, such that he will "see" them ("he shall see his seed"). And these prophets he then praises in explicitly Isaianic terms: "These are they which hath published peace, that hath brought good tidings of good, that hath published salvation, that saith unto Zion, 'Thy God reigneth!' And O! How Beautiful upon the mountains were their feet!" (Mosiah 15:14–15). For Abinadi, the key to understanding Isaiah 52:7, with its talk of publishing peace and beautiful swift feet on the mountains, is Isaiah 53:10, understood as a prophecy of a "first resurrection" at the time of Christ's rising from the dead.

As he continues, Abinadi turns next to the scandal of particularity. That is, he recognizes that the Christian story of salvation seems to leave whole swaths of the human family entirely out of account.[50] His first response to this worry simply insists (like other voices in the Book of Mormon) that all who "have died, before Christ came, in their ignorance, not having salvation declared unto them," will nonetheless "have part in the first resurrection" along with the prophets and their disciples (Mosiah 15:24).[51] But then Abinadi goes on to claim that particularity will be swallowed up in universality after Christ's resurrection: "I say unto you that the time shall come that the salvation of the Lord shall be declared to every nation, kindred, tongue, and people" (v. 28). And significantly, Abinadi links this idea directly to Isaiah 52:8–10—especially (it seems) to verse 10: "The Lord hath made bare his holy arm in the eyes of all the nations, and all the ends of the earth shall see the salvation of our God" (v. 31). For Abinadi, when Isaiah speaks of people seeing "eye to eye," he has reference to an eventually universal Christianity, the result of "the watchmen . . . lift[ing] up their voice" to announce that "the Lord hath comforted his people" in redemption from death (vv. 29–30).[52]

---

50. The scandal of particularity was a constant concern for Mormonism's founder, Joseph Smith. See Samuel Morris Brown, *In Heaven as It Is on Earth: Joseph Smith and the Early Mormon Conquest of Death* (New York: Oxford University Press, 2012), 203–47.

51. For similar passages in the Book of Mormon, see 2 Nephi 9:20–27; Mosiah 3:9–12; and Moroni 8:20–23.

52. It is tempting to suggest that Abinadi is supposed to understand Isaiah's talk of seeing "eye to eye" as a description also of the first resurrection, of the prophets

Through the story of Abinadi, the Book of Mormon thus develops a rich and complex Christological interpretation of Isaiah 52:7–10, placing it alongside and in tension with the entirely non-Christological interpretations of Noah's priests and of Nephi. Viewed through the lens of Isaiah 53 (also interpreted Christologically), Isaiah 52:7–10 first praises pre-Christian prophets who explicitly anticipate the coming of the Messiah. It then goes on to describe how the same prophetic message, after the Christic event, will spread through the world, until all human beings see "eye to eye" and recognize that "the Lord hath comforted his people." The eventual spread of the Christian message then amounts to the making bare of the Lord's arm before all nations. For Abinadi, apparently none of this has to do with ancient Judah's exile in Babylon or even with any likening of that exile to other moments in Israel's history.[53]

And, as already noted, once the Abinadi narrative comes to a close, the reader naturally feels as if the whole question of Isaiah's meaning has been decided. Not only do references to and discussions about Isaiah largely disappear from the Book of Mormon until the resurrected Christ makes his appearance,[54] but the narrative reports the creation of a kind of Abinadite church—a pre-Christian "church of anticipation"[55]—that solidifies and institutionalizes his message and, presumably, his approach to

---

and their disciples seeing each other eye to eye with Christ, who sees them as his seed when he rises from the dead. It seems more straightforwardly to be the case, however, given the placement of the final quotation if Isaiah 52:8–10 within Abinadi's defense, that he is supposed to understand Isaiah's talk of seeing "eye to eye" to refer specifically to the eventual development of universal Christianity.

53. Occasional references in Abinadi's defense to God redeeming "his people" perhaps suggest that he is to be understood as having an eye to Judah's or Israel's historical redemption, rather than to the redemption of human beings (collectively understood as God's children and therefore as God's people). This remains unclear, however.

54. Significantly, there are two passing references to Isaiah 52:7 in Mosiah 18:30 and Mosiah 27:37, in each case describing as instances of publishing peace the successes of Nephite Christians in preaching and missionizing. These references only suggest all the more straightforwardly that Abinadi's interpretation of Isaiah is supposed to be read as generally accepted after his prophetic intervention.

55. I take this term from Hugh Nibley's analysis of the Nephite church. See Hugh Nibley, *An Approach to the Book of Mormon* 2nd ed. (Salt Lake City: Deseret Book, 1979), 130–33.

Isaiah.[56] Eventually, however, questions about the interpretation of Isaiah are raised anew, and thereafter Isaiah remains a relatively consistent focus in the Book of Mormon. Significantly, the chief focus of the reemergence of Isaianic interpretation continues to be Isaiah 52:7–10.

Isaiah 52:7–10 For and After Christ

As already mentioned, the Book of Mormon comes to an unmistakable climax when Jesus Christ, resurrected from the dead, appears among the children of Lehi. The account of that appearance focuses on the events of just two days, when Christ instructs New-World Israelites. Early in the first day, Christ quotes Isaiah 52:8–10 and offers a preliminary interpretation by clarifying the circumstances of the prophecy's fulfilment. Echoing Nephi's prophecies, he describes a history of Jewish diaspora after Jerusalem's destruction, and then of Josephite devastation when Europeans arrive in the Americas in the early modern period. Christ then speaks of "that day when the gentiles shall sin against my gospel and shall reject the fullness of my gospel," when he will "remember my covenant" to Israel (3 Ne. 16:10–11). Then, he claims, Gentiles in the New World will face destruction unless they "repent" and are "numbered among . . . [the] house of Israel" (v. 13). Describing this destruction of non-Israelite Christians, the Book of Mormon's Christ draws on Micah 5:8: "I will suffer my people, O house of Israel, that they shall go through among [New-World Gentiles] and shall tread them down" (3 Ne. 16:15). And then, when unfaithful Gentiles are eliminated and faithful Israel restored, "the words of the prophet Isaiah shall be fulfilled" (v. 17). Christ identifies the words he has in mind by quoting, specifically, Isaiah 52:8–10 (see 3 Ne. 16:18–20).[57]

---

56. The Nephite Christian church explicitly uses "the words of Abinadi" as their core text according to Mosiah 18:1.

57. There is some difficulty in the text of the Book of Mormon at this point. Recent and current editions of the text have Christ state that it is "then" (that is, at the time of gentile destruction) that "the words of the prophet Isaiah shall be fulfilled." All earlier editions and the only available pre-printing manuscript of the text, however, have the word "when" in the place of "then." See the discussion in Royal Skousen, *Analysis of Textual Variants of the Book of Mormon*, 6 vols. (Provo: Foundation for Ancient Research & Mormon Studies, 2004–2009), 5:3409–11. If one follows the earlier version (which seems clearly to be what Joseph Smith himself dictated originally), then it seems that the fulfillment of Isaiah 52:8–10 is something the visiting Christ introduces as something occurring only *after* the

But as soon as Christ quotes this passage from Isaiah, his sermonizing breaks off. He gazes on his audience and sees that they "cannot understand" his meaning (3 Ne. 17:2). Consequently, he dedicates the remainder of his first day with them to preparations for a second day of sermonizing. And after proper preliminaries on the second day, he returns to the Isaiah text:

> Behold, now I finish the commandment which the Father hath commanded me concerning this people. . . . Ye remember that I spake unto you and said that when the words of Isaiah should be fulfilled—behold, they are written, ye have them before you, therefore search them—and verily, verily I say unto you, that when they shall be fulfilled, then is the fulfilling of the covenant which the Father hath made unto his people. (20:10–12)[58]

In this connection, the Book of Mormon's Christ again quotes from the prophet Micah, but now more fully and more disconcertingly: "if the gentiles do not repent. . . , then shall ye which are a remnant of the house of Jacob go forth among them, and ye shall be in the midst of them as a lion among the beasts of the forest, and as a young lion among the flocks of sheep who, if he goeth through, but treadeth down and teareth in pieces—and none can deliver" (vv. 15–16). Christ's first interpretation of Isaiah 52:8–10 is thus consistent. The passage, for the Book of Mormon's Christ, finds initial fulfillment when the Lord's favor shifts from Gentiles (European Christians) to scattered Israel (in particular the New-World Josephites), with the latter rising up apocalyptically against the former.[59]

Further along in the second day of instruction, Christ again returns to Isaiah 52:8–10, but now apparently by outlining a *second* fulfillment of the prophecy. Describing the time when, after gentile destruction and Josephite restoration in the New World, "the fullness of [the] gospel shall be preached" to Jews returning to Jerusalem (3 Ne. 20:30),[60] Christ says the following:

---

destruction of the Gentiles—rather than as effectively equivalent to or at least concurrent with the destruction of the Gentiles.

58. Other passages from Micah appear in the course of Christ's sermonizing in the Book of Mormon, though relatively little has been written on this subject by interpreters of the text. Significantly, attention is paid particularly to passages from Micah focused on the theme of the remnant, suggesting a deliberate hermeneutic running in clear parallel to that associated in the Book of Mormon with Isaiah.

59. For a brilliant analysis of the Book of Mormon's discussions of this eventual shift away from European religious hegemony, see Hickman, "Book of Mormon."

60. The Book of Mormon, with relative consistency, anticipates the conversion of Jews to at least some form of Chrisitanity. For discussion of the relevant texts, as well

And they shall believe in me—that I am Jesus Christ, the Son of God—and shall pray unto the Father in my name. Then shall their watchmen lift up their voice, and with the voice together shall they sing, for they shall see eye to eye. Then will the Father gather them together again and give unto them Jerusalem for the land of their inheritance. Then shall they break forth into joy. Sing together, ye waste places of Jerusalem! For the Father hath comforted his people! He hath redeemed Jerusalem! The Father hath made bare his holy arm in the eyes of all the nations, and all the ends of the earth shall see the salvation of the Father! (vv. 31–35)

Here Christ in the Book of Mormon takes Isaiah 52:8–10 to be fulfilled a second time by events specifically centered around Jews, rather than (as at first) around other Israelites experiencing restoration. Interestingly, where the first fulfilment of the prophecy identified by Christ arguably understands Isaianic references to Jerusalem as metaphorical, the second fulfilment seems to take the text literally because it occurs along with an actual return of the Jews to Jerusalem.[61] At the same time, where the first fulfilment is identified with a straightforward quotation of Isaiah 52:8–10 as it stands in the King James Bible, the second fulfilment is identified in connection with an altered text of Isaiah 52:8–10 (references to "the Lord" being replaced by references to "the Father," for instance).[62] There are, then, differences between the actual texts of the prophecy fulfilled in each instance, as well as between the way certain common words in both texts are referentially understood. The second fulfilment of Isaiah 52:8–10

---

as of the political and ethical difficulties, see Steven Epperson, *Mormons and Jews: Early Mormon Theologies of Israel* (Salt Lake City: Signature Books, 1992), 19–41.

61. Presumably, the references to Jerusalem in Isaiah 52:8–10 in its first fulfillment are to be understood as references to what Christ in the Book of Mormon calls "the new Jerusalem," to be built in the New World for gathered Josephites (see 3 Nephi 20:22; 21:23, 24; as well as the discussion later in the Book of Mormon in Ether 12:2–10). This theme is one Joseph Smith developed later in more detail in his own revelations and writings.

62. The references in the variant text to "the Father" play into a much larger theme in Christ's two days of instruction. From the beginning of the first day, Christ identifies a Nephite debate regarding the respective natures of the Father and the Son, attempting to clarify things (see 3 Ne. 11:21–39). From there, the relationship between Father and Son is a constant theme in Christ's sermonizing. Note that the quotation of Isaiah 52:8–10 is followed, in connection with the second fulfillment, with "And the Father and I are one" (3 Ne. 20:35), an apparent allusion to John 10:30 (one of the many allusions to Johannine texts in this portion of the Book of Mormon; see the following note).

is immediately followed by quotations of most of the remainder of Isaiah 52, including verse 7 with its talk of beautiful feet and published peace.

At its climax, then, the Book of Mormon adds yet another approach to Isaiah 52:7–10 to the interpretations offered earlier in the volume. Significantly, this fourth interpretation shares some elements with Nephi's approach but other elements with Abinadi's approach, as if it completely fused the two. Unlike Nephi but like Abinadi, Christ does not understand Isaiah's prophecies to require a program of likening; rather, he seems to regard Isaiah 52:7–10 to be a straightforward prophecy of readily specifiable events. But unlike Abinadi and like Nephi, Christ understands the events in question to be not the founding events of Christianity, but those surrounding the restoration of Israelites to situations of peace (Jews *and* Josephites). In another, essential way, however, Christ goes beyond both Nephi and Abinadi in his interpretation, since, as the fully divine Christ,[63] he is free to articulate the fulfilment of Isaiah's prophecy by both quoting it as it stands in the Bible and deliberately manipulating the text to make it say what he wishes it to say. Christ exhibits a certain textual freedom with Isaiah that neither Abinadi nor Nephi exhibits in exactly the same way.[64]

Simultaneously, Christ in the Book of Mormon stages a hermeneutical defense of his interpretation of Isaiah 52:7–10. To secure the meaning of Isaiah's prophecy, he connects it to Isaiah 54 (see 3 Ne. 22), exhibiting a

---

63. In a crucial study, Krister Stendahl has argued that the Christ of the Book of Mormon is emphatically the Christ of the Johannine literature—divine through and through. He makes this case through a careful analysis of the Book of Mormon's presentation of the Matthean Sermon on the Mount, noting the ways in which slight variants in the Book of Mormon's version of the text suggest a kind of Johannine redaction. See Krister Stendahl, "The Sermon on the Mount and Third Nephi," in *Reflections on Mormonism: Judaeo-Christian Parallels*, ed. Truman G. Madsen (Provo: Religious Studies Center, Brigham Young University, 1978), 139–54. On Johannine themes in the Book of Mormon (and Mormon scripture) more generally, see Nicholas J. Frederick, *The Bible, Mormon Scripture, and the Rhetoric of Allusivity* (Madison: Fairleigh Dickinson University Press, 2016).

64. Nephi too exhibits some freedom with certain Isaiah texts, especially with Isaiah 29. See, for instance, the helpful discussion in Grant Hardy and Heather Hardy, "How Nephi Shapes His Readers' Perceptions of Isaiah," in *Reading Nephi Reading Isaiah: 2 Nephi 26–27*, ed. Joseph M. Spencer and Jenny Webb (Provo: Neal A. Maxwell Institute, Brigham Young University, 2016), 37–62. At the same time, there is a different feel about Christ's manipulation of Isaiah 52:8–10 compared to Nephi's handling of Isaiah 29. A defense of this point in full would, however, require too much space to justify including it here.

hermeneutic distinct from Abinadi's, who (as discussed above) connects it to Isaiah 53. The Christ of the Book of Mormon thus appears to see a continuous story that begins in Isaiah 52, leaps right over Isaiah 53, and proceeds in Isaiah 54—a story exclusively (and consistently) about Israel's redemption, whether Old-World Judahites or New-World Josephites. In other words, rather than looking at Isaiah 52:7–10 through the lens of what Isaiah 53 might say about the singular messianic servant of God, Christ looks at the passage through the lens of what Isaiah 54 has to say about the plural covenant-bound servants of the Lord (see Isa. 54:17; 3 Ne. 22:17).[65] And he concludes his recitation of Isaiah 54 with these words: "Ye had ought to search these things diligently—for great is the words of Isaiah" (3 Ne. 23:1). Thus, *the* text to which Christ points his New-World audience—and to which he points the Book of Mormon's modern readership—is Isaiah 54.

Significantly, something of an emphasis on the relationship between Isaiah 52 and Isaiah 54 continues to the end of the Book of Mormon, as if to indicate the influence and centrality of Christ's linking of these two texts. Most illustrative is an example from the final verses of the book. There, Moroni, son of Mormon and the volume's final contributor, concludes the record by weaving language from Isaiah 52:1–2 and Isaiah 54:1–4. First, from the opening of Isaiah 52: "Awake and arise from the dust, O Jerusalem! Yea, and put on thy beautiful garments, O daughter of Zion!" (Moro. 10:31). But then, in place of the promise that follows in Isaiah 52, Moroni draws from the first verses of Isaiah 54: "And strengthen thy stakes and enlarge thy borders forever, that thou mayest no more be confounded!" (Moro. 10:31). This weaving reproduces Christ's hermeneutic earlier in the Book of Mormon, where Isaiah 52:7–10 is quoted alongside both Isaiah 52:1–2 and the whole of Isaiah 54.[66] From Christ's appearance to the end of the volume, Isaiah 54 serves as the hermeneutic key for making sense of the Isaiah passage with which the Book of

---

65. It is often noted that Second Isaiah concludes with a pluralizing of the singular servant that is the focus of much of the text before the prophet's final words. In Isaiah 54:17, the one "servant of the Lord" gives way to "the servants of the Lord." See, for instance, Childs, *Isaiah*, 430–31. For some theologically inflected discussion of the possible significance of this shift from servant to servants, see Edgar W. Conrad, *Reading Isaiah* (Minneapolis: Fortress, 1991), 143–52.

66. As mentioned before, Christ quotes much of Isaiah 52 in the wake of his second quotation of Isaiah 52:8–10, and the very first of what he quotes (in fact immediately after completing the second quotation of Isaiah 52:8–10) is Isaiah 52:1–2 (see 3 Ne. 20:36–37).

Mormon most consistently concerns itself.[67] Similarly, direct echoes of Christ's recommendation to study Isaiah diligently appear in later portions of the Book of Mormon alongside imitations of his hermeneutic.[68]

With this interpretation of Isaiah 52:7–10 attributed to the resurrected Christ himself, the Book of Mormon tallies up four distinct approaches to the passage, only one of which—that of Noah's priests—is ever explicitly rejected as in some way corrupt. Christ's approach in certain ways draws on its predecessors within the volume, but it also forges ahead in new directions as well. A few words of conclusion and synthesis might bring the whole picture into focus.

Synthesis and Conclusion

In her dated but still-popular biography of Joseph Smith, Fawn Brodie suggests that whenever, in producing the Book of Mormon, Smith's "literary reservoir . . . ran dry," he "simply arranged for his Nephite prophets to quote from the Bible."[69] The evidence reviewed here, however, suggests that it is precisely where the Book of Mormon directly interacts with biblical texts that it exhibits its most compelling literary artfulness.[70] But more than art, study of the uses of Isaiah in the Book of Mormon suggests interpretive care and theological novelty.

The Book of Mormon illustrates at least four distinct interpretive strategies for making sense of just one representative passage of Isaiah. One of these is introduced into the story only to be rejected as the work of corrupt priests, but the other three it presents as good and right ways of understanding Isaiah. Significantly, it presents each of the three "approved" approaches to Isaiah as arising in unique circumstances, always at some historical distance from the emergence of the others. The first (originating with Nephi) appears at the volume's outset, presented as taking shape six centuries before the Christian era and motivated by an apocalyptic vision of the future. The

---

67. For a representative Latter-day Saint study of Isaiah 54, see Cynthia L. Hallen, "The Lord's Covenant of Kindness: Isaiah 54 and 3 Nephi 22," in Parry and Welch, *Isaiah in the Book of Mormon*, 313–49.

68. The most significant of these appears in Mormon 8:21–26, again in the voice of Moroni.

69. Fawn M. Brodie, *No Man Knows My History: The Life of Joseph Smith, the Mormon Prophet*, 2nd ed. (New York: Vintage, 1995), 58.

70. See Philip L. Barlow, *Mormons and the Bible: The Place of the Latter-day Saints in American Religion*, 2nd ed. (New York: Oxford University Press, 2013), 26–33.

second (originating with Abinadi) appears four centuries later, in response to corruption of Isaianic interpretation, but it then serves as the foundation for a new spiritual movement. The third (originating with Christ himself) emerges only in the Christian era, refocusing biblical interpretation more generally and remaining normative to the end of the volume. Although this last approach is privileged above the others to the extent that its author is Christ, the Book of Mormon never directly asks readers to prefer one approach above another. Instead, the book invites reflection on the idea that prophets in different contexts—along with Jesus Christ himself—might exhibit different approaches to sacred texts. In a sense, then, the Book of Mormon itself presents a reception history, a history of varying interpretations of one passage of Isaiah over a thousand years.

These three (affirmed) approaches to Isaiah 52:7–10, moreover, cannot be easily reconciled with each other. Christ and Nephi regard Isaiah's prophecies as applicable to both Jewish and Josephite branches of Israel, but Christ understands that double applicability to be the prophet's intention while Nephi understands Isaiah as addressing himself intentionally only to Jewish history. Again, Abinadi and Christ see Isaiah's prophecies as literally fulfilled by events long after Judah's exile in Babylon, but Abinadi identifies those events with the resurrection of Jesus Christ while Christ identifies those events with Israel's eschatological redemption. Nephi regards Isaiah 52: 7–10 as relevant but less central than certain other Isaianic texts (such as Isaiah 11, 29, or 49), while Abinadi and Christ regard Isaiah 52:7–10 as the most central of all Isaianic texts. Abinadi uses Isaiah 53 as a hermeneutic lens for understanding Isaiah 52:7–10, while Christ takes Isaiah 54 as his own hermeneutic lens. Only Christ among the three indicates that the text of Isaiah can be heavily manipulated for purposes of preaching. In short, although there are certain constants in the Book of Mormon's treatment of Isaiah, there is much that varies as well, and in significant ways.

The Book of Mormon explicitly and emphatically presents this whole complex history of Nephite Isaianic interpretation as relevant to the nineteenth-century context in which the book first appeared. Despite the fact that the volume presents its story as occurring anciently, it insists that its history of interpretation speaks directly to the modern world. The volume's final contributor, Moroni, strongly commands the book's latter-day readers to "search the prophecies of Isaiah" (Morm. 8:23) because he has seen such readers' era. "I speak unto you as if ye were present, and yet ye are not—but behold, Jesus Christ hath shewn you unto me, and I know your doing" (v. 35). Much earlier in the Book of Mormon, Nephi similarly explains that he prophetically knows that people living at the time of the Book's publication "shall know of a surety" that "the prophecies of Isaiah shall be fulfilled" (2 Ne. 25:7). Nephi in fact claims that he includes Isaiah in his writings because he knows that it will be "of great worth unto them in the last days" (v. 8). Thus, from beginning to end, the Book of Mormon seems to aim—and perhaps explicitly—at arguing that Isaiah's prophecies are relevant to religious controversies in nineteenth-century Christianity. It seems to see why some might follow the long Christian tradition of interpreting the book of Isaiah as containing prophecies of Christ. But it also seems to see why others might understand Isaiah as focusing more on ancient Jewish history, while seeing his words as applicable to other Israelite groups. Above all, it seems to urge its readers to imitate Jesus Christ in understanding Isaiah's prophecies as focusing on the eventual redemption of all Israel after European Christianity has overgrown its roots. The only approach to Isaiah it explicitly rejects is one that, like that of Noah's priests, uses the prophet to justify corruption.

But more work remains to be done. This paper provides only a sketch of what the Book of Mormon does with one relatively brief passage from Isaiah. Close analysis of its varied uses of other Isaiah passages—and perhaps of biblical texts more generally—should reveal a still-richer picture.

Chapter Ten

The Book of Mormon's Use of Isaiah 53

Latter-day Saints tend to resent the presence of Isaiah in the Book of Mormon except in one case. After King Noah's priests ask Abinadi to explain a certain passage of Isaiah, he responds by turning first to another—and much longer—passage of Isaiah. He quotes in full Isaiah 53, the long song of the suffering servant, tying it explicitly to the coming of Jesus Christ. In part thanks to Abinadi's sermon, but likely just as much due to the popularity of Handel's Messiah, Latter-day Saints know and are comfortable with this particular stretch of the book of Isaiah. Where the long block of Isaiah quotation in the middle of Second Nephi puzzles and frustrates many readers, Abinadi's turn to Isaiah 53 encourages and inspires most readers. Familiarity and comfort, however, can make it difficult to raise the right questions about what Abinadi means to do in quoting and explaining Isaiah. We tend to see him making an obvious move in responding to the priests. The Book of Mormon seems rather to wish us to see him as making a surprising and innovative one.

The importance of Abinadi's quotation of Isaiah 53 begins to become clear when one becomes acquainted with the long history of how Jews and Christians have interpreted that chapter. It should be no surprise that Jews and Christians alike have read this rich and rewarding poem from Isaiah with their own theological questions in mind. What happens, though, when one asks how Abinadi's treatment of the poem compares or contrasts with traditional theological interpretations of various sorts? As I was working on sorting out this issue for myself in the course of a larger book project (still in process, but nearing completion), I decided to write a short essay on the subject to present to non-Latter-day Saint scholars for response. Accordingly, I sketched this paper.

I delivered this previously unpublished paper at the 2018 annual meetings of the Society for Biblical Literature, held in Denver, Colorado.

Drastically underrepresented in the literature on biblical reception is the interpretation of biblical texts in Mormon scripture. Mormons today experience the Bible principally through its re-presentation in these unique scriptures; their experience of the Bible is heavily mediated—especially by the Book of Mormon, first published in 1830. Therefore, not only might one read the Book of Mormon as *containing* a wealth of reception-historical details, one might understand the Book of Mormon to be always *producing* a wealth of further reception-historical details through its influence. There's reason to ask how this volume of scripture recasts the Bible.

Any reader of the Book of Mormon immediately notes that it is deliberately biblical in its self-presentation. It uses the archaic style of the King James Bible throughout, and it's sprinkled with turns of phrase familiar from the King James New Testament. Moreover, many of its stories are strikingly inventive variations on biblical narratives, theologically instructive recastings of familiar biblical stories. Here, though, I'll be reaching for even lower-hanging fruit. The Book of Mormon contains biblical commentary of a more direct nature, though it too has largely been ignored in work on reception history (and though questions of reception history have largely been ignored by those looking at the Book of Mormon). Most important here is the volume's treatment of Isaiah. It quotes from and comments on almost a third of the book of Isaiah. And how does the Book of Mormon understand that particular prophetic book? This question has an answer too complex even to summarize here. But I might lay the foundation of an answer by looking at one particularly well-known Isaiah text in the Book of Mormon. How does the volume react to the so-called "song of the suffering servant," Isaiah 53?

This particular Isaiah text has of course been a bone of contention between Jewish and Christian interpreters for centuries. Already in the second century, one finds it weaponized by Christians against Jews (as in Justin Martyr's *Dialogue with Trypho*), and the earliest great commentaries on Isaiah still extant (from the fourth and fifth centuries) repeatedly contend with "Judaizing" interpreters who would historicize the text. Highly publicized Christian disputations with famous Jews in the thirteenth and fifteenth centuries demonstrate continued focus on Isaiah 53 in adjudicating the relationship between Judaism and Christianity. And little has changed on this score. There appeared as recently as 2012 a semi-academic collection of essays aimed at revitalizing Christian missionizing among Jews with the help of the fourth servant song. For its part, the Book of Mormon also weighs in on the meaning of Isaiah 53, in particular on its relevance to debates between Jews and Christians. But it does so in a theologically provocative way—or so I'll try to show.

One might expect numerous interactions with Isaiah 53 from a book so insistent about its Christian commitments and so interested in Isaiah. But while one finds in the Book of Mormon numerous interactions with Isaiah 52:7–10, repeated explorations of Isaiah 29:11–14, various allusions to Isaiah 49:22–23, and insistent emphasis on Isaiah 11:11, Isaiah 53 becomes the focus of the volume only briefly, in just one narrative characterized by rather particular circumstances. The central figure in the story in question is a prophet named Abinadi, and he doesn't *choose* to discourse on Isaiah; rather, he's *forced* to do so when he's tried for his life by a court of corrupt Mosaic priests. The priests demand that Abinadi explain a few verses from Isaiah 52. Abinadi offers a Christological interpretation in response, turning to Isaiah 53 to secure the relevance of Christological interpretation in general to Isaiah in particular. It's to be noted, though, that Christological interpretation of Hebrew scripture isn't what Abinadi normally does. He's on trial because he's spoken simile curses against the corrupt king presiding over the priests. Abinadi's a threat to political stability, but his legal defense comes to focus on whether Isaiah should be interpreted in a Christian fashion.

The scene has many trappings of the just-mentioned late-medieval trials in which Isaiah 53 functions. Abinadi's controversy concerns the gap between what's presented roughly as a traditional Jewish approach and what's presented as a complexly Christian approach. In effect, the Book of Mormon, in what it presents as a singular scene, portrays in its own way a relatively conventional event, a standard feature of the West's history of Jewish-Christian interactions. An informed and thoughtful reader of the Book of Mormon at the time of its publication would certainly have reflected on the type-scene of sorts proposed by the book. And yet there are two striking departures in Abinadi's story from the traditional Jewish-Christian disputation. First, in Abinadi's trial it's the *Christian* (or at least: the one who believes Jesus is the Messiah) rather than the Jew who's on trial, and so it's *Jews* (or at least: non-messianic adherents to the Law of Moses) rather than Christians who hold the trial. Second and more radically, Abinadi's trial occurs sometime in the second century *before* Christ, that is, in the *pre*-Christian era, long before such an event would have been possible in the West. These two variations on an otherwise familiar theme have major theological implications—confirmed by the particulars of Abinadi's Christological interpretation of Isaiah 53.

First the inversion of roles played by Jews and Christians in the scene. This is perhaps unsurprising, given the storyline within the Book of Mormon.

Christian preaching in the book is the work of a minority religious tradition, one that occasionally becomes mainstream but that usually remains one of several religious options. But the civilization whose history the volume principally recounts is generally made up of adherents to Mosaic Law (until the advent of Jesus Christ at the volume's climax). It's therefore natural, so to speak, for the trial scene to make the characters who are most reminiscent of Jews-as-traditionally-understood into figures of power and judgment, and to make the character most obviously Christian-as-traditionally-understood into a figure of marginality. Of course, the configuration of the situation complicates any too-quick assimilation to traditional categories of "Jew" and "Christian." The figures roughly portrayed as Jewish in the scene aren't traditional since they don't believe, in the words Nahmanides uses in describing a thirteenth-century disputation, that "the Messiah . . . is yet to come." Neither does the figure roughly portrayed as Christian believe that, in Nahmanides's words, "the Messiah . . . has already come."[1] Instead, it's Abinadi who anticipates the coming of the Messiah (but identifying him with Jesus), while the antagonistic priests find straightforwardly non-messianic meaning in Isaiah's words. What gives? What complicates matters is simply the second point: the whole scene is presented as occurring before the birth of Jesus Christ, in advance of the existence of anything that could strictly be called Christianity.

This point requires particular comment. It's this that's especially surprising about the story—and about the Book of Mormon's theology more generally. In the Abinadi story, the Book of Mormon poses the question of loosely Jewish-versus-Christian interpretation of Isaiah 53, but it poses it from within the pre-Christian context. There's no investment here in the idea that the New Testament lies concealed in the Old, while the Old Testament is laid bare in the New. Instead, already in an Old Testament context, it's possible to hold a public theological debate about the typological significance of the Hebrew Bible. Abinadi in fact explicitly speaks of "types of things to come" (Mosiah 13:31) and claims that many in Israel only fail to "understand the law . . . because of the hardness of their hearts" (v. 32). In fact, when the priests first ask him about how to read Isaiah, he initially responds with a couple of sarcastic rhetorical questions: "Are you priests and pretend to teach this people, and to understand the spirit of prophesying—and yet desireth to know of me what these things mean?" (12:25). The Abinadi story assumes that a good Old Testament priest would already fully anticipate the New Testament.

---

1. For the relevant texts, see Hyam Maccoby, ed., *Judaism on Trial: Jewish-Christian Disputations in the Middle Ages* (Portland, OR: Littman Library, 1982).

It's no surprise, then, that Abinadi offers a Christological interpretation of Isaiah 53, one that in many ways fits comfortably into the Christian interpretive tradition. After explaining that "all the prophets" have said, "more or less," that "God himself should come down among the children of men and take upon him the form of man" (Mosiah 13:33–34), Abinadi asks this rhetorical question before quoting Isaiah 53 in its entirety: "Yea, even doth not Isaiah say . . . ?" (14:1). Immediately after the quotation, Abinadi's next words are: "I would that ye should understand that God himself shall come down among the children of men and shall redeem his people" (15:1). Abinadi offers, in general terms, a strictly traditional Christian interpretation of Isaiah's song of the suffering servant. In some ways, he offers a *quaintly* traditional interpretation of Isaiah 53. After quoting the text, Abinadi provides a few words of commentary. In a first sequence, he focuses on Isaiah 53:8: "And who shall declare his generation?" I haven't the space to argue for this here, but Abinadi seems to understand this question to ask about the mysterious nature of Christ's birth, about the mysteriously split nature of God dwelling in flesh. Unpacking the word "generation," that is, he spells out a theology according to which Christ is at once "the father and the son" (Mosiah 15:2), in some way *his own* father as the son, and in some way *his own* son as the father. This is a peculiar sort of "generation," no doubt, the generation of God-in-the-flesh—a mystery, to be sure.

What makes this interpretation *quaintly* traditional is the way it would sound in the early nineteenth century, to the Book of Mormon's first readers. Already by the second century of the common era, Christians are interpreting the passage like Abinadi. From Justin Martyr to Augustine, Isaiah's question signals the "ineffable origin" of Christ. Saint Jerome sums up: "This [question] is understood in two ways: one should either interpret it concerning [Christ's] deity, that it is impossible to know the mysteries of the divine generation . . . ; or it should be understood concerning his birth from a virgin, that it could scarcely be explained."[2] So consistent is this line of interpretation in early Christianity that Isaiah 53:8 became a prooftext for *both* parties in the Arian controversy. But then, a couple of centuries before the publication of the Book of Mormon, this patristic interpretation began to fall out of favor. John Calvin in fact directly ridiculed the way Isaiah's words were "stretched and . . . tortured into various meanings."[3] With the

---

2. St. Jerome, *Commentary on Isaiah*, trans. Thomsa P. Scheck (New York: Newman Press, 2015), 671 (14.24).

3. John Calvin, *Commentary on the Book of the Prophet Isaiah*, vol. 4, trans. Rev. William Pringle (Edinburgh: Calvin Translation Society, 1853), 120.

shortly subsequent rise of full-blooded biblical criticism, the once-popular interpretation retreated more or less definitively. Although it would still appear in the eighteenth and nineteenth centuries in occasional sermons or popular Christian magazines, it most often appeared in such contexts in the English-speaking world only to be dismissed or argued against. When the Book of Mormon first appeared, a reader familiar with the interpretive tradition would have seen Abinadi's interpretation of Isaiah 53:8 as *stubbornly* traditional, an against-the-grain appeal to a quaint patristic view of the text.

At the same time, because of the pre-Christian context from which Abinadi speaks in the Book of Mormon, his Christological interpretation of Isaiah 53 is radical and startling. This concerns the other major axis of Abinadi's interpretation, Isaiah 53:10, which speaks of the servant "see[ing] his seed." Abinadi quotes the line and then asks, "And who shall be his seed?" (Mosiah 15:10). His answer is that the mysteriously generated Christ finds his seed among "all the holy prophets which have prophesied concerning the coming of the Lord," and among "whosoever hath heard the words of the prophets . . . and believed" (v. 11). This interpretation has temporal boundaries, however, as Abinadi makes clear. Christ's seed is made up only of pre-Christian Christian prophets and their pre-Christian Christian followers, "those that have been and which are and which shall be, even until the resurrection of Christ" (v. 21). These, Abinadi says, "shall come forth in the first resurrection" (v. 22), a resurrection of pre-Christian Christian believers, *with Christ*, at the moment of the latter's resurrection.

Here Abinadi looks thoroughly non-traditional. The more or less universal Christological interpretation of Isaiah 53:10 identifies Christ's seed with the apostles and their Christian heirs, those who spread the news of Christ throughout the world in the Christian—not the pre-Christian— era. So far as I can find, *no one* in the Christian interpretive tradition reads Isaiah 53:10 as Abinadi does in the Book of Mormon. Thus, when the volume first appeared in 1830, a reader familiar with the interpretive tradition would have to reconcile in her mind the quaintly or even stubbornly traditional element of Abinadi's interpretation with its revisionary and even radical element. How might a stubbornly Christological interpretation of Isaiah look if it took shape *before* the actual coming of Christ?

The Book of Mormon's interpretation of Isaiah 53 is thus doubly out of synch with the time of its first circulation. It defends a strictly Christological approach that was largely defunct by that time, fallen out of favor before the commanding force of increasingly historicist readings of biblical texts. But it also proposes a deeply unorthodox view that questions the Christian hermeneutic tradition, dependent as the latter is on the typological understanding of the relationship between the two testaments. Is there a way of reconciling these two gestures? I think so. The *traditional* interpretive gesture would have been read as contesting rising biblical historicism at the moment of its earliest arrival in the American context (and just decades before its first saturation of the American context). In a similar vein, the *radical* interpretive gesture outlines a new historical and even historicist narrative, a counter-historicism perhaps, one according to which Christian theology was available in advance of Christianity. What the two gestures share is an antipathy to available historicisms, and what they therefore jointly offer is a new historical-and-historicizing narrative, in fact a new master narrative for biblical religion.

This new master narrative ends up playing an influential role in early Mormonism and beyond. Joseph Smith, after publishing the Book of Mormon, turned his attention to producing a revision of the Christian Bible. He focused much of his attention on recasting its Old Testament in the Book of Mormon's mold. Its prophets, after Smith's revision, have clear prophetic knowledge of Jesus; they aren't just typologically oriented in a direction that might later be brought into full clarity with the revelation of God in Christ. And in so many ways, adherents to the religious tradition inaugurated by Smith have generally reproduced his revisionary gesture—albeit at the level of interpretation rather than of direct alteration to the biblical text. They tend to believe that biblical prophets all had clear knowledge of the Christian future, and so—in the words of a Book of Mormon prophet—"many hundred years before his coming . . . they believed in Christ and worshipped the Father in his name" (Jacob 4:4–5). Smith's version of Genesis has Adam and Eve receiving Christian baptism, tells how in the first generations of humanity some saw Abel's death as effecting Christian atonement, recounts a clearly Christian vision had by Enoch before his walk with God, and so on. Terryl Givens sums up:

> Whereas previous thinkers had emphasized the fragmentary nature of prior revelation and its final consummation in [later] scripture, Joseph [Smith] pushed . . . in the other direction. "From what we can draw from the Scriptures relative to the teaching of heaven," [Smith] said, "we are induced to think that much instruction has been given to man since the beginning *which we do not possess now.*"[4]

---

4. Terryl L. Givens, "Joseph Smith: Prophecy, Process, and Plenitude," in *Joseph Smith Jr.: Reappraisals after Two Centuries*, ed. Reid L. Neilson and Terryl L. Givens (New York: Oxford University Press, 2009), 114–15.

This is itself interesting. But what seems to me to be *really* at stake in all this is less a rewriting of the historical timeline than a contest over the nature of the prophetic as such. A crucial difference between the traditional disputations over Isaiah 53 and the one staged in the Book of Mormon is that, while traditional disputations concern Jewish and Christian *scholars* who argue about the *correct* interpretation of Isaiah 53, the Book of Mormon offers a scene in which *priests and a prophet* argue about what it means to receive *the spirit of prophesying*. In the traditional disputation, the two parties readily agree that the prophetic remains in the past, and what there is now is a question of sorting out *best* or *most reasonable* interpretations. But the Book of Mormon suggests that what's at stake in any real debate about the interpretation of Isaiah is whether the prophet's word can be *repeated*, repeated *prophetically*. Abinadi confronts priests who reduce prophetic activity to the past and ask only what the text means. But he declares that prophetic activity continues into the present, that Isaiah's word is alive only where it's taken up again by another who's inhabited by the same spirit of prophesying. Whether Isaiah himself is supposed to have seen clearly the coming of God in Jesus Christ, *Abinadi* does, and that's what makes him a good interpreter of the text, according to the book. He prophetically sees the possibilities bound up with Isaiah's words, not just their actualities responsibly interpreted.

The Book of Mormon thus poses, in the context of its first appearance, a question about the status of prophecy. It asks whether Isaiah—and all of biblical scripture with him—must be trapped in the past. By creating an absolute historical timeline, moreover, at every moment of which Christianity can be fully alive and well, this question becomes perennial, a question to be asked by every generation. Is the Book of Isaiah a word that remains open, alive, and prophetic? Is there any way for it to be these things if it isn't taken up anew by prophets? Abinadi's commentary on Isaiah 53 moves rapidly from quoting lines from Isaiah with phrases like "even as *Isaiah* said" to quoting lines from Isaiah that are introduced with "Behold, *I* say unto you!" In the end, it's less that the Book of Mormon introduces and then insists on a set of Isaianic interpretations than that it calls for a revival of prophetic use of the prophets. Its moment in the history of Isaiah's reception is one calling for a prophetic doubling of the prophetic word rather than a responsible hermeneutics. And that remains a consistent call in the larger Mormon tradition.

Chapter Eleven

"After This Manner Hath the Prophet Written"
Isaiah 48 in the Book of Mormon

When the Book of Mormon draws nearest to the biblical text, even the tiniest differences between the two texts take on major significance. The long quotations of Isaiah in the Book of Mormon are thus freighted with potential significance. In such contexts, for verses and chapters, the texts of the Book of Mormon and the (King James Version of the) Bible are so astonishingly similar that it becomes possible to ask about the theological significance of there being an "and" in one and a "but" in the other. When one lays the Isaiah texts in the Book of Mormon side by side with their equivalents in the Bible, all kinds of tiny differences of potential theological significance leap out. And when one considers all of the tiny differences over the course of a single chapter, there are sometimes remarkably suggestive patterns. There is good reason to think that patterns in such variation are particularly important theologically.

In the course of my own studies of Isaiah in the Book of Mormon, I have come to see Isaiah 48 as particularly provocative in this regard. When compared with other full chapters of Isaiah quoted in the Book of Mormon, its presentation in Nephi proves itself the most consistently unique (with the obvious exception of Isaiah 29, where Nephi seems straightforwardly to be altering the text of Isaiah in the course of likening it to his own prophecies). And the little variants scattered throughout Isaiah 48 as Nephi quotes it add up to an interesting picture, suggesting that the version in Nephi's record has a different theological agenda than its biblical counterpart. This has obvious theological significance, for which this paper is a relatively informal examination, sorting out its basic implications.

This previously unpublished paper is one I have delivered a few times at relatively informal groups—especially in a public talk at Pioneer Book in Provo, Utah, and at a private study group in Seattle, Washington.

The Book of Mormon, you're probably aware, demonstrates some interest in Isaiah. Unfortunately, it seems to be precisely to the extent that the Book of Mormon demonstrates interest in Isaiah that we as readers lose interest in the Book of Mormon. You've heard the jokes—you've probably passed them on, in fact: even a bullet can't get through the Isaiah chapters, and all that. The fact is that we resent there being anything in the book that isn't plain by our standards. And so we read the Book of Mormon more or less as if Isaiah weren't there at all. When Nephi or even Jesus Christ himself starts quoting from *that* prophet, we start skimming. We're uneasy about it, but we don't change much about it.

Or rather, we make *some* effort at changing it, but not enough to get anywhere, really. All the LDS book publishers know that there's a market for books on Isaiah, perhaps especially for books on Isaiah in the Book of Mormon. They know Mormons will buy these books—buy them over and over again—even if they never really learn anything from them. Always buying books on Isaiah, but never coming to a knowledge of what Isaiah's up to: that's us. But like with so much in life, we're hoping, collectively, that we've shown enough initiative to be blameless even while we've made no actual effort and we've gotten more or less nowhere.

There. Do I sound arrogant and self-serving enough yet? Because you know I'm planning on speaking on Isaiah in the Book of Mormon. What else would you expect me to do at the outset of my presentation but tell you all that you're ignorant of Isaiah and that I've got the secrets? You all might *think* you know something about what Isaiah's up to, but I've done the work necessary to *know* what he's talking about, and I'm here to tell you what I've learned so that you can all bask in my wisdom—perhaps in my spiritual superiority. Right? Not at all. I'm earnest when I say that we're hoping, collectively, to show enough initiative with Isaiah to be regarded as blameless, even as we make no real effort and learn basically nothing about him. But while I've done a good deal of work on Isaiah (it seems to be *all* I'm doing lately), I think I've made headway only to the extent that I've *unlearned* things. What I've got is an always-growing set of *questions*, not a bunch of answers. I think I've developed some understanding, but the sort that helps me finally to see what we ought to be asking, not what would leave me feeling settled.

So, here's what I'd like to do tonight: I want to look at Isaiah 48, at how it's used in the Book of Mormon, to begin to make clear what we ought to be doing with this prophet that drives us all mad. And my hope is just that I can get us to the point where it's possible to start asking the right questions about Isaiah, about Isaiah in the Book of Mormon or about Isaiah in the Restoration. If that sounds alright to you, I'll get started.

The Book of Mormon, as you know, quotes often and with relish from the writings of Isaiah. In First Nephi, we get two full chapters of Isaiah. In Second Nephi, we get sixteen chapters, along with a host of lesser allusions and borrowings. In Mosiah, we get another chapter and a half. In Third Nephi, we get almost two more chapters. And, of course, you can find other allusions and borrowings through much of the last part of the Book of Mormon. Setting aside allusions and borrowings, the Book of Mormon gives us nearly a third of the Book of Isaiah in full quotation. A third! The Book of Isaiah has sixty-six chapters in it, and the Book of Mormon quotes twenty-one of those in full. That's really quite striking.

But here's something equally striking. Of all the chapters of Isaiah that get quoted along the way in the Book of Mormon, there's just one that gets quoted without any obvious purpose. You might guess what it is: Isaiah 48. Nephi alone reproduces eighteen chapters of Isaiah in his record, and there's a clear reason for every one of those chapters—*except* Isaiah 48. Every other chapter of Isaiah that he quotes he explains, however briefly. 1 Nephi 22 gives us commentary on Isaiah 49. 2 Nephi 6 provides a clear motivation for the quotation of Isaiah 50–51. 2 Nephi 25 provides a rather deft outline of the whole of Isaiah 2–14. And 2 Nephi 26–27 weaves Isaiah 29 into a plainer prophecy that makes its relevance perfectly clear. But Nephi never gives us so much as a word of justification for his quotation of Isaiah 48. Why is it there at all?

It gets weirder. Isaiah 48 is the *first* full chapter of Isaiah we encounter in the Book of Mormon. Nephi quotes it in 1 Nephi 20, long before the so-called "Isaiah barrier" of Second Nephi. The very first words of Isaiah we're asked to grapple with in the Book of Mormon are those that make up Isaiah 48, and yet we're never given any indication as to their meaning or importance. Perhaps, however, we might come to the conclusion that Isaiah 48 isn't terribly important. Sure, it gets quoted first, but it's clear that Nephi's got no real investment in this particular chapter. Yet here's another peculiarity: Isaiah 48 receives more revisionary attention than all but one other chapter of Isaiah that's quoted in the Book of Mormon. What does that mean? You might be aware that when Isaiah's quoted in the Book of Mormon, there are often differences between the text there and the text as it appears in the Bible. If you look at *how many* differences there are in various chapters of Isaiah, it turns out that Isaiah 48 is the second-most-altered one. Despite the fact that we get no explanation of its content or even of its inclusion in the Book of Mormon, it's one of the two most systematically revised texts of Isaiah in the book. For that reason at least, I don't think we can say that it wasn't of much importance to Nephi.

So Isaiah 48 puzzles. There's more that's puzzling about it, in fact—more than what I've already mentioned. This will take a moment to set up, but bear with me.

If we take a few steps back to look at patterns, at patterns of what from Isaiah interests the writers of the Book of Mormon, we might notice that its lengthy quotations come from two stretches of Isaiah. In Second Nephi, we get a long quotation of Isaiah 2–14 (which Nephi then couples with Isaiah 29, a text closely related to Isaiah 6–12). And then over the course of the whole of the Book of Mormon, we get quotations in bits and pieces of the whole of Isaiah 48–54—interestingly, in order. So the Book of Mormon is interested, apparently, in two major parts of the Book of Isaiah: chapters 2–14 and chapters 48–54. That second block of Isaiah text, from chapters 48–54, is fascinating. Isaiah scholars more or less universally regard Isaiah 40–55 as a larger unit (usually going by the name of "Second Isaiah"), a larger unit that divides into two halves. Isaiah 40–48 is regarded as a coherent subunit with clear boundaries, and then Isaiah 49–54 is regarded as an equally coherent subunit. (Isaiah 55 is taken to be a kind of conclusion or epilogue to Second Isaiah.) Now if you look again at the blocks of Isaiah text that show up in the Book of Mormon, it's clear that there's deep interest in the second subunit of Second Isaiah. It's quoted, in bits and pieces, over the course of the whole Book of Mormon. All of Isaiah 49–54 shows up, and in order! But here's the weird thing. The Book of Mormon quotes nothing from the first subunit except Isaiah 48. Just that one chapter. But then it tells us nothing by way of explanation about that chapter. It's entirely out of place, as well as unexplained.

The fact of the matter is that the inclusion of Isaiah 48 in the Book of Mormon gets weirder and weirder the longer you look at it. Nephi makes it the very first Isaiah chapter we encounter, and he presents it to us as strikingly different from the biblical version of the text, and yet he never says anything about its importance or its meaning, and it's the only chapter from its particular part of Isaiah that gets quoted in the Book of Mormon. It's like we're supposed to see this chapter as *especially* significant and *especially* insignificant, all at once. If that isn't odd, I don't know what is.

So, what should we make of Isaiah 48 in the Book of Mormon? Well, the fact is that I don't know. I don't have any particular wisdom to share on that point. But I *do* have a lot of questions. And what I'd like to do for the remainder of our time together today—I already told you this—is to work our way toward those questions, as carefully and as productively as possible. I think it'd be best if we begin with a review of Isaiah 48 itself, independently of the Book of Mormon. What's going on in this chapter on its own terms? Taking a look at that first will allow us then to make better sense of how the text is reworked or alternatively presented in First Nephi.

Commentators almost universally agree that this chapter is plagued with a host of interpretive difficulties. There are those, of course, who attempt a straightforward reading of it, finding some kind of coherence or another that allows them to present a unified interpretation. But, as Brevard Childs nicely puts it, such interpretations end up "far removed from the difficulties of the actual text," and they "cloak the text with a homiletical coating without deep exegetical probing."[1] A more honest appraisal confesses that Isaiah 48 is something of a mess. And perhaps the Book of Mormon's revisions to the text should lead Mormon interpreters to make the same confession. As we'll see, the Book of Mormon version of Isaiah 48 helps to introduce a certain thematic unity that's arguably missing in the biblical version of the text.

Now, how to organize this mess? Well, it seems to me that, at least with an eye to the King James rendering of the chapter, Isaiah 48 can be divided into several shorter units. It arguably comes in two halves, verses 1–11 and verses 12–22. And there's a kind of gravitational center to the first half. Verses 1–2 provide an assessment of Israel's unfaithfulness and hypocrisy (they "swear by the name of the Lord . . . but not in truth"), but then verses 9–11 offer a few words regarding the Lord's fidelity to the covenant people ("for my name's sake will I defer mine anger"). In between these contrasting-but-parallel bits of text, verses 3–8 outline a kind of double strategy on the Lord's part for ensuring Israel's compliance despite its infidelity, exhibiting the Lord's commitment to his wayward people. The strategy outlined there at the heart of verses 1–11 is double, I say, because it entails the Lord *first* declaring "former things" long in advance, early enough in the game to prevent apostate Israel from attributing them to false gods they've only recently become attached to, and then *second* declaring "new things" only now, late enough in the game to prevent apostate Israel from claiming that the prophets only recirculate used material.

This same division between *then* and *now* permeates the second half of Isaiah 48. It opens with the Lord describing himself as "the first" and "the

---

1. Brevard S. Childs, *Isaiah* (Louisville: Westminster John Knox Press, 2001), 371.

last," and then it sets up a contrast between what God's declared "from the beginning" (described in verses 13–16a) and what he's only "now" having his prophets declare (described in verses 16b–19). From the beginning, God announced that he'd raise up a deliverer to bring Israel out of foreign captivity, and now it's coming to pass. But even as prophecy from an earlier era sees its fulfillment, God now sends a new prophet or servant who laments Israel's continued stubbornness and calls them to repent and to enjoy the deliverance God's granting them. After these two sequences, in verses 20–21, we get the new prophet's command to "go forth" and "flee" from Babylon, where Israel's held captive, followed by a description of God's care for them as they make their way back to their promised land. They're to experience a new exodus.

Finally, the chapter ends with a word of warning—"There is no peace, saith the Lord, unto the wicked" (v. 22). It's likely that this apparently out-of-place statement is there in the text primarily for structural reasons. It appears again, more or less word for word, in Isaiah 57:21. Many interpreters think that the two instances of the formula are meant to divide the whole of Isaiah 40–66 into three larger blocks of text: Isaiah 40–48, Isaiah 49–57, and Isaiah 58–66. That may well be right. Or it may be just that the prophet felt it necessary to balance the promise of deliverance with a warning that the wicked would still be left without peace.

Alright, so maybe we've made some preliminary sense of Isaiah 48 here—or at least we've been able to impose a little bit of order on the text. The basic organizing principle seems to lie in the difference between two eras of prophetic activity: a past era when the prophets spoke of what would happen now and the present era when the prophets come to clarify the nature of those other prophecies' fulfillment. Now, we might want to ask next about *what* the prophets of old predicted, about *what* the prophets now hope to clarify. But here's the odd thing about Isaiah 48. There's little if nothing in this chapter about the actual *content* of these prophets' message. At best we have an indication that it has something to do with deliverance from exile in Babylon. The real focus of Isaiah 48 isn't on *what* the prophets have said in the past or are saying now, but simply on *the fact that* the prophets said something in the past and are saying something now. The theme of the chapter concerns both *declaring* and *hearing*, and these are the two words that appear with the greatest frequency in the chapter.

So the basic organizing principle of Isaiah 48 turns out to be closely connected to the chapter's principal theme. The chapter's *subject* is declaring and hearing, and its material seems to be *organized* around a distinction between two periods of time during which such declaring and hearing are at issue. What's in question, of course, is whether Israel will now hear what the Lord's declared through his prophets, both in the past and in the present. The first words of the first half of the chapter are, after all, "Hear ye this, O house of Jacob!" And the first words of the second half of the chapter are, in a similar vein, "Hearken unto me, O Jacob and Israel!" The chapter presents us with a question. Will Israel listen now that deliverance is nigh? Or will Israel continue to resist the Lord's messengers?

Perhaps that's enough by way of review? Have we got a basic sense for what's there in Isaiah 48 as it stands in the Bible? So now our question becomes this: What does Isaiah 48 look like in the Book of Mormon? If, as we've said, this chapter differs from its biblical counterpart much more than most of the chapters of Isaiah that show up in Nephite scripture, what needs to be said about the differences? Is there a kind of coherence to them? Is there perhaps a discernible program at work in them? I think the answer is yes. And that's quite peculiar. So let's get to work, shall we?

Let's start with some numbers, abstract but perhaps informative. There are 621 words in the English text of Isaiah 48 as found in the King James Version. Twenty-three of those words are simply deleted in the Book of Mormon, whether individually or in whole phrases (three short phrases get deleted entirely). Another eleven words are removed from the text just to be replaced with totally different words. Five more words just change in grammatical nature (change of tense, alteration in pronoun). And three words simply get moved from one place to another in the text. And then ninety-nine words get *added* to Isaiah 48 in the Book of Mormon. Twelve of these are replacement words, but the other eighty-seven *augment* the text. Interestingly, fifty-four of those eighty-seven augmenting words come in whole phrases added to the text. There are ten added phrases, ranging up to the largest single addition: thirteen words added in one go.

That's a lot of change, and it's difficult to know exactly how to turn it into a set of statistics. And anyway, for our purposes, a *qualitative* study will be worth a good deal more than any *quantitative* analysis. So, let's take a look at where there are differences between the biblical and Book of Mormon versions of Isaiah 48.

The differences are so frequent, so consistent, that there's only *one* verse that's exactly the same in the two versions of the text: verse 18. Every *other* verse contains variants when the two texts are set side by side. (I might note between parentheses that I'm using Royal Skousen's critical apparatus to look at differences between the biblical and the Book of

Mormon versions of the text. There are variants in the current edition of the Book of Mormon that weren't there in Joseph Smith's original dictation, just as there are variants in Joseph Smith's original dictation that aren't in the current edition of the Book of Mormon. Maybe I should note also that I don't use Skousen's critical apparatus uncritically. I've used his helpful resources, but I haven't always agreed with his conclusions about the so-called "earliest text.") Now, given that all but one of the twenty-two verses making up Isaiah 48 exhibits variation when we compare the Bible and the Book of Mormon, we *can't* just work through the text line by line. That'd take us much longer than you've got patience for. So instead, we'll have to be choosy, highlighting patterns and looking at more obviously significant differences.

Verses 1–2 provide us with a good introduction to what variants in this chapter look like, so let's spend a minute or two there, even though these aren't the *most* significant passages we might consider. If you read these two verses in the King James Version of the Bible, you'll pretty naturally feel that there's something wrong. Verse 1 calls Israel out for hypocrisy; they "make mention of the God of Israel, but not in truth, nor in righteousness." But then verse 2 goes on just to say that "they call themselves of the holy city, and stay themselves upon the God of Israel," with no clear indication that they do any of this in an inappropriate fashion. Verse 1 suggests hypocrisy, but verse 2 suggests faithfulness. And even weirder, the two verses are linked by the causal word "for," which seems to indicate that it's *because* "they call themselves of the holy city, and stay themselves upon the God of Israel" that they're hypocritical. Even if there's a way to make sense of this (and some suggest that there *is*), it's unquestionably awkward in the version that was most readily available to nineteenth-century readers.

Two differences in the Book of Mormon's version of verse 2 do away with the awkwardness. First, the causal "for" that opens verse 2 in the biblical version is replaced with the contrastive "nevertheless." And second, the "and" that links "they call themselves of the holy city" to "stay themselves upon the God of Israel" is replaced with "but they do not." The first of these two differences sets up the first claim in verse 2—the claim that Israelites *do* "call themselves of the holy city"—as a point of apparent contrast with Israel's real lack of commitment. And then the replacement of "and" with "but they do not" makes the second claim in verse 2 negative: Israelites *don't* "stay themselves upon the God of Israel." With these two changes, the awkwardness of the biblical text disappears. The opening verses straightforwardly call Israel out for hypocrisy.

But they do more than just that in the Book of Mormon version. The contrast there between "they call themselves of the holy city" and "they do not stay themselves upon the God of Israel" introduces an explicit gap between what Israel *says* and what Israel *does*. Verse 1 *gestures* toward hypocrisy by claiming that Israel swears neither "in truth" nor "in righteousness," but it doesn't *explicitly identify* any particular distance between saying and doing. Strictly speaking, we could interpret verse 1 as accusing Israel just of insincerity—or perhaps worse but more specifically, of perjury. We don't *have* to conclude from verse 1 alone that there's any actual *hypocrisy* characteristic of Israel. It may be that the nature of the accusation lies elsewhere. But with the Book of Mormon's version of verse 2, it's quite clear that Israel's talk that's neither "in truth" nor "in righteousness" is closely linked to an egregious pattern of hypocrisy—to a consistent mismatch between what Israel *says* and what Israel *does*.

"Fine," you might say. "So what?" Well, we've already seen that there's a strong emphasis throughout Isaiah 48 on what God *says* through his prophets and then on whether he *does* what he says. The Book of Mormon version of this text thus doesn't just get rid of a kind of awkwardness in the text. It also sets up a clear contrast between Israel, with whom there's no real equivalence between what's said and what's done, and Israel's God, who does what he says. That, I think, is quite interesting.

It's interesting, but these aren't the only differences you find in the opening two verses. There are actually *three more* differences between the biblical text and the text in the Book of Mormon.

The biblical version of verse 1 opens with "Hear ye this!" The Book of Mormon gives us instead "Hearken and hear this!" There's a doubling of verbs in the Book of Mormon version (Israel's to "hearken" as well as to "hear"), and there's an elimination of an unnecessary pronoun in the Book of Mormon version (no "ye" after "hear"). Is this significant at all? Actually, it might be. Let's note that the second half of Isaiah 48 opens with a command to "hearken," rather than with a command to "hear," so the added verb sets up a clearer link between the opening lines of the two halves of the chapter. That's potentially important. But then maybe this is *also* important. Once elsewhere in Isaiah there's a close coupling of these two verbs: "to hearken" and "to hear." It's in Isaiah 42:23, where this question appears: "Who will hearken and hear for the time to come?" Are we supposed to understand that in the Nephites' copy of Isaiah there was an implicit link between Isaiah 42:23 and Isaiah 48:1? Perhaps we're supposed to find in Isaiah 48 the beginning of an answer to the question posed in Isaiah 42. That's interesting as well.

Another variant appears toward the end of verse 1 in the Book of Mormon version. The King James Version, remember, describes Israel as those who "swear by the name of the Lord, and make mention of the God of Israel, but not in truth, nor in righteousness." But now note this. The "but" that precedes "not in truth, nor in righteousness" is italicized in the King James Version. Perhaps you're familiar with this. The King James translators italicized words that they felt were necessary to capture the sense of the underlying text but that didn't actually represent any underlying word. In short, there's no "but" in the Hebrew text at this point in Isaiah 48:1, though the King James translators saw the need to insert one in the English rendering so that there'd be no mistaking the meaning of the text. The Book of Mormon version, however, eliminates the italicized "but" and replaces it with "yet they swear"—so that the verse ends: "yet they swear not in truth, nor in righteousness." Now, this doesn't change the meaning of the text in any terribly substantive way, but it alerts us to the fact that the Book of Mormon version of Isaiah often provides variants at those places, precisely, where the King James Version contains italicized additions. This is worth noting because it happens several times in Isaiah 48. But it's also worth noting because differences between the texts appear much more frequently in connection with non-italicized parts of the text than with italicized parts.

Okay, there's one more difference between the two versions of verses 1–2. The Book of Mormon version contains an entire clause in verse 2 that's lacking in the biblical version of the text. Verse 2 ends in the King James Version this way: "The Lord of hosts is his name"—referring back to "the God of Israel" mentioned immediately before. The Book of Mormon version follows "the God of Israel" with the clause "which is the Lord of hosts." There's then an emphatic "yea," followed by the remainder of the biblical text: "the Lord of hosts is his name." Now, notice that there isn't any obvious motivation for these changes. This is the sort of thing that leaves you scratching your head. It seems that the Book of Mormon version wants us to take seriously the identity of "the God of Israel" as "the Lord of hosts," and perhaps to regard that as primary with respect to the fact that God's *name* is "the Lord of hosts," but why should that be important?

As I look at verses 1–2, then, I find a nice little catalog of the sorts of differences we can expect when we set Book of Mormon Isaiah side by side with biblical Isaiah. First, there are differences that seem to be motivated by confused or confusing aspects of the biblical version—but those differences often prove to be theologically significant beyond the fact that they patch up the text. Second, there are differences that indicate links among scriptural passages in light of the Book of Mormon version, links that suggest larger textual structures that otherwise don't exist in biblical Isaiah. Third, there are differences that highlight the importance of places in the text where translators have traditionally had difficulty, signaled most classically by the King James Version's use of italics. And fourth, there are differences that seem difficult to explain in any easy way, that make for rather stark differences in meaning but that don't seem to have any obvious motivation lying behind them.

There. Four kinds of variation in Book of Mormon Isaiah that serve as general types for more significant changes. We've tracked them here, for a few minutes, in just the first two verses of Isaiah 48, but there they're *relatively* insignificant because they don't seem to add to anything like a discernible *program*. Nonetheless, with these basic categories of variants in hand, perhaps we can turn to differences in the rest of Isaiah 48 that seem more systematic in nature.

So, what I'd like to demonstrate now is that the differences between the Book of Mormon and biblical versions of Isaiah 48 focus almost exclusively on one theme: that of *declaration*. It's not always the *word* "declaration" that's the focus of the differences between the two texts, but it's often enough that word and more or less always that theme. So, let's take a look at this, moving sequentially through the Book of Mormon's version of Isaiah 48 line by line, noting how each of its variants focuses, generally speaking, on this theme.

We've already seen a first one, actually. The differences we've already tracked between the Book of Mormon and the biblical versions of verse 2 focus us anticipatorily on the theme of declaration. Why? Because they bring out of Isaiah's words a stronger emphasis, in the Book of Mormon version of the text, on the gap between what Israel *says* and what Israel *does*. The theme of declaration—that is, of what God and his prophets *say*—is closely related to this, since it prods its readers to think about whether God, unlike Israel, *does* what he *says* he'll do. What's the status of *divine* declaration, especially when it's set side by side with *human* declaration (even that of the covenant people)? That's a question that's already raised uniquely—or at least with a unique emphasis—by the Book of Mormon version of Isaiah 48, as early as verses 1–2. But this is only anticipatory.

Programmatic attention to this point comes only after these introductory verses end, when we turn to the verses that follow.

The first variant after verses 1–2 appears at the beginning of verse 3. It might seem simple enough. An instance of "behold" shows up at the outset of the verse in the Book of Mormon that's entirely lacking in the Bible. "Okay," you might say to yourself, "so Nephi—or maybe Joseph Smith, acting as translator—really liked the word 'behold.'" But hang on. Note the way the "behold" in the Book of Mormon version makes for a stronger sense of transition from verses 1–2 to what follows after. There's an abruptness about the biblical text here that's missing in the Book of Mormon version. Still more, the "behold" of the Book of Mormon version arguably lays an emphasis on the first line of verse 3 that's lacking in the biblical version. For some reason, it seems we're supposed here to think there's something important about this line: "I have declared the former things from the beginning." We're both being told *and* being asked to focus our attention on the fact that God declared things.

Already with this first variant, we're being alerted to the centrality of or the emphasis on the theme of declaration in the Book of Mormon version of Isaiah 48. And the other variants in the Book of Mormon's rendering of verse 3 refer back to this question of declaration. The biblical text here goes on to distinguish between God's declaration ("they went forth out of my mouth, and I shewed them") and the later fulfillment of that declaration ("I did them suddenly, and they came to pass"). The Book of Mormon version, however, eliminations this distinction, focusing the whole of this verse just on the act of declaration. How? "I did them suddenly," from the biblical version, becomes "I did *shew* them suddenly." And then the whole line, "and they came to pass," present in the biblical text, simply disappears in the Book of Mormon. The first of these two variants turns the biblical version's statement that God went about doing what he'd declared he would into yet a further insistence on the fact of declaration, while the second variant here simply eliminates the other biblical statement that God did something beyond declaration.

The point of all the variants in the Book of Mormon's rendering of Isaiah 48:3 is thus, pretty clearly, to focus us on declaration alone (figured both as a matter of saying and as a matter of showing—that is, both as a kind of verbal communication and as a kind of visual demonstration). We're not only to be aware of but to focus on the fact that God declared or showed something from the beginning. And then we're told three times over that God declared them or showed them to and through the prophets.

We're not to move too quickly to questions of action or doing. (Let me note between parentheses that the verb "to show" is clearly being used here in parallel to the verb "to declare," though you might be tempted to hear in it a reference to God's actually *doing* something. This becomes clear in verse 5, where "I have even from the beginning declared it to thee" is supposed to be equivalent to "before it came to pass I shewed it thee.")

Alright. So we've got a feel for verse 3. And similar variants can be found in verses 4–5, which I'll summarize quickly. There's an addition or a deletion here, a changed pronoun or a differently tensed verb there—and more or less all of these differences between the two texts concern the theme of declaration. The one variant in verse 4 turns it into a motivation for the Lord's acts of declaration. And then there's some difference in the objects of declaration and showing in verse 5, and there's a whole line present in the Book of Mormon version of that verse that's lacking in the Bible, one that makes unambiguous what the verse has to say about declaring or showing.

But let's slow down with verse 6. There's a sense of transition in verse 6, both in the biblical text and in the Book of Mormon. To this point, everything has been about what *the Lord* has declared or shown. And verse 6 appropriately follows this up with two verbs that describe the way human beings are supposed to receive what the Lord's offered, with talk of *hearing* and *seeing*. But here again there's an important difference between the two versions of the text. The biblical version suggests that hearing has taken place only in the past ("thou hast heard"), while it makes seeing something that remains to take place ("see all this," it commands). This follows the biblical version of verse 3, where there's a distinction drawn between what was declared before and what's happening, visibly, right now. But the Book of Mormon version reworks all this. "Thou hast heard and seen all this," it says, making the parallel gestures of declaration and demonstration—declaring and showing—past things that have already made things known. And *then* the Book of Mormon version asks a question that makes the pressing issue in the present not one of seeing what the Lord's doing, but one of willingness to declare in turn what's been declared. "Thou hast heard and seen all this," it says, "and will ye not declare them?" This question is also there in the biblical version, but its role is substantially less significant there.

So here we begin to get a sense for the transition that verse 6 effects. After several verses emphasizing the Lord's making things known through word and vision, the prophet now asks whether Israel is ready to pass the word and the vision along. And this is a good deal more emphatic in the Book of Mormon version. This is not only because of its consistency in making both declaration and demonstration a matter of the past, but also because *Israel's* task of passing God's declarations on is *double* there. In the biblical version, verse 6's question about whether Israel will make its own declaration precedes an abrupt announcement about the new things that God's showing now. But the Book of Mormon version adds "and that" to this announcement, expanding the focus of Israel's responsibility to declare. The prophet asks not only whether Israel will declare what God's declared and shown in the *past*, but also whether they'll declare what God's declaring and showing *now*, the "new things."

Are you noticing how consistently the differences between the two versions of Isaiah 48 concern the matter of declaration? Just in verses 3–6, we've seen the Book of Mormon version (1) lay a unique emphasis from the beginning on the theme of declaration, (2) carefully align showing and declaring as parallel ways of God's making things known, (3) eliminate any rush to turn from speech to action, (4) disambiguate the text so as to make perfectly clear what God's motivations for declaring things are, (5) subtly revise the specifiable objects of declaration and demonstration, (6) definitively set both declaration and demonstration in the past, (7) highlight in a unique fashion Israel's responsibility to declare what's been declared to her, and (8) double the content of what Israel's supposed to declare. All that in just four verses! And don't forget that the variants in verses 1–2 weren't without their connection to all this, since they helped to emphasize from the very beginning the importance, for this chapter, of the relationship between words and actions.

So much in just a few verses! And yet, we're only getting started—getting started a little slowly, sure, but really only just getting started! Take a look at verse 7. It's an odd verse as it stands in the Bible, and the Book of Mormon version doesn't really get rid of that oddity. But it *does* add a whole line that's of particular interest to us here. The last part of the verse seems in the biblical version to be abrupt and out of place: "lest thou shouldest say, 'Behold, I knew them.'" But the Book of Mormon has this before that line: "They were declared unto thee." So, we're told in the Book of Mormon version of the text that God did some declaring so that Israel couldn't claim to have known the new things of their own accord. Note that at this point, we're not just getting differences between the two versions that are *connected* to what's said in the biblical text about God declaring things. Here we get in the Book of Mormon version of the text an actual *instance of the word "to declare"* that's entirely missing in the Bible. And this is something we'll get several times over as the chapter continues.

In fact, since the differences between the two versions of the next several verses are pretty minor—we haven't the time to spell out their basic nature, but take a look sometime, and you'll see that they're relatively light fare, despite their frequency (well, verse 10 might be an exception; there's a more significant difference there, but not one with major implications, I think). Well, anyway, since the differences between the two versions of verses 8–13 are pretty minor, let's move ahead to verse 14 and what follows it. And we'll just leave off the whole of verses 18–22 for our purposes as well tonight. The differences between the biblical and the Book of Mormon versions of *those* verses are, with one exception, all quite minor also. (There's a pretty major difference between the two versions of verse 22, but it's pretty self-explanatory, so we won't spend any time on it today.) So, what we'll do with the time we've still got together tonight is look now just at verses 14–17. It's in these verses specifically that we find the major transition we flagged a bit earlier. I hope you haven't forgotten already, but there's a major transition in these verses from what God's said through his prophets in the past to what God's saying now through his prophets. This is marked especially by that "and now" in verse 16.

So, it's verses 14–17 we want to consider now. And what we find there—surprise, surprise!—is more focus on the theme of declaration. Here's the biblical version of verse 14: "All ye, assemble yourselves, and hear; which among them hath declared these things? The Lord hath loved him: he will do his pleasure on Babylon, and his arm shall be on the Chaldeans." You might note that this verse is a bit peculiar in the biblical version. Who's supposed to assemble and hear? And are they the ones "among" whom there's someone who "hath declared these things," or are they simply to hear that there's someone among some other group who's done such declaring? And what are "these things" that've been declared? And then does the "him" of "the Lord hath loved him" refer to the person that's done some declaring or to someone else? And why is all this interrupted with a word about God doing his pleasure on Babylon? Well, and might we interpret "the Lord hath loved him" as an interruption itself, since everything else in the verse seems to be the Lord speaking in the first person? So, here's the set of difficulties in this verse: there are too many ambiguous pronouns here, there isn't a lot of helpful punctuation, and there doesn't seem to be real consistency in the identity of the speaker. As you can imagine, this has led to a good deal of interpretive confusion, with commentators proposing all kinds of wild approaches to the text.

The Book of Mormon version is less ambiguous in some ways. Here it is (with a bit of emphasis to highlight the points of difference):

> All ye, assemble yourselves, and hear; which among them hath declared these things *unto them?* The Lord hath loved him—*yea, and he will fulfill his word which he hath declared by them. And* he will do his pleasure on Babylon, and his arm shall *come* on the Chaldeans.

Does this clear anything up? Maybe. But let's leave aside questions of interpretive clarity for a moment to make one point *very* clear. The Book of Mormon version introduces *another* instance of the verb "to declare" that isn't there in the biblical version. We're told not only that "the Lord hath loved him"—presumably "hath loved" the one who's "declared these things"—we're not only told *that*, we're also told that the Lord "will fulfill his word which he hath declared by them." That's entirely unique to the Book of Mormon text. And note that it clarifies at least a thing or two about the text. It seems that, for Book of Mormon Isaiah, there are *several* people declaring "these things"—several, rather than just one. And Book of Mormon Isaiah makes clear that it's really *God* who does the declaring, since it's "his word which he hath declared by them." Where the biblical text just tells us that there's declaring going on, the Book of Mormon version tells us something more substantial about it all.

Well, it tells us *something* more substantial about it all, but there are important ambiguities left to deal with. "The Lord hath loved *him*"—note the singular pronoun, the same in both versions of the text—and yet the Lord "will fulfill his word which he hath declared by *them*"—here we get a plural pronoun, in tension with the singular "him" that's there in both the Bible and the Book of Mormon. It's clear that there are *several* declarers in the Book of Mormon version, and yet the Book of Mormon version retains the *singular* pronoun when speaking of the Lord's love. This difficulty is compounded by verse 15. There the biblical text talks about some kind of calling: "I, even I, have spoken," the verse reads in the biblical version," yea, I have called him: I have brought him, and he shall make his way prosperous." The Book of Mormon version makes clear that it's the Lord talking, first by opening the verse with "'Also,' saith the Lord," and then by inserting "the Lord" after the first "I, even I." (The Book of Mormon also replaces the italicized "even" of "I, even I" with "yea.") These first differences between the two texts just clear up ambiguities. But then we get this: where the biblical version has "I have called him," the Book of Mormon version has "I have called him *to declare*." Here *again* we get an extra instance of the verb "to declare" in the Book of Mormon version, and that's already quite interesting. But this additional instance of the verb attaches it again to a singular pronoun, "him," reinforcing the tension of the previous verse. Is it one or many who declare God's word? God's called "him," in the singular, to declare. And yet God plans to fulfill the word he's declared by "them," in the plural.

All this is all the stranger because it suggests that the Book of Mormon version of the text means something rather different from the biblical version. Commentators pretty universally recognize in verses 14–15 some kind of reference to Cyrus of Persia, the royal figure who toppled Babylon and then made Judah's return from exile possible late in the sixth century. Some have suggested, in fact, that the prophet gives Cyrus a nickname of sorts: "The-Lord-Hath-Loved-Him." At any rate, it's usually assumed that it's Cyrus who will "do his pleasure on Babylon," whose "arm shall be on the Chaldeans." And it's usually assumed that it's Cyrus who's been "called," "brought," and whose "way" will be made "prosperous." But none of that's really possible in the Book of Mormon version of these verses. Certainly, in the Book of Mormon version, "the Lord hath loved him" can't be a name or a nickname, since the phrase is followed by a "yea" that then explains that the Lord's love manifests itself in divine fulfillment of what's been declared. And the added line in verse 14 makes it pretty clear that, for Book of Mormon Isaiah, it's God rather than Cyrus who'll "do his pleasure on Babylon." Further, in the Book of Mormon's verse 15, it isn't Cyrus who's been "called," since the called one is called specifically "to declare"—not to topple empires or to restore Judah to its lands of inheritance. Semi-obscure references to Cyrus have been replaced, as it were, with a clearer focus just on declaration.

So, the Book of Mormon version has an intense focus on declaration throughout verses 14–15, but we're still left with a puzzle about exactly who's doing this work of declaring. Is there some kind of prophetic figure who's received a singular call to declare? Or is there a whole group that's been called to declare—a group that, for whatever strange reason, can nonetheless be referred to as a singular "him"? Or maybe there's a singular prophet figure who's been called to declare, but he's set up a larger group of disciples who declare his message alongside him? Are we looking at the formation of a small group of the faithful within larger Israel, gathered together by a prophet as a kind of core? Is this something like what Isaiah elsewhere calls the remnant?

The fact is that all these questions can receive, for the moment, only tentative answers. And what happens with verse 16 in the Book of Mormon only makes things more difficult. Earlier I mentioned that interpreters generally see in verse 16's "and now" a kind of transitional point in Isaiah 48—or at least in its second half. From verse 12 through the first part of verse 16, interpreters usually see a focus on what the Lord's said "from the beginning"—those "former things" discussed also in verses 3–6a. And then, beginning with the "and now" that opens the last line of verse 16, they see a change of focus, now on those "new things" discussed in verses 6b–8. Moreover, the best interpreters—"the best" as I rank them, anyway—the best interpreters see in the passage beginning with verse 16's "and now" a sudden and mostly unprecedented focus on a *servant* figure. This servant is at the center of the story told in Isaiah 49–54, and so it seems the point of Isaiah 48:16–19 is to introduce him to readers. The "and now" of verse 16 is thus crucial because it marks the point in the text where former things, things from the beginning, give way to *this* new thing specifically, the intervention of the servant: "And *now* the Lord God, and his Spirit, hath sent me."

If all that's relatively clear, then let's note this right away: the "now" of verse 16's "and now" isn't there in the Book of Mormon. We just get "and the Lord God—and his spirit—hath sent me." And that changes everything. There's no sharp transition here, no introduction of a new focus. But perhaps that's no surprise, since we've seen that the variants in the Book of Mormon's version of verses 14–15 have *already* introduced a servant figure. Someone's *already* been "called to declare," an individual or perhaps a whole group of individuals whose declarations amount to God's very word, and they come with a promise of fulfillment. So, in the Book of Mormon version of verse 16, perhaps we shouldn't expect any *new* servant figure—just a clarification of the one that's already been introduced.

And that's exactly what we get. If you read verse 16 as it stands in the King James Bible, it seems pretty clear that we're hearing the voice of God. "I have not spoken in secret from the beginning," he says. "From the time that it was, there am I." That's divine talk, don't you think? God's asserting his permanence, his eternality. He was there from the very beginning. But then this is what we get instead in the Book of Mormon: "I have not spoken in secret from the beginning. From the time that it was declared have I spoken." This isn't about the divine being, but about divine speech—that is, it's about, *once more*, declaration. Here for the third verse in a row, the Book of Mormon version has an instance of the verb "to declare" that's entirely lacking in the biblical text. And here it turns our attention from divine being to divine speech. But then that divine speech is what's uttered by the prophetic servant. Immediately following this line, "From the time that it was declared have I spoken," we get: "And the Lord God—and his spirit—hath sent me." This makes perfectly clear that, for Book of Mormon Isaiah, the divine speech that's been coming since the very beginning and continues into the present is what's being spoken by this servant fellow. The biblical text, by way of contrast, sets up a pretty sharp distinction between God's being and the servant's sending—and of course, it says nothing in verse 16 about declaration.

The Book of Mormon thus presents a version of Isaiah 48 that's far more consistently focused on this servant figure than can be found in the Bible. Rather than being suddenly introduced just at the end of verse 16—and then only briefly, so that verses 17–19 are supposed to constitute the first speech of the newly-introduced servant—the servant of the Book of Mormon's version of Isaiah 48 is the focus of the whole chapter, anticipatorily in the first half of the chapter and then forcefully and consistently in verses 14–16. Importantly, this continues right into verse 17 as well. Interpreters who take the last part of verse 16 to introduce the servant figure generally see in verses 17–19, as I just noted, the first divine word uttered by that servant. But in the Book of Mormon version of the text, verse 17 is instead a directly divine testimony, uttered by the Lord himself, by way of confirming the approved status of the servant. Here's how the Book of Mormon renders verse 17:

> And thus saith the Lord, thy Redeemer, the Holy One of Israel: 'I have sent him.' The Lord thy God—which teacheth thee to profit, which leadeth thee by the way thou shouldest go—hath done it.

We get here divine confirmation that the Lord is the one who's sent the servant figure. (The biblical version of verse 17 lacks any reference to sending. Instead, the Lord just confirms *his own* identity: "I am the Lord thy God," etc. And there's no "hath done it" at the end of the biblical version of the verse—no further confirmation, then, of the sending of the servant.)

From verse 14 through verse 17, Book of Mormon Isaiah asks his readers to reflect on the sending of a servant, a servant with divine approval. And the task of the servant throughout is that of declaration, underscored over and over in the Book of Mormon version of the text. There's a message that needs declaring. This is *far* more emphatic in the Book of Mormon than in the Bible, as I hope we've made perfectly clear.

But it remains a question *what* it is that's being declared, or that's supposed to be declared. So, let's close up these reflections by saying *something* about that remaining question, and then I'll look to you to ask some questions to keep us going a little longer.

Where have we gotten tonight? I believe I've made the case sufficiently well that there's something like a discernible *program* at work in the Book of Mormon's version of Isaiah 48. Almost *every* difference between it and the biblical version of Isaiah 48 concerns declaration. And we've seen that the variants in the Book of Mormon version focus major portions of the chapter on the theme of declaration in a way that's basically foreign to the biblical version. Although Nephi never quotes from or alludes to Isaiah 48 after he copies it as a block into the last part of First Nephi, it seems there's something systematic or programmatic about its function in the Book of Mormon. Can we say something about that program by way of conclusion?

I think we can. What we've begun to see, just in the last few minutes, is that the intense focus on declaration throughout the Book of Mormon version of Isaiah 48 places the theme of the *servant* at its heart in a crucial way. Where, in the biblical version of Isaiah, chapter 48 seems to be largely *transitional*, attempting to summarize themes from chapters 40–47 before abandoning them to turn to themes from chapters 49–54, chapter 48 seems in the Book of Mormon to be largely *introductory*. Isaiah 40–47 is ignored more or less in its entirety, and Isaiah 48 appears principally as an introduction to the central theme of Isaiah 49–54—those several chapters from late in the Book of Isaiah that get quoted in bits and pieces throughout the Book of Mormon. In the end, there's a kind of *independence* about the Book of Mormon's version of Isaiah 48, an independence from the chapters that precede it in its canonical presentation in the Bible. And that independence allows it to serve as a programmatic introduction to the themes of the chapters that follow it in its canonical presentation in the Bible. There's thus, in the Book of Mormon, a deeply suggestive presentation of an *alternative* canonical situatedness of Isaiah 48. It's one that I think we should take very seriously.

So where might we go from here? Obviously, our work here tonight has been fast and furious, and a major part of what's needed is a slower, more dedicated study of every one of the differences between the two versions of Isaiah 48. But once that's done, what seems to me especially worth pursuing is the possibility that the Book of Mormon presents a *coherent* version of Isaiah 48 that's theologically productive, interpretively astute, and historically significant. I'm convinced that the Book of Mormon's presentation of Isaiah is, quite generally, far more sophisticated than we've allowed for. It's time we began looking seriously at what it's doing with Isaiah. Really, it's time we just began *figuring out the questions that need asking*, as I said at the outset of my remarks tonight. That might be enough for now. And I hope I've begun outlining the sorts of questions we need to ask tonight.

Isaiah 48 is certainly a good starting place, a good place to begin asking questions. And perhaps, in response to our questions, we might begin to hear what the Lord's been declaring to our deaf ears through the Book of Mormon for almost two centuries.

Chapter Twelve

Biblical Contributions to the Book of Mormon's Presentation of Gender

It was only in the second half of the twentieth century that a specifically feminist style of analyzing the Bible gained real recognition in the field of biblical studies. Once this major development occurred, it was not long before feminist studies of the Book of Mormon—largely following the basic methods on offer in biblical studies—began to appear. As readers have noted for a long time, few women appear in the Book of Mormon, certainly as major characters. Much early feminist writing about the Book of Mormon worked principally to draw attention to that fact and to offer possible explanations for it, whether in defense of the book or by way of critiquing it. To take either a defensive or a critical position is ultimately, though, to assume a theological stance, to begin to explain in theological terms what the Book of Mormon has to offer about questions of gender.

As gender-focused research on the Book of Mormon has continued to develop in the twenty-first century, and especially as various schools of theological interpretation have arisen within the Latter-day Saint context, there has emerged a more self-consciously theological style of studying gender-related issues in the Book of Mormon. Although earlier research on women in the Book of Mormon often drew comparisons (and emphasized contrasts) with the Bible, fewer in the more recent generation of interpreters have asked how the Bible might have shaped the picture the Book of Mormon presents of women. This essay, bringing together my interests in Isaiah's role in the Book of Mormon and my interests in the Book of Mormon and gender, tries to remedy that situation. It turns out that there may be reason to think that the Book of Isaiah significantly shapes the roles played by women in the Book of Mormon. In this context as in so many others, Isaiah seems to lie at the root of the Book of Mormon's theological commitments.

I presented this previously unpublished essay at the 2016 annual meetings of the Society for Biblical Literature, held in San Antonio, Texas.

Readers of the Book of Mormon often criticize its apparent andro-centrism. Few women appear in the book, and those who do are often the unfortunate subjects of violence and abuse. This sad situation has led at least one commentator to argue that feminism might well have saved the book or the people whose history it recounts. Nonetheless, some recent interpreters—largely in papers that aren't set to appear in print until next year—have begun to demonstrate the overlooked complexity of the role played by gender in the Book of Mormon.[1] There seems to be a deliber-ate critique within the book of its own androcentrism, for instance, and evidence suggests that it implicitly inveighs against certain received con-ceptions of masculinity in the context of its appearance in the nineteenth century. Of course, it remains to be seen whether a fully redemptive gen-dered reading of the book can be worked out, but it can at least be said that what the book does with questions of gender is far more interesting than has been previously recognized or assumed.

Welcome as such recent studies obviously are, they remain as yet largely cut off from the unmistakable biblical roots of the Book of Mormon. That is, although they occasionally mark out connections or offer comparisons with the biblical text, they provide no systematic analysis of how the Book of Mormon's presentation of gender is shaped by its inclusion of passages familiar from the Christian Bible. In the course of this paper, I mean to provide a preliminary (but substantial) analysis of what biblical texts bring to the Book of Mormon's portrayal of the sexes. Naturally, avail-able time imposes certain limits. I will therefore focus here solely on "the book called Isaiah" (to borrow Hugh Williamson's useful phrase) and limit myself to commenting on how the presentation of women in Isaiah might be said to shape the Book of Mormon's own presentation of women. I'll further end up limiting myself primarily to what might be said of the Book of Mormon's presentation of gender in light of just Isaiah 3. Despite these limitations, I hope that what I outline in the following few minutes

---

1. [This line refers to two essays that actually did not appear until 2019: Kimberly M. Berkey and Joseph M. Spencer, "'Great Cause to Mourn': The Complexity of *The Book of Mormon*'s Presentation of Gender and Race," in *Americanist Approaches to* The Book of Mormon, ed. Elizabeth Fenton and Jared Hickman (New York: Oxford University Press, 2019), 298–320; and Amy Easton-Flake, "'Arise From the Dust, My Sons, and Be Men': Masculinity in *The Book of Mormon*," in *Americanist Approaches to* The Book of Mormon, 362–90. Today I would add Deidre Nicole Green, *Jacob: A Brief Theological Introduction* (Provo, UT: Neal A. Maxwell Institute, 2020).]

might serve as a useful foundation—both thematically and methodologically—for further, more exhaustive work.

Every reader of the Book of Mormon recognizes its investment in Isaiah. The volume opens with an uncomfortable story about how its chief protagonists came to possess a copy of Isaiah's writings, which they carried away from Jerusalem early in Zedekiah's reign. According to the book, they soon wove together what they found written under Isaiah's name and what they experienced in their own dreams and visions, ultimately producing a peculiar fusion of prophetic traditions. The first major expositor of this nearly-systematic interpretive program—the prophet Nephi—even provides his approach to Isaiah with a name: "likening." He and his associates liken the written text of Isaiah to the oral text of their own apocalyptic visions, providing their readers with a double prophetic witness. Their focus is on the ultimate redemption of Israel—of both Judah and Ephraim—through Gentile conversion. These are unmistakably Isaianic themes, though the Book of Mormon weds them to a vision of European history I can't take the time to summarize here.

This inaugural Isaianic project, front and center for the first hundred and fifty pages of the book, eventually falls out of favor—apparently because it becomes corrupted by power-hungry priests and so must be replaced by another interpretive program. The result is the rise, about a century before the birth of Jesus, of an anticipatorily Christological program of interpretation. Almost immediately after its introduction, however, this interpretive project falls into the narrative's background, such that Isaiah largely disappears from the volume until the visit of the resurrected Jesus to the ancient Americas at the book's climax. At that point, Isaiah returns to center stage, with Jesus himself offering an outline of how to interpret the prophet's writings. For the most part, his approach mirrors that of Nephi, arguing that events in and after the history of European Christianity follow the basic outline of Isaiah's prophecies—especially prophecies from the second half of Second Isaiah. From that point through the remainder of the volume, Isaiah's influence can be felt rather strongly.

Where in all this does one find women? The Isaiah passages drawn on in the Book of Mormon come primarily from two blocks of text. Early in the book, the focus is largely divided between a sustained engagement with Isaiah 2–14 and a sustained engagement with Isaiah 48–51, but to these is added a remarkably complex midrash on Isaiah 29. The Christological approach to Isaiah espoused somewhat later in the book focuses on Isaiah 52 and 53. And then the resurrected Jesus and the voices that appear following his visit focus more or less exclusively on Isaiah 52 and 54. Taken together, then, the Book of Mormon lays emphasis on Isaiah 2–14 and Isaiah 48–54, with additional interest exhibited in Isaiah 29. Close investigation suggests that four passages in particular form the chief points of emphasis: Isaiah 11:11; Isaiah 29:14; Isaiah 49:22–23; and Isaiah 52:7–10. The first three of these passages are the primary focus of Nephi's interpretive program, while the last serves as the focal point throughout the remainder of the volume.

Significantly, one of the four passages that especially draw the Book of Mormon's attention focuses rather heavily on gender. Isaiah 49:22–23 portrays Israel's redemption as occurring because Gentile rulers carry them home. But the passage emphasizes gender parity several times over, mentioning "daughters" as well as "sons," "mothers" as well as "fathers," and "queens" as well as "kings." Further, at least in the somewhat peculiar King James rendering, the male "kings" referred to in the text are only unstably masculine, since they become Zion's "*nursing* fathers" in parallel to the queens who become "nursing mothers." (Note that distinct adjectives appear in the underlying Hebrew, with the result that more recent translations distinguish "foster fathers" from "nursing mothers"; Joseph Blenkinsopp translates, "Kings will look after your children, their queens will serve you as nurses." Yet the Book of Mormon follows the King James rendering here, reproducing the fascinating image of "nursing fathers.") And then, still further, this focal passage from Isaiah emphasizes gender because its promises are addressed to daughter Zion, a central figure in the drama of Second Isaiah and the clear counterpart to the male figure of the servant who has been studied to exhaustion for the past two centuries.[2]

In this particular passage, then—that is, in Isaiah 49:22–23—one might expect to find the strongest Isaianic influence on the Book of Mormon's presentation of gender. Perhaps unfortunately, however, this is not the case. The images Nephi most often draws from this passage are simply those that concern signaling: lifting up the hand, and setting up a standard. He seems largely uninterested in the rich use of gendered imagery in the Isaianic text. And something much the same has to be said for most of the Book of Mormon. Throughout the volume, extensive quotations from Second Isaiah draw on passages in which Israel or Jerusalem is figured as a woman—a woman divorced or abandoned, a woman recovered and remarried, a woman once-barren but now fruitful,

---

2. See John F. A. Sawyer, "Daughter of Zion and Servant of the Lord in Isaiah: A Comparison," *Journal for the Study of the Old Testament* 14 (1989): 89–107.

and so on. But, peculiarly, the heavily gendered character of these passages never seems to seep from the quoted Isaiah passages themselves into the Book of Mormon's own discussions of Israel's dramatic history—that is, whenever it discusses Israel's history in its *own* voice, rather than in Isaiah's. Thus, it is certainly significant that the resurrected Christ who sermonizes at length at the climax of the Book of Mormon quotes Isaiah 54 in its entirety, thereby utilizing what is perhaps the richest of Isaianic texts for use of feminine imagery. But neither he nor any other voice in the Book of Mormon ever uses that same imagery when not directly quoting Isaiah. In fact, in the only passages where the Book of Mormon uses feminine imagery to figure Israel that aren't direct quotations of Isaiah, the text explicitly identifies other biblical or pseudo-biblical sources: the Book of Revelation for a few such references in Nephi's writings, and the writings of a certain Israelite prophet Zenos for a few such references in the writings of Nephi's brother Jacob.

Must one therefore conclude that the Book of Mormon quotes Isaianic material that's saturated with gendered talk, but that this material has not really affected the Book of Mormon's own presentation of gender? I think not, in the end. I want to outline two possible connections between passages in Isaiah 3 and the larger Book of Mormon narrative that, although they're implicit at best, perhaps rather weak at worst, seem to me nonetheless rather suggestive. These are connections that together suggest some kind of continuity between the presentation of gender in the Isaianic corpus and the presentation of gender in the Book of Mormon. They both concern the category of gender talk in Isaiah that Irmtraud Fischer nicely names "Sociocultural Conditions of Women's Lives."[3] In essence, I think there's reason to believe that some of the sociocultural presuppositions about gender put on display in Isaiah 3 are carried over into the Book of Mormon's narrative. This perhaps wouldn't be surprising in and of itself, but I will make a case that the Book of Mormon rather deliberately and inventively explores the larger implications of these sociocultural presuppositions.

Before turning to the two texts from Isaiah 3 that concern gender, let me note that the Book of Mormon exhibits some rather apparent interest in the description of social conditions in Isaiah 3. At one point in Nephi's writings early in the Book of Mormon, as already noted, the whole of

---

3. Irmtraud Fischer, "Isaiah: The Book of Female Metaphors," in *Feminist Biblical Interpretation*, ed. Luise Schottroff and Marie-Theres Wacker (Grand Rapids, MI: Eerdmans, 2012), 307.

Isaiah 2–14 is quoted in one block. Significantly, *only a single clear allusion to the first sequence of these chapters*—that is, to Isaiah 2–5—appears anywhere in Nephi's subsequent discussions of Isaiah's larger meaning. And this allusion is to Isaiah 3, specifically to the moment where Isaiah speaks of the wealthy in Jerusalem as "grind[ing] the faces of the poor." Nephi refers to this passage when he speaks of "the Gentiles" as "preach[ing] up unto themselves their own wisdom and their own learning, that they may get gain and grind upon the face of the poor" (2 Ne. 26:20). There's thus already some evidence that the Book of Mormon as a text is in important ways interested in the sociocultural presuppositions of Isaiah 3—and that it shares with Isaiah a certain indignant response to oppression.

With that introduction of sorts, let me begin with the passage from Isaiah 3 most often criticized by feminist interpreters: Isaiah 3:16–4:1. Here the prophet castigates "the daughters of Zion" in rather apparent disgust at their finery. In Fischer's words, "the text reads like a fashion-magazine reporter might write watching from the edge of the runway; every item worn by the noble women is discussed in detail, as is their behavior, and the perversion of it all is named."[4] You know the passage, I assume. Isaiah speaks of these "daughters of Zion" as having "stretched forth necks and wanton eyes, walking and mincing as they go, and making a tinkling with their feet." His near-obsession with the full catalog of their adornments naturally appears to the twenty-first century as symptomatic: "the chains, and the bracelets, and the mufflers, the bonnets, and the ornaments of the legs," and so on. Susan Ackerman says that "the misogyny here seems unrelenting" and calls Isaiah's words a "highly denigrating polemic."[5] In its lengthiest quotation of Isaiah, the Book of Mormon contains this passage, reproduced more or less exactly as it stands in the King James Version.

Now, the Book of Mormon never exhibits a kind of obsessiveness about *women's* finery, although it occasionally critiques the desire for "costly apparel," apparently with reference to both men *and* women. In fact, the only passage in the Book of Mormon where there seems to be a direct critique of female finery comes in an unmistakable allusion to the Book of Revelation, rather than to this passage from Isaiah.[6] So why make note of the Book of

---

4. Fischer, "Isaiah," 307.

5. Susan Ackerman, "Isaiah," in *The Women's Bible Commentary*, exp. ed., ed. Carol A. Newsom and Sharon H. Ringe (Louisville, KY: Westminster John Knox Press, 1998), 171.

6. See 1 Nephi 13:7 and Revelation 18:12.

Mormon's inclusion of this passage? Because of the possibility that it serves a rather different purpose in Isaiah's polemic than is generally assumed. Hans Wildberger notes the possible connection between Isaiah's prediction that these women's "beauty" will be replaced with "burning" and the final moments of Jezebel's life in the Deuteronomistic history. "The story about Jezebel," he says, "describes how women, in wartime, came to meet the enemy, provocatively dressed, but also points out that such a dubious attempt to save one's skin could very easily go awry."[7] Second Kings reports: "When Jehu was come to Jezreel, Jezebel heard of it; and she painted her face, and tired her head, and looked out at a window." The situation, as you know, does not end well. And something similar happens in Isaiah 3. Zion's daughters come walking out of the city with their "stretched forth necks and wanton eyes," wearing their "round tires like the moon," but it does nothing to produce deliverance. "Thy men shall fall by the sword," Jerusalem is told, "and thy mighty in the war."

If Isaiah 3 is read as integrated into its canonical context—which is reproduced in the Book of Mormon—then it seems best to read it as a description of women's behavior in a war situation, rather than as a description of the usual practices of women among the social elite. The women make an attempt at seduction in the hopes of placating the enemy, perhaps even in the hope of seeing their men spared. Perhaps one could even suggest that women are here sent *by force* to seduce the approaching army, in the oppressive hopes that their charms might make for the men's survival. Is it significant that, in the larger canonical context, this passage follows close on the heels of a claim that Jerusalem's sin is "as Sodom," that city where Lot attempted to send out his daughters for abuse in the hopes of protecting two men who had come to lodge with him? At any rate, there is good reason to wonder whether there isn't in Isaiah 3 a portrayal of just such a use of women, coupled with an implicit condemnation of the practice.

Significantly, this sort of practice appears several times in the Book of Mormon, and in more straightforward ways than it ever does in the Hebrew Bible. Early in the book, Nephi is delivered from his violent brothers only when certain women "plead" on his behalf. Later in the volume and more explicitly, one finds a situation where a group of Nephi's descendants faces a group of his brothers' descendants, the Lamanites—the latter presented, throughout the Book of Mormon, as the ethnically and racially other. The

---

7. Hans Wildberger, *Isaiah 1–12: A Commentary*, trans. Thomas H. Trapp (Minneapolis: Fortress Press, 1991), 150.

men on the defense "cause that their fair daughters should stand forth and plead with the Lamanites that they would not slay them," and the Lamanites end up "charmed with the beauty of their women" (Mosiah 19:13–14). Just a few chapters after this story, a similar one appears, where another group of Nephi's descendants is faced in conflict by another group of Lamanites, and they "send forth their wives, who were the [kidnapped!] daughters of the Lamanites, to plead with their brethren, that they should not destroy their husbands"; and here again, the Lamanites "have compassion" on them "because of their wives" (23:33–34). The Book of Mormon exhibits a clear pattern of men having women plead on their behalf, using their charms and beauty in order to see men delivered from violence. In this it is not difficult to see an echo of Isaiah 3, despite the fact that such attempts are successful in Book of Mormon narratives and entirely unsuccessful in Isaiah's prophecy.

Let me turn now to a second possible connection between Isaiah 3 and the larger shape of the Book of Mormon's narrative. The second half of Isaiah 3 seems to focus on war—and on women's fate in the course of war—but the first half seems to focus on internal disorder in Judah, disorder that apparently results from disparity between the wealthy and the poor. Because "the spoil of the poor" is in the "houses" of the rich, and because social elites (as we've already seen) "grind the faces of the poor," Judahite society is turned upside down. "I will give children to be their princes," the Lord says through the prophet, "and babes shall rule over them." But then note this further description of social upheaval, far less comfortable in the modern context: "As for my people, children are their oppressors, and women rule over them." Here again Fischer provides a helpful ideological critique: "The catastrophic conditions in the political elite of the people are demonstrated . . . by the fact that even women rule. The (considerable) exclusion of women from public office is not understood [here] as discrimination but is justified by an interpretive ideological framework that allocates gender roles within a patriarchal viewpoint: women are unfit to govern because of their gender."[8] Of course, as many commentators note, some of the ancient versions of the text have "usurers" or "creditors" in the place of "women" in this passage (the two words are nearly identical in Hebrew).[9] But whatever that might suggest about the

---

8. Fischer, "Isaiah," 308.

9. For a representative treatment, see Joseph Blenkinsopp, *Isaiah 1–39: A New Translation with Introduction and Commentary* (New York: Doubleday, 2000), 198.

original text, the Book of Mormon here follows the King James Version, speaking of women as ruling over men in situations of social disorder.

There may be an important echo of this passage at a crucial turn in the Book of Mormon's larger narrative. At one point in the volume, Nephite Christian missionaries determine to go among the aforementioned Lamanites in the hopes of turning them from the traditions of their fathers. Due to a miraculous series of events, one of them succeeds in converting a regional Lamanite king, who consequently collapses in a Spirit-induced swoon. The king's people, however, believe him to be dead, and they prepare for his burial. At this point, the Lamanite queen emerges as the ruling figure—rather than one of the king's "sons," who *are* in fact mentioned in the text. She takes charge and becomes, quite frankly, one of the most developed female characters in the whole of the Book of Mormon. At a point of profound Lamanite social disorder, women in fact become rulers. Significantly, this occurs again just a few chapters later, as if to underscore the importance of the first instance. The king over the whole of the Lamanite people ends up converted in much the same way his son does, thanks to the work of another Nephite Christian missionary, and this king too collapses in a swoon. Here again the Lamanite queen takes charge and becomes the ruler until disorder is quelled—at which point rule reverts to the Lamanite king, who passes rule to his son when he dies later under normal circumstances. Further, the same situation occurs one more time still later in the narrative (in fact, in a story the text sets up as a parallel to the two just considered). When a Lamanite king is murdered and the Lamanite capital is invaded by the king's murderer, it is the Lamanite queen who initiates diplomatic interactions with the invader, making clear that she has assumed rule in the profoundly disordered political situation.

Here, in three distinct but related moments of intense social disorder among the Lamanites, women come to possess political power—much as Isaiah 3 describes happening in Judah at times of social upheaval. Conflict within this Israelite society, just as pressure exerted from without this Israelite society, reproduces social conditions described in some detail in Isaiah 3.

Now, the question is whether the connections I've traced here are as suggestive as I've tried to make them. Is there any reason, really, to think that these aspects of the societies portrayed in the Book of Mormon are meant to be connected to Isaiah's writings, or to Isaiah 3 in particular? It might be a good deal easier to think either that the parallels are coincidental or predictable for other reasons (simple features of patriarchal social structures, perhaps). Yet I believe there's reason to think that the parallels are significant. What should be striking in the discussions above to anyone familiar with the Book of Mormon's narrative is that these apparent echoes of Isaiah 3 occur only in connection with the Lamanites, the racial and ethnic others of the book, rather than with the light-skinned protagonists of the Book of Mormon: Nephi's descendants, the Nephites. It is only Lamanites who are ever presented as responding to women's pleas on behalf of their men, and it is only in Lamanite society that women assume rule during times of social disorder. Never once are Nephites described as being charmed by Lamanite women in a situation of conflict, and, despite the Book of Mormon's *constant* talk of social disorder among the Nephites, there's not one story in which a Nephite woman assumes a position of political influence. These apparently Isaianic sociocultural traces are, in the Book of Mormon, exclusively associated with the Lamanites.

This seems to me significant for two major reasons. First, a recent study of patterns of language use in the Book of Mormon has suggestively shown that, with the exception of Nephi himself, Isaianic turns of phrase appear most frequently in the one sermon the Book of Mormon attributes to a *Lamanite* prophet—as if Isaiah's writings had somehow had a deeper (and perhaps unconscious) effect on the Lamanites than it ever did on the Nephites.[10] This is, I think, suggestive. But second and still more significant, recent work has shown that the Book of Mormon centers its investigation into questions of gender profoundly on the Lamanites.[11] Every significantly developed female character in the book is a Lamanite, and prophetic critiques of Nephite culture focus crucially on the way that Nephite men abuse both Nephite and Lamanite women. Every story the volume contains regarding Nephite women, or regarding Lamanite women in relation to Nephite men, is a story of violence or abuse. There's reason to think that the book as a whole deliberately foregrounds its androcentrism, precisely so that intermittent prophetic voices within the book—one of them, significantly, the voice of a Lamanite—can then critique Nephite misogyny. The fact, then, that Isaiah 3's discussions of women's sociocultural conditions find echoes only in situations involving Lamanites may well be quite suggestive.

---

10. See Shon Hopkin and John Hilton III, "Samuel's Reliance on Biblical Language," *Journal of Book of Mormon Studies* 24 (2015): 31–52.

11. [This refers again to work cited in footnote 1.]

Especially interesting in this connection is the fact that the Book of Mormon's sociocultural echoes of Isaiah 3 are positive and affirmative, rather than negative and critical. Where Isaiah 3 predicts that women's unique approach to deliverance will fail, Israel's enemies succeeding in war, the Book of Mormon narrative points to Lamanite compassion in such circumstances—and in a way that doesn't allow for the sexual abuse that would certainly have resulted from any such self-offering on the part of women in situations of war. Further, where Isaiah 3 predicts women's political power in times of social disorder with the possible implication that this is inherently wrong, the Book of Mormon narrative presents women rulers among the Lamanites as competent and faithful—precisely what's needed in the moment to stabilize situations that are terribly out of balance. If Isaiah 3 finds traces in the Book of Mormon, it would seem that the latter outlines a possible redemptive hermeneutic, almost feminist in orientation, in its attempt at interpreting the prophet.

Or so it seems to me. I believe I have, at any rate, made a sufficient case here that the Book of Mormon's use of Isaiah may have much to add to studies of gender in Mormonism's found text.

Theological Invitations

Chapter Thirteen

On a Dawning Era for the Book of Mormon

After decades of historically focused research on the Book of Mormon, the late 1970s and early 1980s saw a sudden flurry of publications that examined the Book of Mormon from a specifically literary angle. Then-new institutions offered to shelter such work, and all the evidence suggests that there was a good deal of excitement surrounding what looked like an emerging movement. It was only a couple of years after the seed of literary Book of Mormon studies was planted, however, that weeds grew and choked what had sprung up. The Book of Mormon's historicity came under heavy fire in the early 1980s, in no minor part due to forged documents created by Mark Hofmann. In the midst of a cultural storm where many felt that the Book of Mormon was hanging in the balance, the often nonconfessional framework of literary studies of the Book of Mormon made it an uncomfortable or unwise one for many scholars to take up. Literary study of the Book of Mormon largely disappeared for more than a decade.

During the late 1990s, a handful of committed scholars began to clear a new space of ground where the seeds of literary scholarship on the Book of Mormon might again be planted. By the first years of the twenty-first century, the soil was ready and waiting. In 2010, Grant Hardy showed that the literary seeds would in fact yield much fruit when he published *Understanding the Book of Mormon*. For theologically inclined readers, Hardy's book is loaded with good fruit, ripe and ready for the picking. Such literary fruit, however, remains only pre- or proto-theological. The theologian has to carry a good harvest of Hardy's fruit home and then decide on what recipe might bring out its theological flavor best. Naturally, some prefer their literary fruit raw, fresh from the tree. Theologians, though, ask what kind of a theological pie such fruit might make. This essay, formally a review of Hardy's book, was my attempt to wrestle as a theologian with the remarkable literary work Hardy had begun to produce in abundance with his deeply important book. It serves also as a gentle invitation to the literarily inclined to join the theologian in the kitchen.

This essay originally appeared in *Mormon Studies Review* 1 (2014): 132–43.

G. W. F. Hegel famously said that the owl of Minerva takes flight only at dusk, that it is only as a historical sequence comes to a close that it becomes possible to reflect fully on its meaning and implications.[1] In this sense, Terryl Givens's 2002 *By the Hand of Mormon*, a full-blooded reception history of "the American scripture that launched a new world religion," marked an important break in the history of academic study of the Book of Mormon.[2] Its appearance significantly coincided with the slowdown of the most intense and productive period of investigation the Book of Mormon has witnessed in the almost two centuries of its circulation. Givens thus attempted in his book not so much to take the pulse of a flourishing movement as to eulogize what had been generally regarded as a great era for academic study of the Book of Mormon. Inaugurated by Hugh Nibley and Sidney Sperry in the 1940s, becoming dormant for a period beginning in the 1960s, and reemerging with peculiar force under the guidance of John Welch and John Sorenson in the 1980s, the era whose end Givens effectively announced was dominated by an unmistakable apologetic impulse and aimed at defending the plausibility of the Book of Mormon's ancient origins.

A year after Givens's reception history appeared, the University of Illinois published Grant Hardy's *The Book of Mormon: A Reader's Edition*, a reformatting of the Book of Mormon text that, more implicitly than explicitly, outlined a possible new direction for academic study of the Book of Mormon.[3] By aiming to provide a readable presentation of the text of the Book of Mormon, one that aimed to give center stage to the scripture's narrative, Hardy quietly announced his intention to help inaugurate an era of literary study of the Book of Mormon. Thus, at the very moment that Givens marked the end of one era of Book of Mormon study, one focused particularly on questions of historicity, Hardy launched a project to establish the foundations of another era of Book of Mormon study, now to be focused particularly on questions of narrativity. And what Hardy outlined

---

1. See G. W. F. Hegel, *Elements of the Philosophy of Right*, trans. H. B. Nisbet (New York: Cambridge University Press, 1991), 23.

2. See Terryl L. Givens, *By the Hand of Mormon: The American Scripture That Launched a New World Religion* (New York: Oxford University Press, 2002).

3. See Grant Hardy, ed., *The Book of Mormon: A Reader's Edition* (Urbana: University of Illinois Press, 2003).

implicitly and announced quietly in 2003, he proclaimed unequivocally in 2010 with *Understanding the Book of Mormon: A Reader's Guide*. This clear companion to the *Reader's Edition* is as much a manifesto as a monograph, as much an intervention as an investigation. Of course, literary treatments of the Book of Mormon have been available for a long time, some more compelling than others.[4] What is unique about Hardy's study, however, is that it explicitly presents literary work on the Book of Mormon *as a way forward* for students of the Book of Mormon after a rather different era of study has passed. And Hardy makes a compelling case.

What Hardy means when he speaks of a literary reading of the Book of Mormon is in important ways different from what others might mean when using such language; what he presents is not a work of theory-laden comparative literature but a model of what he calls "narrator-based reading." Arguing from within the field of religious studies, Hardy marks the uniqueness of the Book of Mormon among volumes of recently produced world scripture by pointing to its narrativity. Even though more ancient volumes of world scripture bear the characteristic of narrativity, Hardy argues that the Book of Mormon's "extended, integrated, non-mythological, history-like narrative makes it quite distinctive."[5] Motivated by this heavily narrative flavor, Hardy identifies as the key feature of the Book of Mormon's literary structure its presentation as the work of three distinguishable narrators with different personalities and divergent agendas.[6] Thus in nine chapters, an introduction, and an afterword, *Understanding the Book of Mormon* focuses its efforts on discerning the characters and interests of the Book of Mormon's three major narrators: Nephi, Mormon, and Moroni. The bulk of the book is divided into three main parts, each a study of one of these figures.

On Hardy's reading, the Book of Mormon's major narrators—carefully and revealingly constructed within the text—are presented as drastically distinct. Nephi is a tragic figure, failing to fulfill his father's dying request that he keep the family together and so burying himself ever deep-

---

4. See Madison U. Sowell, review of *Feasting on the Word: The Literary Testimony of the Book of Mormon*, by Richard Dilworth Rust, *FARMS Review of Books* 9, no. 2 (1997): 29–32.

5. Hardy, *Understanding the Book of Mormon*, 12.

6. Rosalynde Welch has pointed out some philosophical difficulties with this approach. See Rosalynde Welch, "Grant Hardy's Subject Problem," Times and Seasons, August 16, 2011, https://www.timesandseasons.org/harchive/2011/08/grant-hardys-subject-problem/.

er in the writings of arcane prophets from a tradition foreign to his own
people. Mormon, in turn, is a dedicated historian with a moralizing message, struggling and often succeeding to make the recalcitrant documents
of history bear witness to God's faithfulness. Moroni, finally, is a self-
conscious finisher, fretting about the myriad ways the whole project of the
Book of Mormon might fail if its first readers misunderstand or dismiss
it. All three figures are handlers and transmitters of texts, but each with a
unique approach to the texts in his possession: Nephi focuses primarily on
the texts produced by the Israelites of the Old World, relishing both their
messages of doom and their messages of hope; Mormon weighs the textual
remains of the thousand-year history of the Israelites of the New World,
his own people; and Moroni turns his attention to a non-Israelite nation
that bridged the Old and the New Worlds, a clear parallel to the Book of
Mormon's earliest nineteenth-century readers.

If Hardy has a hero, it is Mormon, whom he presents as particularly
complicated and especially skilled. Where Nephi artfully but ultimately
unconvincingly makes himself the uncontested hero of his writings, and
where Moroni aptly but not remarkably works out his own prophetic
concerns, Mormon's deft construction of his moralizing history—especially as Hardy analyzes it—takes one's breath away. Hardy gives whole
chapters to Mormon's use of embedded documents of various kinds, to
his construction of parallel narratives to encode moral messages, and to
his constant struggle with the relationship between prophecy and history.
And he provides a list of other historical, literary, and moralizing strategies
in Mormon's writing that could receive as much attention (geographical notes, genealogical details, flashbacks and flash-forwards, the length
of textual units, selective attention, repeated phrases, editorial insertions,
typological interpretation, and so on). Whatever Nephi and Moroni have
to contribute to the Book of Mormon is, on Hardy's interpretation, an-
cillary to Mormon's purpose: Nephi's writings are primarily prefatory to
Mormon's history, and Moroni's writings are first and foremost a kind of
appendix to Mormon's history.

Hardy's portraits of the Book of Mormon's chief authorial or editorial
figures are very responsibly painted. They are products of sustained close
reading of the text, always undertaken with an eye to large-scale questions
concerning themes and motifs. Hardy thus admirably weaves together
detailed readings of relatively short passages (as with, for instance, his remarkable analysis of "the record of Zeniff" in Mosiah 9–10, which reveals
a profoundly sensitive voice in an often black-and-white narrative) and

sweeping characterizations that make sense of whole swaths of the Book of Mormon at once (a good example is his argument that Helaman, son of Alma, is subtly presented as a poor record-keeper whose failure to produce a narrative from the records he gathered and kept left Mormon with more original sources to use in constructing his own narrative). Invariably, local, detailed work grounds broad, global claims. There is little question whether Hardy has read the Book of Mormon well—certainly according to Hardy's own definition of "reading well," namely, "following the contours and structure of the text, perceiving how the parts fit into the whole, and evaluating fairly the emphases and tensions within the book."[7]

In the end, however, Hardy's good reading, compelling as it unquestionably is, represents only one sort of good reading, and it should be asked both exactly how Hardy's approach differs from what precedes it and exactly how Hardy's approach differs from other ways one might go forward with the Book of Mormon. To what extent does *Understanding the Book of Mormon* break with the apologetic impulse? To what extent does it dispense with the historical (or perhaps historicist) commitments of its predecessors? And how might it be situated among the variety of proposals currently on offer for moving forward with academic study of the Book of Mormon?

First, then, it should be said that Hardy's work surely remains within the category of apologetics, albeit not of apologetics in defense of specific *religious* claims. In other words, while it must be said that Hardy expresses no interest in establishing the *historical veracity* of the Book of Mormon (with all that historicity would imply about supernatural events like the visit of the angel Moroni to Joseph Smith), it cannot be said that he expresses no interest in establishing *a certain truthfulness* of the Book of Mormon. His appeals to the book's complexity and interest, its intrinsic worth and literary merits, its compelling construction and occasionally forceful ideas—these are apologetic gestures, instances of a polemic undertaken on behalf of a book few academics believe deserves sustained attention. Simply by taking as his thesis that the Book of Mormon is "better than it sounds,"[8] Hardy defends the book as a source of truth—albeit neither as an unequivocal source of purely objective truth nor as an uncontestable source of divinely revealed truth. The truth of the Book of Mormon as Hardy unveils it is something more like the truth about which

7. Hardy, *Understanding the Book of Mormon*, xiv.
8. Hardy, 273.

Hans-Georg Gadamer philosophizes in his work on the aesthetic.[9] To that extent at least, if Hardy's approach marks an appealing way forward for academic study of the Book of Mormon, it does not definitively dispense with the apologetic impulse.

As it turns out, Hardy's approach to the Book of Mormon does not entirely dispense with questions of history either. As he explains, his approach to the text is "not quite historical and not quite literary, because neither exactly fits the Book of Mormon."[10] It is, he says, a wrong-headed move simply to "read [the book] as a product of the nineteenth century," since "this requires treating it as an indirect or coded source; one must start with the assumption that it is something very different from what it professes to be."[11] It is better, on Hardy's account, to confess the "history-likeness" of the Book of Mormon.[12] But this he takes as a spur to study the story the book sets out to tell, not as a spur to search through ancient texts or archaeological sites for corroborating (or conflicting) evidence. Hardy is more concerned to ask how the history-likeness of the Book of Mormon demands a certain sort of reading than to ask how it demands a certain set of beliefs concerning ancient history.

It should thus be said that Hardy inherits from his predecessors both a certain apologetic orientation (albeit not a traditional apologetics in defense of what are usually taken to be the Book of Mormon's truth claims) and a certain commitment to the historical nature of the Book of Mormon (albeit not overtly to the claim that the Book of Mormon makes ostensive reference to events, people, and places recoverable through the usual means of historical inquiry). He thus remains within the tradition

---

9. For a summary of the relevance of Gadamer's work to Mormonism, see James E. Faulconer, "Recovering Truth: A Review of Hans-Georg Gadamer, *Truth and Method*," *The Mormon Review: Books and Culture from an LDS Perspective* 2, no. 2 (September 27, 2010): 1–7. Perhaps particularly helpful is the exchange between Faulconer and Richard Bushman at the conclusion of the essay.

10. Hardy, *Understanding the Book of Mormon*, xvii.

11. Hardy, xvii. A good example of what Hardy seems to have in mind when he speaks of "treating [the Book of Mormon] as an indirect or coded source" is Clyde R. Forsberg Jr., *Equal Rites: The Book of Mormon, Masonry, Gender, and American Culture* (New York: Columbia University Press, 2004).

12. Hardy borrows the term "history-likeness" from Hans Frei, who helpfully distinguishes between "history-likeness (literal meaning) and history (ostensive reference)." See Hans W. Frei, *The Eclipse of Biblical Narrative: A Study in Eighteenth and Nineteenth Century Hermeneutics* (New Haven: Yale University Press, 1974), 12.

of Book of Mormon studies even as he transforms the basic stakes of the gestures made by his predecessors. In each case, Hardy's efforts undertaken in the book's defense or in the study of the book's history-likeness are oriented by the overarching imperative to always understand the Book of Mormon better in its own right, regardless of the relationship the text might sustain with what lies outside the text. In this sense, he definitively (if not even defiantly) reverses what Givens claims has been the dominant, almost uncontested approach to the Book of Mormon: to take it as sacred signifier (of the truth or falsity of Mormonism) rather than as sacred signified (a text deserving of sustained study). For Hardy, the Book of Mormon should be signified before and almost to the exclusion of its being signifier.

On that score, Hardy finds himself in company with many other emerging students of the Book of Mormon. Even where the focus of recent Book of Mormon scholarship is on ancient history (as in, for instance, the most recent work by John Welch or the commentary produced by Brant Gardner), the focus is on elucidating the text of the Book of Mormon much more than on establishing the historicity of the text.[13] And among those approaching the Book of Mormon from disciplines other than those focused on ancient history (e.g., Jad Hatem, working in comparative religion, or myself, working in philosophy—not to mention Hardy himself), it is even clearer that the chief aim is to see what the Book of Mormon might have to say if it is read closely and inventively.[14] How, though, might Hardy's work be distinguished from other approaches to the Book of Mormon with which it nonetheless shares a commitment first and foremost to elucidating the text?

Here it might be helpful to distinguish, as is commonly done in biblical studies, among three distinct "worlds" to which the student of the text might address her attention. First is the world *behind* the text, the world that *produced* the text. In terms of the Book of Mormon, one might in this regard look either to the ancient world (whether to the Old or to

---

13. See John W. Welch, *The Legal Cases in the Book of Mormon* (Provo, UT: Brigham Young University Press and Neal A. Maxwell Institute for Religious Scholarship, 2008); and Brant A. Gardner, *Second Witness: Analytical and Contextual Commentary on the Book of Mormon*, 6 vols. (Salt Lake City: Greg Kofford Books, 2007).

14. See Jad Hatem, *Postponing Heaven: The Three Nephites, the Mahdi, and the Bodhisattva*, trans. Jonathon Penny (Provo, UT: Neal A. Maxwell Institute, 2015); and Joseph M. Spencer, *An Other Testament: On Typology* (Salem, OR: Salt Press, 2012).

the New World) or to nineteenth-century America (the latter not necessarily in a critical vein: many believing scholars find themselves asking
what role Joseph Smith's own cultural inculcations played in the shape of
the translated text of the Book of Mormon). The idea here would be to
elucidate the text of scripture by looking at how its meaning is (at least in
part) determined by the forces that produced it. Second is the world *of* the
text, the world *portrayed by* the text, as it is portrayed by the text. In terms
of the Book of Mormon, one might in this regard look at the narrative
structure of the book, or perhaps attempt to establish the critical text of
the book, or perhaps compare the text to other scriptural texts (the Qur'an
or the Daodejing, for instance).[15] The idea here would be to elucidate the
text of scripture by giving attention uniquely to what it presents (and
perhaps to how what it presents differs from what other texts that make
similar claims to being scripture or history present). Third is the world
before the text, the world *inhabited by the readers of* the text. In terms of the
Book of Mormon, one might in this regard look at how the stories or ideas
or structures found in the book have helped or might still help to contest
contemporary thought and practice. The idea here would be to elucidate
the scriptural text by showing its relevance and force, by revealing the
ways in which it resists its readers.

　　All three of these approaches to scripture aim at elucidating the meaning of the text, though each takes the meaning of "meaning" to be slightly
different. Where those interested in the world behind the text focus on
the way that meaning is determined by the causal weave of history, those
interested in the world of the text focus on the way that meaning is the
product of complex structures, identifiable through comparative study
of similarly structured texts. Different from both of these are those interested in the world before the text, those who focus on the way that
meaning is constituted through the dynamic relationship between a text
and its readers. In terms of this triple typology, Hardy's work—and larger
interests—can be said to fall within the second category, interest in the
world *of* (rather than *behind* or *before*) the text. That Hardy has expressed
deep interest in and appreciation for Royal Skousen's critical text project
and that he has stated his interest in turning his attention to comparative

---

　　15. One might well wonder whether comparative scripture uniquely pays
attention to the world of the text. But lateral comparison, rather than moving
into the world *behind* or *before* the text, establishes a differential network of how
various (similar) texts work on their own terms, allowing for investigation of an
individual text's meaning in a revealing way.

scripture should come as no surprise, then. Hardy's sights are set squarely on the study of the world *of* the text of the Book of Mormon.

There remains, however, important work to be done on the world behind the text of the Book of Mormon. And promising young scholars have emerged in recent years to undertake that sort of work: Michael MacKay, working on the nineteenth-century context of the Book of Mormon's emergence; David Bokovoy, working on how ancient Near Eastern history might still elucidate the text of the Book of Mormon; and Mark Wright, working on how ancient Mesoamerica might help to clarify the meaning of the text. Obviously, some of this work will have appeal primarily—if not only—to believing Latter-day Saints. It is, nonetheless, work that deserves to be pursued. But more promising in my view, if only because it has been so little pursued as yet, is work on the world before the text of the Book of Mormon.

To return to Terryl Givens, it should be said that *By the Hand of Mormon* does more than just identify the transition from one era of Book of Mormon study to another; it also contributes to the conversation about what a new era of Book of Mormon study might be. Givens does this in part through his construction of a reception history. Such an approach to the Book of Mormon is itself a way of taking seriously the world before the text: a study of how the Book of Mormon has motivated believers and unbelievers alike to respond in a variety of ways.[16] But what was perhaps most interesting about Givens's book was not the history of the Book of Mormon's reception so much as his provocative chapter on the Book of Mormon as "dialogic revelation," as a text that has real ideas to contribute to the ongoing conversation about the nature of God.[17]

There is, I think, much, much more work to do in this vein. There is, in other words, much, much more work to do on the *theological* productivity of the Book of Mormon—work that will more often than not be predicated on the kind of close textual analysis Hardy has modeled. And I find myself convinced that it is only as the Book of Mormon is given to speak directly and forcefully to the world before the text that it might gain the kind of universal appeal Hardy argues it should have. To put the

---

16. Paul Gutjahr's *The* Book of Mormon: *A Biography* has recently expanded the purview of the Book of Mormon's reception history. Where Givens focuses almost exclusively on intellectual history, Gutjahr looks at the history of translation, of missiological usage, and of artist appropriation. See Paul C. Gutjahr, *The* Book of Mormon: *A Biography* (Princeton: Princeton University Press, 2012).

17. See Givens, *By the Hand of Mormon*, 209–39.

point polemically, Hardy's work on the Book of Mormon—its brilliance and fruitfulness notwithstanding—cannot alone accomplish its primary purpose, which is to allow the Book of Mormon to speak with a universal voice. It cannot accomplish this purpose, that is, unless it is taken up into a theological project that reveals the ways in which the Book of Mormon contests contemporary thought and practice.

I might justify this polemical claim by providing just a brief analysis of what I find to be at once the richest and yet the most disappointing moment in Hardy's book. It comes in chapter 7, "The Day of the Lord's Coming: Prophecy and Fulfillment" (pp. 180–213). There Hardy traces the development of Mormon "from historian to prophet" at the culmination of the Third Book of Nephi. Having developed a pattern of employing the fulfillment of prophecies through history to establish God's Faithfulness, Mormon finds himself forced by the Lord to cut his history short and to assume an unwanted prophetic mantle. In effect, Mormon is forced to abandon his own express design to establish the truth of his record through historically verifiable data and assume a "prophetic pedagogy . . . aimed to produce a more resilient faith, a faith capable of withstanding doubts and temptations, one that transcends the historical moment."[18]

Hardy's readerly abilities are here at their peak. The details, which must be omitted here, deserve close attention, and Hardy must be said to have discovered one of the most forceful moments in the whole Book of Mormon. Nonetheless, there is something disappointing about the way that Hardy simply leaves this pregnant transformation of the Book of Mormon's explicit project undeveloped. He notes it as if it were little more than an interesting fact. Why no discussion of how this moment in the Book of Mormon speaks to questions of what it means to write and to read texts? Why no discussion of how the transformation Mormon is forced to undergo might speak to two centuries of debate about the relationship between the prophetic and the historical when it comes to the Book of Mormon's origins? Why no discussion of how this remarkable text might be used as a platform for outlining an approach to the status of religious faith in a world so thoroughly dominated by the scientific outlook? Why no discussion of how Mormon might be thought of as a figure for every religious believer committed to a sacred history of one sort or another? Because he does not pursue the theological implications of his readings—because he remains focused solely on the world of the text, and

---

18. Hardy, *Understanding the Book of Mormon*, 213.

not on the way that that world collides with the world before the text—Hardy misses what might well be the universal voice that speaks in the Book of Mormon, the voice that can speak as much to non-Mormons as to Mormons, as much to the curious as to the deeply interested, as much to the irreligious as to the religious.

In the end, of course, this may be a minor complaint. Even the somewhat disappointed theologian cannot complain too loudly about missed opportunities in Hardy's work—at the very least because she can take those missed opportunities as occasions for her own theological reflection. Nonetheless, from the perspective of the theologian it is worth taking notice of the danger that what Hardy calls the literary approach to the Book of Mormon risks being a bit too academic, a bit too abstract, to have genuinely universal appeal. *Understanding the Book of Mormon* announces the possibility of a new era of Book of Mormon study with great and appreciated fanfare, but the universal voice it attempts to coax out of the Book of Mormon is perhaps still only a whisper out of the dust. If the Book of Mormon is to raise its voice, it seems to me, Hardy and others like him will need as many theologically disappointed interlocutors as they have and will have appreciative readers.

Chapter Fourteen

The Self-Critical Book of Mormon
Notes on an Emergent Literary Approach

Right about the time Hardy's *Understanding the Book of Mormon* appeared, scholars working in the Latter-day Saint context began whispering about a forthcoming essay on race in the Book of Mormon, a heavily theoretical literary study that would appear in a major literary journal and set the whole question on an entirely new footing. While everyone was waiting for the rumored essay to appear, there suddenly appeared in 2013 an entirely unexpected essay on the Book of Mormon in a different literary journal, a fascinating and also heavily theoretical literary study that suggested the Book of Mormon was coming into its own as a literary text. The earlier-rumored essay then appeared in 2014. By that time, though, the authors of the two essays—Jared Hickman and Elizabeth Fenton—had announced their intentions to gather essays for a collection that eventually appeared in 2019: *Americanist Approaches to The Book of Mormon.* Literary study of the Book of Mormon had arrived in earnest as a kind of sub-discipline.

As a theologian—and especially as a theologian trained in the style of contemporary European philosophy that is so often sprinkled throughout theoretically-driven literary criticism—I found these developments particularly cheering. In my own little corner, but with a more strictly theological than a literary aim, I too had been applying thinkers like Jacques Derrida and Gilles Deleuze to the Book of Mormon. It seemed that I now might have interlocutors in the larger scholarly world. When the editor of the *Journal of Book of Mormon Studies* asked me to write a review essay about these developments, I happily and quickly obliged. This essay is, therefore, my attempt to take the measure of the more heavily theoretical literary work of the Americanists at the moment they began to appear. Here again, to address myself to such work was in part motivated by the hope that I might be able to draw out the significance of such research for the theological study of the Book of Mormon.

This essay appeared in *Journal of Book of Mormon Studies* 24 (2015): 180–93.

The names of Elizabeth Fenton and Jared Hickman have quickly become associated in the past couple of years with one another by students of Mormonism. In 2013, as essays on the Book of Mormon by these two scholars were being finalized for publication in *American Literature* and the *Journal of Nineteenth-Century Americanists*, these scholars began circulating a call for proposals for an edited collection of literary essays on the Book of Mormon, then under negotiation with Oxford University Press. In the two years since that time, both scholars' essays have appeared in print, and the proposed Oxford publication—*The Book of Mormon: Americanist Approaches*—has taken shape, with plans in place for its appearance in 2016.[1] Rather quickly, Fenton and Hickman have come to represent jointly the possibility of a first flowering of literary study of the Book of Mormon produced primarily for a non-Mormon readership.[2] While students of the Book of Mormon have to wait a little while yet to see what the coming collection of Americanist approaches will yield, a taste of Fenton's and Hickman's own work can be had by looking at their already-published essays on the Book of Mormon.

More than just a shared editorial project brings Fenton and Hickman into a single orbit. There are striking similarities between their respective literary approaches to the Book of Mormon. Both understand the book to operate in a deconstructive manner (in the technical theoretical sense of the term *deconstructive*), and both argue that the deconstructive operations of the book lend it a peculiar political forcefulness in the context of its appearance in nineteenth-century America. In the following pages, I wish to explore critically the virtues and potential vices of this particular way of making sense of the Book of Mormon. Summarily put, my argument is that the deconstructive approach to the Book of Mormon is revealing in an essential way but that its usefulness encounters certain important limits. On my interpretation, Fenton's work is somewhat more attuned to these limits than is Hickman's, a difference marked in an important way by the fact that the latter scholar makes certain interpretively problematic moves with respect to the Book of Mormon.

---

1. [This book did not appear until 2019, and with a slightly different title: Elizabeth Fenton and Jared Hickman, eds., *Americanist Approaches to* The Book of Mormon (New York: Oxford University Press, 2019).]

2. For a brief survey of literary study of the Book of Mormon, see Michael Austin, "The Brief History and Perpetually Exciting Future of Mormon Literary Studies," *Mormon Studies Review* 2 (2015): 66–72.

Although both Fenton and Hickman develop deconstructive readings of the Book of Mormon, Fenton's "Open Canons" addresses this point in more overtly theoretical terms. Noting the manner in which the Book of Mormon "is preoccupied with the process of compiling and interpreting records," presenting "plates within plates and writing about writing," she argues that the volume "operates both as a history and as an account of history making."[3] Appearing in a geographical place and a historical period characterized by "the impulse to compile and preserve [historical] records" that would attest to the divinely orchestrated history of the young United States,[4] the Book of Mormon undercuts such impulses by both presenting the impossibility of recovering from the archives any full account of providential history and laying out a radically alternative conception of America's past, present, and destiny. The key to both of these moves, on Fenton's account, is the complicated relationship the Book of Mormon establishes between itself and the Christian Bible. Borrowing from the famous allegory of the olive tree in Jacob 5, Fenton uses the image of grafting to clarify this relationship: "Though the grafting process aims to produce a new whole, it is as an act of laceration as well as repair, highlighting the incompleteness of both its source and its recipient."[5] The Book of Mormon's repetition, but "with a difference," of biblical texts ultimately has the effect of "complicat[ing] the distinction between source material and copy."[6]

Although much of her language is perhaps more suggestive of the philosophy of Gilles Deleuze, Fenton ties her presentation to Jacques Derrida, calling the Book of Mormon "a supplement of the Derridean kind, adding 'only to replace,' highlighting the very gap it would address, and compensating 'for what *ought* to lack nothing at all in itself.'"[7] This

---

3. Elizabeth Fenton, "Open Canons: Sacred History and Lay American History in The Book of Mormon," *Journal of Nineteenth Century Americanists* 1, no. 2 (2013): 340–41.

4. Fenton, 341.

5. Fenton, 344.

6. Fenton, 345.

7. Fenton, 344. These last words come from Derrida's *Of Grammatology*, which remains his most important theoretical work. See Jacques Derrida, *Of Grammatology*, trans. Gayatri Chakravorty Spivak (Baltimore: Johns Hopkins University Press, 1974). Fenton's talk of repetition with difference, and especially of blurring the boundary between source and copy, is suggestive of Deleuze's earliest and most influential works. See Gilles Deleuze, *Difference and Repetition*, trans. Paul Patton (New York: Columbia University Press, 1994); and Gilles Deleuze, *The Logic of Sense*, trans. Mark Lester (New York: Columbia University Press, 1990).

is deconstruction of a rather classic sort, according to which careful attention to the details of a text reveals the impossibility of producing a fully complete and internally consistent system of meaning. Fenton argues first that the Book of Mormon performs a deconstruction of the biblical text—that is, it strategically reveals the instability of the Christian Bible by replacing the supposedly inerrant (because quintessentially original) Word of God with an entire network of volumes of scripture, no one of which can be said to be the pristine original from which others are derived. As Fenton puts it, "through the highlighting of fissures in sacred history, [the Book of Mormon] challenges the very notion of textual sufficiency—even when the texts in question are divinely inspired."[8] Once Fenton has established this first point, however, she turns to a still more striking point: that the Book of Mormon systematically deconstructs *itself* just as much as it deconstructs the Bible. The readable text of the Book of Mormon presents itself as suspended between two unreadable poles: the "phantom limb" of the lost "Book of Lehi" on the one hand and the revelatory portion of the volume sealed in "perpetual obscurity" because it remains to be translated.[9] And what stretches out between those two poles as the readable text of the Book of Mormon is presented explicitly and deliberately as "a series of incomplete histories."[10] Still more, the Book of Mormon itself claims that it is to be eventually supplemented by still other books of scripture that would call its own sufficiency into question.[11] Thus the Book of Mormon not only contests the total and inerrant status of the Bible, but it also undercuts its own completeness and consistency in its complex self-presentation.

In the final part of "Open Canons," Fenton brings these several sorts of deconstructive gestures to bear—albeit in a relatively limited way—on the

---

8. Fenton, "Open Canons," 348–49.

9. Fenton, 349, 351. Fenton's presentation of these two poles presents an unresolved tension between the possibility that the Book of Mormon's incompleteness is a product of the contingent circumstances of its production (the loss of the manuscript that shaved off the original opening of the volume was anything but intentional on Joseph Smith's part) and the possibility that the volume's incompleteness is a necessary feature of its own self conception (the postponement of the translation of the sealed portion of the volume is deliberate and organizes the purposes of the entire volume). The relationship between these possibilities remains to be investigated deeply.

10. Fenton, 351.

11. See Fenton, 351–52.

context in which the Book of Mormon first began to circulate. Working against the deep but retrospectively naïve trust evinced by nineteenth-century American historians, the Book of Mormon's deconstruction of the Bible, coupled with its self-critical regard, made it a profoundly counter-cultural document when the first Mormon missionaries began to circulate it. But it is Hickman's "*The Book of Mormon* as Amerindian Apocalypse," more than Fenton's "Open Canons," that takes the measure of the possible countercultural force of the Book of Mormon in the nineteenth-century American context (and beyond). Responding to straightforward accusations that the Book of Mormon contains "patent racism,"[12] Hickman mobilizes the self-critical nature of the volume to complicate its relationship to questions of race. Fenton finds in the book both an attempt at presenting history *and* a complex contestation of every pretension—even its own—to present history in a complete or consistent manner. Hickman, in turn, finds in the book both a text that seems destined to justify racism *and* a complex contestation of every text—even itself—that seems destined to justify racism.

Hickman works out his reading in two sequences.[13] First he presents others' attempts to respond to accusations of racism against the Book of Mormon, systematically arguing that every potential relativization or destabilization or problematization of racial categories in the volume is undercut by the persistent racial binary between white (the righteous Nephites) and black (the wicked Lamanites). Moments that suggest otherwise, he argues, are "counterfactual blip[s]" rather than suggestive resources,[14] drowned in a sea of rigid racial structures. The only possible exception, Hickman claims, is the volume-wide claim that the white Nephites end up eradicated by the black Lamanites, who live on to receive the fulness of Christian truth. Yet even this fails to excuse the Book of Mormon, according to Hickman, because the means for bringing the dark-skinned Lamanites in the last days to the truth of the Christian gospel is the Book of Mormon itself, written by the white Nephites who, as it were, rise from the dead to continue in their paternalistic superiority. Whatever "providential ascendancy" the Book of Mormon grants to the

---

12. Jared Hickman, "The Book of Mormon as Amerindian Apocalypse," *American Literature* 86, no. 3 (September 2014): 435.

13. Hickman divides his presentation of the Book of Mormon's relationship to race into three "levels." Because both the first and the second of his levels achieve the same (negative) results, I group them into a single first sequence here. What I will call the second sequence corresponds to Hickman's third level.

14. Hickman, "The Book of Mormon as Amerindian Apocalypse," 438.

Lamanites, it is "to be mediated by the white Nephite narrative itself."[15] For Hickman, then, the Book of Mormon should be read as deeply and irreparably racist in nature.

This irreparable racism, however, turns out for Hickman to be a virtue due to the self-deconstructive nature of the book, explored in a second sequence. Hickman claims that "in order to dismantle the kind of theological racism the text features, what must be challenged is the very authority of the narrative that elaborates the framework in the first place"[16]—and this the deconstructive nature of the book actually accomplishes.[17] He explains: "Insofar as *The Book of Mormon* purports to be scripture, its self-deconstruction draws attention to that which the literalist hermeneuts of Biblicist America were keen to ignore—the contingent human conditions of scripture writing and scripture reading, in other words, precisely the conditions from which might conceivably arise spurious notions of theological racism."[18] Here Hickman refers to the intense antebellum debate, almost always with reference to biblical texts assumed to be inherently and unquestionably authoritative, concerning the moral permissibility of the institution of black slavery.[19] Hickman's contention is that the Book of Mormon, which presents itself at once (1) as racially problematic scripture (in this way quite like the Bible) and (2) as consciously self-deconstructive text (in this way quite unlike the Bible), had the potential in the nineteenth-century context of its appearance to undermine a crucial presupposition (the inerrancy of scripture, despite its embrace of institutions of slavery) that underlay the defense of American slavery.

---

15. Hickman, 443.

16. Hickman, 444.

17. Importantly, Hickman uses the language of deconstruction in two distinct registers. In the course of the first sequence of his presentation, he speaks of the "self-deconstruction" of the Book of Mormon's narrative, a function of the Nephite authors prophetically anticipating their own people's eventual eradication. This form of deconstruction Hickman places among those that fail to undercut accusations of racism against the book. In the second sequence, Hickman speaks again of the "self deconstruction" of the Book of Mormon's narrative, but there more positively. And it is this second sort that matches up with what Fenton outlines as the deconstructive nature of the Book of Mormon.

18. Hickman, "The Book of Mormon as Amerindian Apocalypse," 444.

19. For a thorough introduction to the basic cultural, political, and religious presuppositions that gave the debate its shape, see Mark A. Noll, *America's God: From Jonathan Edwards to Abraham Lincoln* (New York: Oxford University Press, 2002).

The extension of the deconstructive approach beyond questions of providentialist history writing (Fenton) to questions of race and slavery (Hickman)[20] strains this particular literary interpretation in certain ways. It is difficult to disagree with Fenton's conclusions regarding the manner in which the Book of Mormon contests a certain conception of American history (although believers in the book's historicity will understandably chafe at her suggestion that such contestation locates the volume's origins in the nineteenth century). It is less difficult by far to disagree with Hickman's conclusions regarding the manner in which the Book of Mormon undermines its own scriptural authority in a brilliantly subtle attempt to contest the use of scripture to justify the institution of slavery. Fenton's essay marks the deeply revealing nature of the deconstructive approach to the Book of Mormon; Hickman's essay presses this approach to a kind of extreme, one that at once suggests the radical potential of the deconstructive reading and makes one wonder whether the deconstructive reading does not in the end go too far.

It thus seems to me necessary, in the last analysis, to distinguish Fenton's and Hickman's respective deconstructive gestures, at least in terms of what might be called their tendencies. In effect, Hickman's argument tends toward the claim that the Book of Mormon as deconstructive text fully *undermines* scriptural authority, Fenton's toward the claim that the Book of Mormon simply *recasts* scriptural authority. Both readers find in the Book of Mormon's self-deconstruction a rather direct contestation of a certain conception of scriptural authority: that of inerrancy, according to which the scriptural Word of God remains pure despite its passage through the conflicting vicissitudes of history.[21] But where Fenton appears to see this contestation to be aimed at replacing one conception

---

20. Fenton actually addresses race briefly in the course of her study (see pp. 354–55), a discussion to which Hickman refers in his own study (see p. 457). Importantly, however, Fenton, unlike Hickman, contextualizes the Book of Mormon's presentation of racial matters within the larger frame of providentialist history writing.

21. Although much of Christian biblical scholarship has for centuries abandoned any strict notion of inerrancy, a certain spirit of inerrancy can be said to have remained alive in it until quite recently, at least in the form of a certain (in part Romantic) assumption that the pure Word of God lies *behind* or *at the origin of* the texts that must be said to be impure. The search for the original words of the prophets or of Jesus or of the apostles, assumed to be directly if irrecoverably inspired but then obscured or repurposed in constitutively less inspired ways by editors and redactors, continues in the general spirit of inerrancy. The past few

of scriptural authority (inerrant) with another (deconstructive), Hickman appears—at least at times—to see it as aimed at a kind of total (or at least potentially total) dismantling of scriptural authority as such. Thus, where Fenton might be said to suggest that the Book of Mormon *calls for a deconstructive conception of scriptural authority*, Hickman might be said to suggest that the Book of Mormon *directly deconstructs scriptural authority*. This distinction might seem overly subtle, but it is essential. On the one reading, deconstruction plays a role in a transformation of what it means to speak of scripture. On the other, deconstruction plays a role in under-cutting the very viability of speaking of scripture.

Now, Fenton's interpretation seems to me unquestionably right. On the Book of Mormon's account, the authority of scripture cannot be di-vorced from its passage through the minds and pens of its many (and of-ten irreconcilable) authors. Not only grace but the word of God is stored in earthen vessels. Indeed, voices in the Book of Mormon find themselves wrestling with the doctrine of grace especially when they confront their own ineptitude at writing scripture.[22] In essence, the Book of Mormon dismisses as entirely unnecessary—and in fact undesirable—the extensive machinery that so much of historical Christianity has constructed to de-fend the idea that God saw an inerrant text unscathed through history.[23] The Book of Mormon seems intent on asserting that the divine Word sounds always and only as an echo within unmistakably human words. But whether it is possible to push the Book of Mormon *further*, to find in its humanization of scripture a certain disqualification of appeals to scrip-ture in debates about ethics and politics, seems to me more questionable. Certainly, one must confess that important texts scattered throughout the Book of Mormon aim to work against the kind of secularism that would most naturally approve of what I am calling Hickman's interpretation.[24]

---

decades, however, have witnessed a partial shift in mainline Christian biblical scholarship away from even this form of inerrancy.

22. In this regard, see especially Ether 12. For a good theological treatment of this text, see Adam S. Miller, *Rube Goldberg Machines: Essays in Mormon Theology* (Salt Lake City: Greg Kofford Books, 2012), 99–105.

23. Especially relevant here is Nephi's vision in 1 Nephi 13, where he witnesses the transformation of the Bible into a text stripped of any "purity" (1 Ne. 13:25–28).

24. Such texts have been cataloged most thoroughly in a work that argues for nineteenth-century origins for the Book of Mormon. Whatever its conclusions on this score, it serves as a helpful index of the relevant texts. See Robert N. Hullinger, *Joseph Smith's Response to Skepticism* (Salt Lake City: Signature Books, 1992).

And Hickman himself pulls back from the most radical interpretation of his own gesture in the final paragraphs of his essay: "Paradoxically, *The Book of Mormon* is a scripture whose successful inculcation . . . demands that we not read it as 'scripture' *insofar as that honorific presupposes a naïve literalist cession of transcendental authority to the narrative voice*."[25] This caveat marks Hickman's own recognition that the position toward which his deconstructive reading tends lies outside the scope of what the Book of Mormon presents.

All this makes clear to me that, while the deconstructive reading is immensely productive and revealing, it runs up against a certain limit—a limit that Hickman's essay especially helps to identify because of the way it works at and—perhaps (at times)—beyond that limit. The Book of Mormon is best read as subtly but intentionally calling its own authority into question, but always and only in the literal sense of "calling into question." The Book of Mormon, in other words, poses the question of its own authority, insisting that no assumptions—whether naively for or dismissively *against*—be made too quickly about that question. To trust that the book is simple and didactic, a rather artless pastiche of Christian truisms or even a rather artless container of timeless religious truths, is to miss the volume's complex self-critical nature.[26] Similarly, though, to trust that the book ultimately undoes itself by its own self-critique, dissolving into so many diverse positions that they cannot be critically gathered into a relatively unified project, is to miss the limits the volume imposes on its readers. To embrace the deconstructive reading responsibly is to find a position somewhere between these problematic extremes, to recognize that individual passages in the Book of Mormon—however simple and didactic they might seem on their faces—cannot be interpreted independently of larger structures and frames organizing the volume. Its texts must always be read in the light of their place within an immensely complex, constitutively incomplete, and ultimately self-aware book.

Fenton and Hickman both capitalize on the virtues of the deconstructive reading, demonstrating its real force. Hickman, I have suggested, also illustrates—again, at least in terms of what should be called the ten-

---

25. Hickman, "The Book of Mormon as Amerindian Apocalypse," 454. I have added italics only to the final clause here for emphasis.

26. That close interpretation of the Book of Mormon's narrative strategies can prove rewarding has been abundantly demonstrated by Grant Hardy, *Understanding the Book of Mormon: A Reader's Guide* (New York: Oxford University Press, 2010).

dency of his reading—the potential vices of the deconstructive reading. Unfortunately, exacerbating or at least confirming Hickman's tendency toward a problematic literary construal of the Book of Mormon are a number of interpretive problems scattered throughout his essay.[27] I worry that highlighting what seems to me the more important among these might seem either petty or pedantic—some kind of exercise in dismissive attack. At the same time, I worry that failing to highlight them would be a disservice, since the best literary work—like the best work of any sort—on the Book of Mormon must be grounded on solid exegesis. In the spirit of pushing for an always-more-responsible approach to the text of the Book of Mormon, and fully recognizing the richness of the deconstructive approach Hickman has joined Fenton in promoting (not to mention my admiration for Hickman's success in bringing literary study of the Book of Mormon into the premier journal in his field!), I want to note some places where I think Hickman has in particular misrepresented the text of the Book of Mormon in weaving his literary account.

A first set of interpretive difficulties arises in connection with Hickman's critiques of standard defenses against the Book of Mormon's purported racism. Three of these standard defenses Hickman groups together as attempts at "troubling racial categories."[28] The first concerns the complex place in the Book of Mormon narrative of two peoples of origins quite distinct from that of the Nephites and the Lamanites, the two non-Lehite peoples usually referred to as the Jaredites and the Mulekites. Hickman quite nicely notes that the intersection of these two largely marginal nations takes place in the most "conspicuous narrative seam" in the Book of Mormon—namely, in the transition from the small to the large plates of Nephi, between the book of Omni and the Words of Mormon.[29] According to Hickman, this narrative seam itself "implicitly interrogates

---

27. So far as I am aware, Fenton makes only one interpretive faux pas in the course of her essay. This comes when she interprets references to the Christian Bible in 1 Nephi 13 as references to the Book of Mormon (see p. 357). This misinterpretation of a passage in the Book of Mormon, however, does not affect her argument, since she might well have made exactly the same point with reference to a text only a few verses after the one she cites, where reference is made to the Book of Mormon, and in a way that would substantiate the claim she makes with regard to the misinterpreted passage.

28. Hickman, "The Book of Mormon as Amerindian Apocalypse," 437.

29. Hickman, 438.

the nature and authority of origins."[30] This seems right, but Hickman overlooks the fact that it is at the non-Lehite intersection of the Jaredite and Mulekite stories that some of the most racially charged elements of the Book of Mormon appear. Hickman suggests that the Jaredite record in the book of Ether might be read as "an additional case study of New World declension in which racial curses do not figure,"[31] and yet a close reading of Ether makes clear that the distinction between covenant Israel and noncovenantal peoples with no promises regarding their seed is central to that story—quite as central as elsewhere in the Book of Mormon and with parallel consequences.[32] Still more interesting, it is arguably in the story of the Mulekite encounter with the Jaredites—this supposedly entirely nonracialized story—that the only intentionally Native American element appears in the text of the Book of Mormon. Richard Bushman points out that the Book of Mormon "contains none of the identifying words [associated in the nineteenth century with native culture] like squaw, papoose, wampum, peace pipes, tepees, braves, feathers, and no canoes, moccasins, or corn."[33] Yet one rather apparent exception is the language used to describe the brief encounter between the Jaredites and the Mulekites: the last-surviving Jaredite lived with the Mulekite settlers "for the space of nine moons" (Omni 1:21). Close reading suggests that the Jaredites and Mulekites are deeply entangled in the larger story the Book of Mormon wishes to tell about peoples and races.

Of course, the objection I have just mentioned in no way vitiates Hickman's larger thesis, since he himself goes on to undercut the histories of the Jaredites and Mulekites.[34] Only slightly more problematic are some

---

30. Hickman, 438.

31. Hickman, 437.

32. I have spelled out this interpretation in some detail in Joseph M. Spencer, "Christ and Krishna: The Visions of Arjuna and the Brother of Jared," *Journal of Book of Mormon Studies* 23 (2014): 68–72. [This essay appears in the other volume of *The Anatomy of Book of Mormon Theology*.]

33. Richard Lyman Bushman, Joseph Smith, *Rough Stone Rolling: A Cultural Biography of Mormonism's Founder* (New York: Knopf, 2005), 97.

34. It should be noted that Hickman ignores a host of exegetically rich studies that have closely investigated the role played in the Book of Mormon by the Mulekites. He claims far too simplistically just that "the numerically dominant Mulekites" merge with "relative seamlessness" into Nephite culture (p. 438). For a good recent discussion of the Mulekites with copious references to the literature, see Dan Belnap: "'And it came to pass . . .': The Sociopolitical Events in the Book of Mormon Leading to the Eighteenth Year of the Reign of the Judges," *Journal*

interpretive issues that arise in the last part of his essay, where he reviews the Book of Mormon as a whole, attempting to show the consistent racism of its white authors—interrupted only occasionally by marginalized Lamanite voices and by the visiting Christ of the book's climax. His summary interpretation of Nephi's record is more than a little heavy-handed, especially clear when he claims that the deliberate narrowing of the scope of Nephi's record to "spiritual things" indicates primarily "the profane imperatives of ethnocentrism."[35] Hickman is right that Nephi "unabashedly filters his historical chronicle through that which is 'expedient to [him],'"[36] but he expends no (obvious) effort in uncovering what rather apparently is expedient to Nephi, according to the text.[37] More egregious is Hickman's later citation of what he calls "a rare Lamanite primary document,"[38] Ammoron's letter to Moroni contained in Alma 54. After quite rightly noting "the traces of something like a 'Lamanite view of *Book of Mormon* history,'"[39] Hickman quotes Ammoron's letter at length in order to illustrate "a sophisticated Lamanite worldview,"[40] but this drastically misrepresents the text. Ammoron is not a dark-skinned Lamanite but a light-skinned Nephite

---

of *Book of Mormon Studies* 23 (2014): 117–27. Hickman similarly overlooks the important literature on the Amlicites, the importance of whose curse-related self-marking he overlooks by ignoring the role that the Amlicites (equivalent to the Amalekites, as study of the manuscripts of the Book of Mormon makes clear) go on to play in Nephite-Lamanite relations. For the case that the Amlicites and the Amalekites are equivalent, see J. Christopher Conkling, "Alma's Enemies: The Case of the Lamanites, Amlicites, and Mysterious Amalekites," *Journal of Book of Mormon Studies* 14, no. 1 (2005): 108–17, 130–32. For the best study of the Amalekites among other groups of Nephite dissidents, see John L. Sorenson, "Religious Groups and Movements among the Nephites, 200–1 B.C.," in *Disciple as Scholar: Essays on Scripture and the Ancient World in Honor of Richard Lloyd Anderson*, ed. Stephen D. Ricks, Donald W. Parry, and Andrew H. Hedges (Provo, UT: FARMS, 2000), 163–208.

35. Hickman, "The Book of Mormon as Amerindian Apocalypse," 448.

36. Hickman, 447.

37. The best analysis of Nephi's expedients available in print is Hardy, *Understanding the Book of Mormon*, 58–86.

38. Hickman, "The Book of Mormon as Amerindian Apocalypse," 449.

39. Hickman, 449. Hickman rightly cites the crucial study of this topic: Richard Lyman Bushman, "The Lamanite View of *Book of Mormon* History," in *Believing History: Latter-day Saint Essays*, ed. Reid L. Neilson and Jed Woodworth (New York: Columbia University Press, 2004), 79–92.

40. Hickman, "The Book of Mormon as Amerindian Apocalypse," 449.

who has (through his brother) usurped the Lamanite government. That Hickman calls the letter's writer "the Lamanite Ammoron"[41] seems to indicate that he is unaware of the racially problematic status of Ammoron and the voice he provides to readers of the Book of Mormon.

In these last-mentioned cases of interpretive difficulty, Hickman mingles interpretive acuity (recognition of Nephi's vexed relationship to the story he tells, attention to occasional traces of the Lamanite view throughout the Book of Mormon) with misleading suggestions (that Nephi's "spiritual things" are primarily racial in nature, that the most deplorable instance of Nephite paternalism represents a quintessentially Lamanite perspective). These interpretive mistakes again do not strongly affect Hickman's thesis, though perhaps they weaken it in certain ways, suggesting that there is complexity that Hickman's reading does not accommodate. But one interpretive move in particular, made right at the end of Hickman's essay, is more problematic than these, and it threatens his thesis in a serious way. Essential to his apocalyptic reading of the Book of Mormon is the way in which a racist element supposedly remains operative in the volume's claim that the light-skinned Nephite scriptures will eventually play a paternalistic role in the latter-day redemption of the dark-skinned Lamanites.[42] Yet this very aspect of the Book of Mormon Hickman makes central to his deconstructive reading in the end, finding in the Lamanite prophet Samuel's presentation of this same paternalistic redemption of the Lamanites an indication that "the Nephites [are] mere instruments in the hands of the Lord to restore the Lamanites to their rightful place."[43] Are we to understand that one and the same aspect of what the Book of Mormon has to say about Nephite-Lamanite relations serves as both the last indication of its patent racism at one level (when presented by the Nephite narrators) and the first indication of its metacritical rejection of racism at another level (when presented by a Lamanite prophet)? However important the actual bearer of the voice is in each case (first Nephite, then Lamanite), the message is unmistakably the same, and there is real inconsistency on Hickman's part when he takes that same message to indicate ineradicable racism in one instance and inventive antiracism in another. Here if anywhere, Hickman's tendency to make the text of the Book of Mormon work to his own deconstructive ends, rather than to trace what genuinely and unmistakably is deconstructive in the text, makes itself known.

41. Hickman, 449.
42. See Hickman, 443.
43. Hickman, 453.

These criticisms are, I think, important. Recent academic work on the Book of Mormon has often suggested that little of value (apparently because little of a nonapologetic nature) has been written on the Book of Mormon, but this is simply untrue. For the still-young field of Book of Mormon studies directed primarily to non-Mormon readers to do its work the best way possible, it will be necessary to learn from all the essential exegetical work that has been done on the Book of Mormon over the past century. Only with the most responsible readings possible will literary work of real genius—like that of both Fenton and Hickman—receive a ready reception.

I sincerely hope it does.

Chapter Fifteen

A Mormon Reads *A Pentecostal Reads The Book of Mormon*

In the same year that Elizabeth Fenton's first essay on the Book of Mormon appeared in print and that Jared Hickman and I crossed paths at a conference in Washington DC, I met also the Pentecostal scholar John Christopher Thomas. This last scholar was, like Fenton and Hickman and Grant Hardy, pursuing a literary study of the Book of Mormon. Thomas was already at the time a well-established scholar of the New Testament, deeply interested, though, in making sense of a book that lay far outside his own faith tradition. From our first meeting, we discovered that we were kindred souls, and we soon began corresponding with some regularity about the Book of Mormon. In 2016, his deeply important book *A Pentecostal Reads The Book of Mormon: A Literary and Theological Introduction* appeared. It is, to date, the most substantial treatment of the Book of Mormon written by someone outside the faith tradition. It is in itself a remarkable gesture of goodwill and generosity.

Chris Thomas's commitment to Book of Mormon studies would soon reveal its longevity. He had more than just the one book in him (he is currently laboring on a second), and he and I have worked together in founding the Book of Mormon Studies Association, formally organized in 2018 at a conference held at Utah State University (he is the founding president of the organization and I one of its founding vice presidents). In the midst of so much camaraderie, both personal and professional, I found myself honored by the invitation to say a few things about *A Pentecostal Reads The Book of Mormon* at a meeting of the Society for Pentecostal Studies. Because the book is more literary than theological (although it is theological), I took the occasion to make my usual invitation: to call for increased theological sensitivity in reading the book. It was also, however, a good opportunity to honor a close friend (and I might note here again that it is to this same Chris Thomas that I have dedicated this collection of essays).

I originally read this unpublished paper at the annual meeting of the Society for Pentecostal Studies, held adjacent to the 2017 annual meetings of the Society for Biblical Literature in Boston, Massachusetts.

I first met Chris just over four years ago, at the 2013 meetings of the Society for Mormon Philosophy and Theology. Since that time—and especially since reading his book when it appeared last year—I've been overwhelmed, and sometimes made anxious, by the gift he's offered to the various branches of the Restoration movement, my own included.[1] Let me explain what I mean, and let me do so in my native intellectual language: that of contemporary French philosophy. I promise I'll avoid jargon.

A few years back, a couple of major French philosophers carried on a prolonged exchange about the nature of the gift.[2] The philosophical problem motivating the exchange was the question of the gift's *impossibility*. The idea, put in a nutshell, is that there accompanies every reception of a gift an inevitable desire to cancel the gift as gesture. Every gift, if it's truly and radically given, ruptures the economic order that in fact provides all objects with their social meaning. And so, every reception of a gift comes with a deeply felt need to reciprocate, to counter the gift. That is, we experience gifts as excessive, in a way that makes us anxious about how prodigal we're not. And to rid ourselves of the anxiety, we attempt to match the prodigality of the giver through a counter-gift. Of course, such a well-balanced counter-gift ultimately works just to inscribe the gift in a higher-level economy, a banal socio-economic exchange that eliminates every sense of prodigality in the original gift.

There's the philosophical problem that spurred a remarkable exchange among several French thinkers. You might guess at how something like the drama of this problem has played out in my own weak mind in the wake of Chris's remarkable offering to my religious tradition. His gift reveals my own lack of prodigality. I *want* to give myself to the charitable study of religious traditions that aren't my own, but I seldom find myself doing anything like serious work to understand them. I've certainly done *nothing* like what's necessary to produce a book akin to Chris's. I justify myself by insisting that Mormonism remains a remarkably young tradition, so understudied in its own right—especially its scripture, including the Book of Mormon. And then a gift like Chris's comes my way, written by a

---

1. See John Christopher Thomas, *A Pentecostal Reads The Book of Mormon: A Literary and Theological Introduction* (Cleveland, TN: CPT Press, 2016).

2. [For the two most important contributions to this debate, see Jacques Derrida, *Given Time I. Counterfeit Money*, trans. Peggy Kamuf (Chicago: University of Chicago press, 1992); and Jean-Luc Marion, *Being Given: Toward a Phenomenology of Givenness*, trans. Jeffrey L. Kosky (Stanford: Stanford University Press, 2002).]

faithful adherent to a tradition that in many ways is historically *younger* than my own (depending, of course, on how one traces the beginnings of Pentecostalism)! My justifications suddenly feel rather ad hoc, obvious rationalizations for my selfish interests. Ashamed, I've felt—*I mean this*—I've felt like I should respond with a counter-book, a book that matches the gesture. I've literally thought about what such a book would be, about how to work into my research trajectory a sustained project on Pentecostalism. It's been hard, in short, to receive this gift as graciously as it's been given.

But let me try. After all, the gift of all gifts—I have reference, of course, to Christ's saving gift—the gift of all gifts isn't rightly received by offering up some kind of counter-gift. It's received in submission and gratitude, and in the charism of the Spirit. That's the great theological contribution of Saint Paul, to be sure. The Book of Mormon, incidentally, offers its own version of this same theological insight, in a sermon given by an exemplary king. He says this:

> In the first place, God has created you, and granted unto you your lives, for which you are indebted to him. And secondly, he requires that you should do as he has commanded you—for which, if you do, he immediately blesses you, and therefore he has paid you, and you are still indebted to him—and are, and will be, forever and ever. Therefore, of what have you to boast? (Mosiah 2:24)[3]

Significantly, when this king's subjects come fully to understand their ruler's message and so cry to God for forgiveness, "the Spirit of the Lord came upon them, and they were filled with joy." They testify of this experience later in these words: "We ourselves also, through the infinite goodness of God and the manifestations of his Spirit, have great views of that which is to come, and were it expedient, we could prophesy of all things" (Mosiah 5:3). That's a beautiful Pentecostal moment in the Book of Mormon.

But I digress. I mean here to try to receive rightly the gift of *A Pentecostal Reads The Book of Mormon*. What would that mean? I think this. First, just to express my gratitude to Chris for the care with which he's handled a book I regard as sacred, as genuinely revealed from God. Thank you. And second, I think that to receive this gift rightly is to receive the charism of the Spirit it helps me to see and to experience. What Chris's book does—what Chris himself does—in an unprecedented way is to read

---

3. Throughout this essay, I cite the text as it stands in Royal Skousen, ed., *The Book of Mormon: The Earliest Text* (New Haven: Yale University Press, 2009).

the Book of Mormon with an eye to gifts. And in that regard, he's opened my eyes. When a Pentecostal reads the Book of Mormon, the result is that the Book of Mormon reveals its Pentecostal proclivities. Whatever might be said about the various religious bodies that trace themselves to the book's emergence in the early nineteenth century, *the book itself* is arguably charismatic.

So, here's what I'd like to do for a few minutes by way of response to Chris's book. Where on a few previous occasions, I've responded directly to the book *as* a scholarly book, analyzing its claims and contribution by trying to take its measure, today I wish to say a few things about what Chris's book gives me to see in the Book of Mormon that I didn't know enough to look for. He's himself traced a number of charismatic themes in the book, reading as a Pentecostal. What, in turn, happens when a Mormon like me reads his own sacred book through the lens provided to him by a Pentecostal?

Before turning directly to the text, let me note between parentheses that the branch of Mormonism from which I hail—namely, The Church of Jesus Christ of Latter-day Saints, by far the largest branch of the movement—has a complicated history when it comes to the charismatic. For its first seven or eight decades, it was emphatically charismatic. The muting of this feature of the religion during the first decades of the twentieth century arguably has much to do with a felt need to assimilate to American culture in the wake of intense persecution during the last decades of the nineteenth century. I'll confess I find it deeply ironic that at least my own branch of Mormonism retreated from outward charismatic experience more or less at the time of the Azusa Street Revival and its aftermath. But so it is. At any rate, I want to mention this point to make clear that, although contemporary Latter-day Saints are generally uncomfortable with charismatic Christianity, it wasn't always so—and that's something the Book of Mormon underlines. It emphasizes spiritual gifts in a straightforward way, and it even offers a critique of modern Christianity for its general rejection of spiritual gifts. Latter-day Saints today often see themselves, for that reason, as fully embracing spiritual gifts, although they generally understand them in a way at odds with the Pentecostal tradition, despite what once were remarkably similar approaches to such spiritual phenomena.

But let me turn directly to the Book of Mormon and say something about what Chris's book has helped me to see there.

Let me note first what's begun to strike me as a remarkably consistent pattern within the Book of Mormon. You may or may not be aware that the Book of Mormon has the literary form of a lengthy history. It recounts the thousand-year story of an Israel colony settled in the ancient Americas, led by a family that left the region of Jerusalem on the eve of the Jewish exile in Babylon. Consequently, the book contains numerous opportunities for characters in the narrative to offer a word of farewell. Strikingly, it's at these points of farewell that the most consistent emphasis is laid on spiritual manifestations more generally, and on glossolalia in particular.

Amaleki's a good example. He's the final contributor to a sacred record the volume calls "the small plates of Nephi." This record is largely the work of two first-generation figures, Nephi and Jacob, but various other figures add a handful of verses to it over the course of another three or four centuries. Amaleki is the last. As he finishes the record and hands it off to the same already-mentioned exemplary king who spurred a charismatic response in his people, Amaleki writes this:

> I shall deliver up these plates . . . , exhorting all men to come unto God, the Holy One of Israel, and believe in prophesying and in revelations, and in the ministering of angels, and in the gift of speaking with tongues, and in the gift of interpreting languages, and in all things which is good—for there is nothing which is good save it comes from the Lord, and that which is evil cometh from the devil. (Omni 1:25)

Something similar comes much later in the volume from Mormon, the man who gives his name to the book. Concluding his account of the visit of Jesus Christ to the ancient American Israelites, he issues a warning:

> Woe unto him that shall deny the revelations of the Lord, and that shall say: "The Lord no longer worketh by revelation or by prophecy, or by gifts or by tongues, or by healings or by the power of the Holy Ghost." (3 Ne. 29:6)

Rather devastatingly, Mormon even goes on to suggest that the basic motivation for claiming that spiritual gifts have ceased is "to get gain," comparing such to "the son of perdition for whom there was no mercy" (v. 7).

Mormon's son Moroni, the final contributor to the volume, produces a kind of epilogue to Mormon's autobiography, which appears late in the book. There, writing to his anticipated modern audience, he says this:

> I speak unto you who deny the revelations of God and say that they are done away, that there is no revelations nor prophecies nor gifts nor healing nor speaking with tongues and the interpretation of tongues—behold, I say unto you: He that denieth these things knoweth not the gospel of Christ. (Morm. 9:8)

Echoing the Gospel of Mark, he promises some verses later that certain "signs shall follow them that believe," among which can be found a promise that "they shall speak with new tongues" (v. 24; see also Mark 16:17). Although Moroni writes these words in what presents itself as the intended conclusion to the whole book, he finds himself later with more time to add to the record. He again concludes his further additions to the book with a word about charismata. "Again I exhort you," he writes, "that ye deny not the gifts of God" (Moro. 10:8). In a passage clearly reminiscent of Paul in First Corinthians, he outlines a whole list of spiritual gifts, including the gift to "work mighty miracles," to "prophecy concerning all things," to speak "all kinds of tongues," to interpret "languages and . . . divers kinds of tongues" (vv. 12–13, 15–16).

The most remarkable instance of this pattern is found in the writings of Nephi, the first voice in the book and the most theologically interesting in the volume. In his concluding reflection on "the doctrine of Christ," after more than fifty chapters of material, he provides an explanation of how water baptism should be accompanied by "the baptism of fire and of the Holy Ghost" (2 Ne. 31:2, 13). With such an experience, Nephi explains, one can "speak with the tongue of angels and shout praises unto the Holy One of Israel" (v. 13). Further, he warns:

> After that ye have repented . . . [and received] the baptism of water, and have received the baptism of fire and of the Holy Ghost and can speak with a new tongue—yea, even with the tongue of angels—and after this should deny me, it would have been better for you that ye had not known me. (v. 14)

In a related way, Nephi's brother Jacob concludes his own, much shorter writings with a warning not to "deny the good word of Christ and the power of God, and the gift of the Holy Ghost"—as well as not to "quench the Holy Spirit" and thereby "make a mock of the great plan of redemption" (Jacob 6:8).

I see a consistent pattern here. Glossolalia makes numerous appearances in the Book of Mormon, and these appear to be clustered most particularly around moments of farewell and closure. They're consequently most often tied to exhortation and warning formulas, and they're most often directly addressed to "latter-day" readers, those who would read the Book of Mormon beginning in the early nineteenth century. There's a real feeling in the book that every *final* word ought to say something about making space for charismata, and about the serious dangers associated with dismissing or eliminating the gifts of God.

If that's right, then here's what strikes me as a reader of the whole book, of the book taken as a literary totality: Despite the fact that the book exhibits consistent interest in calling on its readers to take glossolalia seriously—despite the fact that the book demonstrates a near-anxiety regarding spiritual gifts with every farewell gesture it makes—despite all this, the larger story the book tells only *very seldom* actually describes glossolalic events. In fact, so far as I'm aware, there's only one. Further, although the book contains many lengthy sermons, sermons addressed by characters within the book to various groups, it only *very seldom* mentions glossolalia in those sermons. In fact, here again, so far as I'm aware, there's only one such mention. So, here's what we have in the Book of Mormon, if I'm not mistaken. On the one hand, the book exhibits a clear and consistent impulse to tell its readers that *they* need to seek earnestly all spiritual gifts, privileging glossolalia in a striking way. But on the other hand, the book at the same time never really demonstrates that those whose story it recounts *themselves* sought or much experienced glossolalia (although certain other spiritual gifts *do* receive attention in the narrative). There's a spirit of do-what-I-say-but-not-what-I-do about the Book of Mormon when it comes to glossolalia: consistent direct recommendation to readers to seek the gift, but no real demonstration of the gift's frequency or even nature in the stories and sermons recounted for readers.

What to do with this? Well, I don't have a lot of time to develop my ideas here, but let me outline a possible explanation of what might be at stake. There's begun to emerge in recent years an interesting literary approach to the Book of Mormon that, in my view, proves quite fruitful. I've elsewhere tried to summarize this approach by speaking of the "self-critical" Book of Mormon.[4] The idea is basically this: The Book of Mormon presents not a history of *good* examples, but rather a history of *bad* examples—and then it makes efforts to show that it's the problems in the societies it describes that lead to their eventual destruction. Crucially, the way it does this is by associating all *bad* examples with the Nephites, the *apparent* protagonists of the volume, from whom are drawn more or less all prophetic voices and certainly all authorial and editorial voices. At the same time, when the book gives glimpses of life among the Lamanites—the *apparent* antagonists of the volume, culturally other than the Nephites and consistently presented as a benighted people—there, among the Lamanites, *good* examples begin to show up. When prophets occasionally critique the dominant attitudes

---

4. [See, naturally, the essay "The Self-Critical Book of Mormon," in this volume.]

among the Nephites, they cite the Lamanites as a people where things are right, and they even predict consequent preservation for the Lamanites, but eradication for the Nephites.

An example or two might illustrate. Jared Hickman, in a remarkable essay on race in the Book of Mormon, has shown that the volume *at once* exhibits a host of racist tropes (spoken by Nephites about Lamanites) *and* provides crucial prophetic voices—both Nephite and Lamanite—who identify and condemn the racism of those tropes.[5] Similarly, Kim Berkey and I myself have in a jointly written essay argued that the Book of Mormon presents a deliberately misogynistic history among the Nephites only in order to point out through certain prophetic voice that Nephite misogyny motivates their eventual destruction, while right relationships between the sexes among the Lamanites motivates their preservation.[6] Such readings effectively privilege a key line included in Moroni's epilogue: "Give thanks unto God that he hath made manifest unto you our imperfections," he tells his readers on behalf of his people, "that ye may learn to be more wise than that which we have been" (Morm. 9:31). Moroni writes this, by the way, shortly after watching the Nephites' extermination.

Now, hoping all that is clear, I wonder if a similar sort of reading might make sense of the Book of Mormon's apparent ambivalence about glossolalia. The volume's authorial and editorial voices, when addressing the reader directly, are clear and conscious of the need to recommend and to defend the gift of tongues. But the history they tell apparently isn't the history of a people often given to seeking spiritual gifts—tongues above all. I think I find this confirmed, actually, in the two instances—one narrative and one sermonic—where the Book of Mormon *does* focus in on glossolalia (but not in a deliberate farewell).

The sermonic instance comes in the middle of an address in which a Nephite high priest condemns a wayward group of Nephites by contrasting them with the Lamanites. The Nephites, he says, have been "a highly favored people of the Lord"—signaled in part by the fact that they have had "many gifts," including "the gift of speaking with tongues" (Alma 9:20–21). It's unclear how often that particular gift is supposed to have

---

5. Jared Hickman, "*The Book of Mormon* as Amerindian Apocalypse," *American Literature* 86, no. 3 (2014): 429–61.

6. Kimberly M. Berkey and Joseph M. Spencer, "'Great Cause to Mourn': The Complexity of *The Book of Mormon*'s Presentation of Gender and Race," in *Americanist Approaches to* The Book of Mormon, ed. Elizabeth Fenton and Jared Hickman (New York: Oxford University Press, 2019), 298–320.

been manifest among them, but it's clear that the speaker believes the Nephites have ignored its importance. And therefore "the promises of the Lord are extended to the Lamanites," he says, "but they are not unto you if ye transgress" (v. 24). The only moment in the whole book where Nephites are said to have had the gift of tongues, then, it's presented as something generally neglected, and as a reason for God to withdraw his favor from the Nephites. By contrast, the one narrative instance of glossolalia in the volume comes in a story about Lamanites. A Lamanite queen—both racially *and* sexually other than the privileged figure of the Nephite man— experiences a profound conversion experience. Rising from a swoon, "she clapped her hands, being filled with joy, speaking many words which were not understood" (v. 30). Here, in one of the Book of Mormon's very few glimpses into Lamanite culture, there's an indication of the presence of glossolalic experience among the volume's supposed antagonists. The Nephites flout what the Lamanites embrace.

Now, I'm worried I'll go on too long if I say much more here, so let me sum up and conclude. Here's what Chris has given me to see in the Book of Mormon—and it's something I'll be struggling and wrestling with, both as a scholar studying the book, and as a devoted believer seeking out genuine encounters with God—here's what Chris has given me to see in the Book of Mormon: It's a book that not only *explicitly* and *frequently* encourages its readers, like me, to seek out glossolalic experience; it's a book that also *implicitly* and *discouragingly* tells of a people that ignores glossolalic experience and therefore finds itself to be only hypocritical believers. That's something I trust will work on me.

More, for present purposes, it's something I could never have given myself. My religious tradition can't give itself to see what it naturally overlooks. And so, I'm glad—exceeding glad, as the Book of Mormon would say—I'm glad to have a reader with a rather different set of eyes looking at a text I hold sacred. By listening in when a Pentecostal reads the Book of Mormon, I find myself a better reader of the book. And that's reason to celebrate Chris's volume, to be sure. And, again, to give thanks. Once more, then: Thank you, Chris.

Chapter Sixteen

Notes on Novelty
Regarding Adam Miller's
Rube Goldberg Machines

On the cover of Adam Miller's book *Rube Goldberg Machines: Essays in Mormon Theology* are inscribed words by Richard Bushman: "Adam Miller is the most original and provocative Latter-day Saint theologian practicing today." Miller's theological work is indeed original, and it is indeed provocative. His careful articulation of the idea of grace deserves the attention of every Latter-day Saint. I have had the curious privilege of being among Miller's close interlocutors during all the years he was developing his basic theological outlook and key theological methods. We began corresponding in 2005, and we began conspiring on projects soon after. I have been among his closest readers from the very beginning.

Over the years, I have had a good many opportunities to speak at public events about my own way of making sense of Miller's theological work. In all of those opportunities, I have taken basically the same approach: I have argued repeatedly that Miller's theological commitments are not the products of his own individual thinking, reasoning he has merely spun out of his own brilliant mind, but rather the result of his having dwelt for years with the Book of Mormon. His theology of grace is the Book of Mormon's theology of grace. Or rather, what he has to say about grace only makes full sense if it is read and understood against the background of what the Book of Mormon has to say about grace. In all of these public appeals—all of which I offered while Miller sat nearby in the audience—I had really one and the same aim: to call the best theologians in the Latter-day Saint tradition to keep their thought in constant conversation with the Book of Mormon. This essay was the first such public appeal I made, which I originally titled simply "Adam Miller, Book of Mormon Theologian."

I originally delivered these remarks as part of a panel discussion of *Rube Goldberg Machines* at the 2012 meetings of the Society for Mormon Philosophy and Theology, held at Utah State University. It was subsequently published online in *SquareTwo* 6, no. 1 (Spring 2013).

In the introduction to his recent book, *Rube Goldberg Machines*, Adam Miller makes the following claim about his work: "These essays offer a coherent vision of an alternative path for the future of Mormon theology. Rather than taking their cue from the generally systematic, analytic work of David Paulsen and Blake Ostler, they borrow from and extend the hermeneutic approach advocated by James Faulconer."[1] Being myself a fellow-traveler on this "alternative path," and especially being one who is driven by the specifically *scriptural* commitments of Faulconer's approach, I find myself asking as I read Miller's essays the following question: *How does Miller's work relate to scripture?*

I might rephrase this question in terms of faith. Miller is quite forthcoming that the sort of theological reflection he pursues in his work is meant to model charity. Indeed, according to Miller, charity is the very "measure" of a theology's "strength."[2] But might one not justifiably worry that unreserved commitment to charity too easily lends itself to a kind of unfaithfulness, a kind of infidelity—breaking the rules to keep the commandments, as it can be paradoxically put?[3] My question, then, might be phrased as follows: *How does Miller's theology model faith as much as charity?*

My aim in this brief essay is to begin to construct an answer to these two interchangeable questions: How does Miller's work relate to scripture? That is, how does Miller's theology model faith as much as charity? The answer I attempt here to construct will, whether fortunately or unfortunately, be needlessly complex—a little Rube Goldberg machine of my own. I aim to show that Miller's work is faithful to a uniquely Nephite theological gesture, one often mentioned but seldom investigated. My argument is that an apparent theological ambivalence in Miller's work can be viewed as an echo of the essential ambivalence of Nephite messianism. Importantly, lying at the heart of that Nephite ambivalence is the key theological virtue of hope. It is hope, I intend to make clear, that binds faith and charity together in Miller's book.[4]

---

1. Adam S. Miller, *Rube Goldberg Machines: Essays in Mormon Theology* (Salt Lake City: Greg Kofford Books, 2012), xv. For a good sampling of Faulconer's work, see James E. Faulconer, *Faith, Philosophy, Scripture* (Provo, UT: Neal A. Maxwell Institute, 2010).

2. Miller, *Rube Goldberg Machines*, xv; see also 59–62.

3. I draw this formulation from Richard Dutcher's 2005 film *States of Grace*.

4. Revealing the role played by hope in Miller's thought is, I think, an important exercise. In the course of a panel on *Rube Goldberg Machines* at the 2012 meetings of the Society for Mormon Philosophy and Theology (in which the original version of

Obviously, I have some building to do.

Rube Goldberg Machines gathers essays older and newer, something the careful reader can sense. The stylistic difference between the more and the less recent is perhaps most obvious. Newer essays blend the aphoristic and the conversational in arresting prose poems; older essays expound, in prose sharpened to cut to the quick, straightforwardly novel theses. But it is not style that draws my attention here. (Indeed, I was just as jealous of Miller's ability with words some years ago as I have been more recently.) Rather, what draws my attention is an apparent incommensurability between the theological positions assumed, respectively, in the older and the newer essays. This apparent incommensurability concerns the question of *the new, of novelty.*

Compare two essays from the book: "Humanism, Mormonism" (chapter 11) and "Groundhog Day" (chapter 13). These two essays were originally produced within four years of each other, but the apparent difference between them is startling. The thesis of "Humanism, Mormonism" is, straightforwardly, that novelty is the focus of everything worthwhile—Mormonism included. "Joseph Smith's claim," Miller states there, "is that revelation . . . is absolutely essential to the vitality of Christianity. Christianity without revelation is vanity. [And] here, it is necessary to understand revelation as novelty itself."[5] But then contrast this thesis with the repeating refrain from "Groundhog Day": "Novelty is a red herring: the last refuge of that dream that is your ego."[6] Novelty is good, novelty is bad. The contrast, it seems, could not be starker.

In his early embrace of the new, Miller marks his interest in *the succession of worlds.* Convinced with Saint Paul that "the present order of things is passing away" (1 Cor. 7:31), Miller in his earlier essays focuses on how the eternal ruptures the homogeneity of history and gives human beings to reconstruct the order of things—the world itself!—in a novel way. According to this vision, the faithful are either looking to receive the promise or the new or militantly reordering things so that the already-

---

this paper was delivered), Rosalynde Welch described Miller's theology by referring to the image (drawn from Beverly Cleary's *Ramona Quimby* books) of someone trying to ride a tricycle turned into a bicycle through the removal of one of the wheels. Miller's theology, she said, rides tipsily on the wheels of faith and charity. Although she did not say so directly, Welch's image implies that Miller's theological project begins with his removal of the wheel of *hope.* I want to suggest otherwise.

5. Miller, *Rube Goldberg Machines*, 110.

6. Miller, 124.

received promise of the new will be fulfilled. The faithful, in other words, anxiously keep the vigil of the time-between.

But Miller's more recent work begins from a worry about the harried anxiety of, precisely, the vigilant faithful extolled in his earlier work. In their passion for the promise of the new, the vigilant let pass too much of the old. Consequently, Miller has come to focus not on the word that announces the possibility of a new world, but on *the actual experience of the world we human beings already inhabit.* Convinced with the Buddha that the body's several physical senses are "called the all,"[7] Miller in his more recent essays focuses on how attention to the eternal givenness of experience conditions the homogeneity of history. According to this vision, the enlightened are those who reject the lure of the new so as to be where they already are. The enlightened, in other words, see that the world is always new, but never in a new way.

Two successive visions, then, have animated Miller's work, and each of them guides certain essays that appear in *Rube Goldberg Machines.* In the first, earlier vision, Miller sees world succeeding world, the second transcending the first in truth, beauty, and goodness. In the second, more recent vision, Miller sees only one always-changing world, but sees also that that world is transcendentally conditioned. In both visions, attention to the eternal problematizes the homogeneity of temporal history, but while it is *truths* that are eternal in the first vision, it is *the conditions of experience* that are eternal in the second. It is as if, reversing philosophical history, Miller has experienced a conversion of sorts from Hegel to Kant, from (1) thinking the instability of a history whose end in eternity can be thought, to (2) thinking the possibility of being oriented to the eternal conditions of the world of sensory experience.

But one might well ask whether these two visions are really incommensurable. Is the difference between them real or merely apparent? Does the Buddha, the unmistakable hero of the more recent essays, *crowd out* or *commune with* Saint Paul, the unmistakable hero of the earlier essays?

Is Mormonism Pauline?—that, it seems to me, is the question. If it is, then it would seem that the development from Paul to the Buddha marks a shift from faithfulness to something else—enlightenment, as I put it before. But if the relationship between Mormonism and Saint Paul is more complicated, then there are other ways of understanding the development of Miller's thought. Indeed, I want to argue that Miller has, in

---

7. See Glenn Wallis, ed., *Basic Teachings of the Buddha* (New York: Modern Library, 2007), 27.

the Buddhist turn of sorts that has marked his recent work, not so much *abandoned* as *proposed a profoundly Mormon reading of* Saint Paul.[8] He has, in other words, begun to reproduce one of the essential moves made by the Book of Mormon itself.[9]

At first glance, one might take the Book of Mormon to indicate the irreversibly Pauline character of Mormonism. The book is deeply messianic, unmistakably meant to restore Christianity after the Enlightenment to its erstwhile robust faith. Diatribes against corrupted churches, sermons about God's gifts, passionate criticisms of the closed canon, accounts of anti-Christs struck down—all this can only be understood as a massive apologetics for the ancient Christian faith, which took its earliest definitive shape in Paul's letters. How, then, could the Book of Mormon *not* commit Latter-day Saints to Paul's basic conviction that Christ's resurrection heralded the definitively new? And yet there is something odd about Nephite Christianity. What can it mean, for instance, to talk about *another*, a *third* testament that troubles—if not trumps—the binary of *old* and *new* that shapes the Christian Bible? All parties interested in the tired question of whether Mormons are Christian have to agree that if Mormons are Christian, they are Christians with a difference, since their faith complicates or even cancels the old/new polarity that undergirds the traditional Christian faith.

How do the old and new testaments of the Christian Bible work? The classic formulation is simple: In the Old Testament, the New Testament lies hidden; in the New Testament, the Old Testament stands revealed. This formulation is as much the announcement of an interpretive strategy as anything else: the old should be read as an obscure anticipation of the new, the new as the fulfillment of and key to the old. The saving event of Christ's resurrection breaks history in two and allows for everything before the event to be seen as anticipating everything after the event. Now, what

---

8. This marks, I think, an important improvement on Miller's most sustained—but still early—treatment of Saint Paul, that to be found in his book *Immanent Grace*. There he makes Saint Paul's thought a first, abandonable step on the way to thinkers more strictly amenable to his (Mormon) commitments. See Adam Miller, *Badiou, Marion and St Paul: Immanent Grace* (New York: Continuum, 2008). (It should be noted that Miller never mentions his specifically Mormon commitments in Immanent Grace. It is a book on philosophy for a non-Mormon audience.)

9. I spell out the relationship between the Book of Mormon and Saint Paul in some more detail in my forthcoming book, *For Zion: A Mormon Theology of Hope*, to be published by Greg Kofford Books. [This volume appeared in 2014.]

does the Book of Mormon do to this delicate balance between before and after? Most of the book's narrative occurs before Christ's coming, and yet its characters are already fully Christian. The event that should provide the key for understanding the old remains for the Nephites on the horizon, and yet they already understand the old. Consequently, when that event takes place, there is no real change in theology; nothing becomes old when the new arrives.[10]

All this might be put another way: The pre-Christian Nephite prophets emphatically did not anticipate Christianity; they were Christians. From very early in Nephite history, believers were told "to look forward unto the Messiah, and believe in him to come *as though he already was*" or "*even as though he had already come among them.*"[11] Thus, paradoxically, the Nephites embraced in their faith *both* the affirmation *and* the negation of the new. They asserted *both* that something real would be accomplished in the Christ event, something that would change material reality itself, *and* that nothing real would be accomplished in the Christ event because its effects were somehow already operative.

The Jew, according to a useful caricature, understands the Messiah to mark the limit of history, to be an always-deferred figure still to come who orients human desire to God's justice. The Christian, according to a similarly useful caricature, understands the Messiah to mark the past interruption that has broken history in two and introduced into the otherwise closed world God's mercy. Perhaps it is worth creating a third useful caricature: the Nephite understands the Messiah to have always already come in an immemorial-because-pre-historical past, laying the foundation of a world woven of both mercy and justice.

Nephite Christianity thus refuses to see the world as irreparable, and yet it denies that anything else is on its way. Redemption is not to be accomplished, for the Nephite, through the breaking in of something transcendent, but through the reemergence of the overlooked. It is true that

---

10. It is, I believe, for this reason that the Nephites "understood not [Christ's] saying [to them] that old things had passed away, and that all things had become new" (3 Ne. 15:2). It is not that they did not understand the dawn of the new, but rather that they had had the new all along and so could not make sense of the claim that anything was changing.

11. See Jarom 1:11 and Mosiah 3:13 (the emphases are mine). [Miller would seem to have conceded my point, making Jarom 1:11 central to his recent study: Adam S. Miller, *An Early Resurrection: Life in Christ before You Die* (Salt Lake City and Provo, UT: Deseret Book and Neal A. Maxwell Institute, 2018).]

Nephite prophets from the beginning look to an eschatological era ushered in by divine intervention in the last days, but that intervention is only the divinely guided promulgation of an ancient book, the universal announcement of what has passed unnoticed. It could therefore just as easily have been a Nephite as Adam Miller who proposed the idea that "novelty is a red herring." Christ's atoning work, according to the Nephites, was less the dawn of the new than the worldly manifestation of the most ancient and immanent thing of all: the Lamb's being slain *from the foundation of the world*.[12] History is, on the Book of Mormon's vision, neither open-ended (as in Jewish messianism) nor interrupted (as in Christian messianism) but *inconsistent*—divided against itself and troubled by its transcendental conditions, from the outset and intentionally.

Nothing is on its way? Does the Book of Mormon, then, launch a polemic against hope? If it, like Miller, really does claim that novelty is a red herring, does it not reject every orientation to possibility? Indeed, if, as Alma argues most fascinatingly in his discussion with Corianton (see Alma 40–42), the eschaton is an era of restoration, of repetition, for what can one genuinely hope? But, no. The Book of Mormon emphasizes hope as much as Paul does, apparently thanks to Mormon's particular concerns. Because he was himself "without hope," as he says, hope was one of his principal concerns—not only in letters and sermons his son would include in the volume's appendix of sorts (see Moroni 7–9), but already in the theological shape he gave to the editorial project he assembled.[13] Details can be dealt with elsewhere.[14] For now suffice it to say that the Book of Mormon can be read as much as a treatise on the centrality of hope to Christian experience as it can be read as a complex rejection of novelty.

But this should give us pause. Although hope is, according to the Book of Mormon, hope "for a *better* world," it is not hope for *another* world (Ether 12:4). What the Nephite anticipates in hope is not the dawn of the new, but the transformative restoration of the ancient, reemergence

---

12. This language is used in the Book of Mormon over and over again, and not only with reference to the gospel as known by the Nephites. It is found also on the lips of the Christ who visits the brother of Jared long before Lehi is born (see Ether 3:14), as well as on the lips of the angels God sends still earlier to Adam and Eve outside the garden of Eden (see Alma 12:30)!

13. See especially the several references to hope in the Book of Alma.

14. See, again, my forthcoming book, *For Zion*.

of the passed-over, thematization of the foreclosed.[15] There is no hope for a tomorrow with everything set right; there is hope only that the repetition of today will allow it to be done better—more justly, more mercifully, more faithfully, more charitably. Indeed, it is *this* sort of hope, precisely because it is *Nephite* hope, that binds the charity Miller intends to promote to faith.

At any rate, it is this vision of things that, I believe, animates both earlier and later Miller. Careful reading of the earlier essays shows that Miller's approbation of novelty was a first attempt to outline what has become his theme since. This could not be clearer in what I think remains his most provocative essay, "Messianic History" (chapter 3 of *Rube Goldberg Machines*), an essay that was produced three years before "Humanism, Mormonism" and a full seven years before "Groundhog Day."[16] Miller there argues that the Book of Mormon is "messianic" precisely in that it is "rediscover[ed]" as "what was lost,"[17] in that it interrupts time "by way of a pure repetition,"[18] in that it "exposes homogeneous 'progress' as vain,"[19] in that it "carefully collects the heterogeneous debris of history,"[20] in that it, in a word, "is anachronistic."[21] This essay alone shows that Miller's project has not so much changed as sharpened. Novelty—if it is understood as *progress*—has always been vain in Miller's eyes. And novelty—if it is understood as the promised reemergence of what is consistently overlooked—has always been worthy of celebration, on Miller's account.

Miller thus shares his vision with—and perhaps adopts it from—the Book of Mormon. Willing to take Nephite scripture seriously enough to contest every narrative of linear progress, every destructive trust in the present world order, every arrogant reverie in visions of a future conform-

---

15. On this theme, see Richard Lyman Bushman, "The Book of Mormon in Early Mormon History," in *Believing History: Latter-day Saint Essays,* ed. Reid L. Neilson and Jed Woodworth (New York: Columbia University Press, 2004), 65–78; and Terry L. Givens, "Joseph Smith: Prophecy, Process, and Plenitude," *BYU Studies* 44, no. 4 (2005): 55–68.

16. "Messianic History" was originally delivered at the 2004 meetings of the Society for Mormon Philosophy and Theology. It originally appeared in James M. McLaughlan and Loyd Ericson, *Discourses in Mormon Theology: Philosophical and Theological Possibilities* (Salt Lake City: Greg Kofford Books, 2007), 227–45.

17. Miller, *Rube Goldberg Machines,* 21.

18. Miller, 24.

19. Miller, 25.

20. Miller, 26.

21. Miller, 32.

ing only to one's own selfish fantasies, Adam Miller is a Book of Mormon theologian, an exemplary hermeneut, and a worthy traveler of the road Faulconer has paved. Though I wish his work more consistently plunged its spade in the soil of the scriptural text—how I wish he would write commentaries![22]—Adam Miller never fails to teach me to read more attentively, with more faith, more hope, and more charity.

---

22. [Miller has, in fact, written something like a commentary more recently: Adam S. Miller, *Mormon: A Brief Theological Introduction* (Provo, UT: Neal A. Maxwell Institute, 2020).]

Chapter Seventeen

"And it Came to Pass"
A Response to Adam Miller's
"Theoscatology"

The 2013 project sponsored by the Latter-day Saint Theology Seminar involved two parallel investigations—one on 2 Nephi 2, and one on Genesis 2–3. I helped to direct the investigation of 2 Nephi 2, while Adam Miller helped to direct the investigation of Genesis 2–3. As these two on-line seminars drew to a close, we planned a two-day symposium for the summer of 2013 at Utah Valley University. Participants from the seminar on 2 Nephi 2 served as respondents to the papers generated by the seminar on Genesis 2–3, while participants from the seminar on Genesis 2–3 served as respondents to the papers generated by the seminar on 2 Nephi 2. I thus found myself with another opportunity to respond publicly to the work of my friend Adam Miller. His paper, a fascinating and brilliant reflection on just one moment in Genesis 3, immediately struck me as yet again rooted in the Book of Mormon in non-obvious ways. Even when Miller reads the Bible, it seemed to me, he is really reading the Book of Mormon.

This short essay thus began as a formal response to Miller's paper "Theoscatology: On Dirt, Dung, and Digestion in God's Garden." It was a second public opportunity to call for a gifted Latter-day Saint theologian to see his work as ultimately rooted in the Book of Mormon, and so to begin to draw himself closer—in whatever ways possible—to Book of Mormon studies. It was also, however, an opportunity to do some theological work on the text of the Book of Mormon myself, of a microscopic sort. The essay thus takes on the Book of Mormon's most common formula, a formula that few if any have seen as bearing any kind of theological significance: "and it came to pass." This kind of close theological reading was exactly the sort of reflection that Miller and I had developed in conversation over the years, and so it seemed a fit tribute.

I originally presented this essay at "Mormon Conceptions of the Fall" in June 2013 at Utah Valley University, a symposium hosted by the Latter-day Saint Theology Seminar. The essay then appeared in more polished form in *Fleeing the Garden: Reading Genesis 2–3*, ed. Adam S. Miller (Provo, UT: Neal A. Maxwell Institute, 2017), 96–101.

Describing what he called the "prosy detail of imaginary history" he found in the Book of Mormon, Mark Twain said the following of the formula that marks the narrative movement of the book: "'And it came to pass' was [the translator's] pet. If he had left that out, his Bible would have been only a pamphlet."[1] Twain is, of course, hardly the only reader to have noted—and to have complained about—the ceaseless repetition of this formula in the text of the Book of Mormon. Some French editions, for instance, have replaced the formula with an asterisk, not quite making a pamphlet of the book, but shortening it substantially nonetheless.[2] "Scores" of the iterated formula were removed by the Community of Christ committee tasked with producing a reader-friendly Revised Authorized Version of the Book of Mormon.[3] And Joseph Smith himself removed a number of instances of the formula from the Book for the second edition in 1837, presumably in part because he had already begun to hear complaints (if not to make them himself!) regarding the frequency of the formula's appearance.[4]

Frankly, readers of the Book of Mormon very quickly get tired of the phrase—"and it came to pass," "and it came to pass," "and it came to pass." When we set out from Jerusalem with Nephi at the book's beginning, we feel its pinch. By the time we've crossed a desert and an ocean and arrived in the New World, we can tell that it's giving us blisters. When we later find ourselves trudging back and forth between the lands of Nephi and Zarahemla, or marching on the campaign trail with Captain Moroni, or standing precariously atop the wall with Samuel the Lamanite, the phrase has long since rubbed our flesh raw. Much as we might hope for healing from the visiting Christ of 3 Nephi, we never find release. Right through the end of the Book of Mormon, we're reading the refrain: "and it came to pass," "and it came to pass," "and it came to pass."

---

1. Mark Twain, *Roughing It* (New York: Signet, 1980), 103.

2. See Grant Hardy, *Understanding the Book of Mormon: A Reader's Guide* (New York: Oxford University Press, 2010), 5.

3. See Richard P. Howard, *Restoration Scriptures: A Study of Their Textual Development* (Independence, MO: Reorganized Church of Jesus Christ of Latter Day Saints, 1969), 62.

4. See Royal Skousen, *Analysis of Textual Variants of the Book of Mormon, Part I: Title Page, Witness Statements, 1 Nephi 1–2 Nephi 10* (Provo, UT: FARMS, 2004), 207.

But I find myself wondering, after reading Adam Miller's reflections on "theoscatology," whether the often-mentioned Mormon appreciation for the body shouldn't make us pause reflectively at every "and it came to pass." "We need bodies to become like God," Miller says, "but bodies are organs of passing." What's packed into the Book of Mormon's repetitive formula, this textual and narrative remainder that we'd prefer to elide or at least replace with a contentless asterisk? What might we find if we were to read "and it came to pass" as a *theological* formula?

The construction of the formula is important, I think. The only parallel construction to "it came to pass" of which I can think is "it came to be." Note the difference, however. In "it came to be," we have a certain formulaic dismantling of becoming, a certain cancellation of the dynamic and the mobile. The formula opens ("it came . . .") with change and modulation, in fact, with *becoming*, but it closes (". . . to be") with an interruption of change and modulation, in fact with *being*. "It came to be": static being, as a kind of telos, brings becoming to an end. All transformation culminates in a certain state, a final form. It came, yes—but it came only in order to *be*.[5]

What, though, of "it came to pass"? Here the dynamic is succeeded not by the static but by the dynamic. Change and transformation culminate in change and transformation. It came—not *to be* but *to pass*. Might we say, "it came *in order* to pass"? Its purpose or its telos, if *it* can be said to have one, *is* to pass, to remain in the flux of becoming. There's no shift from becoming to being, no end of history. There's only coming and going, the approach of the open from the future and the passage of the closed into the past. There's only, in other words, the persistent punctuation of what, in an earlier version of "Theoscatology," Miller called "intrathoracic time."

But that's too simple, isn't it? What of the tension between the infinitive *to pass* and the conjugated *it came*? Might there be a kind of shift as becoming gives way to passing—a shift, though, not from becoming to being but from the actual to the potential? The formula speaks not of what is *coming* but of what *came*. The first part of the formula—"it came"—already freezes becoming, calcifies the impersonal *it*, stops the heart whose pulse marks the rhythm of time. In "it came" we have the full realization of the actual. But then the frozen, the calcified, the stopped, the fully realized, the actual—*this* passes from actuality to potentiality,

---

5. We find something much the same in constructions that replace the impersonal *it* with the personal pronoun: "I came to realize" or "I came to see."

from finitude (the closedness of what *has passed*: "it came") to the infinite (the neither-past-nor-present-*nor*-future status of what remains *infinitive*: "to pass"). In "it came to pass" perhaps we witness the determinate become indeterminate, the decided become undecidable. In pass*ing*, what *came* (what, indeed, came *to be*) reclaims potentiality (and therefore power?) by a Bartlebian "preferring not to,"[6] by passing over its being and retrieving the becoming it would seem to have given up in the *past* tense of "it came," transforming "the past" (or "the passed") into "to pass."

What is it "to pass," then? A first question. And a question, I fear, that's made relatively little sense as I've tried to develop it here. But let me complicate it further, nonetheless. What of the impersonal *it*? If it's difficult enough even to know what it means to speak, infinitively, of passing ("What is it 'to pass'?"), it's more difficult still to guess at what it means for *it* to pass, or for *it* to have come. What lies behind the *it* of "it came to pass"—or of "it came to be," for that matter? Why is *it* singular? Why is *it* neuter? Why is *it* indeterminate? More baffling, perhaps, why is *it* there *at all*? Why not speak rather of what exactly is that comes, that passes, that is? Why is it only *it* that "comes to pass"?

There's likely little to be decided immediately about *it*, so let me also leave it to one side in order to complicate things further in a second way—in a way that might be less confusing. Notice that I have simplified the Book of Mormon's formulation in much of this brief discussion—giving attention not to "*and* it came to pass" but simply to "it came to pass." What of the *and* of "and it came to pass" that largely prescribes the frequency of its repetition in the Book of Mormon narrative? (Indeed, we might well wonder whether it's the "it came to pass" or merely the *and* that drives us mad as readers of the Book of Mormon.)

Hiding behind the word *and* is a logical function, an operator that marks the status of statements whose connectedness serves as a condition of their collective truth. Things are a little more complicated than just that, since logical conjunction is actually a simplification of a more complex operation (to be specific: the negation of a positively conditioned negation).[7] For the moment, however, it suffices to say that *and* weaves into a kind of totality of causative and conditioning relations all of what

6. See Giorgio Agamben, "Bartleby, or On Contingency," in *Potentialities: Collected Essays in Philosophy*, ed. and trans. Daniel Heller-Roazen (Stanford: Stanford University Press, 1999), 243–71.

7. See Gottlob Frege, "*Begriffsschrift*, a Formula Language, Modeled upon That of Arithmetic, for Pure Thought," in *From Frege to Gödel: A Source Book in*

language might correctly say about the world—the world of becoming as much as of the world of being.[8] What we have in "and it came to pass" is the continuing concatenation of statements about how history might be potentialized, might be given *to pass*.

It is thus in a double sense that we find in "and it came to pass" something like the *remainder* of the Book of Mormon. It's the book's remainder in that it's what we fantasize about flushing away, but it's also the book's remainder in that it's what marks the Book of Mormon's consistent attempt to repotentialize what might too easily become mere actuality. It's what, if we pay attention to its talk of passing, may alert us to how the book not only *reports* but also *questions* or even *contests* history. It's for that reason that, even and perhaps especially in reading the Book of Mormon, we need to shift our attention, as Miller says, from "high drama" to "low comedy," giving our attention to the excessive and overdetermined narrative the Book of Mormon weaves.

A final thought: Here, as elsewhere, I've tried to read Adam Miller as a Book of Mormon theologian—as a thinker of the tensions and stresses at work in the text that launched the history through which *we* are all passing, through which we'll *always* be passing.[9] Perhaps it's only wishful thinking on my part that finds me bringing Miller's thinking back to the Book of Mormon, a too-invested plea that he read less of Bruno Latour and David Foster Wallace and more of the brother of Jared and Alma the Elder. I think not, though. The more time I spend in conversation with Miller, the more I find the image Walter Benjamin took from Edgar Allen Poe to describe his own thought to be appropriate for making sense of Miller's work.[10] His readers and listeners experience him as an elaborately dressed Turk, playing a game of chess he always seems to be winning. But

Mathematical Logic, 1879–1931, ed. Jean Van Heijenoort (Cambridge: Harvard University Press, 1967), 19.

8. See Alfred Tarski, "The Concept of Truth in Formalized Language," in *Logic, Semantics, Metamathematics*, 2nd ed., ed. John Corcoran, trans. J. H. Woodger (Indianapolis: Hackett, 1983), 187–88.

9. See Joseph M. Spencer, "Notes on Novelty," *SquareTwo* 6, no. 1 (Spring 2013), http://squaretwo.org/Sq2ArticleMillerSymposiumSpencer.html. [This essay appears in this volume.]

10. See Walter Benjamin, "Theses on the Philosophy of History," in *Illuminations: Essays and Reflections*, ed. Hanna Arendt, trans. Harry Zohn (New York: Schocken Books, 2007), 253; and Giorgio Agamben, *The Time That Remains: A Commentary on the Letter to the Romans*, trans. Patricia Dailey (Stanford: Stanford University Press, 2005), 138–45.

I've peeked under the table on which the chessboard sits, and I've seen that the Turk they see is only a massive puppet, entirely controlled by a little hunchback dwarf crouched beneath the table. It stays out of sight, for the most part, but it's what makes every successful move. And its name is the Book of Mormon.

Chapter Eighteen

Sin

It is one thing to construct a theological account from sin beginning from what the Book of Mormon has to say on the subject. But is there a theological account to be constructed about ways we might sin against the Book of Mormon? Some would certainly want to say that we sin against the Book of Mormon when we claim to believe it but reject its historicity. For my part, I am inclined to agree. I am unsure, however, about exactly how serious that sin is. It is something I work to stay safely far away from, to be sure. But I wonder about this question because I worry about how we sometimes treat those who question or doubt the Book of Mormon's claim to be ancient. At such times, I find myself wondering whether we do not overstate the nature of this sin, sometimes even making it into a—or even *the*—unforgivable sin. If we do so, do we not run the risk of neglecting the weightier things—say, the Book of Mormon's truth, the way it ought to shape our very lives?

Shortly after Adam Miller's book *Speculative Grace: Bruno Latour and Object-Oriented Theology* appeared, I found myself with a third opportunity to respond to his work in public. Again I wanted to make my usual argument that Miller's theology is ultimately a reflection on the Book of Mormon's own theological commitments and sensibilities. In this case, however, Miller had written a theoretical work for the larger academic world, not a work of specifically Latter-day Saint theology for an insider audience. I had my work cut out for me. Given the claims Miller makes in his book, though, it was not difficult to find an angle from which I could bring him once more directly into the orbit of Book of Mormon studies. His work gave me a way of talking quite directly about the weightier matters when it comes to the Book of Mormon. This essay resulted.

These previously unpublished remarks I originally delivered as part of a panel on Adam Miller's book *Speculative Grace*. The panel occurred as part of the annual conference of the Association for Mormon Scholars in the Humanities, which was held at Claremont Graduate University in March of 2014.

Twice before—once on a panel reviewing *Rube Goldberg Machines* and once as a respondent to a paper—I've publicly argued that Adam Miller, despite his pretensions otherwise, is a Book of Mormon theologian. Given the opportunity to respond directly to Miller's work in another public setting, I've decided to pursue this same thesis again today. Every time I read Miller's writings, I find his thought deeply rooted in—or at least startlingly anticipated by—the Book of Mormon. In a recent paper, Miller drew on an image from Giorgio Agamben to suggest that the Book of Mormon is like the light of the most distant stars in our expanding universe.[1] We don't see that light because the stars that emit it are moving away from us so quickly that the light never reaches us. Although we're in a universe filled with light, we're still waiting—and will always be waiting—for that light to appear. The Book of Mormon is just the same. We live in a world that's filled with evidence for the Book of Mormon's truth, but we're still waiting—and will always be waiting—for that evidence to appear. Meanwhile, the book recedes from us in such a way that we'd have to hie to Kolob in the twinkling of an eye even to catch a glimpse of its real meaning. Miller's work, again and again and again, hies to Kolob. In passing textual twinklings of an eye, glimpses of the Book of Mormon's truth and force and, let's not hesitate to say it, *reality* can be caught in Miller's writings.

We're here to talk about *Speculative Grace*, though, a book that likely wouldn't sound Mormon to most Mormons. Let me explain what I mean with a slightly irreverent whirlwind review of the theological options set forth in our history.[2] The God of *Speculative Grace* is not the best-known God of Mormonism, the scientific, progressive God of James E. Talmage, John A. Widtsoe, and B. H. Roberts. Even less, though, is this God the theologically conservative God of Joseph Fielding Smith and then of Bruce R. McConkie, a God drawn in equal parts from scientific progressivism and Evangelical Christianity. Still less is Miller's God the God of millennial Mormonism, of Mormonism after *Mormon Doctrine*—the God of devotion that many find in the Book of Mormon today. Agreeing with many that the portrayal of God requires rethinking after postwar Mormonism, too serious to allow God to evaporate in the indistinct

---

1. See Adam S. Miller, *Future Mormon: Essays in Mormon Theology* (Salt Lake City: Greg Kofford Books, 2016), 40.

2. [I must confess that I wince today as I read this summary. In writing it, I used hyperbole to keep the story moving. In keeping with the archival nature of *The Anatomy of Book of Mormon Theology*, I leave the text intact. I would write it differently today, to be certain!]

"spirituality" of millennial culture, and yet theologically uncomfortable with what's recently—thanks to Terryl and Fiona Givens—become a call to the scientific, progressive God of a hundred years ago, Miller would *seem* to be leaving Mormonism's God behind.

Seem. Let me underscore that word. Because what I find in *Speculative Grace*—continuing with my sweeping and slightly irreverent historical gestures—is a revitalization of a Mormon theological tradition that was largely buried during the difficult transitional period between 1880 and 1930. When Talmage and Widtsoe and Roberts invented twentieth-century Mormon theology, and especially when that theology found itself in conflict with the rival reflections of Smith and McConkie, the death of nineteenth-century Mormon theological reflection was effectively complete. Miller announces its resurrection. Or rather, he announces the resurrection of a certain strain of nineteenth-century theological reflection. As is well known, there was no more a unified Mormon theological tradition in the nineteenth century than there has been in the twentieth. I think it's important for a host of reasons that in reaching into the communal grave of nineteenth-century theological speculation, Miller's sought to raise with his strong hand only what was even in its first life an institutionally marginalized form of reflection.

I'm referring in all this talk, of course, to the "conflict in the quorum" that set Brigham Young and Orson Pratt at odds for so many of their later years. Not without some institutional force, Brigham's theology officially carried the day. But Orson's theological reflections enjoyed a fair bit of underground approbation, and he certainly couldn't shake his convictions concerning them. On the margins and in a deliberate attempt to dialogue with the philosophers and scientists of his own day, Orson Pratt attempted to systematize Joseph Smith's so-called "Nauvoo theology" in a way that could speak with a universal and academically viable voice. Not only has Miller resurrected Orson's actual theological claims, generally speaking, he's also, it seems to me, resurrected Orson's universalizing attempt to speak to the academy. We're living through the 1840s and the 1850s again, but this time without the conflict that once slowed the pursuit of a Latourian metaphysics.[3]

I imagine it seems like I've long since left the Book of Mormon far, far behind in this discussion. There's a general consensus these days that the Book of Mormon has nothing to do with Joseph Smith's Nauvoo theology, and there's no question but that Orson Pratt saw his theological reflections

---

3. [For a broad and responsible survey of all the theological history covered in these paragraphs, see Terryl L. Givens, *Wrestling the Angel: The Foundations of Mormon Thought: Cosmos, God, Humanity* (New York: Oxford University Press, 2015).]

as an attempt to work out the implications of Joseph's sermons and teachings in Nauvoo. And yet, I think it's crucial to recognize that there was no more serious a student of the Book of Mormon in nineteenth-century Mormonism than Orson Pratt—including, most tellingly, Joseph Smith! It'd be a mistake to think that Orson's work was representative of a general trend *away* from the Book of Mormon in nineteenth-century theological reflection after Joseph's death. As his pamphlets and essays and sermons make quite clear, Orson Pratt was a major—perhaps the only public—point of resistance to precisely that trend. He went where he went in his theological musings because he felt it was the only way to reconcile the explosive theology Joseph Smith announced in Nauvoo with the Book of Mormon that had first converted him. And what makes Orson's theological work so interesting, in my view, is the way that he creatively and productively found Nauvoo right in the Book of Mormon, as if the Book of Mormon were the first great study of Joseph Smith's Nauvoo theology.

Enough preface. You see the general connection I want to draw between *Speculative Grace* and the Book of Mormon. Adam Miller is the Orson Pratt of our own generation, and that means that he's wildly experimental in his theological work while he's insistently attentive to the Book of Mormon. Or that, at any rate, is what I've argued again and again. What I want to do with the rest of the time I've got here, though, is to give my attention to just one moment in *Speculative Grace*, a moment where Miller uses a striking formulation to reconceptualize the notion of sin. I'll argue that he's implicitly suggesting something concerning the way we might think about our own collective relationship to the Book of Mormon.

Here's the passage I've got in mind: "Sin is the dream of an empty black box, of a black box that is absolute rather than relative, permanent rather than provisional."[4] Miller's point, in context, is that sin should be thought of as an essentializing encrustation of unquestioned habits and traditions. Or better, sin is the knowing fantasy that the supposed essences that precipitate out of tired habits and traditions are actually divine and eternal, the well-behaved citizens of Plato's heaven. We take those "forms," imagistic (not to mention imaginary) in nature, and we use them to cover the drastically complex and essentially unstable structures that are our practices. Beneath that beautiful lid, we pretend, there's nothing—or rather, there's only an empty black box. The image, the form, is *sui generis*, without depth and hiding nothing of actual complexity. It thus serves as a

---

4. Adam S. Miller, *Speculative Grace: Bruno Latour and Object-Oriented Theology* (New York: Fordham University Press, 2013), 144.

kind of mirror, a polished glass in which we observe nothing but ourselves while we pretend we're looking as far into the distance as we can.

Dreams, fantasies, mirrors, the imaginary—all this language is crucial. Sin is something we enjoy. Sin is the narcissistic pleasure we take in finding the perfect angle from which to view just the most flattering part of ourselves in a mirror, fantasizing that what we see for a moment if we hold still just long enough in that awkward position reveals the plain truth about ourselves. Sin is the pleasure we take in focusing in on what we think we can flaunt so that we're sufficiently distracted from the massively complex rest of us: the hobbit-hair adorning the feet, the departed septum that makes symmetry impossible, the scars that have never disappeared, the patch of skin where facial hair refuses to grow, the uneven hairline—to mention a few of the "more uncomely parts" I see in the mirror if I'm honest with myself. Of course, to fix on any of those is just as problematic, since they too cover over a million and more complexities that make up the frozen image of my body. And there's certainly as perverse a pleasure in staring at an uncomely as a comely part. The dis-form as much as the form serves as a lid to cover a black box.

Repentance, for Miller, would then be figured in every lifting of the lid, every renewal of the attention that can be given to the complexity of the world—not only of beings, but of being itself. (It's with the latter that religion deals, on Miller's Latourian account.) Repentance is called for by the very texture of the world, of what's in the world and of the world itself—of the world and of the worlds within the world. We're to change by coming back to things, by seeing how much more is at work in them than we're wont to see, by seeing how much we overlook thanks to the fact that we've long since accustomed ourselves to things. We've got to wonder again, giving up our pragmatic conclusions for philosophic questions.

I want to think about this image of the "empty black box" and the assignation of sin to its production. Miller draws the image from Bruno Latour, of course, but it's a poignant image for a Latter-day Saint to fix on. Secularizing skeptics have long argued that Mormonism is built on a *literal* empty black box: an empty wooden chest that Joseph Smith insisted on carrying around when he was at work on the Book of Mormon in order to give the deceptive impression to his nascent following that he had the plates he had supposedly taken from a similarly empty black box in a nearby hill. Even more important—and painful—is the fact that devoted believers have long treated the text of the Book of Mormon as a *metaphorical* empty black box: a signifier exhausted by its role in a whole system of signifiers pointing everywhere but to the complex contents of the Book of Mormon. The cardinal sin of Mormonism, in which believers and skeptics alike find delight, is the refusal to take the lid off the Book of Mormon. We don't read the Book of Mormon; we stare in a mirror we've placed in front of it, such that we magically—and self-servingly—find in what we think is the book only reflections of our current practices and ideologies, whether those be conservative in nature or essentially progressive.

"Repent and remember the new covenant, even the Book of Mormon," God was already telling the Saints in 1832 (D&C 84:57). And you're all aware of the fact that the associated condemnation was said not to have been lifted as recently as the 1980s. What if we were to hear in Miller's talk of sin and in his implicit call to repentance first and foremost an echo of God's revealed words about the Book of Mormon? Might we not suspect that it's precisely the complicated status of the empty black box on which Mormonism is supposedly built that drives Miller's interest in an object-oriented theology? Miller has himself, in an important paper, issued a call to "make the Book of Mormon true," a task that becomes clear only if we take a Latourian object-oriented theology seriously.[5] And his beautiful advice concerning scripture in his *Letters to a Young Mormon* is especially suggestive.[6] There's work to be done on the world, on our practices, on everything. But there's work above all to be done on the keystone of our religion.

A particularly suggestive piece of evidence that I'm on the right track here can, I think, be found in a chapter from *Speculative Grace* entitled "Hermeneutics." Miller there says the following:

> Anyone who has tried to write is familiar with the way that words are 'opaque, dense, and heavy.' It is difficult work to wrangle errant words into lines on a page and stack them in a way that will hold. This recognition of an irreducible errancy—an errancy that results from the fact that words, as material objects, are both resistant to domestication *and* available for seduction—is aptly referred to as a semiotic materialism.[7]

I hear in these words an unmistakable allusion to Moroni's fretful worries in Ether 12:

> Lord, the Gentiles will mock at these things, because of our weakness in writing; for Lord thou hast made us mighty in word by faith, but thou hast not made us mighty in writing. . . . When we write we behold our weakness,

---

5. See Miller, *Future Mormon*, 105–11.

6. See Adam S. Miller, *Letters to a Young Mormon*, 2nd ed. (Salt Lake City and Provo, UT: Deseret Book and Neal A. Maxwell Institute, 2018), 25–30.

7. Miller, *Speculative Grace*, 109.

and stumble because of the placing of our words; and I fear lest the Gentiles shall mock at our words. (Ether 12:23, 25)

Is Miller reminding us, we Gentile readers, that the Book of Mormon is more complex, more deeply structured, than we allow? At any rate, some of you will remember that Miller has dedicated a beautiful essay to Moroni's words, now found in *Rube Goldberg Machines* but originally presented at a meeting of this very organization.[8] It's also worth noting that Miller's phrase I've just quoted, "semiotic materialism," first appeared in an essay he produced for a volume on Mormon scriptural theology.[9]

Speculative Grace pleads for a rethinking of theology that abandons ontological commitments foreign to Miller's Mormon faith. That's its message to the world, we might say. But its message to the Saints who read it, I can't help but conclude, is that we've got to get serious about the Book of Mormon.

And we might say that Miller provides us with a set of concrete instructions for doing so, even if it would have been entirely out of place for him to have provided a concrete example of how it can be done. The task, he suggests, is to look for *structure*. "Objects," he says, and the text of the Book of Mormon is no exception, "are constituted as such by [the] double-bind of *resistant availability*."[10] What we're to look for in our hermeneutic work on the Book of Mormon is precisely the way that resistance and availability weave themselves together, and it seems clear to me that they do so in textual structure. We're all too familiar with the story of Nephi retrieving the brass plates. We've read it too many times, sung the silly primary song over and over, worried the same tired worries about Nephi's willingness to kill Laban or to attribute the constraint to the divine. In a word, the story has become *only* available, *no longer* resistant. If the book is to become anew the source of grace, that availability has to be tangled with resistance.

Historians have perhaps given us a few points of resistance: surprising connections with the ancient world *or* with nineteenth-century America have shocked us out of our comfort with the text. But they've hardly done enough. At best, they've given us to wonder whether the Book of Mormon isn't itself a lid covering an empty black box—the empty black box of a

---

8. See Adam S. Miller, *Rube Goldberg Machines: Essays in Mormon Theology* (Salt Lake City: Greg Kofford Books, 2012), 99–105.

9. See Adam S. Miller, "'Take No Thought,'" in *Perspectives on Mormon Theology: Scriptural Theology*, ed. James E. Faulconer and Joseph M. Spencer (Salt Lake City: Greg Kofford Books, 2015), 57–67.

10. Miller, *Speculative Grace*, 39.

complex history. What we need instead is to see the actual resistances the text offers to us. We've got to remove the mirrors we've placed in front of this narrative and look into the network of semiotic material that structures this text. I'll illustrate again by referring to Nephi's first story: How do we make sense of the original chapter breaks (1 Nephi 1–5 was one chapter in the original), especially in light of the fact that the narrative opens and closes with the same image—a figure coming down to Lehi with a book that, once he read it, filled him with the Spirit and set him prophesying? How do we make sense of the word that's repeated again and again and again through the narrative—most crucially when Nephi is standing over the body of the drunken Laban: "commandments"? How do we think about the structural *inclusio* between this story and the originally planned closing story of the whole Book of Mormon, Coriantumr's beheading of Shiz, especially in light of the complicated political dynamics that differentiate the two stories? How do we think about the structural place of this story in Nephi's remarkably structured first book, since the aim is eventually to reveal the parallelism between Lehi's and Nephi's prophetic visions and the writings of Isaiah retrieved from Jerusalem? And so on.

A finally resistant Book of Mormon! We've had enough—this is what I hear Miller telling us—we've had enough of people saying that the Book of Mormon is so much simpler than the Bible. Frankly, it's not. We're just better at placing mirrors in front of this book than the other. And we've had enough of trite readings, forcing us to listen to predictable moral lessons or commanding us to believe or disbelieve in the book's historicity again and again. This empty black box, of all empty black boxes, is the one we need to peer into.

And here I'll go one step further than what I find in Miller's reflections in *Speculative Grace*. We need to find resistance in the Book of Mormon not only so that we'll find it itself a manifestation of grace. We need to find resistance in the Book of Mormon because its structures provide us with the means for tracing the contours—the topology—of the life of faith. Our cardinal sin lies in our refusal to read the Book of Mormon well. But we only escape from that sin when we read it well *and* draw the consequences for the life of faith. That, I think, is what it means to trust in faith that this book came from God. It's a privileged object, an object unlike others. It needs to be made true, yes, but by our coming to conform our lives to the terrain the book lays out for us. We repent first in our reading of it. But we'll repent fully only when we let the book live in our lives. Then the book will be as true in this world as it is in its own.

An Epilogue of Sorts

Chapter Nineteen

Mormons, Films, Scriptures

Theology too easily looks like a purely academic affair, even when it focuses its attention on something as popularly devotional as the Book of Mormon. The essays gathered in *The Anatomy of Book of Mormon Theology* are no exception. Although they labor—some more and some less—to make themselves accessible and of interest to non-specialist and non-scholarly Latter-day Saints, the fact is that theological reflection on the Book of Mormon in its most traditional guise can look far from inviting to those sitting in the pew. And yet the Book of Mormon is a vibrant and living text, the kind of thing that Latter-day Saints, alone and in community, read carefully and thoughtfully every day. Are there ways to do real and rigorous theological work on the text of the Book of Mormon without removing it from the hands of the Saints to put it into the hands of scholars alone?

An abiding interest in the medium of film—arguably the most popular art form in today's world—provides a unique opportunity to reflect on how movies use and think about scripture, the Book of Mormon in particular. Might film provide a promising site for theological reflection that refuses to remove itself from the main body of the Church to do its work solely within the academy? The very first years of the twenty-first century gave rise to what has sometimes been called a "Mormon film movement," a short-lived but culturally interesting affair. Scattered throughout the films the movement produced are references to—and occasionally whole films dedicated to—the Book of Mormon. Watching these films, I naturally found myself asking what they tell us about the opportunities for serious reflection on scripture in so popular a setting. What messages do such films send to their viewers about the status of the Book of Mormon in Latter-day Saint culture? And what messages might they send about the meaning and depth of the book. I wrote this essay by way of exploring these questions.

I originally delivered this paper at the annual conference of the Association for Mormon Scholars in the Humanities, held at Southern Virginia University in May of 2012—part of a panel on Latter-day Saint films organized by Matthew Bowman. It then appeared in *Dialogue: A Journal of Mormon Thought* 45, no. 3 (Fall 2012): 171–79.

I asserted without argument a few years ago at the annual meeting of the Association of Mormon Scholars in the Humanities that the Mormon film movement of 2000–2005 witnessed the production of only one truly Mormon film; namely, *Napoleon Dynamite* (2004).[1] The claim for which I did provide an argument was that the bulk of the movement launched by Richard Dutcher's *God's Army* (2000) and brought to its culmination with Dutcher's (thankfully-later-re-titled) *God's Army 2* (2005) was principally a study in the possibility of introducing into Mormonism, for ostensibly pastoral reasons but with theologically fraught consequences, an arguably non-Mormon sense of religious transcendence. What I did not note then, but would like to reflect on now, is the curious role scripture played—and did not play—in this short-lived movement.

I want to consider both what I believe all would consider the movement's most impressive production, as well as what I believe all would consider the movement's least impressive production—respectively, Richard Dutcher's *States of Grace* (née *God's Army 2*) and Gary Rogers's *The Book of Mormon Movie: Volume 1, The Journey* (2003). By way of conclusion, I want to say a word about *Napoleon Dynamite*—that most Mormon of films that, nonetheless, had not a word to say about scripture. If, as I suggested a few years ago, the Mormon film movement was as much a theological venture as a filmic one, what can be said about it in terms of specifically *scriptural* theology?

It is relatively easy to set up as polar opposites *The Book of Mormon Movie* and *States of Grace*, and not only in terms of aesthetic merit. Where the one is ostensibly conservative, the other is ostensibly liberal; where the one, not unproblematically, reproduces and reinforces Mormon culture, the other, also not unproblematically, contests and ultimately parts ways with Mormon culture. But despite such clear differences in both talent and approach, Rogers and Dutcher wrestle, in many ways, with the very same problem: What is the relevance of Mormon scripture to contemporary life?

Rogers poses this question in *The Book of Mormon Movie* in three different ways.

---

1. See Joseph M. Spencer, "Alfred Hitchcock in the Legacy Theater: Mormonism, Film, and 'Religious' Criticism," unpublished paper presented at the annual conference of the Association of Mormon Scholars in the Humanities, "Religions and the Practices of Criticism," Brigham Young University, May 8–9, 2009. See also Michael De Groote, "Dynamite, Dutcher, Hitchcock and the Failure of LDS Movies," *Mormon Times*, May 14, 2009.

First, through the liberties automatically taken in any dramatization of a scriptural text, he introduces into the scriptural narrative distinctly modern concerns that arise in the setting of contemporary Mormon culture. The most poignant—and, frankly, painful—example comes in the portrayal of 1 Nephi 18:9–10, that less-than-memorable moment in Nephi's narrative when some of his party began, during the ocean voyage to the New World, "to make themselves merry, insomuch that they began to dance, and to sing, and to speak with much rudeness." In Rogers's adaptation, this scene becomes less a worry about "forget[ting] by what power" the group had been brought out of Jerusalem and more a study in young women's modesty—with two of Ishmael's daughters dancing in quasi-ancient-looking denim skirts that do not reach their knees and not-at-all-ancient-looking tops that leave not only their arms and shoulders but also their midriff bare. Significantly, in Rogers's version, before Nephi chastises his brothers, Ishmael's wife, the rightly-concerned Mormon mother, intervenes, instigating a dialogue too precious not to quote: "What are you doing down here?" "We're just having some fun, mother." "Fun? Look at you! You're half-naked! You know better than this!" "Oh, mother. We're going to a new world. You're so old-fashioned." "The Lord would not be pleased with this." "We're out here in the middle of the ocean. Do you really think anyone cares how we dress?" "Yes. I do. And the Lord does." With this most-awkward scene and others like it, Rogers addresses the relevance of the Book of Mormon to contemporary life simply by projecting onto the scriptural text, in good Sunday-School-discussion fashion, distinctly contemporary and ultimately non-scriptural concerns.

The second way Rogers poses the question of the relevance of scripture to contemporary life is more subtle. Though reviewers of the film have often said that "much of the film's dialogue is taken directly from the *Book of Mormon*'s actual wording,"[2] that is not, strictly speaking, true. The words of the Book of Mormon are more often adapted, abridged, or replaced, both in voice-over narration and in dialogue. Thus "As the Lord liveth, and as we live, we will not go down unto our father in the wilderness until we have accomplished the thing which the Lord hath commanded us" (1 Ne. 3:15) becomes "No. We can't leave. Not like this. Just because we didn't succeed the first time doesn't mean the Lord won't provide a way." With so much adaptation, abridgment, and replacement, those instances where the wording of the scriptural text actually does make

2. Paul C. Gutjahr, *The Book of Mormon: A Biography* (Princeton: Princeton University Press, 2012), 186.

its way into the film are particularly interesting. Such instances are, almost universally, of two kinds. First, the most familiar or most-often quoted texts from Nephi's writings find their way more or less unedited into the film. Viewers are not alienated by a reworded "I, Nephi, having been born of goodly parents" or "I will go and do the things which the Lord hath commanded." Second, whenever a divine figure speaks—God, the Spirit, an angel—the words are generally taken unaltered from the scriptural text. The double implication of Rogers's use of the actual words of the Book of Mormon is that there is a kind of immediate relevance at all times of both what is spoken by actually divine persons and what has come, by dint of constant quotation and repetition, to be recognized as always and immediately relevant.

The third way Rogers poses the question of the relevance of scripture to contemporary life weaves the first two ways together. On rare occasions in the film, well-known and culturally-affirmed scriptural passages are introduced into foreign contexts. A simple example of this is found in the slaying-of-Laban scene. In response to the Spirit's injunction to kill Laban, Nephi responds by asking, "Is not the word of God written, 'Thou shalt not kill'?" while the Book of Mormon text has Nephi say in his heart only "Never at any time have I shed the blood of man" (1 Ne. 4:10). A more interesting example comes when Rogers has Nephi quote himself in response to Lehi's announcement that his sons would have to return to Jerusalem a second time, this time in order to bring Ishmael's family—in particular his daughters—into the wilderness with them. After stating that Lehi's announcement followed "the best vision [he] ever had," Nephi quotes his own words at 1 Nephi 3:7 as a quasi-humorous response: "I will go and do the things the Lord hath commanded," and so forth. To have Nephi parody himself is cute, but it makes little sense of the actual story, of course. It is only *we* who have privileged Nephi's words in such a way that the parody makes any sense. The most fascinating example, however, is to be found in the prefatory scene of the film, the introduction of sorts that explains how Joseph Smith became aware of and received the task to translate the Book of Mormon. In response to the angel's explanation of the record, Joseph asks: "But, who would believe that? A record such as this, delivered from an uneducated farm boy?" To this, Moroni answers: "There is a promise, Joseph, a marvelous promise found at the end of the record. Anyone—*anyone*—who reads this book and asks of God with real intent whether or not it be true will receive an answer to their prayer." Moroni thus, like any good missionary, turns directly to Moroni 10:4–5, to what Latter-day Saints generally regard as the *only* immediately relevant passage in the whole of the Book of Mormon because it provides the outline of a mechanical operation through which anyone can receive a testimony of Mormonism's truth.

What is the theological significance of Rogers's three ways of addressing the relevance of scripture to contemporary life? Despite the film's apparent conservatism, the obvious sense in which it was meant to bring the Book of Mormon narrative to life, there are important ways in which it effectively undercuts the Book of Mormon's relevance. In order to address contemporary concerns, it has, rather violently, to insert scenes and sequences into narratives where they fit uncomfortably at best. Moreover, the bulk of the narrative, as well as of the actual dialogue recorded in the text, is taken to be largely dispensable or made better through summary or rewording; only those passages that Latter-day Saints have collectively affirmed or that record the actual words of divine beings are sacred enough not to be altered. Finally, it makes clear that there is a sense in which the whole text of the Book of Mormon—as Terryl Givens taught us a decade ago[3]—can be set aside so long as one is familiar with Moroni 10:4–5. To the question of how relevant Mormon scripture is to contemporary life, Rogers's film, despite being a staging of precisely Mormon scripture, responds with the answer: "Not that relevant." The perfunctory production of the film thus mirrors the perfunctory relationship Mormons too often have to the Book of Mormon—the book has to be read, the narrative has to be filmed, but nothing here is really supposed to change us or the world we live in. Indeed, I find it beautifully ironic that Rogers's plan to film the whole of the Book of Mormon petered out somewhere around the Isaiah chapters, just like most efforts to re-read the Book of Mormon do in January or February every year.

Much more critical—and in more than one sense of that word—is Dutcher's film *States of Grace*. The film is, on my interpretation, a double critique of the missionary program as an emblem for Mormon culture. First, Dutcher provides a critical study of what leads up to the moment of baptism—a critical study, that is, of how Mormonism, in the form of its missionaries, understands scripture. Second, he provides a critical study of baptism and its aftermath—a critical study, that is, of how Mormonism understands ritual.

---

3. See Terryl L. Givens, *By the Hand of Mormon: The American Scripture that Launched a New World Religion* (New York: Oxford University Press, 2002).

States of Grace opens with a series of suggestions that scripture is completely irrelevant to contemporary life. The first word of or about scripture in the film comes from a homeless street preacher: "'In the beginning, God created the heavens and the earth'—the book of Genesis, chapter 1, verse 1. Verse 2? I can tell you all about it, brothers and sisters, I can tell you all about it: one bible, two testaments, fifty-eight books, eleven epistles—and then the glorious book of Revelation, the glorious book of Revelation." The response is a chorus of different voices, all off-screen, saying "Shut up" in English and Spanish and culminating in someone saying: "No one is listening." Shortly afterward, the two Mormon missionaries who are the film's main characters are shown teaching discussions. In the first, in the middle of Elder Ferrell's reading James 1:5, the investigator falls asleep, snoring loudly; in the second, the same elder's reading of John 10:16 is interrupted by the beer-drinking beach bum that is their investigator with a too-hopeful question about Mormon polygamy.

This negative assessment is, however, complicated shortly afterward when Elder Lozano tells his companion his conversion story: he was converted when, while he lay in the hospital for six weeks, a Mormon missionary convalescing in the bed next to him made him memorize scriptures with him. The possible promise of scripture is then explained when the elders, a few days later, meet with a new investigator—a gang member named Carl who had only just survived a drive-by shooting thanks to the elders. Carl begins their first real discussion with the following words: "I read some of this book that you gave me. It wasn't that easy to read—all that 'thee' and 'thou' stuff. But my grandma—she's religious and all, so she just changed it for me." "She translated it for you?" Elder Lozano asks. "Yeah. Just takes some getting used to. That's all." Given the first dismissive and then more subtly affirmative attitude toward scripture in the film, this exchange is crucial. Dutcher here proposes, finally, that scripture can and should be relevant, but it is necessary for it to be "translated" for it to have any real force. Only then, it seems, can one "get used to it."

This crucial moment gives way to a still more crucial one. Elder Lozano asks, "You have any questions about what she read?" But before Carl can answer, Elder Ferrell intervenes with "How did it make you *feel*?" to which both Elder Lozano and Carl respond by turning to look at him as if he were completely clueless. Here, in an almost passing moment, Dutcher distinguishes two apparently radically opposed understandings of scripture—on the one hand, scripture as signifi*ed*; on the other, scripture as signifi*er*, to put the point in Terryl Givens' terms. Elder Ferrell sees the Book of Mormon as a sacred sign whose truth, learned by attending to one's feelings, serves principally to identify for its readers which institutional church one should join. For him, translation of the book into contemporary life is not terribly important. Elder Lozano sees the Book of Mormon as a collection of sacred teachings whose truths, severally studied, can and should have a real effect in life. For him, clearly, translation is exactly what needs to be done with the book.

It is not difficult to guess which of these expresses Dutcher's own convictions. This is indicated powerfully when, not much later, Carl is shown reading James 1:5 and then kneeling beside his bed to pray. Whereas an earlier investigator had fallen asleep sitting up when this verse was read to her, the same passage brings Carl to his knees. But this is just an introduction of sorts to two subsequent "translations" of the Book of Mormon into a contemporary context Dutcher goes on to present.

The first happens when the street preacher from before is reading in the Book of Mormon while alone in the elders' apartment. Borrowing, but of course without asking, a white shirt, a tie, and a name badge, he goes out into the street to beg for money while preaching from Mosiah 4:16–19: "But I say unto you, ye will not suffer that the beggar putteth up his petition to you in vain, and turn him out to perish. Therefore I will stay my hand, and will not give unto him of my food. I say unto you, O man, whosoever doeth this the same hath great cause to repent. Do we not all depend upon God?" The scene is, largely, presented as a bit of humor: a homeless Pentecostal preacher using the Book of Mormon to guilt passersby into giving him money. Its poignancy, though, should be noted. Unsurprisingly, but in an ominous echo of the first part of the film, the preacher is still without listeners, and there is no suggestion that anyone passing by gives him a cent in response to King Benjamin's words.

More touching is the second "translation" of sorts. When Carl goes to have his baptismal interview, he has to confront the seriousness of his gang activity. In response to his worries, Elder Banks tells him the story of the Anti-Nephi-Lehies burying their weapons of war. To Carl's question about what happened after that, Elder Banks responds: "Somewhere out there, deep in the earth, those weapons are still buried. They all kept their promise, every single of them, even though it cost some of them their lives. But their children—their children grew up strong and happy and good." Later that night, Carl buries his own weapons—guns, magazines, knives—in his backyard, preparatory to his baptism the next day. Here, so literally it borders on cheesiness while remaining moving, Dutcher translates the ancient into the modern, the scriptural into the mundane. What makes this last scene all the more poignant is the fact that it follows on a brief confrontation between Carl and his little brother: "What is wrong with you?" his brother asks. Referring to the drive-by shooting that injured Carl but left others dead, he offers the sort of criticism that appears early in the film but by this point has lost its real force: "They killed Abe, and all you want to do is sit around and read the Bible." While his brother pushes Carl to *do* something, he has no idea that Carl is about to *do* the most difficult thing of all: *stop*. This is a literalism and a kind of translation that one could well "get used to."

But then all of this beauty is called into question. When, just after being confirmed and given the Holy Ghost, Carl finds out his brother has been murdered by a rival gang, he digs up his weapons anew in order to exact revenge. When, with his gun pressed against the forehead of his brother's murderer, he hears his would-be victim both explaining that he has an eight-year-old sister and praying to God, he finds he cannot kill him, but his refusal to do so only leads to his friend's doing the deed. Tormented by what has thus taken place, he goes to the beach where he was baptized and throws his weapons irretrievably into the ocean. The Anti-Nephi-Lehies' act of burying their weapons in the ground was not enough—nor was, incidentally, the ritual of baptism. Bodies buried in the sea and weapons buried in the earth tragically give way to bodies buried in the earth and weapons buried in the sea. Only then can Carl see, as he puts it, how "messed up" everything is. Neither scripture nor ritual can face up to the violent reality of contemporary life, of life in a fallen world.

Dutcher's film thus ends more or less where it begins, in terms of its take on scripture. Though the first half of the film would seem to suggest that scripture can serve a redemptive purpose as far as it is translated into contemporary life, both of Dutcher's "translations" ultimately suggest that there is little reason to have hope in scripture. Right as Benjamin's words may be, they ultimately do little to turn people to the overwhelming need of the poor surrounding us. And beautiful as it might be to think of a gang member burying his weapons of war in a contemporary reenactment of an ancient covenant, it is more sentiment than solution in Dutcher's eyes. It thus appears that the first half of the film is aimed less at showing how scripture might be used rightly than at showing that most Mormon interpretation of scripture is shallower than shallow, so distantly removed from the real problems of life that it is more symptomatic of unthinking arrogance than of misguided or immature charity. The film is thus characterized by anything but the subtly despairing perfunctory element of Rogers's *The Book of Mormon Movie*, but it is not clear that explicit, outright despair is an improvement.

But I do not want to end on a note of despair, so let me conclude with just a word or two about *Napoleon Dynamite*. I lack the space to argue for its Mormonness or for its rightful place in the Mormon film movement—and others have already made that argument anyway. But what relationship does it bear to scripture? On the surface, none. It is arguably more *culturally* Mormon than anything else. And yet the hope that pervades the film is most crucial. It cannot be said to be culturally Mormon in anything like the sense that *The Book of Mormon Movie* is culturally Mormon. There is something more at work there. It outstrips the perfunctory while nonetheless refusing to assume a merely critical position.

What does *Napoleon Dynamite* present, then? Though I lack the space to spell out the details, I think it is a most beautiful filmic presentation of the so-called psalm of Nephi, a study—not anything like as powerful as Malick's *Tree of Life* (2011) but not for that reason unworthy—of Paul's theological self-interpretation in Romans 7. It traces the pathway every Latter-day Saint travels when she finally hears King Benjamin and all his talk about nothingness in the way Benjamin intended. Our worries that we are not good enough are all more than justified. But the problem is not that we are not good enough. The problem is that we think we are supposed to be good enough. And thus, *Napoleon Dynamite* demonstrates, without ever stating what it is up to, the way in which scripture is the most relevant thing of all. It shows us grace.

Subject Index

Pentecostalism, 269–72, 277, 311
Plato, 298
Poe, Edgar Allen, 293
possibility (or potentiality), 47, 64,
  67–70, 95–96, 98–111, 126, 270,
  285, 291–93
Pratt, Orson, 48–53, 115, 297–98
Presbyterianism, 140
priesthood, 84–85

Q–S

Qur'an, 250
race in the Book of Mormon, 255,
  259, 261, 265, 275–77
resurrection, 41, 104, 115, 188–89,
  204, 283, 297
Ricoeur, Paul, 30
Roberts, B. H., 296–97
Rogers, Gary, 306–9, 313
Sanders, E. P., 176
Sawyer, John F. A., 149
Schleiermacher, Friedrich, 97
Schmitt, Carl, 127
secularity, 44, 47, 140, 172
Septuagint, 148
sin, 79, 110–11, 117–18, 123–24,
  295, 298–300, 302
Skousen, Royal, 7, 48, 120, 153–54,
  160, 213–14, 250
Smith, Joseph, 7–8, 21, 37, 48, 74,
  91, 118, 125–26, 133–34, 138–40,
  153–55, 171, 173, 175, 181, 188,
  191, 193, 196, 205, 214, 218, 247,
  250, 258, 281, 290, 297–99, 308
Smith, Joseph Fielding, 296–97
Smith, Julie M., 56
Smith, Robert F., 153
Society for Mormon Philosophy and
  Theology, 4, 90, 270, 280
Sorenson, John L., 244

Southern, R. W., 124
sovereignty, 116, 119, 123–29, 147,
  149, 156, 161–62, 165
Sperry, Sidney B., 20, 244
States of Grace (2005), 306, 309–13
Stendahl, Krister, 12, 194
Sweeney, Marvin A., 60

T–Y

Talmage, James E., 296–97
Tanner, John S., 20
Targum Jonathan, 155–56
Taylor, Sheila, 79
temporality, 25–29, 34–35, 46,
  72–73, 82–87, 92, 107–11, 206,
  282, 284, 286, 291–92
theology of the Book of Mormon,
  3–16, 252–53
Thomas, John Christopher, x, 269–72,
  277
trauma, 26–35
Tree of Life (2011), 313
Twain, Mark, 8, 185, 290
typology, 84, 202, 205
Von Rad, Gerhard, 147
Wallace, David Foster, 293
Walters, Wesley P., 154
Warner, C. Terry, 20
Welch, John W., 183, 244, 249
Welch, Rosalynde, 245, 281
Wesley, John, 118–19
Widtsoe, John A., 126, 296–97
Wilcox, Miranda, 52
Wildberger, Hans, 235
Williamson, Hugh, 230
Witherington, Ben, 13
Wittgenstein, Ludwig, 97
Wright, Mark, 251
Wright, N. T., 13–14, 42, 90, 176
Young, Brigham, 297

Scripture Index

Doctrine and Covenants

Pearl of Great Price

Also available from
GREG KOFFORD BOOKS

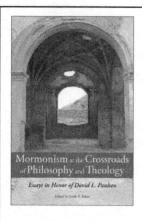

Mormonism at the Crossroads of Philosophy and Theology:
Essays in Honor of David L. Paulsen

Edited by Jacob T. Baker

Paperback, ISBN: 978-1-58958-192-0

"There is no better measure of the growing importance of Mormon thought in contemporary religious debate than this volume of essays for David Paulsen. In a large part thanks to him, scholars from all over the map are discussing the questions Mormonism raises about the nature of God and the purpose of life. These essays let us in on a discussion in progress." —RICHARD LYMAN BUSHMAN, author of *Joseph Smith: Rough Stone Rolling.*

"This book makes it clear that there can be no real ecumenism without the riches of the Mormon mind. Professor Paulsen's impact on LDS thought is well known. . . . These original and insightful essays chart a new course for Christian intellectual life." —PETER A. HUFF, and author of *Vatican II* and *The Voice of Vatican II*

"This volume of smart, incisive essays advances the case for taking Mormonism seriously within the philosophy of religion—an accomplishment that all generations of Mormon thinkers should be proud of." —PATRICK Q. MASON, Howard W. Hunter Chair of Mormon Studies, Claremont Graduate University

"These essays accomplish a rare thing—bringing light rather than heat to an on-going conversation. And the array of substantial contributions from outstanding scholars and theologians within and outside Mormonism is itself a fitting tribute to a figure who has been at the forefront of bringing Mormonism into dialogue with larger traditions." —TERRYL L. GIVENS, author of *People of Paradox: A History of Mormon Culture*

"The emergence of a vibrant Mormon scholarship is nowhere more in evidence than in the excellent philosophical contributions of David Paulsen." —RICHARD J. MOUW, President, Fuller Theological Seminary, author of *Talking with Mormons: An Invitation to Evangelicals*

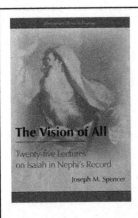

The Vision of All:
Twenty-five Lectures on
Isaiah in Nephi's Record

Joseph M. Spencer

Paperback, ISBN: 978-1-58958-632-1
Hardcover, ISBN: 978-1-58958-633-8

In *The Vision of All,* Joseph Spencer draws on the best of biblical and Latter-day Saint scholarship to make sense of the so-called "Isaiah chapters" in the first two books of the Book of Mormon. Arguing that Isaiah lies at the very heart of Nephi's project, Spencer insists on demystifying the writings of Isaiah while nonetheless refusing to pretend that Isaiah is in any way easy to grasp. Presented as a series of down-to-earth lectures, *The Vision of All* outlines a comprehensive answer to the question of why Nephi was interested in Isaiah in the first place. Along the way, the book presents both a general approach to reading Isaiah in the Book of Mormon and a set of specific tactics for making sense of Isaiah's writings. For anyone interested in understanding what Isaiah is doing in the Book of Mormon, this is the place to start.

Praise for *Gathered in One*:

"With this book, Joseph M. Spencer has accomplished a remarkable feat. He has produced a reader-friendly, engaging study of the writings of Isaiah in the Book of Mormon that makes Isaiah accessible without overly-simplifying his theology and message." — Nicholas J. Frederick, Assistant Professor of Ancient Scripture, Brigham Young University, author of *The Bible, Mormon Scripture, and the "Rhetoric of Allusivity"*

"Spencer has produced by far the most helpful examination of the theological significance of Isaiah within the Book of Mormon. . . . In the emerging field of distinctively theological readings of the Book of Mormon, Joseph Spencer has made a major contribution, suggesting that conversations about the Book of Mormon are far from over." — John Christopher Thomas, *Journal of Book of Mormon Studies*

Made in the USA
Las Vegas, NV
24 December 2021

39305317R00198